www.wadsworth.com

www.wadsworth.com is the World Wide Web site for Thomson Wadsworth and is your direct source to dozens of online resources.

At *www.wadsworth.com* you can find out about supplements, demonstration software, and student resources. You can also send email to many of our authors and preview new publications and exciting new technologies.

www.wadsworth.com
Changing the way the world learns®

Understanding Generalist Practice with Families

Grafton H. Hull, Jr.
and Jannah Mather
University of Utah

THOMSON
BROOKS/COLE™

Australia • Canada • Mexico • Singapore • Spain • United Kingdom • United States

Executive Editor: *Lisa Gebo*
Assistant Editor: *Alma Dea Michelena*
Editorial Assistant: *Sheila Walsh*
Technology Project Manager: *Barry Connolly*
Marketing Manager: *Caroline Concilla*
Marketing Assistant: *Rebecca Weisman*
Advertising Project Manager: *Tami Strang*
Project Manager, Editorial Production: *Christine Sosa*
Art Director: *Vernon Boes*
Print Buyer: *Lisa Claudeanos*
Permissions Editor: *Stephanie Lee*
Production Service: *Mary Deeg, Buuji, Inc.*
Photo Researchers: *Alma Dea Michelena and Sue C. Howard*
Copy Editor: *Kristina Rose McComas*
Illustrator: *Eunah Chang, Buuji, Inc.*
Cover Designer: *Design Associates*
Cover Image: *Corbis, Getty Images*
Compositor: *Buuji, Inc.*
Text and Cover Printer: *Transcontinental Printing/Louiseville*

© 2006 Thomson Brooks/Cole, a part of The Thomson Corporation. Thomson, the Star logo, and Brooks/Cole are trademarks used herein under license.

ALL RIGHTS RESERVED. No part of this work covered by the copyright hereon may be reproduced or used in any form or by any means—graphic, electronic, or mechanical, including photocopying, recording, taping, Web distribution, information storage and retrieval systems, or in any other manner—without the written permission of the publisher.

Printed in Canada
1 2 3 4 5 6 7 09 08 07 06 05

For more information about our products, contact us at:
Thomson Learning Academic Resource Center
1-800-423-0563
For permission to use material from this text or product, submit a request online at
http://www.thomsonrights.com.
Any additional questions about permissions can be submitted by email to
thomsonrights@thomson.com.

Library of Congress Control Number: 2004111503

ISBN 0-534-57937-X

Thomson Higher Education
10 Davis Drive
Belmont, CA 94002-3098
USA

Asia (including India)
Thomson Learning
5 Shenton Way
#01-01 UIC Building
Singapore 068808

Australia/New Zealand
Thomson Learning Australia
102 Dodds Street
Southbank, Victoria 3006
Australia

Canada
Thomson Nelson
1120 Birchmount Road
Toronto, Ontario M1K 5G4
Canada

UK/Europe/Middle East/Africa
Thomson Learning
High Holborn House
50/51 Bedford Row
London WC1R 4LR
United Kingdom

To our children,
Michael, Patrick, R.J., and Jake

Contents

CHAPTER 10

CHAPTER 11

CHAPTER 12

CHAPTER 13

CHAPTER 14

Preface

This book is oriented to beginning students of the family, whether at the undergraduate or graduate level. It reflects the vast diversity of families that graduates will encounter as they enter the practice arena. The text is built upon a generalist perspective that reflects our belief that families require help at micro, mezzo, and macro levels. Social workers and other professionals play multiple roles when working with families, and we have tried to identify and describe those that we think are most applicable. The planned change model used in the text will be familiar to practitioners as it is used in many different areas of social work.

Those working with the family require a thorough grounding in the major theories employed in this area of practice. They also must have a solid understanding of the practice skills that are required to assist families. Because families can present with a large number of challenges, it is also important to be aware of intervention approaches that can be used in various situations. This includes single parents and stepparents, families facing divorce and extreme distress, those experiencing death of a loved one, and those being served by programs emphasizing family preservation and wrap-around services. We also provide information on some of the ways that communities and organizations can facilitate the development of healthy families.

Because so many families are affected by social policy decisions at various levels, we have included a chapter discussing some of the primary programs relevant to families. This includes public assistance and child welfare programs operated by federal, state, and local governments. Finally, we look at some of the future trends involving families and family practice.

There are many books on family available to professors and students, and each differs in significant ways from the others. We believe that a grounding in the generalist perspective allows students to better understand how family practice fits into the larger picture of human service practice. We have also devoted large sections of the book to culturally competent practice with families of color. Almost every chapter has a specific component related to ethnic-sensitive practice. In addition, the Theory in Action highlights found in most chapters help to illustrate the concepts and principles discussed in the text. Finally, we firmly believe that a strengths perspective should pervade work with families, and this focus is clear throughout the book. It is our hope that students will find the content of the text interesting and accessible and that it will whet their appetites for generalist practice with families.

ACKNOWLEDGMENTS

While authors routinely receive credit for their books, it is rare that any project of this magnitude is completed without the help of many people. We would like to acknowledge the contributions to this work of the many people who worked tirelessly and often within limited time frames to assist us. We start with Lisa Gebo and Alma Dea Michelena of Brooks/Cole, who waited patiently for us to turn in the manuscript and forgave our elastic deadline. Their support and encouragement and prodding helped bring the project to fruition. We would like to thank the reviewers whose comments and observations improved the manuscript immeasurably. They include John Carmack, John Brown University; Diana R. Gehart, California Sate University-Fresno; Mildred Joyner, West Chester University; Mark Kaufman, Washburn University; Sharon Pond, Southside Virginia Community College; Catherine Sori, Governor's State University; Myrna Thompson, Southside Virginia Community College; Paul Peterson, our graduate assistant, who helped us gather materials and ideas; and Cheryl Gibson and Becky Lübbers, who assisted by typing, copying, and indexing portions of the manuscript. We should acknowledge the patience of our three dogs, Prince, Christie, and the late Amanda, who have endured countless late suppers waiting for us to turn off the computer and attend to their needs.

Finally, we would like to thank our parents, children, and their spouses, and the clients, theorists, and students who, across the years, have added to our understanding of the complex institution known as the family.

Working with Families

CHAPTER 1

© Michael Newman/Photoedit

I Love Lucy, Father Knows Best, My Three Sons, The Partridge Family, The Brady Bunch, The Fresh Prince of Bel Air, Everybody Loves Raymond, King of Queens, The American Family, Will and Grace, That 70's Show, and Malcolm in the Middle.

From its beginnings to the present, American television has offered a steady diet of shows chronicling the foibles, challenges, and drama of families. The attraction and long tenure of soap operas such as *General Hospital, As the World Turns,* and *All My Children* suggest just how enamored we are with seeing the function or dysfunction of other families. This interest exists whether we are laughing at the antics of family members or thanking our lucky stars that we grew up in somewhat healthier or less problematic units. And it is not just Americans who are fond of shows focused on the family. While several American shows are popular in other nations, many country-specific programs have been developed and broadcast throughout the world. The keen interest that we have in families probably reflects the reality that families are the foundation of most societies. Whatever the form or membership characteristics, families have served as the surviving institution across centuries.

INTRODUCTION

In the quest to provide services to individuals, many helping professions, including social work, have focused their energy on the family and its interacting systems. This text places working with families within the *generalist practice* framework used in many helping professions while presenting a *family-in-environment* approach that helps in understanding family systems. This approach is consistent with the *person-in-environment* perspective common in social work practice.

The text begins with an examination of the history of family practice (intervention with families) to place work with this system in context. In discussing generalist practice with families, we will use a planned change model that can help families in different situations and under different conditions. It is our belief that the model's six-stage process allows the helping professional systematically to aid a family in building their strengths and in resolving issues and concerns. We will also provide an overview of the theories upon which generalist practice with families rests. As you read the text, you will learn about biological, psychological, sociological, and environmental factors and their impact on families. Ways to use theories, knowledge, and skills to create change with a family are then presented in detail. Later we will discuss working with families posing special challenges.

In this chapter, we will lay out the history of family practice. We will also discuss typical definitions regarding the family, family practice, and family therapy. Finally, the chapter will provide an overview of the Family in Environment Practice Framework, the roles of the family practitioner, and the stages of the planned change intervention model. Each will serve as foundation content for the rest of the text.

A BRIEF HISTORY OF FAMILY PRACTICE

Families have a history of serving as the entry point for social workers, teachers, psychologists, and other human service professions to aid individuals in need. Historically, religion and churches played a significant role in providing a means for helping individuals and their families. The church's role clearly was in the forefront during the 1800s, when individuals in both England and the United States sought to set up supportive services for families. The Elizabethan Poor Laws, established through the church in England, did very little to support or tie families together. As a result, Thomas Callers, a minister of the Church of Scotland, developed a different means of serving needy families. Callers created programs that functioned more effectively through keeping families together and outside of an institutional setting. The Charity Organization Society (COS), beginning in England and later imported to the United States, also had its inception through the church. Reverend Gurteen, an Episcopalian minister living in the United States, set up a process to evaluate the needs of each individual and family and provide supports through charity organizations and wealthy donors. He organized the resources and used home visits to help identify the needs of specific families. The individuals visiting these families were known as "friendly visitors." While serving the poor through in-home services was important, often the issues identified by these visitors were moral ones that too often blamed individuals for their circumstances. Mary Richmond, a director of COS and a strong believer in the charity movement from the beginning, emphasized the importance of counseling the family in the home to create change for needy individuals (Richmond, 1917).

While many believe the COS was the forerunner of intervention and practice with the family, the English Settlement House movement, which began in 1884, strongly advocated for changes in society that would benefit the family. Perhaps one of the best-known Settlement Houses was Hull House, founded in 1869 in Chicago by Jane Addams and Ellen Gates Starr (Davis, 1973). Work at Hull House during the Industrial Age focused on supporting families through services offered within their neighborhoods and through programs designed to teach families how to support themselves. Settlement houses were generally set up within immigrant neighborhoods, and members of the community came to the houses to learn to speak English and to acquire other skills that might help them support their families. Unlike the COS, the Settlement Houses saw family problems as a function of environmental conditions and worked to create changes within society without blaming the individual or family. Some would come to view this as the beginning of the family-in-environment perspective, as the focus was on the individual and family and how their surrounding environment affected them.

Help for families was not limited to the development of services for the poor and needy. In 1911, the Family Service Association of America arose from the Charity Organization Societies, whose family agencies had focused their work on counseling any family in need. This association was later incor-

Table 1.1 | Historical Development of Family Practice

Organization	Responsibility
Churches	Religious responsibility
Charity organization societies	Moral responsibility
Settlement houses	Societal responsibility
Welfare agencies	Governmental involvement
Child guidance clinics	Community responsibility

porated in New York State in 1924 (Popple & Leighninger, 2002). An early pioneer of this association, now known as the Alliance for Families, was Mary Richmond, author of *Social Diagnosis* and creator of casework roles and skills. This organization sought to create change by helping to support families, whatever their income level. These different components of family practice history shaped the structure of intervention with the family.

Additionally, other agencies formed around the idea of providing services to keep families together. The Child Guidance Clinics emerged from the mental hygiene movement in the early 1900s. The clinics viewed meeting the counseling needs of the child as a way of providing service to families (Dain, 1980). These clinics served the mental health concerns of children by offering therapy to children and their families and providing community intervention (Popple & Leighninger, 2002). Table 1.1 highlights the differences among these various organizations with respect to their views regarding the root cause of family problems.

DEFINITION OF THE FAMILY

One of the most argued points during the last several decades has been how to define the family within the context of modern society. While many theorists have offered definitions of the family, many are based upon preconceived notions that fail to capture the richness of the term. The U.S. Census Bureau (2000) applies the following definitions to its report on households and families:

> **Household.** A household consists of all the people who occupy a housing unit. A house, an apartment or other group of rooms, or a single room, is regarded as a housing unit when it is occupied or intended for occupancy as separate living quarters; that is, when the occupants do not live and eat with any other persons in the structure and there is direct access from the outside or through a common hall.
>
> A household includes the related family members and all the unrelated people, if any, such as lodgers, foster children, wards, or employees who share the housing unit. A person living alone in a housing unit, or a group of unrelated

Table 1.2 | America's Families and Living Arrangements*

Family Households	
Married couples	55,311
Male householder	4,028
Female householder	12,687
Total	72,025

Nonfamily Households	
Male householder	14,641
Female householder	18,039
Total	32,680
Total all householders	**104,705**

*In thousands

Source: U.S. Census Bureau (2000).

people sharing a housing unit such as partners or roomers, is also counted as a household. The count of households excludes group quarters. There are two major categories of households, "family" and "nonfamily."

Family household. A family household is a household maintained by a householder who is in a family (as defined earlier), and includes any unrelated people (unrelated subfamily members and/or secondary individuals) who may be residing there. The number of family households is equal to the number of families. The count of family household members differs from the count of family members, however, in that the family household members include all people living in the household, whereas family members include only the householder and his/her relatives.

Household, nonfamily. A nonfamily household consists of a householder living alone (a one-person household) or where the householder shares the home exclusively with people to whom he/she is not related.

These definitions are then used to determine families and households noted in Table1.2. As you might expect, the limits of these definitions and the numbers they produce do not do justice to what families are really about.

The concept of *families* (not *family*) is a fluid notion based on relationships between and among individuals. Aldous and Dumon (1990) define *families* as cohabitating groups of some duration, usually economically dependent on each other, whose intimate relationships are based in custom, biology, law, or choice. It is critical for practitioners to recognize the many different configurations of the family. The family's constantly changing shape gives us the opportunity to work with many different types of "families" within our society.

Currently, multiple types of patterns fit under the umbrella of the term *families*. Stepfamilies; same-sex couples; nuclear families made up of mother, father, and children; cohabitating couples; and single-parent families are among the most common examples. This broad definition, however, does not always fit the changing face of family. The notion of the family must be "fluid" and open to change based on the interpretation of characteristics that make up the family. Highlight 1.1 presents an example of how fluid the definition of a family can be.

Sam and Lauren's fluid family constellation is not particularly unusual today, but it does stretch the traditional definition of the family. In many ways, narrow definitions of the family represent a carry-over from the Elizabethan Poor Laws. Those laws defined some families as "worthy" and thus eligible for help, while those who fell outside of the common definition, the "unworthy," received little or no attention. Today, the United States has 105 million households, of which family households comprise 69 percent (U.S. Census Bureau, 2000). These figures changed from the last census particularly in the makeup of family members. The number of married couples with their own children and those without children both decreased. The number of single-parent homes increased to 16 percent of all families. Nonfamily households composed of men living alone and **cohabitating households** (unmarried partners) increased substantially since 1990, according to the U.S. Census Bureau (2000). (See Table 1.3).

These percentages reflect the growing increase in nonfamily households as defined by the government. However, for those of us whose practices focus on families, these percentages also represent an increase in different types of families. For example, we might work with a family consisting of two cohabitating females and two children from a prior marriage (see Hightlight 1.2).

Alternately, we might work with a grandmother who is raising her two grandchildren and living with a man to whom she is not married (see Highlight 1.3).

Understanding how families define themselves is important, and while governmental statistics are useful, they often do not capture the fluid nature of families in actual practice. Those who work with families, in whatever context, need to understand how definitions of the family influence social and agency policy, and affect the scope of family practice.

Highlight 1.1 A Fluid Family Example

Sam and Lauren were married in 1990 at the age of 25. They had two girls, Mary and Laurie, in 1992. When Lauren's dad died in 2000, her mother moved in with the family. Sam and Lauren separated in 2002, divorced, and each remarried. Lauren is now living with her new husband, Ted, her two daughters, her mother and, on every other weekend, with Ted's two boys from a previous marriage, Tom and Fred.

Table 1.3 Changes in Family and Nonfamily Households between 1990 and 2000

	1990	2000
Family		
Married couples without children	29.8%	28.7%
Married couples with own children	26.3%	24.1%
Other family	14.8%	16%
Nonfamily		
Other nonfamily	4.6%	5.7%
Women living alone	14.9%	14.8%
Men living alone	9.7%	10.7%

Source: U.S. Census Bureau (2000).

Highlight 1.2

Joan and Sue: A Nontraditional Family

Joan and Sue have been living together for the past four years. They see themselves in a committed relationship and held a wedding ceremony about a year ago. Joan has two children from her previous marriage to Ray. While she and Ray share the children's custody, Joan spends more time with the kids at her house because Ray travels a lot for business. Two days a week, the children spend time with their paternal grandmother when Ray is not in town.

Highlight 1.3

Sandra and Allen: A Nontraditional Family

Sandra is the 45-year-old grandmother of three children. Her daughter, Tara, left them with her to raise when the kids were 7, 4, and 2. Sandra has not seen Tara in two years and knows that she will not be coming home to take the children back. About a year ago, Sandra met Allen at a single's church supper. They moved in together about six months later.

SCOPE OF FAMILY PRACTICE

Families are at the center of activities within our society. Knowing how to work with families is important to anyone in social work or other helping professions. When we think of family practice, it is easy to think only of public welfare, where the needs of the poor are most concentrated. However, social workers work with families in all types of situations. Most of the work done in schools, hospitals, nursing homes, detention centers, mental health facilities, counseling centers, prevention agencies, and the legal system is with the family. Family practice takes place in all types of institutions where individuals may receive service.

In school systems, teachers provide feedback to families on their child's needs and ways in which learning can be most effective. Social workers work with children and their families on learning problems, truancy, and family needs. School counselors provide the child and family with information to enable the child to be more successful in school. A school psychologist tests children for their abilities and works with the family to provide the best learning experience. Teacher aides support children within the classroom and help the family understand the difficulties their child may be having.

The role of the family within the educational system became even more important in 1975 with the adoption of the Education for All Handicapped Children Act (PL 94-142). This act helped mainstream children with disabilities back into the public school system after years of relegation to special education classes or schools. Families were strong advocates for adoption of this law, and they continue to play a vital role in its implementation for each individual child.

In hospitals, doctors, nurses, psychologists, rehabilitation workers, social workers, and health care workers serve families across the life cycle. From determining the medical needs of pediatric ward infants to planning for an elderly patient's convalescence, family practice is pivotal to decision making and planning. Attention to families within the medical setting occurs within the emergency room, in the doctor's office, on patient floors, and through outpatient preventive care.

In the mental health system, work with a patient usually includes the role and involvement of the family to one degree or another. The role of family members in substance abuse cases has also been identified as critical to continuing remission. Within the social welfare system, social workers and human service workers practice family intervention in all areas of family life. This may include assessing a family's financial needs or providing such child-protection services as family preservation. It may also involve teaching parenting skills, providing family planning assistance, and supporting older clients and those with disabilities.

In the legal system, lawyers and mediators counsel and support families through divorces and child-custody battles. Adolescents violating societal norms receive family intervention from social workers, counselors, and probation officers. Within the institutional setting, families can play an important role in the individual's rehabilitation and re-entry back into the community.

The list of areas where families play a crucial role in the healthy growth and development of their individual members is endless. Family practitioners provide critical assistance to families by helping them deal with difficult situations and enhancing the individual members' growth and development.

THE ROLE OF INDIVIDUAL DEVELOPMENT IN UNDERSTANDING FAMILIES

During the early development of social welfare services, practitioners began to see the family as a means of helping the individual. As the primary support system for the individual, it was only natural that the family would become the first place practitioners looked for resources and supports. Today, as the major social institution for the individual, the family supplies much more than financial resources. It also is designed to provide those components and skills necessary to meet the developmental requirements of an individual, such as physical, social, and emotional needs. Additionally, the need to be cherished, supported, and aided by others points to the reality of basic survival with others in a family-like context.

Developmental stage theorists such as Freud, Piaget, Kohlberg, and Erikson all considered the family's role as crucial in a child's development. Freud saw the psychosexual drives of the individual as the impetus for development. These drives were most often related to both the internal development of the id, ego, and superego and the individual's interactions with family members. Piaget, who studied the cognitive development of the child, viewed this development as occurring not only within the child but through the child's social interactions with others. Children, within the context of the family, develop their cognitive abilities not only on their own but also from interactions within their family. Kohlberg, who studied the moral development of the individual, saw the stages as a reflection of the child's inner discovery and a desire to be seen as "good" in the eyes of others. For example, stage one of moral development suggests that the individual behaves based on the "good boy, good girl / bad boy, bad girl" perception of others. Erikson, in his view of psychosocial development, saw each age-related stage as a crisis that must be resolved in order for self-development and enhanced social interaction with others to occur.

Other theorists have noted the importance of the individual's growth within the family context. A noted play therapy clinician, Melanie Klein, believed that the child's development and ability to cope with difficult situations grew out of the child's development within the family. Carl Rogers, founder of person-centered therapy, noted the important role played by the person's "phenomenal field." He believed the person's interactions with this field, composed of the family, environment, and other systems, greatly influenced the individual's development. Therefore, it is within these structures that the family becomes the individual's first line of support. The whole sense of self that the individual develops depends upon interactions with the family.

FAMILY LIFE CYCLE

Determining the life cycle of the family has become ever more complicated as the definitions and configurations of families have changed. Carter and McGoldrick's (1980) early work on understanding family life produced six specific stages:

1. Unattached Young Adult
2. Newly Married Couple
3. Family with Young Children
4. Family with Adolescents
5. Launching Children and Moving On
6. Family in Later Life

Carter and McGoldrick defined each stage as an "emotional process of the transition and the second order change required to proceed developmentally" (Armour, 1995, p. 29). What becomes obvious when we look at these stages is the role that societal norms played at the time of their development. While many families in western countries move through these stages, many do not. For example, some couples or partners do not marry. Others decide to never have children. For some, the family becomes the center of their emotional lives, while others, influenced by their respective cultures, place no such expectation on the union. Because of these choices, individuals create many differing families patterns at various points along their life spans.

Carter and McGoldrick (1999), later writing extensively on what they term "the expanded family life cycle," highlight the vast diversity apparent in how families actually go through their own life cycles. Depending upon a variety of factors, families may begin their developmental processes at different ages, while some families conclude their stages prematurely. Some couples elect not to have children while others plan on large, culturally or religiously sanctioned families. Carter and McGoldrick's observations about the reciprocal influence of individuals, families, communities, and societies are consistent with the family-in-environment model described in this chapter. They clearly see how issues such as poverty may influence family development or even prevent some individuals from making the choice to start their own family. Carter and McGoldrick also recognize how cultural patterns can directly impact the choices families have and those they make. To more fully understand why the family life cycle must be defined differently, we only need to look at differing theorists and their views of other developing family structures. Visher and Visher (1982), for example, note the necessary tasks stepfamilies must achieve:

1. Mourning of the losses involved
2. Development of new traditions
3. Formation of new interpersonal relationships
4. Maintenance of relationship(s) with child(ren)'s biological parents
5. Satisfactory movement between households

Still other theorists, such as Becvar and Becvar (2003), have focused their attention more closely on the developmental stages associated with marriage (p. 114). Table 1.4 shows these stages.

Table 1.4 | Stages of a Marriage

Stage	Emotional Issue	Stage-Critical Tasks
Honeymoon period (0–2 years)	Commitment to marriage	a. Differentiation from family of origin b. Making room for spouse with family and friends c. Adjusting career demands
Early marriage period (2–10 years)	Maturing of relationship	a. Keeping romance in the marriage b. Balancing separateness and togetherness c. Renewing marriage commitment
Middle marriage period (10–25 years)	Postcareer planning	a. Adjusting to mid-life changes b. Renegotiating relationship c. Renewing marriage commitment
Long-term marriage (25+ years)	Review and farewells	a. Maintaining couple functioning b. Closing or adapting family home c. Coping with death of spouse

Source: Becvar and Becvar (2003), p. 114.

Becvar and Becvar (2003) also note that the many differing structures of families now require that the family life cycle be seen as dynamic if the social worker is to assess accurately a family's stage of development. They propose that "a single-model perspective of the family no longer provides sufficient information but rather must be enhanced by models that include the tasks faced by different types of families" (p. 118). For example, models of individual development, such as Erikson's psychosocial model, must be taken into account when assessing a family situation. In other words, to assess how a family is functioning and developing we must consider such things as the individuals' developmental stage, the stage of the marriage, and the stage of the family life cycle. We must also take into account the environmental pressures facing the family.

FAMILY-IN-ENVIRONMENT PRACTICE FRAMEWORK

This section will approach the topic of families in their environment from several perspectives. We will first define what we mean by a family-in-environment practice framework. Within that approach, we will discuss the value of a generalist perspective and viewing families as client systems. We will also review briefly the knowledge, skills, and values important to family practice.

A variety of family practitioner roles will be described, and the chapter will conclude with a discussion of the structure of family practice.

Definition of Family-in-Environment Practice

This book argues that families are best understood within an environmental framework. This is consistent with social systems theory used in much of the human services. That is to say that one cannot adequately assess a family without recognizing the multiple influences that affect the lives of family members both individually and collectively. To paraphrase Garbarino (1992), the success of any family system "depends in large measure on the character and quality of the social environment" in which we live (p. 15). The social environment can present barriers or assist families in achieving success in fulfilling the tasks associated with this social system. A family-in-environment practice perspective means that we acknowledge the mutual interaction between and among family members and their social environment. The perspective also takes into account the risks and opportunities inherent in living in a social environment. It also allows us to value the myriad influences that affect every family. These include cultural and ethnicity factors, economic and political systems, and other social institutions, such as schools and churches. Thus, the family-in-environment practice framework is *an approach to understanding and working with families that acknowledges the mutual influence of families and their social environments and seeks to use this knowledge to assist families in better achieving their life goals.*

We will also address the family-in-environment perspective in subsequent chapters of this book. For example, Chapter 2 discusses in greater depth the importance of social systems theory as an underpinning of the family-in-environment approach and Chapter 4 examines the multiple ways in which the environment can significantly affect a family's ability to function effectively. In particular, we will consider how economic and social problems impede family functioning.

Generalist Practice Model

The generalist practice model is described by Kirst-Ashman and Hull (2002) as

> the application of an eclectic knowledge base, professional values, and a wide range of skills to target systems of any size for change within the context of four primary processes:
>
> 1. Working within an organizational structure and under supervision;
> 2. Utilizing a wide range of professional roles;
> 3. Utilizing critical thinking skills within a planned change process;
> 4. Emphasizing client empowerment. (p. 7)

The value of a generalist practice model is that it helps identify many fundamental aspects of family practice, including a varied knowledge base, a set of practice skills, and an overarching value framework. Generalist family practitioners also employ a variety of roles to help families, and many practice theories stress the importance of empowering families to solve their own problems.

Obviously, critical thinking is important because family practitioners must carefully weigh information and evidence they encounter and select theories and skills that clearly match family needs. In addition, each practitioner uses a model of practice that orders his or her work with families. We will discuss this model later in the chapter under the structure of practice.

The degree to which a social worker works within an organizational setting and under supervision is often a function of educational level, licensure requirements, and practice auspices. For example, family practitioners with a bachelor's degree in social work will likely operate in some sort of organization and with a moderate level of supervision. Those possessing a graduate degree and sufficient experience may find themselves in private practice with a much lower level of supervision. It is important to keep in mind, however, that even a solo practice is an organizational structure with requirements superimposed by outside entities such as managed care agencies and state licensing bodies. In addition, wise social workers utilize supervision and consultation to improve their own practice, even when this is not imposed by the organization with which they work.

Likewise, the knowledge and skill level will vary depending upon the practitioner's educational preparation, training, and auspices. Interventions, for example, involving family therapy are more or less restricted to those holding graduate degrees, while many other professional activities, such as case management or brokering, can be accomplished by either a bachelor's- or master's-level practitioner. In the next section, we will suggest areas of knowledge, skills, and values that are essential to most, if not all, family practitioners.

Knowledge, Values, and Skills

Generalist family practitioners need knowledge in several areas to practice effectively with this target system. This knowledge includes a familiarity with typical lifespan development and the ways in which this development can vary from culture to culture and individual to individual. In other words, family practitioners must be aware of the wide range of typical development for human beings. In addition, practitioners should have a solid understanding of the risks and problems that individuals may encounter in their developmental processes. Such things as illness, death or divorce of parents, or poverty can leave nearly indelible marks on individuals and families.

Social workers must also possess a broad understanding of what makes up a family and how that definition has changed over the decades. The supposedly picturesque family portrayed on television from 1950–1970 may have rarely existed in reality, but it produced a very limited definition of a family. As previously pointed out, today's families are likely to include single parents, stepparents, gay and lesbian families, aging nuclear families, and extended families in some shape or form. Of course, the "traditional" family model can be found, but it is much less common than many might expect.

A generalist family practitioner must also understand the developmental tasks and life courses of families themselves. As we have mentioned, these tasks and life courses of families vary and must be understood within different contexts. Social workers must develop an understanding of family dynamics. They also must learn theories proven useful for assessing and intervening with families, plus strategies and approaches that can be employed in various situations. To the extent possible, family interventions should be based on models that have undergone careful research rather than on the latest "hot" theory. Basing our work on evidence instead of anecdotes is an ethical responsibility of the social worker.

Likewise, practitioners will need a repertoire of intervention skills for helping individual families. Many of these are the same skills used in working with individuals, such as reframing, confrontation, active listening, paraphrasing, questioning, and probing. Others are specifically designed for use with families and include realigning subsystems, joining, and using narratives. Chapter 7 addresses these techniques at length.

Finally, family practitioners always operate within a value structure that influences every action they take. For social workers, this is the Code of Ethics of the National Association of Social Workers. In the case of human service practitioners, it is the National Organization for Human Service Education Ethical Standards. The American Association for Marriage and Family Therapy also provides a Code of Ethics for its members. Each profession providing family services has its own set of ethical guidelines. Most ethical standards share a clear understanding of the family practitioner's obligations to clients. These include the primacy of the client's needs, the importance of confidentiality, and the expectation of practitioner competence (Nichols & Schwartz, 2001). They also prohibit sexual intimacy between practitioner and client, encourage the avoidance of conflicts of interest, and respect the client's right to self-determination. While each professional code of ethics differs in some aspects from the others, the commonalities exceed the differences in number and scope. Clearly, those entrusted with the sanction to work with families must also be guided by rules that reflect respect for the client's well-being. Actions counter to the client's well-being are usually unethical, regardless of the educational background or training of the family practitioner. Commonly, ethical violations may also subject the family practitioner to legal punishment or loss of one's professional license.

Generalist Family Practitioner Roles

As might be expected, generalist practitioners play many roles when working with families. In the following section, we will discuss several of these roles, including counselor, educator, broker, case manager, mobilizer, mediator, and advocate. We should note at the outset that these roles may be played simultaneously or consecutively, depending upon the family's needs. A family without shelter or food, for example, might require the practitioner to play the broker role first to solve the immediate problem facing the family. Thus, this would occur before engaging in counseling or other roles.

Counselor The *counselor role,* sometimes called family therapy or treatment, requires that the practitioner employ one or more theories to understand and help the family improve their functioning. Along with a theory, the practitioner will use techniques that promise to be effective in helping the family manage a particular problem. Which theory and techniques will be used are often dependent on the educational and professional background of the practitioners, the setting in which they work, and the family's needs. In the counselor role, the practitioner is focused on improving relationships within the family, enhancing family cohesion, and encouraging effective communication among family members. Sometimes this involves showing the family that old ways of interacting are ineffective. Goldenberg and Goldenberg (2002) refer to one of the counselor's activities as helping "families get unstuck" (p. 39) so that they can relate to one another differently. For example, Amanda, a social worker with the local school system, plans to work on the acting-out behaviors of Tim, age 9, by meeting weekly with him and his family to explore what factors are playing into this behavior. Amanda's plan for the counseling includes seeing Tim in play therapy, doing family therapy with Tim and his parents, and having Tim work with another group of children once a week.

Educator While the *educator role* with a family may seem straightforward, it is often not. This is because, as Kinney, Haapala, and Holland (1991) note, "[W]e want to do more than teach families. We want them to *learn how to learn.* Ultimately, we hope that they will begin to understand the learning process so well that they will continue to learn productively long after we are gone" (p. 93). Education involves teaching family members more effective ways to attain their individual and mutual needs. In the educator role, the practitioner might teach family members listening skills or how to communicate clearly to other members. Practitioners might also help parents understand the developmental needs of their children or learn more appropriate parenting techniques. Instruction can occur in one of three ways. It can be *direct,* such as when we give clients information on communication skills. Families also learn by our *modeling* of behaviors. This may occur when we demonstrate a new skill or act in a given way toward the family. Finally, learning occurs through *contingency management,* in which the practitioner reinforces specific behaviors, such as actively listening, or ignores behavior considered inappropriate (Kinney et al., 1991). Learning tends to occur most easily when families are not focused on necessities of life, such as food or shelter. "Teachable moments" occur when family members are "alert, focused, and interested in learning" (p. 97). A family member who is crying or angry probably cannot learn until the emotion has subsided, but a family member who expresses a desire to learn how to respond to an angry spouse is teachable (Brock & Barnard, 1999). Learning is also more difficult when the learner has experienced past learning failures.

Learning may take several different forms. For example, a family may learn values from the practitioner, such as using reason and calm in the face of emotionally charged incidents. Another value often learned is that all family members contribute to the family's health or disorder in their own ways. This helps reduce the tendency to make one family member a scapegoat. Families will also acquire knowledge that may be useful, such as a couple who reads about typical behaviors and problems associated with blended families. This knowledge may help prepare them for the challenges they will face with their respective children. Of course, families will also learn skills designed to help them respond to difficult situations. A family might learn how to respond calmly when an adolescent becomes verbally aggressive or demanding. Parents of younger children may learn how to use timeouts and reinforcement measures to alter unwanted behavior and promote positive conduct. As is evident, learning is at the heart of many family interventions. For example, Susan, a human service worker in the hospital, is working with the Mendez family regarding the decisions that must be made about their mother, Celia (age 89), who needs 24-hour care. One of the patterns Susan is noting is that the family does not directly talk with Celia about the issue but seems to ignore her comments. As a way of working with the family, Susan makes a point of speaking directly to Celia and engaging her in the discussion of her care. By modeling this type of interaction, Susan is educating the family about positive communication with their mother.

Broker The family practitioner playing the role of *broker* assists the family by "putting them in touch with people, clubs, specialized self-help groups, and other resources" (Harper-Dorton & Herbert, 1999, p. 165). As Logan, Freeman, and McRoy (1990) have observed, families often face several problems related to resources. These include "(1) the absence of needed resources, (2) the absence of linkages between people and resource systems or between resource systems, (3) problematic interactions between people within the same resource system, (4) problematic interactions between resource systems, and (5) problematic individual internal problem-solving and coping resources" (p. 42). For example, gay and lesbian couples often receive "low levels of support from all types of relatives—less than they got from co-workers" (Bryant & Demian, 1994, p. 110). As a result, gay or lesbian parents may benefit from parenting groups such as the Gay and Lesbian Parents' Coalition International (Patterson, 1994). Others may find it useful to participate in a support group for prospective parents or to access legal advocacy groups.

Clearly, the broker must have a broad knowledge of community resources providing many services. However, simply referring families to a given resource is often insufficient. While a referral may address the first two problems identified previously, it will not resolve the other three problems. Consequently, the practitioner must use other roles, such as case manager, mobilizer, or counselor. For example, as a crisis counselor at the local homeless shelter, Nathan is working with a family without money or a place to live. Nathan decides to refer the family to the local housing authority for lodging and, if that is successful, to the food pantry for basic staples the family will need. Additionally, Nathan knows it will be important to refer the parents to the local school system in order to keep their children in school while they are waiting for more permanent housing. In addition to these brokering tasks, Nathan may need to do some counseling with the parents to help them look at all their options or may need to role play with the family ways to discuss with the school administrators their need for educational services for their children.

Case Manager "Case management is a process for assisting families who have multiple service needs" (Greene & Kropf, 1999, p. 82). Families benefiting from case management include those experiencing severe physical illness, "homelessness, chronic mental illness, or a developmental disability of a family member" (p. 82). Case management can also be useful in helping families weather developmental crises. *Family case management* involves establishing specific measurable goals and creating a formal contract for service. For example, a family coping with an 18-year-old son with a developmental disability might need to begin exploring ways to increase his independence, including opportunities for employment and, perhaps, structured living arrangements. While family case managers may work alone in delivering these services, it is much more likely they will serve in a coordination role, ensuring that assistance provided by others is appropriate and effective. Keep in mind that the case management role is often combined with other family practice roles, such as broker, counselor, and mobilizer.

Mobilizer Social workers also mobilize human resources for families. Social networks and other sources offering families "face-to-face interaction and a sense of commitment" are important components that help family members manage crises (Harper-Dorton & Herbert, 1999, p. 165.). The *mobilizer role* is important because families exist in a web of relationships with individuals and organizations external to the family. Those relationships are mutual in the sense that families are affected by these outside systems while they simultaneously influence the systems (Parke & Kellam, 1994). Human resources can provide financial assistance, companionship, advice, and emotional support, and can fill other social needs of family members. For example, mobilization of social supports may be especially necessary for gay and lesbian couples. These individuals frequently experience discrimination and heterosexism and lack the kinds of family support usually accorded to straight couples. Through the family practitioner's work with support groups, a couple might be able to better deal with their own relationship and the reactions of those surrounding them.

Mediator *Mediation* involves intervening in disagreements among two or more parties with a goal of helping them reach a mutually acceptable agreement. Mediation is based on the principle of win-win solutions, in which both parties feel positive about the outcome and dispute resolution occurs with a minimum of frustration and anger. A mediator helps the family "hear each other and recognize what each considers important so as to effectuate an agreement that both can live with" (Marlow, 1992, p. 183). For example, family practitioners may end up serving as mediators when a couple elects to divorce. In this role, the practitioner helps the family to negotiate the terms of the divorce and plan for their postmarital relationship (Goldenberg & Goldenberg, 2002). The advantage of mediation in these situations is the potential to avoid the adversarial relationships that often accompany divorce. There is nothing inherently wrong in using attorneys to work out divorce arrangements. However, the fact that lawyers are advocates charged with getting the best deal for their client increases the likelihood that the couple will end up angry with each other. The long term consequences may be resentment and hard feelings that impinge on other aspects of the couple's lives, such as relationships with their children.

The goal of mediation in these situations is to resolve issues affecting custody, visitation, financial support, and asset distribution (Emery, 1994). This occurs through the practitioner's efforts to help partners focus on the family system, clarify problematic issues, identify options, and make choices. Like any situation involving divergent points of view, a mediated resolution is usually preferable for several reasons. First, there are likely to be no clear winners or losers, since each party negotiates the agreement in an antagonism-free environment. This reduces the chances of one person leaving the relationship with a high degree of anger. Second, it also increases the likelihood that both parties will abide by the agreement. Third, and equally important, it decreases the chance that the parents' angry feelings will be expressed toward the couple's children.

Mediation is usually a time-limited activity continuing for no more than a dozen sessions. It requires creation of an atmosphere of trust between the mediator and family and requires a thorough airing of disputed issues. Mediators help the couple create or identify options that can ensure that both parties are comfortable with the outcome. Mediators help the parties negotiate their differences and consider ways they may compromise with each other. Ultimately, all agreements reached in mediation should be committed to writing, often followed by a legal opinion from the couple's respective attorneys.

Advocate *Advocacy* is needed when unequal or inequitable distribution of resources prevents family members from having their needs met. For example, a family may be faced with eviction because they lack money to pay the rent, or bureaucratic red tape may prevent family members from getting resources to which they are entitled. A case manager may also need to be an advocate when an agency is not providing needed services or is failing to deliver services in a timely manner. An example is a family member with a developmental disability who is referred to a medical clinic for a potential heart problem. The physician orders a chest x-ray, to be followed by an electrocardiogram and stress test. However, the physician does not follow up with the client and, in fact, waits two weeks to read the x-ray. When the family case manager contacts the physician's office and talks to the doctor, she discovers the delay led to the patient undergoing two needless and expensive additional tests. Had the physician read the x-rays on time, the client would not have had to undergo the electrocardiogram or the stress test. The family practitioner advocates for the client to ensure there will be no charge for the unnecessary tests.

Another potential advocate role concerns work with gay and lesbian couples wishing to adopt children. Family practitioners may need to advocate with adoption agencies uninformed about such adoptions or with legislatures considering prohibiting gay and lesbian parents from adopting.

A social worker may clearly play many roles when interacting with a family. Particular roles employed by the generalist practitioner depend on client needs and the practitioner's ability, educational preparation, and training. Practitioners must know how and judge when to engage in these roles.

STRUCTURE OF PRACTICE

In using the term *structure of practice,* we are referring to a model followed by the many generalist practitioners working with families. Sometimes called the planned change or problem-solving model, the structure of practice provides guidance to both new and experienced practitioners. One objection to the use of the term *problem solving* is the connotation that the major emphasis of a practitioner's work is focused on a family's deficits rather than on their strengths. On the other hand, a family usually comes to the attention of the practitioner precisely because of problems identified by one or more family members or by some outside system, such as a school, medical setting, or protective service agency. The key is to remember that the "problem" always exists in the context of multiple strengths and that the solution to the problem will likely involve these strengths.

Typically, practitioners identify six or seven steps in the structure of practice. These include engagement, assessment, planning/goal setting, implementation, evaluation, termination, and sometimes follow-up. In the following sections, we will provide an overview of each step. Chapters 3 through 7 provide a more detailed discussion of each step.

Engagement

Engagement has been described from many different perspectives with respect to families. Worden (1994) described it as the "forming of a therapeutic alliance between the therapist and family, a trusting alliance that permits them to explore the inner workings of family relationships" (p. 13). The engagement phase, which typically begins with the first interview session, involves both social worker and family evaluating each other and exploring whether they can establish a working relationship. Following a greeting and initial chit chat, practitioners describe the purpose of the meeting, display an openness to hear all parties, and indicate that they will share their observations at the end. The engagement phase is also the beginning of the effort to define the issues, problems, challenges, and barriers confronting the family. Thus, a practitioner might ask, "What brings you here today?" Exploring this can involve all members, since some may have very different perspectives about the meeting's purpose, the nature of the problem, and the degree of commitment to participate.

Skills used during this phase will usually include the same ones employed when working with individuals. Thus, the practitioner will engage in active listening, seek feedback, observe, explain both client and worker roles, and discuss ethical considerations, such as the limits of confidentiality and mandatory reporting requirements. The social worker will display the behaviors characteristic of effective counseling, including genuineness, respect, and empathy.

This phase provides an opportunity for the practitioner to ask questions, request elaboration, and ensure that everyone has a chance to participate. The social worker will remain neutral and not take sides in the family's issues. Eventually, as the family shares more details and family members feel increasingly comfortable with the process, the practitioner will offer them the agency's services. If the family accepts services, the emphasis will then shift to assessment.

Assessment

The purpose of the *assessment phase* is to identify and clarify the issues confronting the family, articulate what they would like to have happen, and gather any data needed to understand the family better. As described in Chapters 4 and 5, assessment is a complex process that involves a bio-psycho-social focus and an exploration of various family dimensions, ranging from roles and norms to rituals and triangles. In this phase, the practitioner may use many sources of information to understand the family better. These include questions, genograms, self-reports, eco-maps, family histories, and observation.

Although we often treat assessment like a discrete stage in the helping process, in reality, it is an ongoing activity. Data initially available may later turn out to be insufficient. First impressions may eventually prove wrong as family members become more comfortable with the practitioner and share other information they were previously reluctant to divulge. In addition, the challenges faced by the family may change while they are working with the social worker. Such changes might include physical or emotional illness experienced by a family member, divorce, loss of employment by one or both breadwinners, and other factors that we could not foresee. We should anticipate the possibility of change even if the actual events do not occur. Even without change, however, assessments should always remain tentative, subject to revision as more information becomes available.

Planning/Goal Setting

As might be expected, the *planning and goal setting phase* involves a joint effort with the family to identify what changes they wish to attain and the steps that are needed to make this happen. Goals should be "clear, specific, concrete, and measurable" (Collins, Jordan, & Coleman, 1999, p. 140). Goals must also be realistic and within the capacity of the family to achieve. Typically, goals specify a time frame for completion and how the goals will be reached. The family must be a full partner in developing goals, and the goals must be open to change as needed. Often, the family's initial goals may be somewhat abstruse or vague. "We want to communicate better" does not provide sufficient specificity for a goal. Neither does "We want to be happier." Both goals do suggest something about the family's desires but do not tell us when they have achieved the goal. The practitioner will need to help the family refine its goals so that they meet the identified standard. A parent who wants her children "to do more around the house" can be helped to identify the specific activities she would like the children to do. When completed, the mother's goal might be revised into two goals. One might read, "Mary will mow the lawn every Saturday by 5:00 P.M." Another would state, "Monday, Wednesday, and Friday, Lorenzo will rinse the dishes, place them in the dish washer, run the dishwasher and empty it."

Sometimes a family's goal is clear from the start. If the goal is to "reduce or eliminate Rudy's temper tantrums," this is a measurable goal assuming that we have some idea how frequently the target behavior occurs. We can ask parents to gather this type of data and use it as a baseline for judging changes that occur following intervention. We can gather the same information during and after intervention and determine whether they have achieved the goal.

A family may end up with several goals, and it will be important to help the family identify those that are most important. Thus, we will prioritize the goals according to the family's preference. While the practitioner can assist the family in articulating specific goals and suggest which should take precedence, families have the final say in what they will work on first. One reason for this guideline is that clients have the right to self-determination, including the right to fail. A family that reluctantly accepts goals imposed upon them by others are likely to have only a half-hearted commitment to change. Finally, recall the importance of the strengths perspective. Goals should build upon the capacities and abilities and resources already possessed by the family.

Some practitioners engage in contracting with families to formalize the plans that they have developed. Contracts may be written or oral, but most important, they describe what the family and practitioner have come to understand about the challenges facing the family, their goals, and who will be responsible for specific activities. A contract, for example, may specify a certain number of family meetings, expectations about attendance, responsibility for homework or activities outside of the family meetings, and who will do what. As with assessments, goals may have to be revised as new information becomes available. Work with families is usually dynamic, rarely static.

Implementation

In the *implementation* phase, the family and practitioner take specific steps to achieve previously agreed-upon ends. Some call this the "doing" phase within the structure of practice, but this is something of a misnomer for two reasons. First, the practitioner must be active and "doing" at each stage of the process from start to finish. In addition, the family must play a major role in carrying out activities and actions designed to reach their goals. In other words, families are also doers in the process. During the implementation phase, the practitioner will engage in several activities (Collins, et al. 1999, p. 143). These include:

- focusing on the family's needs
- respecting the client's right to self-determination
- expanding the family's capacity for working independently
- maintaining appropriate professional distance
- establishing expectations that are reasonable and within the family's capacity
- teaching the family new skills
- connecting families to needed resources
- carrying out agreed upon activities
- monitoring client progress

Evaluation

Evaluation is concerned with determining the worth of an undertaking. An evaluation helps determine not only *what* happened but *why*. If one goal was to have the adults take a united stand when dealing with children in the family, we would want to know if this outcome occurred. If the goal were to reduce the frequency of shouting matches between mother and son, we would like to know if this happened. Simultaneously, we might also want to know why a given outcome occurred. Evaluation is an ethical responsibility of the practitioner, and funding bodies often require it as a condition for providing money. The evaluation phase will be more successful if the goals that have been set are clear and specific. If vague goals were set, no amount of skill in evaluation is going to result in useful data.

Termination

Termination is the ending of the professional relationship. Realizing that this is the only thing being terminated is important, since the family will continue to exist and will struggle with issues in the future (Worden, 1994). Termination generally occurs when families reach their goals or when further progress is impossible. Sometimes termination occurs prematurely when families simply do not return. Ideally, termination ought to occur following an evaluation that has shown the success of the intervention. However, the realities of work with families and other social systems sometimes leave us with different outcomes.

Sometimes, a referral to another resource follows termination. At other times, it occurs because the situation is becoming worse. This might occur, for example, when a family begins to disintegrate further, reaching the point where there is more harm in continuing than in terminating.

Follow-Up

Follow-up is an attempt to maintain contact with a family following termination. The purpose is to help ensure that families maintain progress that occurred during the intervention phase. Follow-ups are built into some interventions at the start and in others never occur at all. Failure to engage in follow-up is often directly related to insufficient funding and lack of agency sanction to pursue this step. When follow-up is possible, it can serve a very effective purpose for the family. It demonstrates the practitioner's continued interest in the family and can serve as a booster to help the family maintain newly learned behaviors. It also helps identify families who need additional assistance to maintain progress on their goals. Finally, it can serve as an invitation for families to seek assistance for new challenges they encounter after termination.

ORGANIZATION OF THE BOOK

This chapter provided an overview of family practice, beginning with a brief history of practitioner's efforts to assist families. Various definitions of family were introduced, and it was emphasized that the concept of what constitutes a family has changed dramatically over the years. The chapter also discussed the family-in-environment framework that is used throughout the text, while reviewing the generalist practice model that is applied so frequently in social work. Finally, the chapter discussed the structure of practice, a model that includes the helping steps of engagement, assessment, planning, implementation, evaluation, termination, and follow-up.

Chapter 2 is dedicated to providing the reader with a solid introduction to a variety of theories used by family practitioners. The chapter begins with a discussion of a multidimensional framework for employing theories and then reviews basic systems theory concepts useful for understanding families. The remainder of the chapter discusses key family theories. These include structural family theory, family communication theory, strategic family theory, cognitive-behavioral theories, cognitive theory, psychoanalytic and psychodynamic family theory, and postmodern theories. Ethnic and cultural challenges related to family theory are also discussed.

Chapter 3 looks at the process of engaging families in a helping relationship. It includes identifying factors that influence the effectiveness of interventions, steps in preparing for the first meeting, conducting the initial session, and gathering information on family needs and strengths. It also looks at ethnic and cultural challenges affecting the engagement process.

Chapters 4 and 5 cover the topic of assessment. Chapter 4 focuses on the structure of assessment, with a review of the ways in which several bio-psycho-social factors influence family systems. The chapter looks at how the development of individual members can affect the family. It also considers the stages or steps that families go through in developing as systems. Finally, the influence of environmental factors on family systems is addressed.

Chapter 5 looks at the targets for family assessment, including family roles, rules, rituals, communication patterns, and common family difficulties such as triangles, secrets, and cutoffs. In addition, the chapter identifies a series of assessment tools that the social worker can employ, including genograms, ecomaps, self-reports, observations, family histories, and the social network map and grid.

Chapter 6 focuses on the planning phase in working with families. This includes the importance of client- and family-directed planning and focusing on strengths. Steps in the planning process are identified, including goal setting, contracting, and developing an evaluation plan. Ethnic and cultural challenges in planning and goal setting complete the chapter.

Chapter 7 deals with the implementation stage where plans made earlier are carried out by the social worker and client. The chapter begins with a review of basic skills and techniques and then looks at how five models approach implementation. The models are psychodynamic/psychoanalytic, experiential, structural, cognitive/behavioral, and postmodern. Objectives, intervention planning, and techniques of each are discussed.

Chapter 8 looks at the importance of evaluating the effectiveness of family practice and identifies a variety of methods that can be used. Methods included are single-subject designs, content analysis designs, and goal attainment scaling, among others. The chapter also discusses some ethnic and cultural challenges affecting the evaluation process. The final section of the chapter covers termination and follow-up, with a specific focus on reactions to termination by family and practitioner, types of terminations, and tasks to be completed.

Chapters 9 and 10 identify and describe several challenging family situations encountered by practitioners. Chapter 9 includes families of older adults, gay and lesbian families, families living in poverty, single parents, stepfamilies, and families with disabilities. Chapter 10 looks at divorcing/separating families, families facing multiple barriers, and families coping with death and mental illness of one or more members. Each chapter looks at specific challenges facing these families, as well as at strategies for helping them.

Chapter 11 is devoted to specialized family interventions. These include family preservation, wraparound services, extended family support groups (kinship care), and multiple family groups. A description of each is presented along with a review of current research.

Chapter 12 looks at the family in the community, particularly the role the community plays in furthering or impeding a family's quest for survival and well-being. The chapter looks at institutional deficiencies found in the community and discusses the family support movement, school-based family support programs, and those developed by employers. Also included is the role of higher education in fostering healthy communities and families.

Chapter 13 examines the role that social policy plays in sustaining family well-being. It focuses specifically on public assistance and child welfare programs enacted to assist families. Limitations, challenges, and problems of each type of program are described.

Finally, Chapter 14 considers a variety of future trends likely to impact families. These cover issues such as family composition, household locations, family demographics, employment and economic factors, and ethnicity. The chapter concludes with a discussion of the evolution of family practice, particularly service-delivery changes, evolving policy issues, and critical thinking.

2 CHAPTER Understanding Family Theories

© Photodisc/Royalty-Free/Getty Images

INTRODUCTION

This chapter provides the social worker with an understanding of the theories essential for intervening with families. While Chapter 7 will address the implementation of several models based on these theories along with specific techniques, conceptualizing theory before implementing models is essential to practice. By connecting theories to models, the family practitioner uses a multidimensional theoretical approach to practice. Viewing families as part of a variety of systems and connecting theories to families within the context of those systems allows social workers to select the most appropriate and broad-based approach to their practice. Gehart and Tuttle (2003) note that family practice models based on theory "encourage a broad view of the problem situation, including family and social influences on the presenting problem" (p. 5). This is consistent with the family-in-environment focus used in this text. Besides examining the significant theories related to family practice, we will define the ideas central to each theory.

MULTIDIMENSIONAL FRAMEWORK

Theories are one of several tools used by social workers to assist families. A *theory* is a collection of concepts and hypotheses that help us to understand the world. Theories help us explain why things happen and give direction to our efforts. Related to or drawn from each theory are one or more intervention models that we can use in our work with families. Finally, each intervention model is associated with a set of specialized techniques used in practice. While some theories are less useful than others, most underlying theories about families are critical to application. We can think about Figure 2.1 as a basic diagram for how frameworks, theories, models, and techniques fit together in a multidimensional theoretical framework for practice. Another reason for understanding theories is their direct link to assessment. Theories are the lenses through which we view and assess a family. Many social workers may ultimately specialize in one model of practice derived from particular theories. Other practitioners will use more than one practice model drawn from a small subset of theories. We believe understanding families and implementing strength-based planned change requires knowledge of many different theories and their subsequent models to give the client the best services available.

A strength-based planned change approach reflects the basic tenets of Saleebey's (1997) work. Saleebey posits several principles that characterize the strengths approach to practice, and we have applied these principles to family practice. Highlight 2.1 identifies these principles and provides a brief explanation of each.

We have said that it is critical to use many lenses to determine the functioning of a family, its members, and the systems surrounding it. Relying, for example, on a deficit model rather than a strength approach overlooks a family's potential capacity to improve. Using a single lens can also limit our understanding of the context in which we work with clients. Table 2.1 is an example of how different lenses (theories) can affect how a social worker thinks about

Figure 2.1 | Multidimensional Theoretical Framework

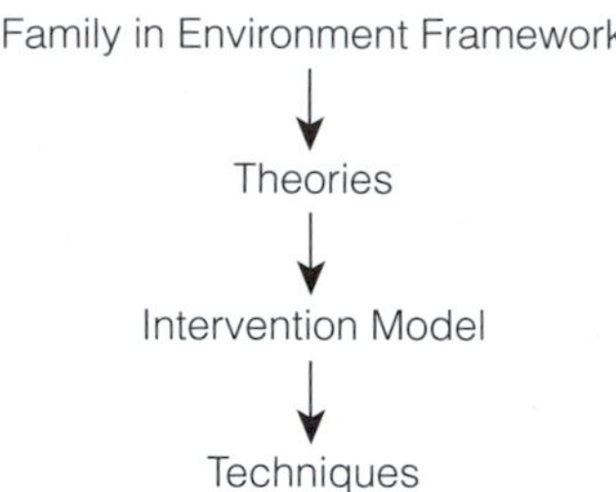

Highlight 2.1 | Strength-Based Family Practice Principles

1. *Strengths characterize every family and every family member.*
   Strengths may take many forms, ranging from financial to emotional resources. The capacity to recognize and seek help for a family problem is one such strength. Empathy, concern for, and sensitivity to the needs of other family members are also strengths.
2. *The possibility for change and growth in families is potentially limitless.*
   Knowing what an individual or family can do is not possible unless we give them the opportunity to show us. Families often rise to the occasion when the practitioner expresses faith in the members' capacities to change.
3. *Families exposed to traumatic events and terrible experiences can develop resiliency and the capacity to overcome the odds.*
   Hardships can both scar families and make them stronger. Assume both are possible and seek the latter. Overcoming trauma, oppression, and misfortune can produce stronger individuals and families.
4. *Family environments are often rich in resources.*
   Resources may range from social networks to institutional services available to help the family. They may be provided by both informal and formal organizations, individuals, other families, and communities.
5. *Family practice is more effective when the family is considered a partner in change rather than a recipient of help.*
   Participating fully in a change effort increases the likelihood that families will reach their goals. Families treated as junior partners by family practitioners may be less committed to achieving goals and objectives.

Source: Based on Saleebey (1997).

Table 2.1 | Different Lenses for Viewing a Family with an Alcoholic Son

Theory	Possible Explanations
Psychoanalytic	Early childhood development difficulties
Cognitive-Behavioral	Cognitive thought dysfunctions
Structural	Power structures define family and contribute to behavior
Systems	Peer systems influence on the individual system (son)
Communication	Interactions between marital couple influence son's behavior
Strategic	Power differentials in the family influence son's behavior
Postmodern	Individual behavior is a function of cultural influences and definitions

and views a family's situation. How one assesses a family situation depends in large part on the theory used. For example, explanations for behavior are usually linked to the social worker's underlying theories of human behavior.

FAMILY PRACTICE

In Chapter 1 we discussed the history of family practice and began to touch on how family therapies are used today. The movement toward family therapy was based on understanding the family through different lenses (theories) and developing related practice models. Early family therapists began their approaches to practice with a common understanding of certain theories and experiences. Primary among these was systems theory and the belief that no entity operates alone but rather exists in conjunction with other entities. Therefore, family members could not behave or change behavior outside of the context in which their family operated.

While both Freud and Jung saw relationships between their psychiatric patients' early development and their current situation, not as much emphasis was placed on the here and now of their family members. This early lens (while a valid part of understanding an individual) did little to change situations if the current family system played a part in the client's life. This view that past family histories were of greatest import for determining individual behavior changed when practitioners began to recognize how the current family constellation influenced the individual's situation.

In 1954, Gregory Bateson, a well-known theorist, scientist, and expert on communication, received a grant to study schizophrenic communication. Bateson had theorized that there were often secondary messages going on between two people in conversations. He believed that these secondary messages were often covert and could be seen in nonverbal ways. Bateson called these interactions "metamessages" and began to study the communication patterns between young schizophrenics and their parents. He theorized that these metamessages had as much of an impact on the young adult as did the verbal expression. Today we recognize that these metamessages occur in almost every aspect of communication between two people and are often more noticeable in family interaction, where emotions (overt and covert) form a major component of family life and interactions. We can see an example of this in Theory in Action: Metamessage.

THEORY IN ACTION | Metamessage

Rachel, age 20, is encouraged by her family to be independent and have her own life. However, the family calls Rachel at least twice a day to find out what she is doing and sends packages with money and other items on a daily basis. When Rachel has an opportunity to take a job several hundred miles away, she hesitates. She is concerned about leaving her family and being completely on her own. Her family's behavior has expressed a message different from the verbal one they provided.

Many psychiatrists, psychologists, and social workers joined with Bateson in attempting to understand how the "metacommunication" phenomenon was affecting their patients. Their research with schizophrenics and their families led them to believe that most things affecting an individual occurred within the context of the family. They also theorized that even dysfunctional family situations could be an effective way of maintaining what we call *homeostasis* (or balance) in the family. We can see an example of this in Theory in Action: Homeostasis.

THEORY IN ACTION | Homeostasis

In the Moreland family, John Moreland's drinking distresses his wife. She is angry with him when he gets home late, cleans him up when he gets sick, and lies for him with his employer when he cannot make it to work. John, facing termination at work, decides to sober up. While his wife is happy about the change in John's behavior, she tends to still keep liquor around the house, fails to attend Alanon meetings, and treats John as she did when he was drinking. The family theorist would argue that the husband's changed behavior had threatened the wife's role in the family and that (consciously or unconsciously) she is attempting to maintain homeostasis (or the same pattern in the family) as she understands it.

These types of theoretical findings, along with other studies that examined family dynamics, communication, family of origin issues, and family roles, led to the development of the family therapy movement. Many early family therapists had worked with Bateson, including Salvadore Minuchin, Jay Haley, and Virginia Satir. While no list is exhaustive, it is important to note that these individuals, plus Don Jackson, Murray Bowen, Carl Whitaker, Robert Liberman, and Neil Jacobson, were pioneers in the field of family therapy. In their own ways, each added to the understanding of family practice/therapy with the application of a major lens or theoretical perspective. The subheadings of theories that follow are attributed to their major theorist, as are subsequent therapies and models of family treatment.

Understanding the basis for family practice models requires understanding the lenses through which each of these models developed. While there is no effective way to highlight all the complexities of particular theoretical bases, we will cover a few of the most prominent theories that family practitioners have used in their models. These include systems theory, structural family theory, family communication theory, strategic family theory, cognitive-behavioral theory, cognitive theory, psychoanalytic and psychodynamic theory, feminist theory, and postmodern theory.

SYSTEMS THEORY AND FAMILIES: COMMONLY SHARED CONCEPTS

Systems theory is a way of looking at individuals, families, groups, organizations, and communities with a view to better understanding how each of these units functions and survives. Originally drawn largely from the fields of biology, engineering, and mathematics, systems theory quickly became a critical tool for explaining family behavior. Many ideas we currently use in family practice are drawn directly from systems theory. One major contribution of this theory is the ability to see the family both as a whole and as a series of component parts (for example, parents, children). A second contribution is the recognition that problematic behavior of any single family member is a reflection of a system (family) disturbance rather than simply a deficit in the individual member. This approach made it much easier to assess and treat a variety of problems, from eating disorders to depression, by making the family the unit of analysis (Holland & Kilpatrick, 1999).

Equally important, systems theory has helped practitioners recognize the influence that ethnicity and culture, family traditions, and environmental factors can have on the stability and health of families and their members. Rather than posit a single explanation for any given behavior, systems theory suggests that multiple perspectives are most important. Highlight 2.2 illustrates how multiple perspectives can be much more helpful than single or unidimensional explanations for behavior.

Highlight 2.2 | **Multiple Perspective**

The Manning family had been referred by the court to see a social worker at the family service agency. The reason for the referral stemmed from a report from the Division of Child Welfare of neglect in the family home. A neighbor had found the children, ages 5, 7, and 9, alone in the family home. The mother had been gone for an hour so she could see her 3-year-old son, who had been hospitalized for pneumonia. The mother had recently been unemployed and was without funds for child care. Her husband had left the family three months ago, and she had no idea of where he was. Awareness of the factors operating in this case can change the way we look at the fact of the mother's court referral for child neglect.

Basic Systems Theory Concepts

Many concepts inherent in systems theory are useful for understanding families. In presenting these examples, we will provide a brief description for each along with general examples of how the concept applies to the family. These concepts and definitions are drawn primarily from systems theorists (Becvar & Becvar, 2003).

Homeostasis *Homeostasis* is the tendency of any system to try to maintain itself in a state of equilibrium or balance. As systems, families are affected by events outside their control, such as economic downturns or the death of loved ones. These events can seriously undermine the economic, social, and psychological resources of the family as a unit and of individual family members. The tendency of all systems to right themselves following stressful and traumatic events is an attempt to get back to some semblance of normality. All families use many methods to maintain their balance. Sometimes these efforts prove futile as the family becomes overwhelmed by events and incapable of adjustment. At other times, they are very effective, at least for the short term, in returning the family to a steady state.

Feedback *Feedback* is essential to family systems, for without it there is no way to know how various members experience family life. Feedback can take many forms—requests for more time or attention, demands for changes in behavior, praise for specific actions, and/or criticisms for perceived problems that are threatening the homeostasis. Sometimes, people give feedback indirectly and thus ineffectively. Consider a partner who withdraws from a relationship with her mate and gradually reduces the time spent with the partner. This behavior is also feedback, but it conveys only indirectly the pain and unhappiness she is experiencing. One goal of helping families is to teach family members how to provide feedback that is more likely to be effective.

Feedback can be both positive and negative. *Positive feedback* can spur family members to attempt new behaviors or to support change already undertaken. *Negative feedback* has the opposite effect in that it reduces the likelihood of change occurring and reinforces patterns of homeostasis (Green, 2003). Thus, a husband who is praised by his wife for talking about his feelings is receiving positive feedback that is likely to result in similar behavior on his part later. A young daughter who is made fun of as a "tomboy" may get the message that her active life in sports is inappropriate. This can lead her to adopt behaviors that are more consistent with her parents' traditional gender role expectations.

Boundaries All family systems have *boundaries,* or ways of demarcating who is in the family and who is not. While invisible, boundaries are often clear, such as when someone asks us to list our family members. We will likely list our parents and any siblings. However, boundaries can be much more complex when the family involves stepparents, stepchildren, new spouses for parents, and perhaps others who are important to the family, such as grandparents. The family might also include nonrelated individuals (fictive kin) to whom they have accorded family status. Boundaries are important in family practice, since it is crucial to know which individuals need to be included and which excluded from our helping activities.

Open and Closed Systems Family systems may be considered along a continuum from open to closed. By *open* or *closed,* we are referring to the degree and nature of interactions with other systems in the environment. These interactions include communication, exposure to new ideas and information, and the sharing of resources. No family is likely to be entirely open or closed because of the impact this has on the family unit. A totally open family, for example, would not differentiate between those who are family members and those who are not. Within a completely open family, it is possible that any child or adult could move into the family and be treated as just another family member. Totally open families would expend resources such as family income and shelter equally on those inside the family and those outside. In fact, there is likely to be no obvious boundary between those comprising the family and those on the outside. This is a model that most of us would find disturbing and uncomfortable.

At the same time, a totally closed family system would have no interaction with the larger environment. Family members would not engage in relationships with anyone outside the family and would never adopt ideas or practices used by outside individuals or families. All family members would be focused on other family members, would be discouraged or prevented from introducing others into the home, and would operate within a tight set of rules about what is right and wrong. The absence of any feedback from the environment can be extraordinarily debilitating for the family. We use the term *entropy* to describe these situations because a totally closed family system is headed for disorganization and disarray. The lack of interaction with the environment prevents the acquisition of new skills and decreases the potential for solving family problems. This is particularly problematic because it is through exposure to the ideas of others that we learn various ways of dealing with life's difficulties. By recognizing that there are often several satisfactory ways of doing things, we are behaving in concert with another systems concept, *equifinality.* This concept is essentially the equivalent of the old phrase "there's more than one way to skin a cat." [Author's note: This idiomatic phrase meant little when I first heard it from my parents, except for a lingering concern that there might be some strange behavior buried in our family history. With experience, I learned that there are often many ways of doing anything; however, the lingering concern remains.]

In practice, most families are somewhere along the continuum, neither completely open nor totally closed. The point on the continuum may change over time, but ultimately survival as a healthy family unit requires some level of interaction with the external environment. As social workers, we may need to help a family become more open to new ideas at one point in their development while assisting members to focus more on their own internal relationships at another point. The particular needs of the family in this regard are likely to become more obvious from a family assessment, a topic that is discussed in Chapters 4 and 5.

When we talk about open or closed systems, we are acknowledging the fact that all systems have some boundaries that separate them from the external environment. Most of us can recognize who is a part of our family and who is not because, while essentially invisible, these boundaries are generally clear to family members. Of course, since all systems have boundaries, this also means that boundaries exist within the family. For example, the adult partners have a boundary that separates them from the children. Siblings may have boundaries that characterize their relationships with each other. For example, a brother and sister about the same age may be very close while another older sibling is not considered a part of this dyad.

Adaptation An important characteristic of a healthy family system is its capacity to adapt to changes, stressors, and other threats occurring either within or outside the family. *Adaptation* is a crucial ability because all systems continually face change. Children are born, reach adolescence, leave home, and marry. Each of these requires a family to adapt. Similarly, serious and/or chronic illness, deaths, and other negative experiences put the family in a position to change some aspects of their behaviors. Job changes, whether positive or not, also require adaptation, as do modifications in one's standard of living. Essentially, all life events and transitions, expected or unexpected, pleasant or not, force the family to cope. Moreover, individual family members may experience different stressors. Adolescents may experience stress related to family expectations, especially if they doubt their ability to fulfill parental wishes (DuongTran, Lee, & Khoi, 1996). Both cultural backgrounds and gender may affect how severely individual family members perceive a stressor. The resiliency and adaptability of the family in the face of these life events are solid measures of strength.

Structural Family Theory

We most commonly attribute *structural family theory* to the work of Salvador Minuchin. Minuchin developed his theory and model by borrowing from "ecological systems theory, general systems theory, network therapy and other approaches" (Jordan & Franklin, 1999, p. 23). Minuchin (1974) stated that he believed family structure to be "The invisible set of functional demands that organizes the way in which family members interact" (p. 51). These functional demands might include such things as who talks to whom, who disciplines the children, what rules are carried out, who is in charge, who protects whom, and which roles are played within the context of the family. These patterns of interactions then structure the ways in which individual family members act with one another and in turn limits the possibilities of changing behaviors. In structural family therapy, the goal is to change the unhealthy structures into healthy ones. There are several concepts in structural theory that must be understood before the family practitioner can view the family through this lens. We have discussed several of these concepts in relation to systems theory, but they garner additional meaning when linked to structural family theory. In structural theory the ideas of boundaries, subsystems, roles, enmeshment, disengagement, hierarchy, and transactions are key to the development of the structural family therapy model (Green, 2003).

Boundaries As discussed previously, boundaries in a family are the lines of demarcation separating systems and subsystems. In structural theory, these boundaries are critical to the lens through which we see the family. A boundary can be open or closed within a family. In structural theory, there is a belief that boundaries are important to the health of the family, and yet simultaneously the family is in constant change influenced by factors in the environment. Additionally, there is a belief that the boundary around the family protects the family from outside intrusion but also allows family members to be free to move outside their own system. Problematic boundaries are often characterized as too rigid or diffused. Rigid boundaries do not allow for free movement between the subsystems, which in turn prevents the individual from connecting to others. This can often cause a person in the family unit to feel disengaged. While disengagement can foster independence, it can also bring isolation. Diffuse boundaries, on the other hand, do not have clear demarcations of subsystems, and the children and parents can be too intrusive in each other's lives. We call this type of family situation *enmeshment* because it does not allow individuals to operate independently.

Subsystems Structural theory holds that families most often operate as an open system with subsystems that perform certain functions. While each individual serves as a subsystem, other subsystems may be based on such factors as generation, gender, parent–child, and mutual interest. Thus, a child may be simultaneously considered part of several family subsystems. One subsystem may consist of all the other children in the family, while another may be based on the fact that both father and son are devoted to sports. Similarly, all the boys in a family may make up a separate subsystem denoted by their shared gender. Depending upon what is happening within a family, these subsystems may shift between members. For example, a trauma in the family, such as divorce, may disrupt the father–son subsystem and bring the son into a subsystem with the mother. The most common subsystems in a traditional family include the couple (who also operate as the parents), the children, and a parent–child alliance.

Within structural theory, awareness of covert subsystems is also important. These subsystems are the ones that are not always obvious. For example, a woman may maintain a closer relationship with her father on an interpersonal basis then she does with her husband. A father may feel closer and more accepting of one child than another. Each subsystem needs its own protection in order for members to develop. If, for instance, parents were constantly playing a group of three siblings against one another, the children probably could not grow and change as needed within this system. In another example, if John's mother is constantly taking him places to get new things and leaving daughter Sarah at home, while the father constantly dotes on Sarah, neither the couple's nor children's subsystem will function as effectively as it might.

In structural theory, two adults make up the couple subsystem that has come together to form a bond. Traditionally, this has been a man and woman but can also be a same-sex couple. This subsystem in the family acts relatively independently from other subsystems. This coming together of two individuals in a bond creates a boundary that both prevents outside intrusion and serves as a protective unit within the family. While this theory presents a logical understanding of the traditional family, we must remember that there are single parents and kinship adults who also serve as the parental subsystems.

The children in the family also form a unit with a boundary where, through their connections, they learn to interact and understand the ways to operate within the family system. This subsystem often serves a supportive function to children when there are difficulties within the family, and it serves as a unit in which children can develop their independence.

The parent–child subsystem is one in which the parents interact with the children based on the needs of the child. Such a subsystem differs from others in that it crosses generational boundaries. While this crossing of generational boundaries can be dysfunctional at times, it can also be very functional if it does not interfere with the other subgroups and their boundaries.

Roles Within each of these subsystems, individuals play different *roles*. A woman might play the role of mother for her child, daughter for her own parents, and best friend for her partner. Each of these roles carries with it particular characteristics that can shift and change over time. If the father is demanding in interactions with his children, he probably cannot act in the same manner as a husband or son. This differentiation occurs in part because of the way others, such as his wife or father, expect him to behave. In a healthy situation, an individual can move between these roles and shift behaviors accordingly. In an unhealthy situation, the father would attempt to carry out his demanding behaviors in all the roles he lives. *Complementarity* is about the members of subsystems developing personalities that complement each other. For example, we may describe one child as "wild" in her behavior whereas her sibling may be considered "someone who is studious and seldom leaves the house."

Hierarchy The *hierarchy* in a family is about who is in charge and who has power. While we generally accept that parents have the power over their children, there can be situations in which a child serves as a "parental child." For example in an alcoholic family, the oldest daughter may look after the younger children because her parents are incapable of doing so.

Transactions All of these components of structural theory are brought to bear on the *transactions* among family members and, as these transactions are done repeatedly, they become patterns. These patterns establish the homeostasis for the family. So whether the patterns of transaction are positive or negative, the family will act as a system to maintain the status quo because that is what they know.

Family Communication Theory

Communication theory serves as one of the prominent theories for understanding families and practicing family therapy. Communication theory's earliest development arose from "cybernetics." *Cybernetics* began as an understanding of self-regulation of machines and moved to an understanding of interactions between people (Becvar & Becvar, 2003). Based primarily on systems theory, cybernetics provides a way of understanding not only how people interact but also how they react to one another. This early understanding of interactional phenomena contributed to Bateson's concept of metacommunication. For Bateson, his study of schizophrenics and their interactional patterns with their families showed clearly how communication (nonverbal and verbal) could lead to specific behaviors. Satir, Stachowiak, and Taschman's (1975) classic book *Helping Families to Change* reflects the different communication stances that verbal and nonverbal interactions can create. The five stances identified during family interactions include placating, blaming, distracting, functional, and super-reasoning.

In communication theory, a major concept is that of the "here and now." Believing that individuals operate primarily from the interactions of their communication, theorists began to define communication concepts better. These included complementary and symmetrical communication, the role of power perceptions of other family members, circular causality, and feedback loops (Nichols & Schwartz, 2001)

Complementary Communication *Complementary communication* refers to those situations in which two opposites fit together. Couples will reflect on how different they are in aspects of their personality and communication and yet match one another in complementary ways. For example, one individual in a relationship may be outgoing and spontaneous, while the partner may be more reserved and organized in his or her approach to an issue.

Symmetrical Communication This term refers to the state of equal communication between partners. Equal communication reduces the likelihood of setting up roles for members. An example of symmetrical communication might include a communication structure within a relationship in which both partners perceive equality in the relationship, talk equally, and communicate decisions in the same way. While this may seem ideal, there are nuances to this that may not be functional.

Power Perceptions *Power perceptions* are the images that individuals within a family have regarding one another. These perceptions may or may not be accurate. For example, while a father in a family may appear to be very powerful, it may be the mother who makes most of the decisions while the father carries them out. We might view a child as having more power because of acting-out behavior and the attention it requires from the parents trying to control it.

Feedback Loop A *feedback loop* refers to the process of communication in which one person communicates to another and the person receiving the message comments back, and so forth. Through feedback loops, communication theorists learn to understand how one form or type of communication affects another person and how it contributes to the response received.

Circular Causality *Circular causality* refers to the process of feedback loops. In families, feedback loops note the ongoing exchanges that occur between individuals as they act and react toward one another. For example, Alice may yell at Bob when he comes in late. To avoid Alice, Bob decides to continue to come home late, hoping she will be in bed. Alice, in turn, becomes increasingly angry and waits up to yell at Bob. This approach to understanding dynamics and communication in a family is a different concept from looking at issues in a linear fashion of direct cause and effect.

Communication theory suggests that individuals in groups or families respond to one another based on their verbal and nonverbal interactions. Underlying communication theory is the acceptance of the premise that no one can understand or feel the way another person does. Therefore, the accuracy of communication becomes crucial in a family's ability to interact with one another.

Strategic Family Theory

Jay Haley is the theorist most often associated with strategic therapy. Strategic theorists embrace more of a behavioral emphasis than most family practitioners. They seek the simplest and most constructive way to resolve a problem. Focused in on problem solving, strategic theorists believe in directly attacking symptoms. Another contributor was Milton Erickson, a well-known psychiatrist who, becoming convinced that insight therapy did little to resolve problems, began to treat symptoms rather than childhood memories and experiences. Bateson's work with cybernetics was also one of the founding stone's of the strategic movement in family therapy.

Using the idea of treating resistance, Haley believed that family dynamics involved the ideas of feedback loops, rules, and hierarchy as defined in structural family therapy (Haley, 1976). In addition, Haley thought that symptoms were the result of a hierarchical difficulty in a family. If, for example, a parent–child coalition against another parent developed, Haley reasoned that symptoms or problems in a family emerged to maintain a particular structure based on individuals' need to control. He set about treating the family's symptom rather than their overall interaction because the symptom represented a problem that the family could change. As an example, Haley might focus the change effort on resolving the problem of a child's bed-wetting without delving into past family history.

Haley also believed in the metaphor of control. He saw members of families as trying to control and define the nature of relationships (Haley, 1976). As strategic theorists believed that symptoms result from the interactions of people striving for control of a situation, his approach was then to create a situation in which neither symptoms nor the dysfunctional hierarchical structure could be maintained. His method for doing this was to "join with the family" through labeling, identifying, or defining a problem (Becvar & Becar, 2003, p. 219). Following the joining with the family, the therapist can create change by attempting to participate in the problem structure.

Several additional ideas familiar to strategic theorists include first-order change, second-order change, problematic sequences, and problem purpose (Goldenberg & Goldenberg, 1991).

First-Order Change *First-order change* refers to change that occurs within the existing rules and patterns of the family. Since the existing rules and patterns are, by definition, ineffective, any change that the person demonstrates is unlikely to be permanent. Consider the case of a child whose parents yell at him about doing his homework but then never follow through to ensure that the child is completing this work. The child learns quickly that the family rule is to yell, obtain temporary compliance, and then return to the usual routine. Thus, the child promises the parents he will work harder on his homework, does so briefly, and then reverts to his old behaviors when the parents cease to pay attention. While making this promise is logical and appropriate for him, his degree of commitment is negligible. When the parents are not around, the child continues to ignore the homework and plays games on the Internet instead.

Second-Order Change *Second-order change* occurs only when the family rules have been modified to support and sustain changes in behavior. Thus, in the previous case, the parents are taught to communicate clearly to the child regarding their expectations, to follow through by ensuring the child completes the homework, and to reinforce the new behavior. The child now learns that the rules have changed and that simple verbal assurances of compliance with the parents' wishes are insufficient. Social workers seek second-order change because it tends to continue for longer periods and represents *real* rather than *token* change in behavior.

Problematic Sequences Individuals within a family system often maintain their own problems by acting out in a patterned sequential manner that tends to increase the rigidity of behavior. For example, a mother wishing her oldest son to become more responsible spends most of their interactional time correcting and taking care of his irresponsible behavior. This interaction increases the son's belief that he is irresponsible, and he does not take more responsibility because his mother always takes care of the situation for him. Thus, the mother's attempts to help her child become more responsible result in his becoming less so.

Problem Purpose *Problem purpose* is a term used to explain how troublesome family issues may actually serve some specific purpose. For example, consider a child in the family who acts out every time her parents argue over money. By misbehaving in such situations, the child successfully gets the parents to focus on her rather than continuing their attacks on one another. Not only does this end the parents' problematic interactions, it also gives the girl the additional attention she craves.

The concepts and theoretical strategies in strategic theory are simultaneously simple and complex in their application. The family practitioner using these ideas needs to be aware of the dynamics of the family and careful in the application.

Cognitive–Behavioral Theories and Families

The use of cognitive–behavioral theories and practice models with families came from the combination of several different theories. The foundation for both behavioral and cognitive theory is learning theory. *Behavioral theory* is based in large part on two central concepts: classical conditioning as theorized by Ivan Pavlov and operant conditioning as described by B.F. Skinner. *Classical conditioning* begins when an unconditioned stimulus (such as food) leads to an unconditioned response (such as salivating) (Nichols & Schwartz, 2001). If we then pair the unconditioned stimulus with another stimulus such as a bell, the result is a conditioned stimulus that can produce the same behavior as the original unconditioned stimulus. In Pavlov's work, he paired the ring of a bell with the presentation of food to a dog. After a while, the dog would salivate whenever the bell rang, even without the presentation of food.

Operant conditioning emerged from classical conditioning and explains behavior largely as a function of its antecedents and consequences. Under this theory, praising a child (consequence) for being polite (behavior) is likely to encourage further such actions by the child. The concepts important to behavioral theory include the following: positive reinforcement, negative reinforcement, primary and secondary reinforcers, punishment, extinction, and the Premack Principle.

Positive Reinforcement *Positive reinforcement* is a term that describes any consequence that is likely to increase the occurrence of the behavior that preceded it. For example, a child receives a piece of candy following the completion of his homework every evening. Candy is the positive reinforcement and an increase in homework completion is the outcome.

Negative Reinforcement *Negative reinforcement* refers to the removal of an adverse or negative consequence with the goal of increasing the occurrence of a positive behavior. Consider a child restricted from watching television until she improves her grade in history. When the child's grade in history improves, the parents end the TV restriction, thereby reinforcing her academic effort. We use both positive and negative reinforcement frequently with children and adolescents.

Primary and Secondary Reinforcers Primary and secondary reinforcers "describe a difference between what is biological and what is learned" (Gehart & Tuttle, 2003, p.174). *Primary reinforcers* are those that are based on common biological needs, such as food and clothing. *Secondary reinforcers* are those items that the individual learns to value, such as good grades.

Punishment *Punishment* is very different from both positive and negative reinforcement. While both positive and negative reinforcement increase the likelihood that a person will repeat a behavior, punishment *decreases* the likelihood. For example, consider a child who got into a fight at school. His parents decide to ground him for a week as punishment. The grounding is designed to discourage fighting and decrease such behavior in the future.

Extinction In behavioral theory, the term *extinction* refers to a complete elimination of a behavior. If we no longer reinforce an individual for a certain behavior, that behavior should cease to occur. An example would be the young wife who every Sunday fixes her husband his favorite meal and is lavishly praised for doing so. After a while, the husband neglects to acknowledge his wife's efforts and eventually she stops making the meal. Behavior that is never reinforced is likely to disappear given enough time.

Premack Principle Gehart and Tuttle (2003) describe the *Premack Principle* as a theory "that a person's preferred or high-probability behavior can be used to reinforce low-probability behaviors that one would like to change" (p. 174). An example of this would be parents who would like a son to clean up his room, so they tie the privilege of playing outside to cleaning his room first. Because the child really enjoys playing outside with his friends, parents can easily use this as reinforcement for the desired behavior.

Cognitive–behavioral family practice tends to be time-limited and scientific in approach and evaluation. It also incorporates education through such activities as parent training.

Cognitive Theory

Added to these concepts are those related to *cognitive theory.* Cognitive theory emphasizes the role that cognitions (thoughts, self-talk) play in producing behavior. For example, a cognitive theorist might explain a client's depression by looking at the repeated negative thoughts and internal messages the client gives himself. Continually telling himself that he is a worthless person and a burden to his family is likely to have a profound impact on his emotions and behavior. Thus, cognitive theory attempts to explain behavior by looking at the thoughts that engender the behavior. While both behavioral and cognitive theory have developed associated models, most theorists and writers use both theories in treatment, as in cognitive–behavioral. This is due in part to the belief by many theorists that without cognitions, there are no behaviors. Albert Ellis (1977) and his A–B–C theory of behavior helped develop the use of cognitive theory in therapy models. *A* represents the Activating Event leading to *B,* the Belief, and this then leads to *C,* the Consequent Emotion. Ellis believed family members create their own situations that in turn affect the whole family. For example, a daughter believes she is stupid and cannot make good grades in school. Consequently, she does not try hard and ends up making poor grades. Ellis's theory is that individuals place irrational beliefs on each other, and these beliefs affect the emotional environment within the family. It then follows that if family members can see the irrationality of their beliefs and come to terms with more rational thoughts, then relationships within the family can improve.

Aaron Beck extended Ellis's work through his efforts to help clients experiencing depression. Beck also believed that cognitive thoughts caused emotions that led to a responding behavior. It is noteworthy that Beck's and Ellis's theories in this area were at odds with traditional views that emotions controlled thoughts.

Some key terms related to cognitive theory include cognitive distortions, automatic thoughts, thought stopping, and schemas (Nichols & Schwartz, 2001).

Cognitive Distortions Both Beck and Ellis theorized that individuals had irrational beliefs *(cognitive distortions)* tied to emotions that affected behavior. Beck (1976) notes the following six distortions as common ones that affect behavior:

1. The mental filter: Taking the negative details of an event and magnifying them while filtering out all positive aspects of a situation.
2. Dichotomous thinking: There is no middle ground. Everything is either/or, good or bad.
3. Mind reading: Believing you know exactly what people are thinking, especially in regard to their thoughts about you.

4. Catastrophizing: Thinking the worst case scenario is going to occur and that it will be intolerable.
5. Blaming: Others are solely responsible for your problems.
6. Control: (a) Out of control, "I am at the mercy of external forces." (b) Need for control, "I must control everyone and everything or the results will be disastrous." (as cited in Green, 2003, p. 157)

Beck viewed these distortions as the primary reason for individuals' distress and saw them as majors factors in creating the family's environment. It follows that changing these distortions or irrational beliefs would change what was happening in the family.

Thought Stopping *Thought stopping* is a concept in cognitive theory based on the idea that if the individual can stop the cognition (an irrational belief or cognitive distortion), then the emotion and subsequent behavior can be stopped also. In cognitive therapy, one method of stopping a thought is for clients to picture a stop sign in their head whenever they recognize the problematic thought.

Schemas Gehart and Tuttle (2003) define a *schema* as a set of beliefs held by the family that sets the rules that regulate a family's behavior. In cognitive therapy, consider a family who appears frightened of outside interference because of an irrational belief that outside influence would destroy the family. In therapy, the practitioner would challenge that belief and encourage the creation of a more rational belief or schema.

Another contribution to cognitive theory is the work of Albert Bandura (1977). His social learning theory has four underlying principles that seek to explain behavior:

1. *Expectancy*—Bandura argued that the mere fact that people expect to be reinforced or rewarded is sufficient for them to behave in a specific way. This suggests the importance of cognitive processes on individual behavior and explains situations where a behavior occurs even though no prior reinforcement has taken place. For example, a child may willingly share her toys with her brother because she believes this will please their mother.
2. *Self-efficacy*—This is the belief that one can achieve certain goals or tasks. The individual may come to believe this through seeing others accomplish these tasks or because he or she has been successful at these tasks in the past. For example, a husband believes that he can smooth over things with his wife by bringing her flowers and telling her how much he loves her because this has worked several times in the past. He therefore believes that no matter how bad his behavior, he will always be successful in mollifying his wife.
3. *Reciprocal determinism*—This is the reciprocal exchange of information between two or more people. It is the response one has to what has been said and the response of the other person to the initial response. For example, a daughter starts calling her father names and waits for his response. Based on the father's response, the daughter then decides what to say next.

4. *Modeling*—Bandura posits that individuals learn to behave in particular ways by watching others. This approach suggests that we learn behaviors, such as drug abuse, by watching others who abuse drugs.

Psychoanalytic and Psychodynamic Family Theories and Families

Like cognitive–behavioral theory, psychoanalytic and psychodynamic family theory are similar and yet different. Sigmund Freud, best known for *psychoanalytic theory,* believed that individuals developed through what he called "psychosexual drives." These drives propel individuals forward through a series of stages of psychosexual development (Nichols & Schwartz, 2001). (Erikson [1950] later anchored each of these stages with a psychological development challenge, such as trust vs. mistrust in the oral phase.) Freud also believed that the personality of each individual was made up of the *id* (the pleasure-seeking part of the individual), the *Ego* (the mediating self between the id and the superego), and the *Superego* (most closely associated with the conscience and the values of right and wrong). Freud, although working with individuals and not families, believed that most issues that human beings develop are related back to our mothers and fathers and early family interactions.

Psychodynamic and psychoanalytic theory are interchangeable in their meaning. While psychoanalytic/psychodynamic theory accounts for intrapsychic makeup of the individual, and family therapy concentrates on relationships between people, psychoanalytic/psychodynamic family theory also uses *object relations theory* to bring both together. (Object relations theory hypothesizes that individual personalities are formed in large part by the perceived relationship between the individual self and the other object [generally the mother] during early development.) In *psychodynamic family theory,* there is a recognition that one's family of origin strongly influences the present family situation, in particular those of the unconscious object relationship between parent and child (Becvar & Becvar, 2003). Theorists further believe that individuals project these early relationships onto their present families. The following are some basic concepts of psychodynamic family theory: insight, transference, counter-transference, introjection, projective identification, collusion. differentiation, splitting, rapproachment, and object constancy.

Insight *Insight* in psychoanalytic theory is the process by which clients become aware of and understand how an early childhood experience affects them now. For example, a father with an emotionally abusive mother comes to understand his strong reaction to any criticism from his wife.

Transference *Transference* is a concept in psychoanalytic theory that refers to the transferring of the client's emotions and feelings onto the therapist. This occurs as clients begin to view the therapist as a figure from their past, generally an early parental figure with whom they bonded as children. Through transference, the client can struggle with unresolved issues from childhood and, overall, transference serves as a positive action in psychoanalysis. For example, a father in a family session might become angry with the practitioner because he sees the therapist as an authority figure. The practitioner, in turn, would work through this issue with the father, and the father would have in essence worked through his issue with his own father.

Counter-Transference *Counter-transference* coveys the same meaning as transference, although now it is the therapist who projects onto the client those characteristics related to the bonded parent. In situations such as this, social workers are no longer helping the family member, having placed their own issues onto the client. For example, a family practitioner may become reluctant to see a family because the mother reminds her of her own mother. The social worker should always be aware of these situations and deal with the issue without harming the family.

Introjection *Introjection* is a defense mechanism in which "an individual derives feelings from another person or object and directs it internally to an imagined form of the person or object" (Barker, 1999, p. 253). This might occur, for example, when children introject feelings of anger from their parents into themselves. In turn, this becomes their personality, that of an angry child.

Projective Identification *Projective identification* is a notion through which people project their own attributes (generally those they do not care for) onto another person and then either induce that person to take on those attributes or believe that person has them whether or not he or she actually does. An example would be a girl who lacks self-confidence accusing her mother of being weak and indecisive.

Collusion *Collusion* occurs when one family member tacitly agrees with the image others have of him/her. For example, in the preceding case the mother's response to her daughter's projection is unconsciously to become weak and indecisive. Another example would be when a father believes a son to be lazy because he sees himself as lazy. The son, in turn, behaves in a lazy manner and colludes with his father's view of him.

Other Concepts Many additional concepts impact family theory and treatment. For example, terms such as *autism, symbiotic, separation/individuation, differentiation, practicing, splitting, rapproachment,* and *object constancy* were part of Margaret Mahler's theory regarding the process of individuation (Nichols & Schwartz, 2001).

Mahler used these terms to represent the process a child goes through in coming to individuation. The beginning stage of this process is that of *autism.* During early infancy, children are totally turned inward, dealing with only their needs. During the *symbiotic* stage (ages 2–6 months), children begin to turn outward and see themselves as one with the bonded parent. The third stage is the *separation/individuation* stage, where the child develops an individual sense of self. This stage begins around the age of 6 months and has four substages. *Differentiation* is the first substage in which children begin to break free of the bonded parent and view themselves as separate. The second substage is that of practicing, when children begin to explore their own world. For most children, splitting occurs between ages 16 months and 24 months, during the *rapprochement* substage. *Splitting* refers to the child's ability to divide the world into all-good and all-bad. An example can sometimes be seen in a store when children around 18 months hug their parent and then, just as suddenly, become furious at the parent for denying them some item or piece of candy. This outburst occurs because in the child's mind, the parent is either all good or all bad. Thus, the child separates from the bonded parent with unease and anger and yet returns to the parent for nurturing and comfort. Eventually, the child sees the parent as someone who can be both good and bad. The final substage (24–36 months) is that of *object constancy,* where children come to view their relationships with the primary object (bonded parent) as more completely separate. It is at this stage that the child moves beyond splitting and sees others as having both positive and negative qualities. The importance of understanding Mahler's stages in family practice lies with the practitioner's ability to grasp the separation–individuation issues between the child and parent and how these issues are currently affecting their relationship.

Postmodern Theories and Families

Postmodern theories are most closely associated with a social constructionist view and second-order cybernetics. *Social constructionists* believe, among other things, that the past does not necessarily provide guidance for the present. Thus, prior ways of doing things can be rejected as reflecting outmoded beliefs and values. The changing landscape of human life and the environment underscore the need for new solutions unfettered by traditions and old paradigms. "The main premise of social constructionism is that the beliefs, values, institutions, customs, labels, laws, division of labor, and the like, that make up our social realities are constructed by the members of the culture as they interact with one another from generation to generation and from day to day" (Freedman & Combs, 1996, p. 16). Brown and Christensen (1999) suggest the following four central ideas in relation to a social constructivist's view of family practice:

1. Reality is subjective.
2. Therapy should be less hierarchical.
3. Change is inevitable.
4. Change is already occurring. (p. 224)

Cybernetics is the "study of the processes that regulate and control systems" (Barker, 1999, p. 115). *First-order cybernetics* is the simpler approach, in which the researcher observes the actions between two systems and, based on this view, analyzes the process. In more traditional family practice, the practitioner would be the expert who was examining the process between and within the family system and making decisions based on these observations. In *second-order cybernetics,* the practitioner serves more as a partner in the family process and thus observes not only the family's behavior but their reactions as well. Second-order cybernetics is a more complex and abstract approach because so much more must be taken into account when studying the systems if one is simultaneously a part of that system and therefore influencing it. For example, even the facial expressions social workers use to convey their feelings when working with a family can affect how the family defines and describes their situation.

In postmodern family practice, Green (2003) notes that the following tenets are crucial to good practice:

1. *Participate with the client.* In postmodern family practice, the practitioner works with the family to reconstruct the stories and beliefs they have about their lives. By being part of the change process, the practitioner also serves as a partner in co-creating new stories.
2. *Reality depends on one's belief system.* Reality as a function of one's belief system stems from the awareness that our reality is always created within the context of our own personal experiences. And as we create this reality with every interaction, we simultaneously form new contexts for understanding our lives. In turn, as this reality changes, so do our contexts. As coworkers in the process of family practice, the practitioner and the family continue to create their own sense of reality.
3. *Language is central to* how *we know* what *we know.* In this tenet, we are saying that our language creates its own reality. As we move through processes, we as individuals both interpret and understand our world by the language we use to describe it. In postmodern family theories, the family and the practitioner collaborate and create the story of the family's life. Likewise, they share in any new stories that emerge.

Feminist Theory As an example of postmodernist theory, *feminist theory* departs in many significant ways from the dominant theoretical paradigms found in family practice (Hare-Mustin, 1978). To begin with, feminist theorists object to what they see as an androcentric domination of practice theories. This critique points out that too many traditional theories use male behavior as the norm with female behavior seen as a derivative (Hooyman, 1994). Feminist theory also rebels against approaches that are based on a view of relationships as (competitive, hierarchical, and authoritarian) (Van Den Bergh & Cooper, 1986, p. 11). One feminist criticism of systems theory is the assumption that there is a mutuality of influence between, among, or within systems. The view of mutuality does not take into account such things as power differentials between males and females, or issues of economic and social dependency. Power distributed unequally among systems, for example, means that one gender or the other exerts greater influence in the world. Another criticism is that "systems theory does not address the nuances of separate gender role socialization" (Worden, 1999, p. 48). Atwood (1992) gives an excellent example of this when she notes that our tendency to define family triangles as dysfunctional overlooks how often gender socialization influences women to take a particular role in family disagreements. Likewise, women often assume responsibility for family rituals, not because they want to but because others assume they are better suited for such roles.

The influence of gender also extends to the behavior of individual social workers who may be unable to escape their own socialized view of the world when working with families. A mind-set based on gender socialization may show up in all stages of the helping process. On the one hand, we may unwittingly stereotype family members based on our own sense of what is appropriate (Worden, 1999). Male practitioners may base assessments on a particular view of what is appropriate behavior for male or female members of the family. Conversely, female practitioners needing to employ skills such as confrontation may find this difficult with male clients because this is not the way we have socialized women to act (Bogard, 1990).

Feminist theorists see failure to address power differentials and the impact of socialization on men and women as a major shortcoming of many theories, including those of Haley, Jackson, Bowen, and others (Atwood, 1992). Assessment tools that are based on biased perceptions of gender-appropriate behavior or that use male expectations as a yardstick are problematic. For example, we may see greater degrees of disturbance in women who do not fit the mold of dependent and nurturing than in those who do. Likewise, we may define women who express anger openly as having more serious issues than a man socialized to handle anger in this manner. Families characterized by closeness and nurturing may be considered enmeshed rather than recognized as expressing high levels of intimacy and sensitivity with each member.

One area of potential agreement between feminist and social systems theorists is the way that larger systems (including the family, church, and schools) can influence the shape of individual behavior. Both would agree that the expectations of other systems shape the behavior of us all. Likewise, both would agree that societal influences define what specific actions merit rewards and which are punished. Germain (1991) made this point clear when she observed that systems theory recognizes that "families, like all human systems, are inseparably embedded in the historical, social, cultural, economic, and political context in which they exist" (p. 123). In other words, systems theory is not automatically antithetical to feminist theory if the former can live up to its expectations.

A key principle in understanding feminist theory is the recognition that men and women have very different experiences throughout their developmental processes, including both their families of origin and of marriage (Goldenberg & Goldenberg, 1991). Feminist theorists begin from this point and strive to help families attain relationships built on equality rather than superiority or presumed gender roles. They recognize that both men and women benefit from being able to express the whole range of human emotions instead of only those permitted under traditional views. Operating from this point of view, feminist theorists emphasize a collaborative style of therapy that seeks to help family members explore new rules and roles while allowing them to jettison culturally prescribed but inappropriate expectations. Feminist theory is committed to social workers examining their own biases and proclivities toward gender-based assumptions about appropriate behaviors (Nichols & Schwartz, 2001).

Narrative Theory *Narrative theory* is also a form of postmodern theory. Narrative theory and therapy are grounded in the realization of how "experience generates expectations and how expectation then reshapes experience through the creation of organizing stories" (Nichols & Schwartz, 2001, p. 387). This quote refers to the way individuals organize what is going on around them. For example, as individuals experience life, they come to form an expectation about themselves (for instance, people who have not had positive experiences in life come to believe through actual situations and cognitive construction that nothing positive will happen to them). A narrative is then created out of all their experiences (so the individuals who do not expect anything positive tell themselves a story about how bad their lives are). This story then colors all their experiences so they cannot see when something is positive. It becomes a vicious circle. The narrative therapist believes that people who want to change their behavior must first change the story they have about themselves and their experiences.

According to Kelly (2002), there are several basic concepts in narrative theory:

1. *Externalizing the problem.* Narrative theory views the person as having an externalized problem rather than being a problem. Nichols and Schwartz (2001) state that narrative therapists "believe that problems arise because people are induced by our culture into subscribing to narrow and self-defeating views of themselves and the world" (p. 392). These people focus on how the problem impacts the family rather than how the problem comes from them.
2. *Problem-saturated stories.* These are the stories individuals tell themselves based on their experiences with others and society. The stories are filled with problems, as that is how individuals sees their lives. In sessions, clients are guided to see beyond these problem-filled stories and see themselves in a variety of different ways.
3. *Mapping the problem's domain.* This involves discussing with clients how the problem has affected their lives in various domains as well as how it has affected them in the past, present, and probable future. This discussion encourages the client to think about what might be done to resolve the problem.
4. *Unique outcomes.* This is the identification of those times in which the problem has not been present or affected the circumstances in which individuals find themselves. It is an opportunity for the client to point to new and different narratives in which the problems do not exist. Clients might, for instance, begin to see aspects of themselves that are positive and strength building.

5. *Spreading the news.* This aspect of the narrative approach calls for clients to share their new story (as it begins to occur) with others. In this way, the story becomes more real and begins to dominate the old story. This may be done in many different ways, including "celebrations, certificates, awards, or even talking to groups of others facing similar problems" (Kelly, 2002, p. 122).

These concepts increase the likelihood that the new stories that are developed and told will affect clients' thinking. In turn, clients will change their behavior towards those interactions with other individuals and society that keep the problem alive.

Ethnic and Cultural Challenges

One of the most important things to understand about theories is the fact that they were created during a certain time period. Another is that those who created the theories were individuals with their own experiences within the context of a society/environmental situation. As in postmodern thinking, theorists bring with them their own set of experiences that create the story they tell. For example, Sigmund Freud, when developing his personality theories, was in essence relating to his own life. This is not to say that Freud's theories are invalid as a means of understanding human behavior. Rather, we are recognizing that he formed them within the context of his own life and times. Because of limitations like this, it is improbable that any single theory can account for all the cultural and ethnic factors affecting families. The stories created by a family would only fit within their circumstances and not for another family. For example, a Caucasian family may be entirely accepting of the idea that their problem stems from differences in power structure within the family (structural theory and model) and be willing to modify the structure. Yet, a Hispanic family might very well see such a power structure difference as entirely appropriate within the context of their culture and be unwilling to change it. Likewise, a postmodern theory base, such as feminist, would seek equality in the relationship between a husband and wife. Such a notion may be unacceptable to other cultures that neither desire nor tolerate equality between spouses.

For families to be accepting and open to different models of family practice, we must take their circumstances into account when selecting the theory or theories we propose to use. Sensitivity to the limitations of theory and subsequent models of therapy is crucial to working with families to achieve their goals.

Engaging Families

CHAPTER 3

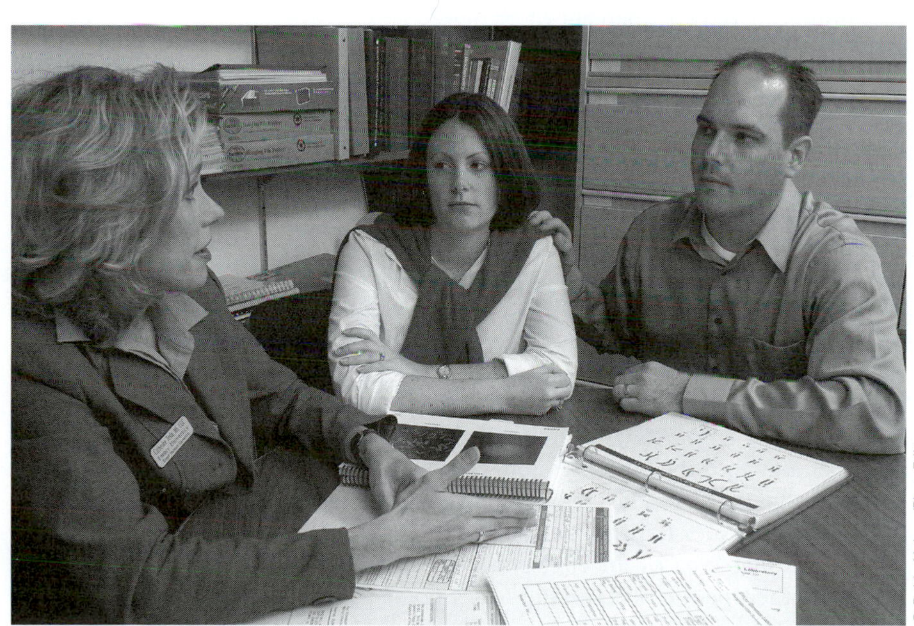

© Robin Nelson/PhotoEdit

INTRODUCTION

This chapter discusses the engagement process and working with families from the initial point of contact. As the first phase in a family practice model, this is the opportunity for the practitioner to make a connection with the family. It is also where the practitioner lets the family members know that he or she will listen and be concerned about who they are and what they are communicating. It is also a time to begin building trust between the practitioner and the family and to make it easier for them to decide to come back.

THE ENGAGEMENT PROCESS

Worden (2003) defines *engagement* as "the forming of a therapeutic, trusting alliance between the therapist and the family that permits them to explore together the inner workings of the family relationship" (p. 17). The research suggests that success in helping clients relies heavily on the relationship between the family practitioner and the clients. Lambert and Andersen (1996) found in their research regarding efficacy that 30 percent of all success in a planned changed intervention relied primarily upon the family practitioner and client relationship. Extra therapeutic factors, such as client's level of motivation, strength of ego, and degree of social support, among others, account for 40 percent of change. Interestingly, techniques and expectancy each accounted for only 15 percent of change.

The Basis of Engagement

Engagement in family practice, as in other areas, may begin in a person-to-person meeting or over the phone. On the surface, the term *engagement* implies the ability to begin an interaction with another individual or family. That interaction is designed to increase communication and build a relationship through an interactive process. These three actions form the basis of engagement, which begins a process of change. Achieving this outcome requires nine additional actions.

Infusing Energy The infusion of energy between the social worker and the family begins as part of the relationship. The practitioner must be able to infuse energy into the initial session. Social workers must also display an activity level that tells family members the practitioner is involved and ready to work on any issues that arise. Infusing energy is a process by which the family practitioner creates an environment where family members are eager to begin the therapeutic process and to set goals they wish to achieve. He or she joins with the family to build rapport that will support later practitioner–client activities (Minuchin, 1974).

Bringing a Sense of Hope to the Situation Without hope, the family will feel defeated before they begin. Research has shown that positive client change

Figure 3.1 Factors Accounting for Counseling Effectiveness

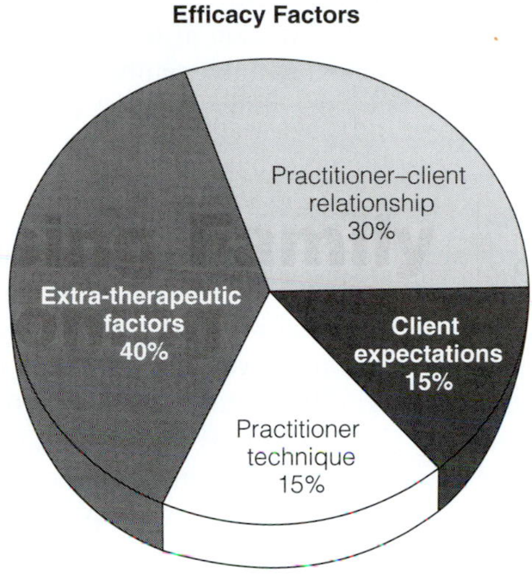

Source: Data from Lambert and Anderson (1996).

generally occurs within the first few weeks of treatment (Fennell & Teasdale, 1987). In fact, up to 66 percent of clients may improve before attending the first session (Lawson, 1994). The client's sense of hope can account in part for this type of change (Ilardi & Craighead, 1994). The social worker must also feel a sense of hope in order to instill it. This is not always easy to do when the practitioner is dealing with a family facing multiple challenges and barriers. An example would be a family where the mother, with limited financial resources, is coping with her own illness, a mentally challenged daughter, and a son who is currently in a juvenile detention center. This type of situation can create a sense of hopelessness not only in the client but also in the family practitioner. Finding hope means finding a way to aid the family in a particular area without getting overwhelmed by all the problems at once. As a family is able to believe the social worker can help them deal with one issue, they become more hopeful that they can deal with others.

Providing the Family with a Sounding Board So They Know They Are Being Heard This is an important step as it means much more than simply listening. It means letting the family feel heard and understood. This builds a sense of trust and clarity for the family about their concerns. Bachelor (1995) has found that clients described a good relationship with a therapist as having the qualities of respect, nonjudgmental attitude, empathic understanding, and attentive listening. These qualities support this sense of being heard. However, using these facilitative methods with families is not always easy. For example, each family member needs to be heard. Moreover, the things different members say may well conflict with one another. Social workers do not have to agree with everything that families say, but they do need to be open to hearing the different perspectives. A social worker also must try to understand how the emotions and thoughts developed. Family members also need to be encouraged to talk about their strengths. In doing this, the family practitioner can lead the family by example.

Demonstrating Support While research shows that a family is more willing to work in therapy with practitioners who are good at displaying supportive types of behaviors, doing so within a family situation can be very tricky (Frankel & Piercy, 1990). Showing support may sound easy; however, being supportive of every member at the same level can be difficult to do. When family members' views on situations differ, being supportive to everyone in the family can seem contradictory. Being supportive, however, is not simply about agreeing with every family member's ideas but is about respecting them for being the people they are. We refer to this type of support as "dignity and self-worth for the client."

Utilizing "Use of Self" in the Process of Understanding Family Members' Concerns *Use of self* is a process of "being with the client" through listening, facilitating, providing feedback, responding honestly, and using some degree of self-disclosure. A key mechanism by which the practitioner connects with the client is through demonstrating empathy. *Empathy* is the ability of the family practitioner to perceive the feelings, behaviors, and experiences of the family members and to be able to respond accordingly. It is the means by which family practitioners establish relationships, build trust, and maintain support. By listening carefully to the family members, the family practitioner can hear beyond the words and pick up nuances in tone and emotion to understand better what family members are saying. Listening occurs not just with the ears but also with the eyes and physical presence. Empathy shares with the family member that the practitioner is not only listening but also understanding what it must feel like to be in the client's situation. Through empathetic responding, individuals are more freely able to be themselves, and a family can achieve greater intimacy through the modeling of these responses (Green, 2003).

Perceiving feelings is a much more complicated process then it sounds. Clients can be relating surface feelings, such as anger, and yet in reality be covering up underlying feelings of sadness. Misreading a client's angry feelings and responding to them without recognizing the emotions that are under the surface would likely be unproductive.

There are five basic levels of empathetic responses, as outlined by Truax and Carkhuff (1967):

> *Level 1.* At this level there is very little empathy going on. The family practitioner does not respond to the words being said through feedback and certainly is not responding to the feelings.

FAMILY MEMBER: I just keep being angry over the way she treats me. She never seems to care about how I feel.

FAMILY PRACTITIONER: Maybe you're not very nice to her and she is just sick of it.

Level 2. Practitioners responding at a minimal level define this level of awareness of the client's needs. They may show some recognition of what the family member is saying but pay very little attention to the meaning.

FAMILY MEMBER: I feel frightened about being alone.

FAMILY PRACTITIONER: I feel frightened at times too.

Level 3. At this level, the family practitioner simply reflects back what the family member says. This is the beginning stage of empathy.

FAMILY MEMBER: I don't want to get involved in anything that could make me anxious.

FAMILY PRACTITIONER: You don't want to become anxious.

Level 4. The family practitioner takes what the client says and mirrors the answer while beginning to interpret deeper feeling.

FAMILY MEMBER: I feel really bad about what happened. I felt so bad I punched a wall.

FAMILY PRACTITIONER: You punched a wall because you felt bad, and that also made you angry.

Level 5. The family practitioner makes responses that are under the surface of the client's statements. Using this type of empathy during initial sessions is a mistake because of the risk of being wrong. First, the family practitioner is unfamiliar with the family members and second, the practitioner's comments may be frightening because she has not built up the requisite level of trust with them.

FAMILY MEMBER: I really don't want to go over there with her. She is always angry. I won't have a good time.

FAMILY PRACTITIONER: It sounds like you are frightened to be with her because she is always being angry. You don't have a good time when you're with her, just like you didn't have a good time with your mother when she was angry.

Knowing how to use empathy is important to building trust. It also gives the family the opportunity to be even more open in their expressions because they know the practitioner is listening. By being empathetic, the family practitioner is bringing hope to the family by understanding their feelings.

Unconditional Positive Regard Unconditional positive regard is about the dignity and self-worth the family practitioner gives the family members. Each person in a family needs to be valued for who he or she is as a human being. Despite his or her behavior, each person needs valuing by others. By valuing a person, we are not implying that social workers accept a behavior or value it. Quite the contrary—being able to understand someone's behavior is different from condoning it. However, by respecting the family members' dignity and self-worth without conditions, the practitioner is valuing who they are and not what they do.

Congruence Congruence is the characteristic of being consistent with what one does and says. *Congruence* is a term that implies the social workers' verbal statements are consistent with their behavior. When practitioners are not congruent, it undermines the family's trust in them. Before family practitioners speak, they need to know that their nonverbal behavior will convey the same message to the family as their verbal statements. For example, a practitioner might say to a family that she is open to their voicing of uncomfortable feelings but simultaneously shows discomfort when they do. Such discrepancies are readily apparent to even the casual observer. While being congruent is critical for a family practitioner, it is also important for family members to learn to be congruent with one another. A mother who smiles when she tells her son she loves him is much more effective as a parent than one who says she disapproves of something the son has done and then laughs about the behavior.

Warmth Hepworth, Rooney and Larsen (1997) note that the "element of warmth is difficult to define, yet it is generally agreed that a warm person is attentive, yet calm and relaxed, and speaks with a well-modulated voice that reflects the nuances of feeling manifested by the client" (p. 61). When working with families, showing this kind of warmth to all family members is critical for the practitioner. The limits of this demeanor must be tempered, however, by the understanding that being warm in nature to clients also means being congruent. Clients quickly identify situations when the practitioner is attempting to force warmth. A practitioner who tells clients she understands their concerns but does not use a corresponding tone or facial expression will be seen as someone who does not care. Likewise, not going overboard with an emotional response is important because faking feelings would be just as detrimental as not having them. Be honest, congruent, and care about family members. This will convey concern to the family members and in turn, the warmth of a person who cares.

Honesty Honesty is an appropriate quality for a social worker to possess. Being honest with family members in a way that is productive is a skill. While honesty conveys respect, unkindness does not. If a social worker does not agree with a family member, sharing concern over this issue is important while simultaneously letting the person know that the social worker understands his or her feelings. Some inexperienced family practitioners can also mistake honesty for self-disclosure. Self-disclosure is the sharing of the practitioner's personal experience to display the helper's ability to understand the client.

However, disclosure itself is a skill that needs careful handling with a family. While disclosure allows the family to feel as if the family practitioner can better understand them, it can also create concern for the family. First, it may sound to the family as if the practitioner has the same problems they have and lead them to question his ability to help them. Second, it runs the risk of the family believing that the practitioner sees his situation and theirs as identical when they do not share this perception.

Self-disclosure needs to be done on a discriminate basis. What is important for the family to know is that the practitioner has been in similar situations or that she has been in a specific situation that is described for the family. It is important to know that disclosure has been found to be helpful to clients but only when it is used to convey understanding and not suggested as a solution to their problem (Knox et al., 1997). Every situation and every person is different, and families can become confused when the practitioner attempts to tie her situation to theirs.

These essential skills create an atmosphere for families that allows them to engage in the intervention. However, many families cannot respond due to the level of their anxiety, anger, and fear. Sharing expectations and giving the family a safe environment are critical steps to helping them overcome these barriers.

PREPARATION FOR THE FIRST MEETING

Initial Contact

There are many different ways a social worker first contacts a family needing aid. For example, the social worker may receive a phone call from the family, another agency may make a referral, the family may walk into the agency without an appointment, or the court may order the family into treatment. When the social worker makes the initial contact, responding to the expressed needs and concerns is important. This is not always easy to do when the contact is made by phone, by outside referral or by court order. In these cases the family members may not have initially met the practitioner personally and may have no sense of who she is or how she can help them. In these cases, understanding the different ways to make that connection stronger is important. Each situation requires special skills to begin an engagement that will prove positive for the intervention.

Phone Contact Most often the initial contact with a family will be by phone, either when they call or when a social worker receives an outside referral. The practitioner's tone of voice in this situation tells the family member a lot about him. When people speak on the phone, most have an image of the person on the other end in their head. They may even subjectively make assumptions based on the person's voice and/or situation. Some of these assumptions are often wrong, and they are based on our own experiences of interacting with other people, how they sound, and what experiences they bring with them. Setting aside one's own experiences formed from other people and keeping an open mind about the family and its members is essential but can be difficult. Generally, once practitioners meet individuals and get to know them, they see them as unique people. However, when a practitioner only talks to one family member on the phone for a few minutes, this is almost impossible to do.

When first working with family members on the phone, it is important to use the voice and tone to convey openness and empathy, whatever their voice or situation. For example in the following phone conversation, the mother who has called is sharing her perception of the situation and her frustration. As you read the mother's comments, think about how you might respond in an initial phone conversation.

MS. WILLIAMS: Hello, I was calling to talk with someone about some problems we are having in our family.

FAMILY PRACTITIONER: I would be happy to speak with you. My name is Hakeem Koizumi, and you are Ms. Williams?

MS. WILLIAMS: Yes, that's right.

FAMILY PRACTITIONER: How can I help you today?

MS. WILLIAMS: My husband and I are constantly fighting about our daughter. We can't seem to ever agree on what her rules are, and she is sixteen and completely out of control. My husband and I had such a big fight last night over her being two hours late with her curfew that I went and stayed all night at my mother's.

At this point, think about what thoughts and reactions you are currently having to this situation. What assumptions are you making and what thoughts might you be having about the family members themselves?

FAMILY PRACTITIONER: It sounds as if your family is going through a very difficult time.

MS. WILLIAMS: We are and I don't know what to do.

FAMILY PRACTITIONER: Well, in situations where everyone in the family is involved in the issue, which is almost always, I initially like to meet with everyone and talk about the situation. Do you think you and your family can do that?

MS. WILLIAMS (*crying*): Well, I would, but I don't know whether my husband and daughter would.

FAMILY PRACTITIONER: This is very difficult for you and I do not want to place you in a more difficult situation, but I know how important it is to solve family problems with all members of the family. Have you talked about this or have you seen a family counselor with your family before?

MS. WILLIAMS: No, but when I called my husband this morning he said he would think about it. I think he might come in with me if he thought it would help and we could bring Jena too.

> **FAMILY PRACTITIONER:** That would be good. Why don't we set up a time now when you might all be available and then talk further with your husband and daughter? It sounds to me like you would all want to make things better, and I just want to express my support for you and your husband to consider ways to do that. It sounds to me as if you both care about what is going on.

This phone conversation contains several items of note. First are the words and tone of voice, which convey support and empathy. Second is the use of reflective listening and feedback. Third is the emphasis on the strengths that the family practitioner has picked up in this short conversation. It is the ability to send this message that will encourage the family member who called to try to bring the whole family. However, it is always possible that the husband and/or daughter may refuse to come. Before ending this conversation, asking the family member what would help her to bring the entire family is also important. The practitioner might talk about certain things that she could say or share some information about the positives of family practice. At this point, however, the family member generally knows how best to approach her family, and the practitioner is there to aid her however possible.

Referral as a Voluntary Family There are many situations where an outside source may refer a family for help. It might be an involuntary referral, as from a court order; it might be a referral from the school or another agency; or it might be a referral from another family. Consider a referral where the family is voluntarily agreeing to come in after having been referred by another agency. In such cases, having as much information as possible before speaking with the family to set an appointment can be very important as it allows the practitioner to give them the best feedback possible. The practitioner must take care, however, not to read more into this additional information than is evident or make major assumptions about the family. It is also important to be sensitive to the possibility that referral sources may have their own preconceptions about the family. To help guard against this risk, some social workers like to see the family first before they gather too much information. By using this approach, they avoid being biased when initially sitting down with the family. Information, however, can prepare social workers for the first interaction, whether by phone or in person. It enables them not to be surprised by certain facts the family members tell them. It also aids in knowing how the family may perceive the difficulties themselves.

Sometimes, referrals send a message to the family that the practitioner is a person they can trust. This is more likely to be the case if someone they value believes in him. Remember, while the social worker is engaging the family, it is also engaging him. How the referring party described the social worker or the agency can be very important. If a former family with whom the practitioner has worked makes the referral, they may have assured the family that he can help them. As social workers, we know that families really help themselves with the strengths they already possess and those they develop. No matter what the family may have been told before coming to the initial session, it is important that the practitioner spends time helping the family identify their expectations. The following example shows how this may be done:

MS. SAMUELS: I appreciate your finding the time to meet with my daughter and me. My friend Sara Williams says you really helped her family. I hope you can help us in the same way.

FAMILY PRACTITIONER: I appreciate the compliment, but I think the Williams family deserves most of the credit. My job is helping families reach their goals. I believe you already have the strengths and skills to resolve your issues, and I want to help you put those skills to work.

Referral as an Involuntary Family *Involuntary families* is the term used to describe families who do not want to see a social worker but are forced to do so. Families might be coerced by a court order, by a possible school expulsion, or for many other reasons. It is important to remember in these cases that the family is still making a choice to see the practitioner. Even under threat, the family or its members can choose to do something else. Their decision to come in under these circumstances is still a choice they are making. This is a strength in a family that decides to seek help despite facing other difficulties. Pointing this out to the family is important in the first conversation. It is also critical to acknowledge the feelings the family and its members are having about coming. By being open to their reluctance and anger, the social worker shows the family that they are important. This approach is also consistent with the belief that clients have the right of self-determination. Although the benefits of seeking help may be substantial, the family always has the right to fail or to refuse to participate.

Additionally, the social worker may have to deal with her own anger or reluctance in seeing a family because of the way in which they approach her. Social workers are human beings who have emotional reactions to being called names or to having to deal with another person's anger. Under most circumstances, family practitioners can differentiate themselves from the family's anger and not take it personally. When this is not so, it may be because the family cannot lay down their anger at feeling forced and/or because the social worker is responding to their venting by becoming angry. That is why it becomes so important for family practitioners to deal with their own feelings and emotions before dealing with those of the clients. The following is an example of a situation in which the involuntary client is placing his angry feelings unto the family practitioner. After each family member's response, consider what you would think and feel as the family practitioner, then look at the social worker's response.

MR. SANDER: I am calling because the school told me we had to meet with you or they would expel John. I just want you to know up front that I will come only because I have to and my wife wants me to. John doesn't have a problem, the school does. He doesn't have any problems at home, and I keep him in line.

FAMILY PRACTITIONER: I can tell you are angry about coming to see me. I just want you to know that I respect the fact that you have chosen to come. I look forward to meeting you and your family.

MR. SANDER: Well, you may not be so happy to see me because you can be sure I do not want to meet with you.

FAMILY PRACTITIONER: I can understand your reluctance and would probably feel the same way myself. Still, I look forward to meeting your family.

Planning

It is important when planning for the initial session to be very clear on the differences and similarities between meeting a family in or outside their home. The family may make an appointment to come to the office or they may request, or the social worker may recommend, that the meeting take place in their own home. The ability to know how to handle these differences and similarities provides the basis for future success in working with families.

Meeting with a family in their own home is quite a common function in child welfare services and when working in a community setting with families. There are many advantages to meeting with a family in their own home. The first benefit is the ability to better assess family life and the environment in which they live. How and where family members sit in relationship to one another is often key in understanding relationships. This is also true in office visits but can be even more important in the home in terms of where chairs are placed, who sits on the couch with whom, or even if there are enough seats for everyone. What is the condition of the house? Are there environmental dangers? Is it a space where the lack of resources makes it difficult for families to feel positive or for children to have enough space to study or play?

Environmental factors can strongly affect a family and their relationships; however, never confuse a poorly cleaned home with bad parenting. As social workers, we can read more into a situation than may be present. A house with unmade beds and clothes lying around might be a response to the parents working several jobs and having little time to pick up. On the other hand, a child left in a dirty diaper or a kitchen where bugs crawl around on dirty dishes may suggest a greater need for some type of family intervention.

Some families may be more comfortable talking with a social worker in their own home. At the very least, they may find it easier to go home than to try to come to an office so that more members of the family can meet. To the extent possible, attempt to accommodate the family's request for a meeting place.

Of course, other families may be self-conscious about their homes and feel uncomfortable having a stranger visit them. How individuals act in their own home may be different from when they are in other settings. Being more natural is always a possibility but they may also be more self-conscious with a stranger in their home. Again, because it is important for the family members to be as comfortable as possible, letting the family decide where to meet may be best.

INITIAL MEETING

The initial meeting with a family has several components and tasks:

- Making introductions and beginning observation of family members
- Establishing guidelines and orienting family members to the process.
- Encouraging interactions between and among siblings and other family members
- Answering family questions
- Learning the family's perception of the problem—it is not unusual for this perception to differ from those of others, including the individual or agency that made the referral
- Identifying the needs of each family member and differentiating them from those of others
- Focusing on family members' strengths
- Gathering initial information for assessment
- Aiding family members in communicating more clearly with one another
- Beginning the process of establishing goals
- Summarizing the session and encouraging the family to see their strengths and coping skills

Introduction and Beginning Observations

When the family arrives for their appointment or when the social worker first arrives at the house to meet with the family, addressing the members of the family on a more formal basis is important. For example, refer to the adults as Mr. Martinez or Mrs. Brown. Introduce yourself in whatever way is the most comfortable for you. My personal approach is to use my first and last name, for example, "Hello, I am Jannah Mather, we spoke on the phone." This does two things: It shows respect for the family members and simultaneously allows some informal interaction with the use of your first name. There may be cases in which utilizing your formal title may be important, for example, if a court has referred a family and you believe that introducing yourself on a more formal basis initially is best. Over time, the family's invitation to use their first names will tell you something about their level of comfort with you. Despite their choice, however, being comfortable with the family's preferences for addressing them is a show of respect.

When first meeting a family, it is also customary to hold out a hand during introductions. This gives family members who wish the opportunity to greet the social worker and introduce themselves. Being conscious of the adult family members and their desire to be addressed first is important to assess. A parent who is reluctant to be at the session may need to receive some extra appreciation for coming, for example, "I am so pleased you came to the meeting today, Mr. Chalabi." Often, the social worker will see an adolescent who is reluctant to be there. Noticing a small thing about a person initially can also lead to small talk and engagement. For instance, the adolescent might be wearing a specific university sweatshirt, so the social worker may observe when introducing himself, "I gather from the shirt you are wearing that you are a big fan of Podunk University."

The introduction is often a good opportunity to observe the family and note the actions and behaviors that set its tone. These are among the things to consider:

1. Who speaks first?
2. How do the members of the family introduce themselves
3. Who appears to have the power in the family?
4. Is the person who arranged the appointment the one who provides the introductions?
5. How are the members of the family dressed?
6. Does the family members' posture provide clues to their attitude toward treatment?

As the family moves into the office or everyone enters their home, allow them to sit wherever they would like. This initial selection of seats and demeanor can tell a lot about the family and the individuals in it. Some things to note include the following:

- Who is sitting next to whom?
- What does their body language say about their response to being in this situation?
- Who speaks to whom during the initial minutes?
- Were the members of the family assigned seating by another member of the family?

Establish Guidelines and Answer Questions

A critical part of a first family session is the establishment of guidelines for the sessions and clarification of any questions the family may have. Explain that the session's notes and records are confidential but may be reviewed by a supervisor or colleague to help the social worker serve them better. If the family has been court-ordered into treatment, then talking about any reports that need to be made is especially important. Answer any questions the family may have regarding confidential information. It is the social worker's ethical responsibility to address issues of confidentiality and privacy and to point out any situation that could require divulging this information. This might include mandated reporting of child abuse, or the practitioner's duty to warn others about threatened violence or to respond to a subpoena. It is important to make these things clear from the beginning.

> **FAMILY PRACTITIONER:** What we talk about in our family meetings will be kept between us. However, there are certain circumstances where others may have access to this information. When you or someone else may be harmed or when a child has been harmed, I am required to share this information. It is also impor-

tant to know that in order for me to aid you to the best of my ability, I may need to share information about your case with my supervisor. If that happens, my supervisor is also bound to confidentiality to the same degree I am.

In an involuntary situation, you might add a statement such as this:

FAMILY PRACTITIONER: As you know, the court sent you for family counseling. While I will maintain your confidentiality to the degree I can, you need to understand that I am required to make a report to the court and will be summarizing our sessions and your progress. I will be happy to share my report with you before sending it to the court.

The social worker must also set parameters around how the session will run, for example, when and where the meeting will be, how and when members may express themselves, and prohibitions against harming one another. This is an appropriate time for the social worker to explain her background and how she approaches family issues. This will likely lead into a discussion of the systems perspective and the belief that problems experienced by a family member often reflect family pain. While the family at this point may not understand or accept that their issues involve the whole family, within the first few sessions the social workers actions can speak for her.

Helping the family understand that a family situation involves all members of a family and not just one is a difficult but necessary step. Most families will enter counseling because they have identified one of their members as the cause of the problems. Interestingly, often an individual member *will* be actively involved in problems as a way to maintain family homeostasis. This process of identifying one member as the problem is known as *scapegoating*. Families and children develop scapegoating stories as a way to keep the family's attention from other issues they may not want to deal with, for example, marital conflict. One way to begin to set a system's framework is to note the differing parts of the family who have taken an active role in its story. Satir (1967) believed that strong subsystems of parents and children in a family could strengthen the family's structure and provide a means for the family to resolve their own issues. She would often pull the parental subgroup away from the children's subgroup to disconnect any inappropriate triangles that might be occurring. An example is the Farley family, who has entered family treatment in response to the acting-out behavior of their 16-year-old daughter, Rachel.

FAMILY PRACTITIONER: I recognize the situation your family is experiencing is very difficult. Have you as a parental team attempted to resolve these issues in any particular ways? (This statement acknowledges the situation the family is in but does not reinforce their belief of the cause. Additionally, the social worker is attempting to help the couple see themselves as a unit.)

MR. FARLEY: Yes, we often try to talk about family problems when we drive home together from work. We have tried a variety of ways to get Rachel to understand the mistakes she is making, but so far nothing has worked.

FAMILY PRACTITIONER: Mrs. Farley, what are some ways you and your husband have attempted to solve the family's difficulties. (Here the family practitioner is pulling the mother into the discussion to show the importance of her role and perspective on the family and to validate her participation.)

MRS. FARLEY: Well, we have tried grounding her and giving her extra chores to do.

FAMILY PRACTITIONER: I realize this might seem a bit unusual, but can you give me a demonstration of a conversation you had together which led to one of these decisions?

From this discussion, the family practitioner has begun to move the identified scapegoat in the family away from the center of attention. The practitioner has also managed to ask the parents to display the strengths they have in resolving the problem and is beginning to aid them in improving their communication skills.

Encouraging Interaction between Siblings

Similarly, the family practitioner in the first session might encourage an interchange between the siblings to identify them as a different subgroup. As he assesses and encourages these subgroups to interact, he can bring the discussion back around to the family as a whole and compliment them on their ability to communicate.

FAMILY PRACTITIONER: Well, I can see that you and your sister must have some things in common, as you both play soccer.

TED: We really don't. She's too little for me to spend time with.

FAMILY PRACTITIONER: So you and Carrie don't play soccer together?

TED: Sometimes we do. Especially if we are practicing. It's just that we can't really play with our friends together 'cause someone always gets hurt.

FAMILY PRACTITIONER: Carrie, what is it like for you to get to play soccer with your big brother?

CARRIE: I don't know but I like it when we can do things together.

FAMILY PRACTITIONER: What kinds of things?

CARRIE: You know, just things.

FAMILY PRACTITIONER: Let's have you sit over here by Carrie, Ted, and maybe the two of you can share with me what those kind of things are.

Following a short discussion in which Ted and Carrie sit together and talk about a game they played yesterday, the family practitioner turns the discussion back to the family.

FAMILY PRACTITIONER: It sounds like Ted and Carrie do some fun things together. How about as a family? Can you tell me what kinds of things you do as a family, Ms. Beckham?

Another task for the first meeting is to clarify everyone's expectations. It is entirely likely that the family may want to know about the practitioner's expectations of them. Does everyone have to come? Can we change times? All of these are valid questions that families may ask. Answering as honestly as possible and setting the guidelines help to build trust and to create an environment in which the family feels safe.

Family Questions

When a family first meets with a practitioner, they are generally apprehensive and nervous. This is a good time to let the family ask questions about what they are going to do in the sessions and about who she is. One way to start is to ask the question, "Have you ever been in family counseling before?" If the answer is no, this allows the family the opportunity to address any questions they may have about what is going to happen in their meetings. If the answer is yes, the practitioner may want to clarify what that experience was like and what they expect to happen in this setting. Another question that can often open communication between the practitioner and the family is to ask how they felt when they became aware they were coming to the meeting today. This type of question often elicits many different responses and in some ways frees family members to talk about being apprehensive or even being angry. If a family member starts to express these feelings, it is good to allow him or her to do so.

Often during a first meeting, a family may have several questions about the practitioner. These may be related to his experience or his expectations of them. They may want to know what the practitioner thinks of them and how he views the family. Some theorists believe it is best not to answer such questions but to turn them around and ask the family what makes them want to know the answers. Others do not believe this is the most appropriate response except in those situations where it is clear that the family's reasoning for asking the question relates to concerns they are experiencing. As mentioned earlier, we must use self-disclosure carefully. There are no definitive answers about when revealing something about oneself is helpful. However, Hepworth et al. (1997) suggest that the practitioner should "precede disclosures of views or feelings with either open-ended or empathic responses" (p. 128). Being honest with a client requires the practitioner to be certain that in answering the question she is doing so as part of a therapeutic need and not simply because she wants to share her own history (p. 130).

The Family's Perception of the Problem

It is important when beginning to work with a family that the practitioner gets a better idea of how they see the "problem." While we emphasize that the family's strengths will aid them the most, the reality is that the family is coming in because they or someone else perceives that they are having a problem. Getting everyone's view of the problem is also imperative. Most family members will not have the same view, and it is as important to understand where the differences are as well as to understand the similarities. This step begins the solution phase of the intervention. Simply by having family members talk about how they view the issue and what methods they have tried to resolve it, the practitioner is creating an environment in which the family begins to think about solutions again. In particular, suggesting that the family describe not only what they have tried but what has been successful in any way gives them a snapshot of their strengths.

Eliciting responses from family members can be difficult at times. Some individuals may want to dominate the conversation while others may get up and leave. Either scenario is difficult, but that does not mean it cannot be productive. The interactions and processes that go on between family members give the family practitioner a better understanding of how the family operates. Who does most of the talking? Who says little? How do they interact with one another? How does the family go about explaining a situation? Very calmly or very loudly? This does not mean we allow someone to dominate the conversation. Speaking politely but insisting that each person share his view of why they are there allows the social worker to set up acceptable guidelines for behaviors toward one another.

The question of who to ask first about the problem or the reason the family is there has been debated in the literature. Whitaker (1977) always started with the father, reasoning that because he was the one most resistant to a treatment intervention, he needed the authority to feel a part of the process. In other cases, to get a better view of how the family functions, it is suggested that the practitioner should simply introduce himself and let whoever wants to, respond. However, most family practitioners would agree that the first interaction needs to be with the parents. This shows respect for their role and that they have a powerful part to play in the family. The practitioner needs to be especially sensitive in these circumstances to any cultural or ethnic preference as to who is first addressed. Ignorance about these issues can ruin the pratitioner's rapport with the family before it has begun.

Summarizing what is heard from each family member helps to clarify what has been said and shows interest in each individual in the family. This is important for engaging each family member. However, following this process, knowing that the practitioner views all of their definitions as valid is important for family members. Summarizing these differing views into one can be difficult but also very valuable for the family.

> **FAMILY PRACTITIONER:** Ms. Darwin, I hear you saying that you want Karen to be happy and you don't want her to get hurt. Karen, I also hear you saying you want to have fun and you don't plan on getting hurt. Your differences then are about how that is going to happen.

Identify the Needs of Each Family Member

Although the family is there to resolve an issue, gathering information from each member about what he or she needs or would like to have happen in the meetings that may go beyond the identified problem is also important. Allowing family members to think about the practitioner's time with them as something that might enhance their lives gives them the opportunity to hope for the future and what they can accomplish. Additionally, as family members recognize common needs they are better able to set common goals, an important step in this process:

FAMILY PRACTITIONER: What would you like to see happen here that could meet your need?

MOTHER: I would just like you to help us find a way to stop fighting. I am so tired of the fighting!

DAUGHTER: I want to quit fighting too. I am sick of it. You are the one that starts the fights!

FAMILY PRACTITIONER: I guess you and your mother must have similar needs, as it seems you would both like to find a way for the fighting to stop.

Focus on Family Members' Strengths

Focusing on family members' strengths is a major part of ensuring that the family understands they can solve their own problems. Begin this process by highlighting those behaviors that are obvious in the first session. For example, consider the following:

The family member who called seeking help.

FAMILY PRACTITIONER: It shows your concern for your family that you sought help in resolving this issue.

The family member who does not want to be there.

FAMILY PRACTITIONER: I appreciate the fact that although you did not want to come, you chose to come for the family.

Strength building is not just about noticing or commenting on a family member's strengths. It is also about putting problems in a certain perspective. Saleebey (1997, p. 46) notes three strategies for working from a strengths perspective:

1. "We recognize problems only in their proper context." What this means is that we should discuss problems in simpler terms. We must discuss problems when they become obstacles to the client's goals but not let them become the main focus of the intervention.
2. Adopt "simpler ways of talking about problems" so they do not define our lives but rather the expectations we might have from the process of daily living in the world. As problems are placed in a simpler everyday perspective, they become part of life's development that can be overcome as part of everyday life.
3. Pay "less attention to the problem" and more attention to the person's strengths. By focusing on strengths and turning away from the problem, we are affirming our view of individual family members and of the family itself.

Begin Gathering Initial Information for Assessment

From the first moment that practitioners speak with a family or receive their file from another agency, they assess what it is like to be a part of that family. While this is natural to do, not having preset ideas about the family is also critical. Practitioners need to inform themselves by spending time with the family and getting to know them individually and as a family unit. Being open to hearing what is said and not said, what processes are occurring, how they handle the dynamics, and what emotions are manifested by the family is the real assessment. They are also responding to their perception of the practitioner, not just as themselves. Considering this, remaining objective is important to building trust with the family so they can share who they are trying to be.

Assessments are important aspects of the engagement process. They are important initial understandings of how the family communicates, relates, and interacts with their present environment. While this beginning assessment is not the extensive piece that will be done with more questioning, it is done so that what the practitioner says will fit with the family and its members.

Beyond the initial observations made when the family comes to the practitioner's office, it is important to more fully assess the family dynamics as they are occurring in the first session. These observations make it easier to understand the communication process and to respond in a manner that fits with the family's method of communication and interaction with the outside environment. This assessment is primarily done through observation during the initial session. The following are guidelines for gathering these assessments:

1. Who talks with whom? Is there a pattern to their interaction? For example, does the son talk with his mother first about something he wants and then she talks with his father?
2. How is the communication handled? Do family members interrupt one another or do they wait until the other person is done talking?
3. What does the family talk about? Are they concentrated on what they perceive as the problem or on the problem person? Do they allow discussion of other topics? Do they talk about their feelings or is everything based on actual events?
4. Are there outside supports for the family, such as an extended family, or does the family appear to limit their outside contact?
5. How does the family describe their hopes? Are they cohesive or do these differ among family members?
6. What stage is the family in according to a fluid life cycle? Do they seem to be handling this well or are they stuck at some particular developmental stage?

The answers to these questions will determine how a practitioner interacts during an initial engagement with a family. Understanding the family's overt as well as covert rules, boundaries, and structure allows him to build an alliance with a family.

Aid Family Members in Communicating More Clearly with One Another

Although this is the first session and the practitioner's primary objectives are to observe, build trust, and engage the client, working with family members to clearly speak with one another can help the process of engagement. By helping family members to be clear in their interactions with each other, the practitioner is encouraging hope in the family and producing some initial positive changes. We can also refer to this facilitation as skill development in the area of communication. Research done on behavioral skills techniques in marital and family communication shows them as having positive short-term effects (Sprenkle, Blow, & Dickey, 1999). Johnson and Yanca (2001) state that "teaching skills to the family or group is essential to improving individual, family, and group functioning" (p. 217).

In helping family members communicate more clearly with one another, the practitioner needs to model good communication skills with the family. One of the most powerful communication phrases that an individual can use is the "I" message. Thomas Gordon (1973) originally developed the "I" message for improving the child-management effectiveness of parents. These messages reflect a communication style by which the speaker shares with another how he is feeling by beginning his statement with an "I" and following it with a description of the felt emotion or reaction. The "I" replaces the pronoun "you" and allows the speaker to state what he wishes without the other person or people feeling attacked. For example, instead of a father saying something like this:

> **FATHER:** You don't listen. You never listen. I feel like I am talking to a wall.

he could say the following using an "I" message:

> **FATHER:** I feel very angry when it seems like you are not listening.

The difference between these statements is small, but they convey very divergent meanings. The following are a few examples of overusing the word "you." Try to think of a different way to say each statement using an "I" message.

> **MOTHER:** You are so mean to your father and me. I just can't stand it anymore. You have to change or I cannot keep going.

> **DAUGHTER:** You never let me do anything. I have to sneak out just to get to do something. You don't really care about me.

> **FATHER:** If you do not listen to me, I will ground you for a year.

Another method for helping families communicate with one another more clearly is to ensure that they are hearing what the other person is saying. A social worker can do this by asking each family member to repeat what he or she heard the person saying.

> **MOTHER** (*to son*): I get very angry when you don't study and do so poorly on your grades.

SON (*to mother*): I don't really care what you think.

FAMILY PRACTITIONER (*to son*): Let's go over what you heard your mother say.

SON (*to family practitioner*): She thinks I am stupid.

FAMILY PRACTITIONER (*to mother*): Can you repeat what you said to your son?

MOTHER (*to son*): I didn't say you were stupid. You are very smart. That's why I get angry, because you could do much better on your grades.

These types of interventions are generally received well during an initial session and can facilitate the family's trust in the social worker and in their ability to relate to one another.

Begin to Establish Goals

Before the end of the initial session it is important to start structuring the family goals and family members' individual goals. When clients personally select their goals, the intervention is much more likely to be successful than if they accept a goal to escape punishment or gain a reward (Rooney, 1992). Hepworth et al. (1997) note that goals need to have guidelines. The following four seem particularly important to setting initial goals during engagement.

1. Goals must relate to the desired end results sought by voluntary clients.
2. Goals for involuntary clients should include motivational congruence wherever possible.
3. Goals should be defined in explicit and measurable terms.
4. Goals should be stated in positive terms that emphasize growth. (pp. 347–349)

By having initial goals (hopes) set, families can see something at the end of the first session that they are working toward. The fact that the social worker is helping them set these early goals gives clients a feeling of hope and belief in themselves. Barnum and colleagues (1998) suggest that individuals can maintain hope and look for positive outcomes when they are able to pursue their goals.

There will be times, of course, when individual goals will not necessarily match family goals. It is the family practitioner's responsibility during the engagement process to help the family find those goals that match both the family's and the family members' needs. These goals need to have the family as the fundamental focus. Many families will be unable to complete this task during the engagement process. It is important to continue to stress how critical family goals are and to suggest that the family be prepared before the next session to establish these goals. Too often, family practitioners start to intervene with a family without goals and find themselves by the third session having to start over. Hanna and Brown (1999) suggest the following questions for helping a family find common goals from a strength's perspective:

1. Ask each family member to describe how he or she would like things to be different.

2. Ask family members to describe changes in positive rather than negative terms.
3. Ask family members to be specific about what they want to change. (pp. 242–243)

Summarize Session and Encourage Family to See Their Strengths and Coping Skills

Summarizing is important in encouraging family members at the end of each session. At the end of the first session, it is critical to let the family know what they have accomplished and to comment again on their strengths and coping skills. Noting the family's strengths and coping skills at the end of this session gives them the message that they have the means to resolve their own issues and achieve their overarching family goals. Comments such as these encourage the family members to acknowledge their skills and, in fact, often causes an increase in the conscious use of those skills over the next few sessions. Whitaker (1982) believed that the goals used in family intervention reflect a sense of self and positive skills.

ETHNIC AND CULTURAL CHALLENGES IN ENGAGEMENT

It is important to recognize that what we have presented are the basic guidelines for engagement. Some families may have different needs and want to interact with the practitioner in different ways. It is important to be in touch with these differences and be sensitive to them. Perhaps one of the most valuable areas a family practitioner can be trained in is issues of ethnic and cultural diversity. In many cultures, norms do not necessarily fit with the basic guidelines.

Let us take, for example, a situation where a Mexican-American family receives an intervention. Research has shown that in Hispanic households, generally the male head of the family is the one with authority who needs to be addressed first in a therapeutic setting. The reasoning behind this is that the family will recognize the practitioner's respect for them and be more open to her involvement. If she decides to hold out her hand to greet a new family and a child shakes it first, then she is not respecting the hierarchy within the family. Goldenberg and Goldenberg (2002) suggest the following list for working with families from different cultural and ethnic groups as a starting point for considering the diversity of experiences to which various cultural and ethnic groups have been exposed (pp. 334; 337).

- Country of origin
- Circumstances of immigration if applicable
- Degree of acculturation
- Generation in the United States
- English fluency

- Sex-role assignments
- Social economic status
- Prejudice or discrimination
- Role and status reversal
- Lack of community support
- Intergenerational conflicts and relationships
- Machismo
- Male-female relationships
- Devotion to church

As one can gather from this list, any number of things may disrupt the basic process of engagement. Not being able to speak the same language or not being able to discern from the language accurate meanings would also have a huge impact on the practitioner's ability to engage the family.

While much has been stated about how the family practitioner should engage with the family, perhaps not enough can be said about the actual relationship between the two. We know that in order to build trust, there must be empathy, genuineness, and warmth; however, a relationship goes far beyond these behaviors. A relationship is about the family and the practitioner coming together in a collaborative fashion. While the social worker has skills to bring to this situation, it is really the family's strengths and their own skills that will make a difference. The practitioner is there to facilitate their coping mechanisms and to provide them with a means of thinking through alternatives, trying out solutions, and not losing faith in the fact that they might resolve their conflicts by using their strengths. The ability to make this happen depends on the engagement processes that have been discussed here. With the appropriate therapeutic alliance built, the family practitioner can move the family forward toward their goals.

4 CHAPTER | Family Assessment Considerations

© Michael Newman/PhotoEdit

INTRODUCTION

As we discussed in Chapter 2, assessment is the second step in the planned change or problem solving process. Assessment of families is a potentially complex undertaking for several reasons. First, families are composed of individual members, each with his or her own experiences, understanding, reactions, and perspectives on the family. Second, families have their own dynamic developmental processes that are both similar to and dissimilar from those of the individual family members. Third, assessment can focus on such diverse elements as development of a child, parent–child relationships, parenting skills, or partner relationships. Fourth, each family exists within a larger environment that may support or undercut the ability of the family to function effectively as a system. Finally, the family theory employed by the practitioner governs, or at least affects, the assessment process. This combination of factors makes work with families a challenging activity.

The major theme of this chapter is looking at the structure of assessment, particularly the importance of using a bio–psycho–social lens to examine and understand individual families. In the process, we consider three significant factors that influence family functioning. The first of these is the role development of the individual and the ways that this can affect the family. This is important because as a system, the challenges experienced by individual family members often influence the whole family to one degree or another. The second factor to be considered is the way in which a family's own developmental process may affect their well-being. The final factor is the way that large environment influences can facilitate or impede effective individual and family functioning. A family-in-environment approach requires consideration of each of these influences if we are to adequately understand and work with families.

USING A BIO–PSYCHO–SOCIAL FOCUS

Assessing families is a multidimensional activity that must take into account a variety of variables. Typically, this means that an assessment must have a *bio–psycho–social focus* that incorporates physiological, psychological, and social/environmental factors and events that affect the family. Without this broad perspective, it is easy to ignore crucial events that impact how well families function and meet the needs of their members. Looking both at the individual family member and at the family as a whole is also necessary.

Using a bio–psycho–social focus on the family allows us to take into account such variables as the influence of environment, family strengths and access to resources, cultural and diversity issues, economic factors, and spiritual concerns. It allows us to understand how, for example, an individual family member's illness can affect the overall family or how employment loss can undermine the family's ability to meet its needs. Only by considering all of the factors that impinge on the family can we truly understand the situation and identify how best to help them.

Influence of Individual Development on Family Systems

Individual members of a family develop within a context of social roles, affected by issues of race, gender, class, and culture (Almeida, Woods, & Messineo, 1998). The consequences of this context are that the ability to develop into a mature human being is fundamentally influenced by experiences and structures beyond the control of the child. By *mature human beings,* we mean the capacity to think and operate within our own values and belief system, to "empathize, trust, communicate, and respect others who are different and to negotiate our interdependence with our environment and with our friends, partners, families, communities, and society in ways that do not entail the exploitation of others" (McGoldrick & Carter, 1999, pp. 27–28).

The learning process that should lead to maturity is influenced by the aforementioned contextual elements. For example, how well we learn to deal with individual differences largely depends on how family members, peers, the community, and society deal with difference. If parents and peers commonly employ racism, homophobia, and gender stereotypes in these contexts, it is likely that such factors will characterize the child's learning. If we raise boys to deny their social and emotional interdependence on others, this will become a problem because developing and maintaining successful relationships requires avoiding the myth of independence and autonomy. There is ample evidence that both parents and other adults treat boys and girls differently. The words we use in discussion with girls, for example, are much more likely to include emotional topics (Lewis & Haviland, 1993). Media, health care providers, educators, and others support differential treatment of boys and girls, and often reinforce the parents' own biases about child rearing.

THEORY IN ACTION | Learning Process

Steven, age 13, was found drunk on the school campus at lunchtime. His parents were called in and when the father showed up, liquor could be smelled on his breath also. Following his expulsion from school for a week, Steve returned to school with two bruises on his arm. Two weeks later, Steve was expelled again for starting a fight in the schoolyard with another student. When Steve returned to school the following week, he was caught with a bottle of liquor in his coat pocket. His father's reaction to being called into school again was to grab Steve by the arm and shake him hard. How much of Steven's behavior is influenced by the way his parents have raised him?

Our understanding of child development has been hampered by the overwhelming tendency of our research to focus on males, to the exclusion of females. Research on women has been much more recent in development and has challenged the historical emphasis on autonomy and independence. It has also rejected theories that emphasize competition, fail to address communication skills, and ignore the need for relationships. There are clearly differences in adults that we can trace back to differential treatment in childhood. Empathy, for example, is much more likely to be evident in males if their fathers were involved in child rearing (Miedzian, 1991). Social patterns emphasize preparing boys for competition and girls for relationships, and these tendencies have major implications for their ability to function in a marriage or other adult relationships.

Societal patterns also influence how we see ourselves. Children who are different because of disability, color, culture, and so on are less likely to see themselves reflected in popular media or as part of a valued segment of society. They will likely face a lifetime in which others have lower expectations for them or in which they experience discrimination and prejudice because of their differences. While parents can help prepare children for these experiences, it is a burden not placed on those who are privileged in society. Similarly, expectations related to gender differences may result in others defining girls in particular ways. For example, a girl may be discouraged from activities or interests typical of boys. Likewise, we may discourage boys from developing their emotional capabilities and their abilities to relate to others.

Children of color also have a major developmental task that is imposed by society and their life circumstances—the need to master two cultures in order to survive and prosper (Hale-Benson, 1986). Commonly these cultures differ drastically from one another. The dominant or sustaining culture values intellectual intelligence, prefers written to verbal communication, and sees events in a linear fashion. The more nurturing African American culture, by contrast, emphasizes verbal communication, body language, and a circular or nonlinear perspective on events. Traditional theories of child development tend not to recognize other types of intelligence, such as interpersonal, emotional, musical, intrapersonal, spatial, or artistic, although these abilities are often correlated with school performance (Ellison, 1984; Gardner, 1983; Goldman, 1997; Hale-Benson, 1986). This failure represents a lost opportunity to recognize and develop knowledge and skills essential for survival and success both in academic and life pursuits. In addition, most theories fail to note how socialization can place obstacles in the way of individuals and groups who are capable of more fully developing their own interdependence and sense of self. Knowing what influences the individual has experienced helps when it comes time to do a family assessment. In this way, we can more readily recognize culturally sanctioned behaviors and patterns based upon life experiences and distinguish them from more serious emotional difficulties.

THEORY IN ACTION | **Culture Socialization**

Tim (an African American), age 15, lives in low-income housing with his mother and three brothers. Tim, with the support of his family, is enrolled in honor courses at the local high school. He also works a four-hour job after school in the afternoon. The high school counselor recommends to Tim that he might want to take classes at the local trade school so he can get himself a job when he graduates. When Tim points out that he would like to go to college, the counselor advises him that this will be very difficult and very expensive. Her views are based on his skin color rather than on him as a person.

Another factor to keep in mind is that the developmental needs of a child may conflict with those of adult caretakers. One example is a 20-year-old mother who loves to party late and sleep in the morning. At 6:00 A.M. she is groggy, disoriented, and generally exhausted but that is precisely when her 2-year-old son and 3-year-old daughter awaken and demand attention. In this situation, the mother's youth and inexperience make it difficult for her to understand her children's needs and developmental requirements. Yet, if she had failed to adjust her own schedule to fit her children's needs, the consequences on their development could have been severe by hampering their sense of trust and security (McGoldrick & Carter, 1999). Likewise, a parent uncomfortable talking about issues such as sex or race may hinder a child's capacity for relationships with the opposite sex or people of color. Parents who unduly value aggressiveness, strength, and independence cannot develop their male child's more emotional side or emphasize values such as fairness and interdependence.

Similarly, adolescent girls need parenting that allows them to see that their own potential for well-being is not connected to the ability to attract and hold a mate. Parents who lack this perspective in their own development will find it harder to understand why it is important for their daughters.

Individual stages of development may also influence family life as both partners cope with physical, social, and emotional changes. For example, decreasing physical strength and agility may make one partner feel less capable of undertaking certain activities. This, in turn, can influence the person's sense of importance since he or she was always known for these now declining abilities. On the positive side, some changes (such as menopause) may lead to a desire for additional challenges and lead a person off in new directions.

Individual developmental experiences can have a major bearing on what occurs within a family. Males who do not develop skills in communication and emotional sharing are more likely to experience problems within their relationships. Females who have incorporated societal expectations about gender-appropriate behavior may find it difficult to meet the needs of children who must be prepared to live in a changing society. Parents struggling with their own developmental stages and tasks can have less energy and inclination to meet their children's needs. Helping families cope with the ordinary and extraordinary challenges they face requires that we acknowledge the role of individual development in creating or diminishing the resources needed to survive and succeed.

Influence of Family Development on Family Systems

Many researchers employ a *family development model* to explain how the institution of the family evolves. Using a model that parallels individual life cycle theories, they identify a series of development stages, each associated with specific tasks and challenges. Recognizing that these developmental stages are likely to have consequences for a family makes it easier to help struggling families. The stages of the family life cycle discussed in the literature vary from writer to writer. However, they all have approximately the same identified challenges with which the family will struggle. We will briefly describe each of these stages and tasks and provide examples of how they may influence the family's capacity to adapt. It is important to keep in mind that any stage's length may vary considerably due to variables such as marriage or remarriage, childbearing later in life, and the decision not to have children, among others. Ultimately, according to Goldenberg and Goldberg (1991), family development "provides the major context and is a major determinant of the growth and development of its members" (p. 14). Thus, a family's dysfunction might be indicative of its own developmental impasse. Perhaps the "problem" is actually a solution to a family problem caused as members grapple with the challenges of achieving their own individual development milestones. This might occur, for example, when an adolescent developing a capacity for independence clashes with parents who want to protect her and forestall future problems.

Marriage and Cohabitation Marriage and cohabitation require similar elements for success, and some research suggests that marital couples do agree on these characteristics (Lavee, 1997; Stinnett, Sanders, & DeFrain, 1981). These characteristics include the following:

1. Love, companionship, bonding, and caring
2. Understanding, agreement on various issues, and support for one another
3. Mutual respect and regard for each other
4. Mutual trust and loyalty
5. Satisfactory sexual relationships and intimacy
6. Cooperation in decision making
7. Intellectual, mental, and worldview compatibility
8. Communication and conflict resolution
9. Economic stability and financial well-being
10. Opportunity for personal autonomy and self-actualization

Family practitioners tend to cite the same items although, interestingly enough, they do not necessarily agree on the relative priority of each one (Lavee, 1997).

Both marriage and cohabitation require a degree of commitment to a new unit. This usually requires both partners to work out new relationships with family members and friends and, in doing so, the commitment is the crucial aspect of this process. Unless it is strong, the challenges of changing old patterns and forming new ones are likely to overwhelm one or both partners. In addition to the importance of this step, it is also important to recognize how difficult it can be. All partners bring into the relationship rules, beliefs, and preferences associated with their respective families of origin. When these factors differ between partners, they must use a negotiation process to arrive at a mutually satisfactory arrangement. These rules may cover almost everything, including such things as "when and how to sleep, eat, have sex, fight, and make up" (Goldenberg & Goldenberg, 1991, p. 20). Couples must adopt new sets of rituals along with whatever traditions they wish to observe. The potential for disagreements is significant. At whose house will we celebrate Thanksgiving? Do we open any presents on Christmas Eve? How should we celebrate birthdays? In one family, for example, birthdays are a major event, with the individual receiving presents, special attention, and other indicators of his special status. In another, the only thing expected is a card or phone call acknowledging the event. These kinds of differences need to be reconciled.

Childbearing and Birth The Gallup and Newport (1990) findings that the vast majority of Americans have children and that only 4 percent neither had nor wanted children suggest the almost universal attraction of children to families. However, when children are born, new challenges face the family. These might include who does what and when. Both partners have to make room for the child in physical, emotional, and temporal ways. Pregnancy affects the physical energy of the woman and may carry with it other unpleasant side effects such as morning sickness. Interest in and capacity for sex may change for one or both partners during pregnancy. The dyadic relationship must prepare to admit a third person to the family system. In such situations, it is common for one parent to be more enthusiastic about these changes than the other. The partners must rearrange the home to provide living space for the child, and the spare bedroom that had been a study may now be returned to its original use. Clearly, the process of preparing for and having a child can seriously disrupt the prior lifestyle of both parents.

Child Rearing Once the child has arrived home, other adaptations become necessary. Childproofing of cabinets is required despite the annoyance that these methods pose for adults. The parents must make decisions about such mundane topics as shopping, selecting a day care or a nursery, and determining who will pick the child up from the babysitter. Later issues involve child-rearing techniques, discipline, and a whole series of tasks with the potential for disrupting the pre-child dyadic relationship. No matter how successful the dyadic adjustment was before children, the adjustment afterward will be difficult. One reason is the very real possibility of a triangle developing, with all the negative aspects of these relationships. *Triangles* are alliances or coalitions among three members of a family that are most noticeable in times of stress. Avoiding triangles requires a degree of maturity and acceptance of one's new role as a parent, itself an important developmental task. We will discuss triangles at greater length in Chapter 5.

With both parents employed in many cases today, there is greater need to organize schedules, assign responsibilities, and still maintain a satisfactory relationship with one's partner. As the children get older, other institutions become involved in their lives. Schools, clubs, peer groups, church, sports, and many other formal and informal institutions begin to have important influences on the child.

Once children get older, other challenges arise. Allowing children to develop autonomy and independence while simultaneously providing them with guidance and oversight is an ongoing obligation that becomes even more stressful during a child's adolescence. Unfortunately, adolescence tends to fall at a point in the family system where other issues are also occurring. For example, partners may begin to question their jobs and their relationship with each other while simultaneously struggling with parenting an adolescent.

The universal attraction for having children discussed earlier appears to be true for both heterosexual and gay and lesbian families. However, the percentage of parents with children in the latter appears to be lower (Patterson, 1992). Lesbian and gay parents experience the same challenges faced by other new parents but with the added force of institutional and individual prejudice and hostility. A couple's own parents, a potential source of strength for heterosexual couples, are often negative toward the idea of their gay and lesbian children becoming parents. The gay/lesbian parents may have their own concerns and questions about raising children in a non-heterosexual family, especially relating to the possible hostility and prejudice the children may experience. These concerns are complicated further by medical and health issues dependent upon the method of insemination used and the legal quandaries that can occur involving parental rights.

Separating from Children Family developmental stages such as the children leaving home may allow the primary caretaker to consider options that were not possible during child rearing. A new job, volunteering, or the opportunity to explore long dormant interests may upset the homeostasis within the family relationship. The separation stage also represents a major life task for the child, one complicated by the longer periods of dependency required by extended educational experiences. The empty-nest experience may force the parents to reassess their relationship. It is sometimes at this point that one or both partners realize that the last decade has been spent in activities that revolve around the children. One possible consequence of this is that the parents may not have nurtured their own relationship. If this happens, they can discover that they no longer have many interests in common, a frequent prelude to divorce.

While the divorce rate for older couples has increased, it does not yet mirror the rate for younger couples (Goodman, 1992). However, when older couples divorce after 20 or more years of marriage, several outcomes are typical (Goodman, 1992). First is a reduction in morale and an overall sense of disruption in one's life. Second is a tendency to see one's life as more negative than it is, an occurrence frequently experienced by men. Third is a trend toward a variety of psychological problems. While many divorced women rate themselves as having a better quality of life following a divorce, men are much less likely to come to this conclusion. Despite this difference in perception, men experience fewer financial problems and are four times as likely as women to be financially secure following a divorce. Factors such as making new friends, receiving financial and social supports from family and friends, and adequate preparation before the divorce seem to be significant factors in one's sense of well-being (Goodman, 1992).

Another developmental task of this phase is to build adult-to-adult relationships with one's children. The transition from parent to confidant is easier if the adolescent years have been weathered successfully and parents have carefully walked the line between protecting and overprotecting their charges.

Relating to In-Laws Relating to in-laws can be an enjoyable developmental phase or a source of stress. When a child marries, there may be great joy and a welcoming of the child's spouse and family. Simultaneously, there is always the possibility of strife, especially when parents have difficulty relinquishing control over their children. Too great a desire to help can be seen as intrusive, and too little involvement may appear to show disinterest. Potential problems are more likely in instances where the parents are unhappy with their child's choice for a mate or when major differences in issues like religion, ethnicity, or class exist (Blacker, 1999). There is also the potential for additional triangles as parents take sides with their own children or grandchildren. Not surprisingly, the burden of maintaining quality in-law relationships usually falls to the wife. While it is not unusual for some families to distance themselves from problems with their in-laws, one family, so stressed over the intrusiveness of the wife's mother, abruptly left the United States to live in Australia. Only after several years apart did the family consider returning to the vicinity of her parents.

In some cultures, such as the Native Americans, families come to expect a close involvement of the in-laws in their affairs. "Elders will influence family decision-making by sharing advice, encouragement, and setting boundaries for intercultural interactions" (Weaver & White, 1997, p. 77). Knowledge of these traditions can prove useful for the social worker. The practitioner can seek sanction and support from significant members of the Native community and encourage the involvement of other Native people when developing family programs. It is also possible that funding and services for Native families may be available through their Nation. These include services for children and families, health care, and job training, among others.

While the topic of in-laws has sparked many jokes and humorous movies and television shows, there is ample evidence that many families have excellent relationships with their in-laws. Often the in-laws represent an extended family resource in a nuclear family age. In-laws often provide financial assistance, emotional support, childcare services, and a host of other benefits. In many families, the inability of parents to care for their own children due to drug abuse or other problems means that grandparents become the full-time caretakers, reprising their earlier roles. Although there are exceptions, typically the birth of grandchildren improves family relationships with in-laws and is seen as very positive by the grandparents. The joy dims a bit when divorce and remarriage occur because of questions about which grandparents are the "real" ones and how visitation arrangements are handled. However, with careful attention, these issues can be resolved if all parties are willing and able to work for the betterment of the family unit.

Caregiving of Elderly Parents It is a truism that as children prepare to depart from the nest, aging parents may begin to need assistance with life tasks. Partners who were looking forward to having time to themselves after the last child leaves home may instead end up caretaking their own aging parents. This can be an enormous burden that falls on women much more than on men, causing conflicts between employment and one's responsibility to a parent (Walsh, 1999). With an average age of 57, these women have often established careers and employment patterns that make it nearly impossible to take on additional burdens. Worse yet, one-quarter of these caregivers are themselves over 65 and at a point where they expected to enjoy their retirement years. Since caregiving often involves an average of 28 hours per week spread across all 7 days, the toll is significant. Intergenerational tensions can arise as parents, once caretakers for their own children, now must rely on their children for help in conducting their lives. On the other hand, children who do too much for their impaired parents may provoke dependency and learned helplessness. If families become overwhelmed by this added responsibility, elder abuse may result. A variety of models of respite care are in use to help caregivers and to reduce the stress associated with this role. These include homemaker services provided in the family's home, sitter or companion services, and parent-trainer services that train and pay family or friends to provide services. Also available are adult foster care, licensed family or group care services, and care offered at the home of another provider. Each of these programs allows caregivers to have time away from their responsibilities, and social workers should be aware of such resources.

Finally, nursing home placement necessitated by continued deterioration of the parent is likely to create a sense of guilt among those making the decision. Those placed may complain about being abandoned, even when institutional care was the only option. Daughters, who most often have primary care responsibilities in these situations, may be particularly susceptible to the idea that they are somehow abdicating their role as caretaker.

The death of the last parent signals the family adults that they are now the senior generation and the next to die. This can be troubling especially when coupled with other life tasks, such as preparing for and entering retirement.

Retirement Retirement can mean a significant increase in time spent with one's partner coupled with a lowered income. Physical health may become a more serious concern and begin to be a limiting factor in relation to previous pursuits. Some retired families become more dependent upon their children, while others must cope with the death of friends and family. Other family developmental milestones can provoke problems. For example, a decision to sell one's home and move to a smaller residence can produce unforeseen conflicts with grown children who feel a sense of loss over their soon-to-be-sold childhood home. It may also lead to stress between the partners because of the need to eliminate household items once considered precious. On the other hand, retirement may be a period of great joy as partners travel or pursue lifelong interests and hobbies. Finally, grandchildren may prove to be a blessing and enliven the retirement years of many families.

Death Preparing for one's own death or that of a spouse is difficult. In many ways, no one is truly prepared to lose a life partner, even if a long period of illness precedes death. A grandparent's death may also have important implications for grandchildren, as this is often the first death they have experienced. A lingering illness before death may have taxed the financial resources of the family. Similarly, assisted living or nursing home care may have depleted family resources before death, leaving the remaining spouse with fewer assets. Most likely, the surviving spouse will be the woman because of that gender's greater life expectancy. The primary tasks of this stage are to "grieve for the loss of the spouse and to reinvest in future functioning" (McGoldrick & Walsh, 1999, p. 196). The grieving process may take as long as a year while the surviving partner mourns the loss of the spouse. Eventually, the focus turns to everyday functioning and new interests. We should note, however, that this pattern is more likely if the woman is the surviving spouse. For men who survive the loss of their wives, the risk of suicide and death in the first year is high. In the first six months of bereavement, widowers have a death rate 40 percent higher than married men their age (McGoldrick & Walsh, 1999).

We must also consider cultural issues during this stage because there are wide differences in how families manage death. Some cultures have strict rules about the timing of burials and common rituals that must be observed. In others, traditions that are followed may or may not be connected with spiritual or religious beliefs. A culture may prescribe the length of mourning periods and expect specific behavior from the surviving family members. Sometimes the death of a family member triggers the involvement of the members of the family of origin, for example, when a brother of the deceased assumes increased responsibility for the family of his late sibling.

In divorced families, issues of bereavement can be confusing. Spouses who have been separated for some time may still experience intense reactions to the death of their former partner. In stepfamilies with children where the biological parent dies, there may be additional legal complications if the surviving spouse has not adopted the children. Without a legal framework such as adoption, the remaining stepparent has no rights to maintain a relationship with the children.

Another complication to be considered is that many spouses end up as caregivers to their own partner in the years immediately preceding death. This can be a tremendous burden on the spouse who is dealing with his or her own infirmities and diminished physical resources. Again, the burden tends to fall most heavily on women. The problem is aggravated if the ill spouse is suffering from Alzheimer's or other forms of dementia. The inability of the ill spouse to recognize his wife or children, periodic expressions of paranoia, and severe memory loss can be depressing and even a source of anger for the caretaker. Elder abuse can occur in these situations, particularly when the cared-for partner is violent or aggressive. If the caregiver suffers from substance abuse or mental illness or, because of his or her new role, experiences financial hardship, the potential for abuse increases. Social workers must be alert to these situations when interviewing family members.

The death of one spouse can lead eventually to a remarriage or at least an ongoing relationship involving the survivor. This new adventure can feel wonderful for the widow or widower, although the reactions of other family members may affect these feelings. Some adult children will consider a parent's remarriage as evidence of disloyalty to the deceased. Others will become suspicious of the motivation of the new stepparent, suggesting that financial reasons are behind the marriage or relationship. In these situations, what should be a joyous period is often characterized by bad feelings and strained relationships.

THEORY IN ACTION | Importance of Family Life Cycle Theory

The Sheffield family was being seen in treatment by family practitioner at the local community mental health center. They had come to discuss the problems they were having following the retirement of the husband two months ago. They stated that they were fighting more and they did not seem to agree on anything anymore. Mrs. Sheffield stated that since her husband had retired, he laid around the house and did not want to do anything. She stated that when she tried to talk with him about her concerns, he just refused to talk. Mr. Sheffield admitted that he had been feeling really down since he quit work. He stated that he did not know how to adjust to being home all the time and resented his wife's ability to get out of the house every day.

Influence of Environmental Factors on Family Systems

The larger social environment of the family can profoundly affect the system's capacity to meet its obligations to its members. In fact, the influence of the environment can be salutary, helping the members by providing employment, quality educational opportunity, and social support for both individual members and the family itself. Unfortunately, the environment may also be destructive to the family by limiting opportunities for employment or offering poor schools, a lack of social services, discrimination, prejudice, and no mechanisms to assist families in meeting their needs. Consider, for instance, the influence on a family in a community where one out of every three adults is unemployed, 30 percent of adult males are caught up in the criminal justice system, most families contain a single adult, and children on their way to school routinely encounter drug dealers and gangs. Contrast this with a community where schools are a high priority, 75 percent of the students go on to college, drug use is low, and social opportunities for children include scouting, boys and girls clubs, and athletics.

It is not difficult to see how one environment can provide a degree of nurturing and support while the other can undermine the best efforts and intentions of both children and parents. This is not to say that the influence of the environment is all-powerful. Many children grow up in unsupportive and dangerous communities and yet do not end up in gangs, on drugs, or in criminal careers. It is difficult to determine conclusively why two children growing up in the same community will turn out differently. However, the fact that this routinely happens suggests the importance of understanding the interaction of physical, social, and psychological influences on the individual. One boy in the community may have parental support that helps buffer the influence of gangs. Another may come from a family with strong spiritual and religious beliefs that limit the attractiveness of drugs. Still another may have skills or attributes such as athletic ability that provide outlets and a route out of the community. The resilience of children in such situations is often a remarkable thing to see.

Consider also the resources available to an unemployed single mother, estranged from her own parents and raising three children under the age of six, and how these can affect her ability to meet all of their needs. Compare this with the same single mother who has a strong, loving extended family to rely on. The resources available to individual families have a lot to do with how successful the family can be in meeting its needs. Financial programs, such as Temporary Assistance to Needy Families (TANF) and unemployment insurance, coupled with social programs such as public housing, low income heating assistance, and others can make the difference between a family that survives and one that disintegrates. The absence of resources, whether familial, informal, or formal, can have a bearing on which families make it and which do not. Societal support for such programs is another factor in determining what governmental and private resources are available to help families struggling to survive.

Open and Closed Systems In Chapter 2, we discussed the notion of open and closed systems. You may recall that these terms refer to the degree and nature of cross-boundary interactions with other systems in the environment. These interactions may take the form of communication, exposure to new ideas and information, and the sharing of resources. A closed family system lacks interactions with the larger environment and consequently may not have access to resources available in the environment. The Figure 4.1 shows a family that resists involvement with outside institutions and remains mostly closed to the environment. The deflected arrows show the direction of effort and the failure of the family to have any significant contact with either the church or school. Systems with closed boundaries are attempting to be independent but at a cost of not receiving resources, information, or other assistance needed for coping with change. A closed system's capacity for adaptation is significantly reduced.

In practice, most families are somewhere along a continuum, neither completely open nor closed. The point on the continuum may change over time, but ultimately survival as a healthy family unit requires some level of interaction with the external environment. It may be necessary to help a family become more open to new ideas or to assist members to focus more on their own internal relationships. The particular needs of the family in this regard are likely to become more obvious as a result of a family assessment.

Disengagement Boundaries also indicate who is not a part of the subsystem. Consider Mike, a 35-year-old man who has become *disengaged* from his wife and daughter who are very close to one another. Disengaged subsystems cease to function with any sense of connection to other family members. Disengaged

Figure 4.1 Closed Boundary

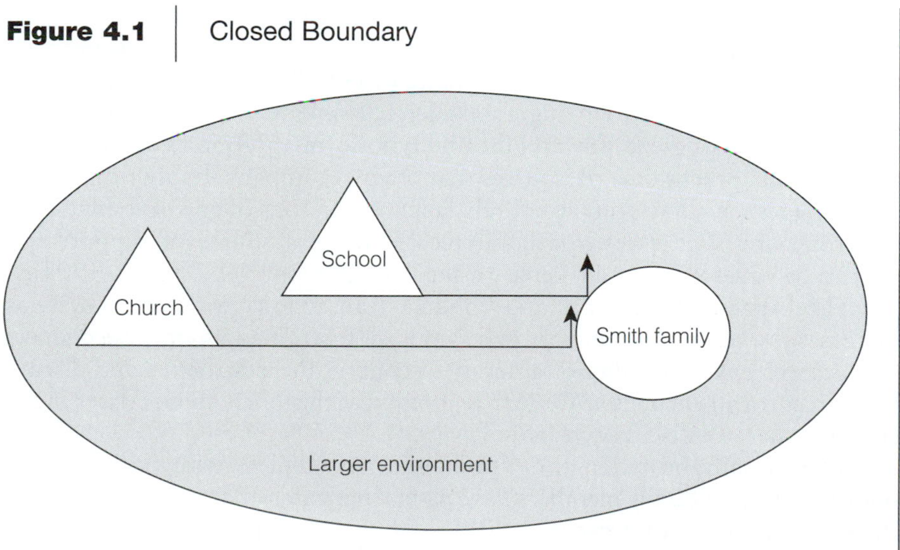

family members are at the opposite end of the spectrum from enmeshed families. Developing close family ties and mutual feelings with the disengaged subset is very difficult. Without further information, it is impossible to tell whether Mike's decision to disengage brought the mother and daughter closer together or if their closeness resulted in his disengagement. It is also possible that both events occurred simultaneously, each contributing to the other. These possibilities illustrate the mutual and reciprocal influence that family members can have on one another. Although each family member is an independent system, all family members are also interdependent. By this, we mean they do not and cannot function completely independently of one another and must rely on each other to meet a variety of human needs (Dell, 1989).

Family Resources and Strengths It is easy to fall into the trap of assuming that a family having problems is very low on resources, like a car low on gas. Operating from a strengths perspective, however, allows a much more realistic view of the resources a family brings to the table (Saleebey, 1997). Resources may be psychological, social, or financial, and they may exist within the family itself or consist of extrafamilial strengths. Intrafamily resources might include the quality of individual relationships within the family, for example, mother and child, as well as the ability to be assertive in identifying one's own needs. The ability to recognize the need for assistance is similarly a resource. A strong connection to one's extended family, spiritual or religious strengths, and a high tolerance for stress are additional possible resources. Of course, a strong work ethic and sense of responsibility for one's family are also assets that might exist (Logan et al., 1990).

Extrafamilial resources could include a stable source of income, extended family members willing to help the family under stress, and friends who can provide emotional or social support. For example, studies by Werner (1993) and Anthony (1987) have shown that "resilient youngsters tend to rely on peers and elders in the community as sources of emotional support and seek them out for counsel and comfort in times of crisis" (Werner, 1999, p. 143). For some families, resources might include accessible services within the financial capabilities of the family and the ability to form appropriate relationships with a family practitioner. Resources that often accompany family rituals such as marriages may, however, be entirely lacking in unions of gay or lesbian couples. In many such cases, the family ceases to be a source of support and instead becomes a major challenge to the couple (Bryant & Demian, 1994).

The capacity to interact and conduct transactions with other systems increases the resources available to a family system. The loss of these connections can cripple the ability of a family to counter the destructive and disruptive forces it will encounter. We will be looking at this phenomenon later in the chapter when we discuss cutoffs.

Every family has strengths. The literature is replete with evidence that both parents and family members have assets that can be harnessed to improve the successfulness of interventions (Briar-Lawson & Wiesen, 2001). And yet, too much attention has been placed on the ability to diagnose and label clients and families using essentially deficit-based tools such as the Diagnostic and Statistical Manual of the American Psychiatric Association. It is perhaps understandable that we have spent inordinate amounts of time focusing on the negative because families often present with some serious problems. However, focusing solely on the problem ignores the reality of family strengths. A strengths focus is important for several reasons. "Strengths are all we have to work with. The recognition and embellishment of strengths is fundamental to the values and mission of the profession. A strengths perspective provides for a leveling of the power relationship . . . between clients and practitioners" (Cowger, 1997, pp. 62–63). In fact, the inherent vulnerability of a family seeking help can be an impediment to the kind of partnership needed to bring about change, especially if we perceive the client as an ineffective or incompetent problem solver.

Cowger (1997, pp. 64–65) provides an excellent set of 12 guidelines for completing a strengths assessment that we can apply to families:

1. *Ensure that the family's understanding of the facts of the situation are the central focus of the assessment.* This means that how the client perceives the situation should be accorded primacy. After all, families tend to know their situations better than anyone else.
2. *Believe the client.* While this may seem easy, there has been a long tradition in the helping professions of discounting the family's account of things. This may arise from a belief that family members lie or are simply too close to the situation to recognize reality.
3. *Determine what the client wants.* This encompasses finding out what the family members want to be different in their lives and coming to understand what they would like the practitioner to do. By doing this we can increase client motivation to work for the desired end. While providing what a family wants is not always possible, it is a good place to begin an assessment.
4. *Move the assessment toward personal and environmental strengths.* This means that the practitioner makes every effort to assess both personal strengths of the family members as well as environmental strengths. The latter might be formal and informal resources and networks the family can probably use.
5. *Provide a multidimensional assessment.* This assessment should take into account the "client's interpersonal skills, motivation, emotional strength, and ability to think clearly," among others (p. 64). It should also identify strengths within each family member as well as those in the larger environment.
6. *Use the assessment to discover uniqueness.* By this he means that the practitioner should look carefully to learn what is unique and different about the family because these characteristics can be the basis for building on familial strengths.
7. *Use language easily understood by families.* This should be obvious, but the nature of professionalization is to create and use a unique language or

nomenclature that clients do not always comprehend. Using such language creates an artificial barrier or distance between the practitioner and client.

8. *Ensure that the assessment is a joint effort between family and practitioner.* By doing so, we increase client motivation and help the family own the final assessment. Failure to make it a joint venture can lead to the family terminating prematurely.
9. *Reach a mutual agreement on the assessment.* This avoids situations in which the family has their understanding of what they need to do while the social worker has another "secret" understanding. This double agenda model has no place in human services and undermines the trust between practitioner and family.
10. *Avoid blame and blaming.* Blaming is associated with the deficit model and only results in defensiveness and individual or family lack of participation in the helping process. Blaming lowers family members' motivation to change and reduces their sense of self-efficacy.
11. *Avoid "cause-and-effect thinking".* This is suggested for several reasons. First, it is difficult to validly assign blame to any single element in the family. Family dynamics are simply too complex to do so. Second, even our best guess is only that—an approximation of what we think contributed to the situation. Third, cause-and-effect thinking often contributes to blaming ("If my wife had not had an affair, everything would be fine.").
12. *Assess; do not diagnose.* Diagnosing is the antithesis of a strengths-based assessment and is derived from a deficit-focused medical model. It encourages labeling with all the negative connotations associated with such appellations. Moreover, it can leave the client expecting the practitioner to solve the problem now identified and labeled.

Assessing strengths is a process that requires forethought and attention to how we interact with families. Being careful to use a strengths perspective is part of what some call *conscious use of self*. By this term, we mean that the social worker must make continuous decisions about the best way to help families.

THEORY IN ACTION | Strengths-Based Assessment

FAMILY PRACTITIONER: Tell me about your family and how you get along, Ms. Taylor.

MS. TAYLOR: We get along fine, but every once in a while we start to fight about money and how much the kids need.

FAMILY PRACTITIONER: It sounds to me that you have some very normal arguments about money, as do most families. I know lots of people struggle with trying to make ends meet, but I think it is also important to recognize how well you are doing.

Culture and Diversity One component of the environment that can affect families is the influence of culture and diversity. The impact of these factors can vary dramatically from one family to another depending on different factors. For example, such things as how much connection a family has to its cultural heritage and the acceptance of diversity within its own membership may be important variables.

Fong (1997) argues that there are two environments that we must take into account in understanding families. The first is the "kind of environment from which the client came and the second is the kind of environment into which the client is moving" (p. 42). The role of the community and larger environment is especially important for cultures in which the individual is not the primary unit of focus. This is true of Native Americans and many Asian cultures, including the Chinese. There are several reasons for this observation. First, the community may represent an extension of the family. This is evident in places like Chinatown in San Francisco and other cities. A person's involvement in the community is a measure of connectedness to and identification with the culture.

A second reason is that for some groups such as Native Americans, the larger environment has had disastrous impacts on the health and well-being of families. As Weaver and White (1997) point out, "the root of many current social and health problems among Native people lies in the past. The United States government made specific and deliberate attempts to destroy Native people both physically and culturally. We cannot minimize the impact of these actions. Although Native people have survived, tremendous damage was done to individuals, families, and communities. The trauma experienced by Native families has never healed" (p. 67). To give a sense of how environmental issues affect Native families, one only has to look at several statistics. More Native families are headed by single females than is true for the rest of the population, and the median income of all Native families is only 62 percent of that of the rest of the population. Native families are two-and-one-half times as likely to live in poverty (Bureau of Census, 1993). Many of today's Native adults were raised in Bureau of Indian Affairs boarding schools, where they not only lost their own culture but were not assimilated into the larger society. Native children were placed in substitute care (foster care or adopted) at a rate 20 times higher than white children (Johnson, 1981). These experiences undercut many traditional Native family values, provided poor role modeling in many case, and taught disciplinary techniques that are at odds with traditional parental approaches. Weaver and White (1997) note that these interactions with environmental forces have left "themes of loss" among Native people.

A third reason is that for immigrant families, adapting to the host cultural community and environment can be a major source of stress and family disruption. Clashing values, a sense of loss of cultural mooring, loss of autonomy, feelings of rejection, role confusion, and the absence of social supports can lead to severe psychological problems, including depression (Choi, 1997). These challenges affect not only the adults but the children of immigrants, who are expected to adopt norms that are at odds with their culture.

A fourth reason for Fong's observation is that the community is also the location of services. Unfortunately, in many communities these may be not be accessible, appropriate, or available, thereby creating major implications for the practitioner interested in connecting family members with community resources. At the same time, for some groups the community is a major source of support and mutual aid in difficult times. The Native American tradition of the extended family means that parents can expect help from community members and do not have to consider themselves solely responsible for decision making about their children.

A fifth reason for the influence of culture and diversity in the larger environment is the enormous role that culture plays in how families function and succeed. Consider, for example, the fact that many Asian cultures place a higher value on men than on women. Women are expected to show loyalty to their own father, to their husband, and to their sons. Power in the family clearly lodges with the male. Individual wishes are subordinated to the overall good of the family. Family harmony is prized over individualization, and all members must bring honor to their families (McGee, 1997). These values are at odds with American expectations about the role of women and beliefs about the importance of self-actualization and independence.

Contrast this with African American families, who have a long tradition of valuing the extended family but also a history of women playing major roles inside and outside the home. Add to this a greater focus on openly expressing feeling as opposed to controlling them, and we see another significant difference between African-Americans and the dominant culture (Majors & Mancini, 1992). Again, many of these characteristics arose from historical factors such as slavery and have been nurtured by racism and prejudice.

Latino Americans also have a tradition of respect for the family system coupled with a strong sense of dignity of the individual. Beliefs in "male machismo" and "female virtue" exist side by side. Family achievement receives greater emphasis than success of the individual member. Reliance on the family for support in times of stress is similar to Native American culture. Although Latino Americans, like Asian Americans, are composed of people from many different countries, these patterns appear to be core elements regardless of group (McGee, 1997).

Understanding cultural differences and effectively employing cultural competence in practice is not always easy. The importance and difficulty of this task are underscored by the research of Bridger et al. (1997), who found that family practitioners who worked with many different cultures possessed only limited knowledge of cultural diversity, often operated with incorrect information, and tended to overgeneralize about ethnic differences. Often, practitioners try to understand different cultures by focusing on specific attributes of each, highlighting the differences without an awareness of how myriad factors can influence each individual and family. Witkin (1989) comments on this tendency by noting:

> The meanings we "observe" or ascribe to the world are not ultimately reducible to simple enumeration of physical events, but are a complex constellation of

> events superimposed on a conceptual field of expectations, beliefs, attitudes, commitments, and feelings. To the extent people act on their perceptions, they shape the very social phenomena they experience. From this perspective, the "reality" which social scientists attempt to discover is not "out there," but a product of collective attempts at sense-making. Understanding such sense-making and how humans create their own realities may be a better use of research energies than attempting to map a purported independent reality. (p. 90)

Witkin is essentially arguing against overgeneralization and is highlighting the need to see each individual and family as unique systems with their own experiences, perceptions, and realities. His observation makes a great deal of sense when we consider the enormous diversity that exists between and among families and family members.

Keep this caveat in mind when reviewing the summary comparison of how culture affects the family shown in Table 4.1. Remembering that the differences and similarities shown in the table are generalizations is important. That means that while they may apply to entire groups, they likely overlook individual differences within subgroups. In addition, single individuals may differ substantially from their putative group. In other words, it is entirely possible, and indeed likely, to meet people who hold some or even none of the traditional values and cultural beliefs of their group. Mixed-culture marriages, generational status, opportunity, and other environmental influences can and do produce wide intragroup variations. This suggests the importance of the practitioner learning as much as possible about the cultural identification and experiences of family members before assuming anything about them based upon external characteristics such as skin color, culture, or ethnicity.

When a family or family member does follow specific cultural values and beliefs, considering this in the helping process is important. Attitudes around gender, proper ways of showing respect, assertiveness, and general experiences with other societal institutions may all have a bearing on whether and how the family responds to the practitioner's offer to help.

Also consider that families whose experiences with social and other institutions have been largely negative might approach a social worker with a degree of hesitance, suspicion, or even anger. Other families may be convinced that the practitioner is unlikely to be helpful because they have perceived other human service helpers as ineffective. One task of the social worker is to gain the trust and confidence of the family while displaying the ability to help them get the results they need.

Economic Considerations As we have noted, the environment can be both a source of strength and a potential detriment to families. Another important aspect of the environment involves economic considerations such as availability of employment, unemployment compensation, and adequate wages and benefits. The gradual replacement of factory jobs, which typically produced higher salaries and benefits, with service industry employment has created an anomaly in which a single parent working 40 hours per week cannot earn sufficient money to support a family. The trend in many business sectors toward hiring part-time rather than full-time workers is also

Table 4.1 Potential Culture Differences and Similarities Affecting Family Life

Native Americans	Latinos	Asian Americans	African Americans	Majority Culture
Family/group achievement	Family achievement	Family achievement	Individual achievement	Individual achievement
Low verbal communication	Low verbal communication	Low verbal communication	Highly verbal communication	Highly verbal communication
Low autonomy	High autonomy	Low autonomy	High autonomy	High autonomy
Thought-oriented	Action-oriented	Thought-oriented	Action-oriented	Action-oriented
Passive work and activity orientation	Passive work and activity orientation	Active work and activity orientation	Active work and activity orientation	Active work and activity orientation
Extended family structure	Extended family structure	Extended family structure	Extended family structure	Nuclear family structure
Lower assertiveness	Lower assertiveness	Lower assertiveness	Higher assertiveness	Higher assertiveness
Focus on present	Past-present focus	Past-present focus	Focus on Present	Focus on future
Flexible time orientation	Flexible time orientation	Flexible time orientation	Flexible time orientation	Rigid time orientation
High fatalism	High fatalism	High fatalism	High fatalism	Low fatalism
Harmony with environment	Harmony with environment	Harmony with environment	Harmony with environment	Mastery over environment

having a negative impact on families. Part-time employees typically receive few, if any, of the benefits provided to full-time workers and thus have fewer of the resources needed to overcome family crises such as illness or unemployment.

Add to this national policies that encourage companies to move to less expensive venues, and we have the common pattern of well-paying employers moving their entire operation outside the United States to countries where labor is cheaper and work regulations more lax or nonexistent. This further erodes opportunities for family members to sustain themselves with gainful employment.

Assessment of economic factors must take into account the role that unemployment and underemployment play in the emotional stability of family members. When the family breadwinner(s) are unable to support their family adequately, other issues may emerge. Role reversals may occur as one partner becomes the major breadwinner while the other loses his or her sense of importance as a provider. Depression, substance abuse, and family violence are all factors that can occur or increase in families faced with severe economic circumstances. The absence of adequate health insurance can contribute to illnesses going untreated, with both short- and long-term consequences.

Similarly, economic factors may have a bearing on a family's ability to offer members a variety of positive experiences. Inadequate income may preclude children's participation in many activities such as sports, music, and scouting. It may mean that older children remain home from school to provide child care for younger siblings or that younger ones become latchkey children. Clearly, economic variables are part of an effective family assessment.

THEORY IN ACTION | Economic Considerations and Child Abuse

Neal was just reported to the Department of Family Services for slapping his 12-year–old son in the face, leaving a bruise. When the local steel plant closed, they laid off both Neal and his wife. Together they had worked at the plant for 10 years, earning a combined $60,000 per year. Neal worked in the forge handling molten steel. Since his layoff, the only job he can get is at McDonald's, where he earns a bit more than a minimum wage.

The bank is repossessing the family home, and Neil has no health insurance for a chronic lung problem he developed from working in the mill. He is depressed, coughing constantly from his illness, and ashamed that he cannot support his family. When his son demanded to know why his parents would not buy him a $150 pair of sneakers, Neil exploded.

It would be easy to focus on Neil's need for help in managing his anger, to consider him a child abuser, or to look for other explanations for his behavior, such as alcoholism. A better perspective is to consider all of the influences that currently affect this family and its ability to function effectively. Contributory factors might include unemployment, serious health care problems, role disruption, potential loss of shelter, and other related explanations. Focusing on anger management with Neil would likely prove ineffective if we ignore the other contributory factors. Multiple perspectives encouraged by systems theory may complicate things but ultimately will lead to more appropriate assessments and interventions.

As is evident in this situation, many factors are at work within this family. Neil's changed status as primary wage earner is affecting his self-concept and his relationship with other family members. The threatened loss of their home is causing stress in all family members, coupled with the normal problems that affect all families. The son's demand for expensive sneakers reflects the influence of his peers coupled with a sense of uncertainty about what is happening to the family. Helping this family requires more than seeking internal psychological explanations or problems. The family needs help on several levels to cope with their situation.

Spirituality *Spirituality* "refers to a search for purpose, meaning, and connection between oneself, other people, the universe, and the ultimate reality . . . " (Sheridan, 2002, p. 567). Spirituality may occur within the context of specific religions but can also be manifest outside of this structure. The topic of spirituality has become increasingly important in assessment as we begin to understand the ways in which people rely on their spiritual beliefs to cope with life events. Attending to spirituality is consistent with a variety of theories, including "existentialism, humanism, and transpersonal" (p. 568). Canda and Furman (1999) note that "spirituality is the heart of helping. It is the heart of empathy and care, pulse of compassion, the vital flow of practice wisdom, and the driving force of action for service" (p. xv). As such, spirituality is compatible with most helping approaches used in family practice.

Many researchers have demonstrated the ways in which spirituality has been a positive force in helping individuals and families cope with substance abuse, suicide, and other traumas (Faiver et al., 2001; Fournier, 1997; Simmons, 1998; Spalding & Mertz, 1997). At the same time, spirituality has been repeatedly recognized as a source of strength and potential area for assessment for various ethnic and refugee groups (Diller, 1999; Potocky-Tripodi, 2002).

We may assess the importance of spirituality and religion for family members through the judicious use of questions such as these:

- Do you participate in any spiritual or religious groups?
- Describe your level of activity in this group.
- How do these activities help you in your life?

- Describe the primary beliefs of this group?
- Do you think it would be helpful to explore your spirituality as we work together?
- Has any event in your life affected your sense of the meaning of life?
- What allows you to continue to make it when so much in your life has been problematic?

Keep in mind that some of these questions are best employed when the practitioner sees some indication that the family does have a spiritual/religious dimension. If, after some preliminary assessment questions, there is no such indication, further attention to the subject is likely to be ineffective. Consider the family's spiritual involvement to be just another potentially important assessment area and therefore worthy of exploration.

A FAMILY ASSESSMENT CHECKLIST

We discussed earlier how a family-in-environment practice framework and bio–psycho–social focus can aid in understanding and intervening with families. The checklist for family assessment (see Table 4.2) is designed to help the practitioner at least consider the factors that can affect how well families perform their functions. As can be seen in the model, the theory employed by the social worker will affect which aspects of a family situation become the primary focus. For example, a practitioner using learning theory is likely to look carefully at the ways that families, peers, and other societal institutions shape,

Table 4.2 | Checklist for Family Assessment

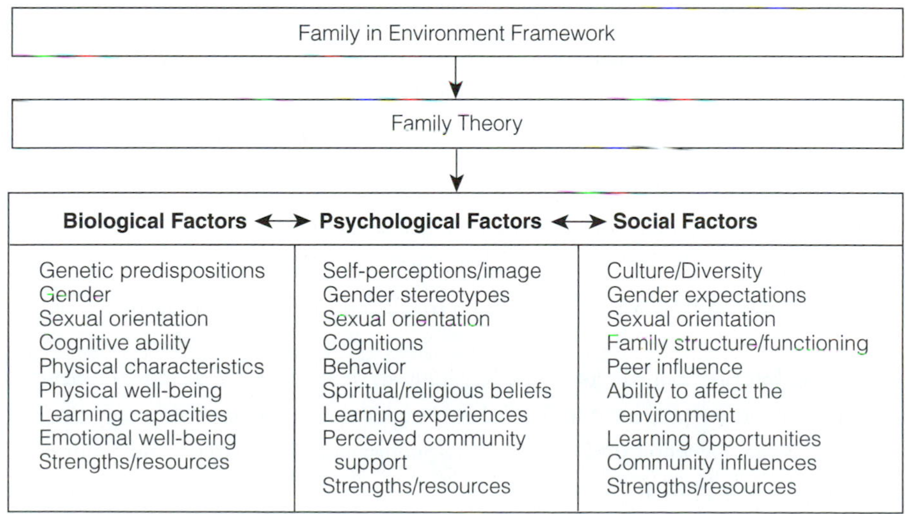

Family in Environment Framework

↓

Family Theory

↓

Biological Factors ⟷	Psychological Factors ⟷	Social Factors
Genetic predispositions Gender Sexual orientation Cognitive ability Physical characteristics Physical well-being Learning capacities Emotional well-being Strengths/resources	Self-perceptions/image Gender stereotypes Sexual orientation Cognitions Behavior Spiritual/religious beliefs Learning experiences Perceived community support Strengths/resources	Culture/Diversity Gender expectations Sexual orientation Family structure/functioning Peer influence Ability to affect the environment Learning opportunities Community influences Strengths/resources

reinforce, or punish specific behaviors. A practitioner using family communication theory might consider how issues such as communication patterns, power, and feedback contribute to the family's difficulties. In other words, the theories that we use guide us as we look at all the factors that can influence family behavior and functioning.

In this checklist, the three column headings are connected by arrows, indicating that factors in one column influence factors in the others. Consider, for example, a child born with a physical disability such as blindness. While the disability may be genetically based and clearly biological in origin, it is affected by how others in society react to the genetic outcome. A family that shelters and otherwise overprotects such a child may be greatly affecting the child's psychological development. If community institutions then limit opportunities for the child because of prejudice, this in turn may affect whether the individual becomes a contributing member of society. Ultimately, the mutual interaction of biological, psychological, and social influences have a great deal to do with how we assess and intervene with troubled families. The checklist is only meant as a guide and is certainly not an exhaustive list of factors that can influence the functioning of a family.

Highlight 4.1 contains a brief assessment plan based on the practitioner's first contact with the family. The assessment notes both strengths and challenges facing the family and suggests areas the practitioner will explore in future meetings with the family. It becomes clear that much more work must be done to accurately determine how best to help this family.

Highlight 4.1 Assessment Plan after First Session

FAMILY ASSESSMENT

Names: Jim (36) and Midge Reynolds (34)
Son Michael (13)
Adopted Daughter Minu (11)

Address: 1322 West Highland, San Diego, California, 23432

Phone Number(s): Family Home Number: (714) 840-9876
Jim's Work Number: (714) 543-6575
Midge's Work Number: (540) 342-3122

Source of Referral: Voluntary referral from friends previously seen at agency.

Identifying Information: Mr. and Mrs. Reynolds arrive on time for the appointment with both children present. Mr. Reynolds introduces himself first, although Mrs. Reynolds is the one who called to make the appointment. Both parents and children are dressed nicely in what appears to be new clothing. Mrs. Reynolds begins the discussion by stating that she is nervous to be here because they have never been to a social worker before. Both children appear uncomfortable in their chairs and are fidgety. Mr. Reynolds is turned sideways in his seat and looks directly at his wife while she speaks. Mrs. Reynolds describes their problem as the "difficulty they are having with Minu." According to Mrs. Reynolds, Minu does not study at school or have friends. She plays by herself at home and hardly has time for any of the family. This behavior started about six months ago. Up until that time, according to Mrs. Reynolds, Minu was very hardworking at school and had a few friends. Mr. Reynolds agrees with his wife's statements and adds that they just do not know what to do with their daughter anymore. Minu turns her back on the family and buries her head during this discussion. When asked about how she feels about being there, Minu has little response, although Michael sighs heavily.

Assessment Information:

Parent(s): Both parents attended college and met right before graduation. They were married at the ages of 20 and 22 respectively. Mr. Reynolds finished college and is a CPA at a small local firm. Mrs. Reynolds did not complete college (saying she had too many other responsibilities). She currently works as a secretary in a law firm. Mr. and Mrs. Reynolds state that they have been happily married for 14 years and have not had any marital problems.

Children: Michael, age 13, is tall for his age and is well-spoken. He appears to engage with his sister from the general gestures and comments he makes when she is spoken to. The parents relate that Michael is a model student and very active in sports. Minu, age 11, was adopted by the Reynolds when she was 2. While Minu is of Korean descent, the Reynolds were allowed to adopt her because of lack of availability of adoptive Korean families. Minu is described as being a model student up until 6 months ago, when she became very withdrawn.

Extended Family: The Reynolds' extended family lives across the country. Both sets of grandparents live in the same city, and the Reynolds report seeing their families at least twice a year. Mrs. Reynolds reports having daily contact with her mother by phone. The parents report that the grandparents are very supportive of the family and children.

Physical Issues: There are no physical issues at this time.

Environmental Issues: The family comes from a middle-income background and reports having no financial problems. They are active in their children's school and in a local church. Both Mr. and Mrs. Reynolds have jobs and report no special problems in the community.

(continued)

Highlight 4.1 Assessment Plan after First Session (*continued*)

Presentation: All members of the Reynolds family present well except for Minu, who appears withdrawn and untalkative. All family members are dressed appropriately and appear articulate, except for Minu. Minu, besides being quiet, has a very sad facial expression and appears fearful in the session. Efforts to engage her are not returned.

Support System: The Reynolds' support system appears strong with attachments to family, friends, and community members.

Strengths: The Reynolds appear very supportive of one another and appear to have a strong sense of family. They have good support systems and many strengths, as shown by their efforts to seek aid for their daughter. Both children have or have had good records at school and positive social relationships. The family's strong desire to support one another is a key strength.

Plan of Action: The initial plan is to meet with the Reynolds family once a week for six weeks. An in-depth assessment will be made of the family and any issues that have arisen specifically in the last six months. Goals for the family intervention will be set with the family, and all efforts to engage each family member in the sessions will be made.

Assessing Family Functioning

CHAPTER 5

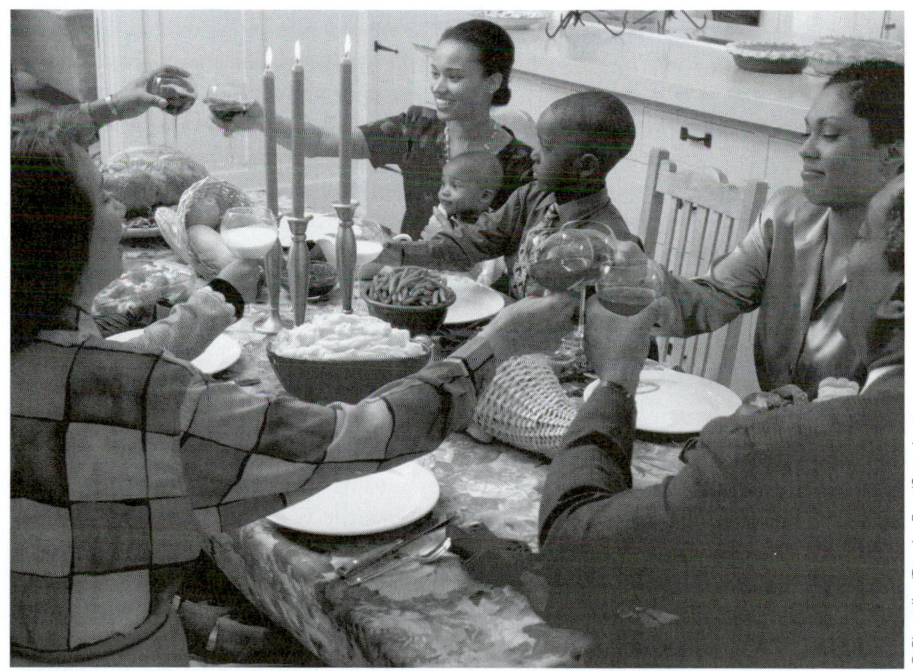

© Photodisc/Royalty-Free/Getty Images

INTRODUCTION

Chapter 4 introduced the structure of assessment and the importance of using a bio-psycho-social focus when working with families. This chapter explores a variety of factors helpful for understanding family strengths and resources. Among the concepts addressed are family roles and rules, communication and interactional patterns, the role of triangles, cutoffs, rituals, family history, and family secrets, among others. The chapter concludes with a discussion of family assessment techniques and tools, including genograms, eco-maps, self-reports, and family histories.

TARGETS FOR FAMILY ASSESSMENT

As we have just noted, families are complex entities that require thorough assessment in order to develop appropriate plans for intervention. In this section we will look at several patterns and processes that deserve attention as part of a comprehensive assessment.

Family Roles

Family roles are important to our understanding of family functioning (Janzen & Harris, 1997). Family roles include the more obvious ones such as parent, partner, spouse, lover, friend, breadwinner, child, and sibling. Each of these roles comes with expectations about specific behaviors that we assume each role player will carry out. At the same time, most people develop into their respective roles over time. Cues to these expected behaviors come from experiences within one's family of origin, modeling by others in one's life, and feedback from family members. One task of the family practitioner is to help members understand the role expectations of the other family members.

THEORY IN ACTION | **Role Expectations**

Nancy expects her partner to sit and watch television with her in the evenings. This is behavior she associates with the role of significant other. On the other hand, Nancy's partner, Sharon, brings work home from the office and expects to spend time on this each evening. Sharon sees the work-at-home behavior as a part of her role as primary wage earner.

Clearly, Nancy and Sharon have a difference of opinion about the behaviors associated with the role of partner and possibly a clash between demands of two different roles. This difference in understanding is perhaps normative, since it is unlikely that each family member is going to behave exactly in line with the expectations of every other family member. Expecting that the other members will behave in a given manner based upon their respective roles is a common source of aggravation for many families.

Family Rules

Family rules are another idea important for understanding families. Every family develops a set of rules that govern their interactions with each other and often with the external environment. Some rules are culturally based, such as the importance of not causing a family member to lose face (be embarrassed) (Fong, 1997). We pass other rules along from one generation to another, never challenging family members' generally accepted beliefs. One example of such a rule is that no one should talk about family issues outside of the family. Of course, some rules we learn from experience. Perhaps the children have learned that they can ignore their mother's calling them to come inside until she finally yells or calls them by their full names.

Sometimes rules are completely unspoken or at least not openly discussed. In other situations, adult family members' reactions to rule violation provide feedback that influences other members. Nichols (1999) notes that regardless of whether rules are spoken or unspoken, they "are tenacious and resistant to change because they are embedded in a powerful but unseen structure" (p. 97). Rules are important because they can govern routine aspects of family life, including discipline, individual responsibilities for daily activities (for example, cleaning the kitchen, doing the laundry, and so on). Rules may also govern whether family members express affection in public and how members address one another.

Family rules are influenced by several variables. These may include the unit's socioeconomic status, its culture and ethnicity, and basic family values. Family rules adopted when a family was more or less affluent may still operate when the financial situation changes. The impact of culture on family rules will be different depending on whether members are recent immigrants or third generation and whether they hold to traditional values and beliefs or are completely acculturated. As might be expected, first-generation immigrants are likely to hold more tightly to traditional family rules than will their children and grandchildren. Within many Asian cultures, respect for authority and harmony governs the behavior of family members. Compare this with the cultural values of many Americans, who are more likely to believe in free expression and "resolving conflict through open debate" (Hitchcock, 1998, p. 7).

Family values, especially those based upon religious or spiritual beliefs, are likely to result in rules. These rules may affect what is eaten or not eaten, child-rearing practices, and relationships with grandparents and other members of the extended family. They may also influence other aspects of family life. For example, members of the Mormon Church identify a specific evening (Monday) to be spent in family pursuits, just as most organized religions identify specific days to be spent in worship or not engaging in work activities.

Family rules are useful because they create a sense of predictability within the family. Each partner knows what to expect from the other, and children can predict what the parents will do. Rules help maintain the family's homeostasis. They become problematic when they interfere with the family's ability to change when confronted with new challenges. They also can limit the ability of family members to attain their individual aspirations and may lock the system into dysfunctional patterns of behavior.

Because these family rules are unwritten, they also can affect the social worker who unknowingly violates them. Rules prohibiting nonfamily members from touching family members of the opposite sex, including shaking hands, or rules related to eye contact can produce negative reactions when violated. Similarly, cultures that rely more on nonverbal communication patterns, including facial expressions, tonal quality, or gestures, are using rules that others are less likely to understand.

Family Rituals

Rituals are repetitive and often a stylized form of family productivity (Berg-Cross, 1988). They may include activities such as eating Sunday dinner together, washing the car on Saturday, and visiting Grandma on Thanksgiving. Rituals can encompass brief events such as attending church on Sunday morning or involve activities that consume several days. For example, one extended family always spends a week together canoeing and camping every summer. They will allow no other activity to interfere with this ritual. In another family, the mother must always visit her grown sons on their birthdays. Still another family drives for six hours to spend Thanksgiving with the husband's sister although they do not really get along well. While the women prepare the meals, the men watch the football game, and the children bicker at one another. After supper, everyone heads back home, regretting the trip. Although they repeat this pattern every Thanksgiving with similar outcomes, the family continues to make the six-hour trek.

Like rules, family rituals serve several purposes. First, they help to organize a family's day-to-day existence and produce a degree of regularity and continuity in its life. Like much else in life, we can view rituals on a continuum. Some families maintain no rituals, operating in a semi-chaotic fashion, while others have found past rituals so unpleasant and constraining that they engage in very few (Imber-Black & Roberts, 2000). At the other extreme are families whose rituals are rigid and highly resistant to change. Somewhere in the middle are families whose rituals are reassuring to family members because they ensure stability and consistency and provide guidance on what to expect in the future. Rituals also provide a sense of belonging because one must be a member of the family to take part in the ritual. Rituals are often the basis for memories about specific life events and are often used when we ask members to describe their families of origin (Berg-Cross, 1988). Rituals give children an anchor they can depend upon, whether bedtime stories or weekend picnics.

Sometimes, rituals can be elaborate, complicated events with carefully scripted communication. Or they may be simple day-to-day activities such as eating dinner at a particular time. We celebrate some only with family members, and we carry others out as part of community events, such as the 4th of July. In some cultures, rituals serve to demarcate status changes such as *rites de passage* from childhood to adulthood. In these cases and others, actual participation in the ritual produces a significant change in one's life.

Later in life, adolescents may reject rituals if they experience them as stifling or old-fashioned. Yet, each new couple tends to either repeat rituals from their youth, create their own rituals, or derive some combination of the two. As Berg-Cross (1988) says, rituals serve as the scripts for many parts of the family drama. Most frequently, women organize and maintain rituals in the family, especially mothers. This is likely a carryover from past generations, when a mother was more likely to stay at home. Today, being in charge of family rituals can be a major burden when coupled with full-time employment outside the home.

Despite the commonplace nature of rituals, many events today have no rituals associated with them. For example, gay and lesbian couples have no formal ritual similar to the exchange of marital vows. Often there is no ceremony, no wedding gifts, and none of the other traditional outpouring of support that typically coincide with marriage (Bryant & Demian, 1994). Physical changes, such as menopause or recovery from surgery, have no rituals associated with them. Neither divorce nor the end of a nonmarital relationship has any connected rituals, thereby making it harder to adjust to the change (Imber-Black & Roberts, 2000). The absence of rituals can be problematic for families and, as will be discussed in a later chapter, new rituals are being used to help families cope with various life issues.

Communication in Families

Communication in families is a major source of problems experienced by partners of all ages. Effective communication requires several qualities from family members. These include listening skills, empathy, warmth, genuineness, and a commitment to empowering the other party.

Listening and Communicating Listening and communicating clearly are essential to family systems, for without these abilities there is no way to know how various members experience family life. This communication process can take many forms. These may include requests for more time or attention, demands for changes in behavior, praise for specific actions, and criticisms for perceived problems that are threatening the family's homeostasis. Sometimes, communication is given indirectly and ineffectively. Consider a partner who withdraws from a relationship with her mate and gradually reduces the time spent with the partner. While this behavior is a form of feedback, it conveys only indirectly the pain and unhappiness she is experiencing. One goal of helping families is to teach family members how to communicate in ways that are likely to be more effective.

Empathy Jordan (1984) has described empathy as "a cognitive and emotional activity in which one person is able to experience the feelings and thoughts of another person and simultaneously is able to know his/her own different feelings and thoughts" (p. 2). Frequently considered a *sine qua non* of good counseling, empathy is also a critical ingredient in a healthy family. To state it another way, empathy is the capacity to put oneself in the shoes of another and to understand how that person experiences an event. "The act of empathy is a powerful tool. If you can feel for someone else, take their feelings into your body and your understanding, it means you can feel for and accept yourself" (Penn, 1998, p. 309).

Empathy in a family is essential to effective communication because it reduces the likelihood that conflicts will get out of hand. Family members who feel understood by parents and siblings are less likely to strike out at others or pursue their own emotional needs at the expense of others. Ferreira (1963) identified three ways in which empathy was important to healthy families: "(1) that family members guess each other with precision better than chance, (2) that children are better guessers than adults, (3) that members of a normal family are better guessers than members of pathologic families" (p. 237). Being understood is an essential condition for an optimum family environment, and empathy is one way of communicating this understanding.

Other researchers go further in their concern about the importance of empathy. According to Dell (1989), "to the degree that parents do manifest significant deficits in empathy toward their children, then, precisely to that same degree will their children be prone to controlling behavior, rage, and violence" (p. 5).

Several family practitioners, and especially Ackerman (1966), have highlighted the importance of mobilizing a family's empathy to cause change. One purpose of techniques such as having family members play each other's roles is helping them develop a degree of empathy for the person they are emulating. By facing the other member's concerns and problems, the individual playing the role is better able to understand what it must be like to be the other person. When this role playing is successful, family members may view the identified patient as a person suffering within the family context and not necessarily as the primary troublemaker. Chasin, Roth, and Bograd (1989) note that when "each partner is charged with listening very carefully to the other and with experiencing the wishes of the other from both the positions of the self and of the other; empathy often begins to replace blame. Each partner is powerfully affected by being gratifying to and gratified by the partner in each one's dreams for the future. When they experience gratification in these roles, they become hopeful. If they experience extreme displeasure in these roles, they arrive perhaps painfully at the possibility that they may have truly irreconcilable goals for the relationship" (p. 128). Gottman (1994) calls this activity "validation" and characterizes it by such actions as showing awareness of how the other person feels, accepting responsibility for one's own mistakes, and apologizing when one is wrong. Each of these actions can empower the partner and increase the satisfaction with the relationship.

Practitioners and researchers have developed a variety of tools that help assess a family's capacity for empathy toward one another. We will discuss these later in this chapter. We should note that differences in empathy are also found cross-culturally. Roland (1988) contrasts the familial self of Indians and Japanese with the individual self of Americans. The *familial self* is the basic inner psychological organization of the Indian and Japanese that involves intensely emotionally intimate relationships, high levels of empathy and receptivity to others, and strong identification with the family's reputation and honor. This characteristic enables them to function well within the hierarchical intimate relationships of the extended family and community.

The *individual self,* on the other hand, involves a self-contained ego boundary and sharp differentiation between inner images of self and others. Such a difference enables Americans to function in a highly mobile society that grants considerable autonomy to the individual.

Warmth Families communicate warmth when members treat other members in ways that help them feel understood, accepted, and safe. Children depend upon parents for safety, acceptance, and understanding. Partners require the same from each other. A communicated message of safety allows for other positive human characteristics to develop, including openness, honesty, and a willingness to take chances. Open expression of feelings requires a sense that other family members will not judge one negatively. This allows both children and adults to make their own choices and decisions without fearing rejection from the very people with whom they are closest. The need for pretense is lessened when family members know that it is okay to feel blue, excited, angry, or to express one's emotional reactions, whatever they may be. Feeling unsafe, on the other hand, curtails one's ability to share feelings and experiences, and to attempt new challenges. This is true for both children and adults.

The absence of warmth in a family has been associated with several potential problems. Some research has identified a parent's emotional withdrawal and failure to provide expected parental warmth as a factor in the development of various psychological disorders, such as borderline personality disorder (Marziali, 1995) and adolescent suicide (Hepworth, Farley, & Griffiths, 1995). Researchers have found similar links between a child's school performance, interactions with others, and social competence (Mrazek & Haggerty, 1994). As is evident, parental warmth is an important factor in ensuring the healthy development of the child.

Genuineness Honesty and a lack of pretense or artifice characterize *genuineness,* sometimes called authenticity. Parents displaying genuineness can share their own feelings and reactions with their children and spouses honestly. They are nondefensive and candid in their actions and discussions with family members, admitting errors and generally modeling behavior that is helpful in furthering intrafamily communications. Johnson (1992) calls this honesty "owning your own shadow" and argues that only when partners take ownership of their own feelings will a relationship improve. The ability to accept ownership of one's feelings is fostered by the other person's efforts to demonstrate empathy.

Guarded communications, defensiveness, and an unwillingness to self-disclose characterize families without genuineness (Kadushin, 1990). In addition, such families also engage in behaviors that reflect distancing and emotional withdrawal from relationships. This is particularly problematic in families with children and adolescents who can recognize artifice and a lack of genuineness. This recognition can lead to acting out and other nonfunctional behaviors. Moreover, developing a sense of closeness and effective communication patterns when one member is incapable of honesty is difficult for other adults in the family.

As might be obvious, the characteristics of empathy, warmth, and genuineness within a family are related and mutually intertwined. For example, a lack of openness impairs honesty, and neither children nor adults are likely to confide in a family member perceived as cold and judgmental. Not surprisingly, the characteristics that help make a good professional counselor are also significant factors in healthy family functioning.

THEORY IN ACTION | Empathy, Warmth, and Genuineness within a Family

The Parsons family meets with the school social worker following the truancy of their daughter. It becomes clear to the social worker during the session that family members have enormous difficulty talking to one another. The social worker attempts to help the family with this during the session.

MRS. PARSONS: We do everything for you, Emma and it's like you just don't care.

EMMA: I care, but you wouldn't know anything about caring yourself.

MRS. PARSONS: You ungrateful girl! I should just let the police arrest you for truancy and take you to jail.

EMMA: You would like that, wouldn't you?

SCHOOL SOCIAL WORKER: I think there are a lot of feelings being expressed in this room right now and I am not sure we are all aware of them. Let's try understanding one another more. Mrs. Parsons, Emma, I would like to ask you to turn and talk directly to one another. Let's begin by you, Mrs. Parsons, telling Emma what you felt today when you discovered she had skipped school.

MRS. PARSONS: I was angry and scared because I didn't know where she was.

SCHOOL SOCIAL WORKER: I heard your mother express that she was scared. What do you think about that, Emma?

EMMA: I didn't know you got scared, Mom. I'm always all right.

MRS. PARSONS: I don't always know that and I worry that you may be hurt. That is what makes me the most upset.

EMMA: I don't want you to worry. I want you to listen to what I tell you are my problems.

Other Dimensions of Communication Within every family, parents have the capacity to communicate many messages to children and their partners. Ideally, parents will communicate in ways that increase the interpersonal capacities of children and other adults. We can see this in the communication patterns of many African American families. These families teach their children to "imitate and function in the dominant culture without believing that its demeaning images of African Americans are true. Another role of the family is to pass along different kinds of successful coping strategies against racism" (Greene, 2000, p. 27).

This effort at empowerment also occurs when parents encourage children to make decisions by themselves. For example, giving a child the choice between wearing red pants or blue pants helps accomplish three things. First, it conveys to the child the parent's belief in his efficacy to make decisions. This is an empowering message, especially coupled with praise for sound decisions.

Second, it helps prepare the child to make other decisions throughout life, many of which will be much more complex and difficult. This too is a very positive process and helps develop in the child strengths that will be important later. From this, children learn that they have within themselves the power to cope with other challenges. Finally, it ensures that when children show up at school, they will not be confused with circus clowns and ridiculed accordingly.

We can also see empowerment in the behavior of couples. One example is allowing and encouraging one's partner to take time for individual (noncouple) pursuits. A second example is encouraging partners to maintain ties with friendships engendered prior to the onset of the couple's relationship. Such opportunities to recharge one's emotional batteries are healthy actions that empower the relationship. A third example is when partners express their feelings accurately to one another without resorting to emotional gasoline.

THEORY IN ACTION | Empowering a Relationship

Consider two couples who have recently been too busy to take any time to spend together. A partner in one couple says, "I would like to spend the evening with you tonight." This message is clearly and simply communicated and encourages a healthy response. Contrast this with a partner in the other couple who states, "We never do anything together any more." The second statement, while essentially but indirectly conveying a similar wish, invites an emotional response likely to drown out the other partner's cry for help.

When partners begin to understand their own needs, learn what triggers their feelings, and think carefully about how and what they are saying, they can empower their significant others to respond in healthier ways (Thomson, 2000). Equally important, they help reduce the fight or flight response that frequently arises in relationships and prevents either partner from hearing or responding to the other.

Other ways that empowerment occurs between partners include efforts to validate one's partner's ideas even while disagreeing with them. Partners who do this send a message that validates the other person even when they do not see eye to eye. Empowerment is a powerful tool for both partners and parents.

As should be clear, empathy, warmth, genuineness, and empowerment are mutually reinforcing characteristics of a healthy family. Each helps the communication process in a relationship and strengthens the ability to weather the typical stresses inherent in any close dyad. Each also contributes to the well-being of other family members, particularly children. Parents are role models that influence children even when they are adults.

Common Family Difficulties: Triangles, Secrets, and Cutoffs

Working with families requires an awareness of common difficulties they may encounter. Often, difficulties arise from family members' unsuccessful attempts at solving problems or dealing with crises. Trying to improve either their own emotional or physical health or that of the family unit, they adopt coping mechanisms that often worsen the situation. Three of the most common ways families handle stressful events or situations include triangles, secrets, and cutoffs.

Triangles As noted in Chapter 4, *triangles* are alliances or coalitions among three members of a family that are most noticeable in times of stress. Atwood (1992) defines them as "A situation in which two people unable to relate to each other use a third person, usually a child, to reestablish contact and restore some kind of homeostatic balance" (p. 26). Conflicts or disagreements that might be amenable to easy resolution if they occurred in a dyad become much more intractable when a third person is added. Ironically, the third person's involvement usually follows a period in which a family dyad becomes conflictual or difficult. Rather than deal with the conflict within the dyad, one person elects to involve a third person to divert attention away from the basic issue. Bowen's theory of triangles argues that the person feeling most anxious will be the one to triangle in another individual. The new person's involvement allows a detour around the conflict but also prevents the original dyad from working out their difficulties (Nichols & Schwartz, 2001).

While triangles are often troublesome for the family, they are also quite typical. The most obvious and significant triangle is the mother-father-child alliance that occurs as soon as a child is born. This triangle becomes problematic when parents, unable or unwilling to resolve their differences, involve the child. This can happen when both parents focus their attention on the child to avoid dealing with their own issues, or attempt to get the child on their side of the dispute. Immature parents may be more tempted to use this method at the cost of learning how to resolve conflicts (Atwood, 1992). At the same time, children caught in this arrangement are inhibited from achieving the differentiation of self that is expected in the developmental process. Triangles become damaging when they prevent a child from successful completion of this developmental task or stage. A child may not develop a sense of autonomy when caught up in parental issues and problems. This can have serious consequences for later relationships. Parent-child triangles are especially difficult because the problematic relationships and issues are often played out in subsequent triangles, thus perpetuating the dysfunction from one generation to the next (Carter & McGoldrick, 1999). As is probably obvious, this avoidance technique is harmful both to the dyad and to the person drawn into the triangle.

THEORY IN ACTION | Dysfunctional Triad

Mr. and Mrs. Charles had been fighting over his drinking for several years. Following the arrival of their first child, Mrs. Charles placed their daughter in bed with them to sleep. Now at the age of 10, their daughter still climbs into bed with her mother to sleep before her father has come to bed. Mr. Charles's drinking has continued and has become worse since the birth of their daughter, with him staying out late to drink and falling asleep on the couch.

We should note that these triangular relationships are more dysfunctional in traditional middle-class families because they think the parental dyad is central to the health and happiness of the family (Berg-Cross, 1988). In traditional families, we would expect that a boundary separates one system or subsystem from another. Thus, we would expect that the adult partners in the family would have a boundary that separates them from children in the family. In other cultures, this is less of an issue because the spousal dyad is less valued than say the father/son (Chinese), brother/brother (some African), or mother/son (Hindu).

We consider three triangles to be particularly dysfunctional (Minuchin, Rosman, & Baker, 1978). The first is the *detouring triangle* that occurs when parents detour from their own marital difficulties by focusing on the child. This can reinforce the child's problem behavior when one parent engages in an emotional battle with the child while the other either ignores the behavior or sides with the child. Detouring can also take the form of both parents focusing on a specific aspect of the child's life, such as sexuality, rather than dealing with their own sexual issues. The primary function of detouring triangles is to allow the parents to avoid dealing with a painful or unpleasant aspect of their own relationship. Unfortunately, the continued parental focus on a child can be so strong that it provokes physical and emotional responses as the child seemingly absorbs the parental stress.

Another dysfunctional triangle occurs when *parent/child coalitions* form. These rigid alliances can replace the parental dyad as the center of the family. They may come about as a parent attempts to pull one child to his or her side of the argument or when a child sides with one parent to forestall conflict between the parents. Sometimes such child-initiated alliances work because they do allow the parents to quit arguing. Ultimately, however, they prevent the parents from working out their difficulties. Research has shown that families experiencing major distress in their lives were likely to have weak marital dyads coupled with stronger parent-child dyads (Gilbert, Christensen, & Margolin, 1984). The authors also noted that the more troubled the parental dyad, the more likely the mother was to vent her disappointments and upset on the child. To the family's detriment, situations requiring collaborative problem solving were most likely to cause dysfunctional alliances.

In unhealthy families, there may be boundaries that separate a parent-child dyad from other family members. Figure 5.1 shows a boundary that includes a mother, Mary, and her daughter, Maria. This boundary appears to exclude the husband and father, Tony, potentially suggesting a very strong relationship between mother and daughter and a weak relationship between husband and wife. While boundaries separating partners from children are the norm, families who are experiencing difficulties are more likely to have unusual boundaries.

The third common triangle involves *split loyalties* in which each parent is pulling on the child to join him or her in an exclusive dyad relationship. This may occur around separation or divorce of the parents, but such drastic events are not always necessary. The impending disintegration of the family, foreshadowed by these parental behaviors, can contribute to acting-out behavior by the children. However, even if the child's behavior brings the parents temporarily together, the result is usually the same—a dysfunctional parental dyad. Interestingly, the composition of dyads within the triangle may change over time. Both the age of the children and the nature of parental issues may result in different alliances at various points in the family life cycle.

While we tend to think that some dyads, such as mother-father, father-son, and mother-daughter, are normative and healthy, this view is culturally bound. For example, in matrilineal societies no one expects fathers to have close ties with their sons. In traditional Cheyenne families, they expect mother-daughter relationships to be "tense or even hostile," with daughters forming much closer attachments to their father's brothers (Coontz, 2000, p. 17). In addition, feminist theory suggests that the notion of triangles carries a negative connotation with the woman being held responsible for the problem. Feminist authors suggest that efforts to stop triangulation should not occur in ways that reduce women's self-esteem (Zucal, 1992).

Family Secrets Family secrets are so ubiquitous that it is unlikely any family exists without some secrets. Family members know the secrets but do not

Figure 5.1 | Boundary Separating Family Subsets

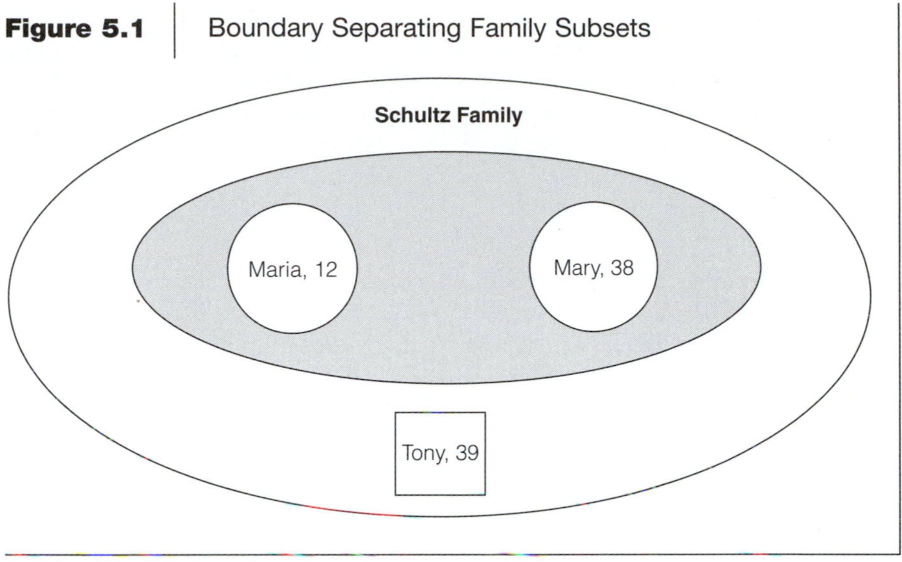

share them with outsiders. Occasionally, only a part of the family knows the secret, such as the parental dyad. Family members closely guard instances of alcoholism, criminal or deviant behavior, emotional problems, and other negatives because they reflect poorly on the family. Imber-Black (1999) identifies four ways that family secrets affect family members:

- They can divide family members, permanently estranging them.
- They can discourage individuals from sharing information with anyone outside the family, inhibiting formation of external intimate relationships.
- They can freeze development at crucial points in life, preventing the growth of self and identity.
- They can lead to painful miscommunication within a family, causing unnecessary guilt and doubt.

Despite their disadvantages, family secrets can serve multiple functions and may be *supportive, protective, manipulative* or *avoidant* in nature (Berg-Cross, 1988). Often, *supportive secrets* do nothing more than maintain the family image to outsiders and may well be harmless in their impact. The family may never share the fact that their daughter had an abortion or reveal that one parent is engaging in illegal gambling. Similarly, one sibling will never tell the parents what really happened at the slumber party when they were out of the country. In addition, sexual proclivities and behaviors of one or both parents will not be shared with the other family members for obvious reasons. In each case, the intent of the secret is to support the individuals involved and the family as a whole, both to internal and to external audiences.

Protective secrets are similar to supportive secrets in that there is an intent to shelter a family member from embarrassment or difficulty. The fact that the family has adopted a child is typical of such secrets, as is a past suicide of a family member. While well-intentioned, protective secrets can evolve into major problems when other family members discover the truth. At the same time, parents often keep protective secrets that enhance the marital dyad. Examples include not sharing with children information about financial status, problems at work, or a partner's previous extramarital affair. Occasionally, children maintain protective secrets such as pretending they do not know what the parents do when they go to bed early on Thursday night.

Manipulative secrets are designed to gain an advantage for the person holding the secret. Watching television soap operas, one would get the idea that all families have multiple manipulative secrets. One parent may never share her true feelings about her sister-in-law nor discuss why she always avoids spending time with certain of her husband's friends. Keeping these secrets avoids family squabbles and stress in the marital dyad. A brother may not share with parents the knowledge that his sister is sexually active because he was the one who introduced her to her first partner. A family member who maintains a secret to blackmail or otherwise coerce another family member is engaging in manipulative behavior. As is evident, some manipulative secrets are relatively harmless, while others can have a devastating impact on the interior life of the family.

Avoidant secrets are those the family maintains rather than dealing with serious familial issues.

THEORY IN ACTION | **Avoidant Secret**

Ruth was a college student with a long pattern of inflicting cuts on her arms whenever she was under stress. Rather than seek help for their daughter, the family decided simply to ignore the behavior that they neither understood nor supported. Unfortunately, by refusing to deal with the problem, Ruth's parents effectively furthered the behavior. Only when the issue came up in an internship did Ruth and her parents have to deal directly with their secret.

A very formidable avoidant secret is that involving sexual or physical abuse. In sexual abuse, the perpetrator and the victim know the secret, but neither is willing to share it with anyone else but for different reasons. The consequences for the perpetrator include both familial disruption and societal condemnation. Embarrassment, fear of punishment, and rejection by others are risks faced by the child. Even if other family members know or suspect the secret, they may avoid exposing it for many of the same reasons.

Secrets are not necessarily bad. Those shared between parental dyads or between siblings may foster closeness and affection. Others prevent children from experiencing feelings for which they are not prepared. Secrets can strengthen the family or undermine it, depending upon the nature and purpose of the secret. Too many secrets can be a burden that causes stress to those who must hide the truth. At the same time, a secret exposed can have unpleasant results. Discovering a secret involving one or both parents can be quite stressful for children, and some parents would rather not know what their adolescent children are doing. One parent, in a long conversation with his adult son, learned of the young man's adolescent drug-taking behavior. Had the son shared this information 10 years earlier, it would have provoked a major family confrontation. Now, a decade later, the father felt safe enough to confess his own adolescent delinquencies, behaviors that he kept from his son during the latter's formative years. Over time, some families maintain secrets by creating myths that paint an idealized portrait of the family's early life. A father who ignored his family while pursuing a career may come to be seen as the heroic figure who helped the family make its fortune. The mother, a would-be singer, is portrayed as someone who gave up her career to raise her children. The fact that no one outside the family ever appreciated her singing is conveniently ignored in the retelling of the myth.

Secrets sometimes lead to inappropriate behavior within a family. For example, a parent suspecting a child is using drugs may invade the child's privacy by searching her room. Another parent, suspecting his wife is having an affair, rifles through her purse searching for evidence (Imber-Black, 1999). In each case, a family tradition of secrets has first set the stage for suspicion and then provoked behavior that otherwise would not have occurred. In addition, some children who are told a family secret may feel the knowledge impairs their ability to be honest and authentic with their other siblings. Family secrets can weigh heavily on family members well after they have grown up and moved away (Imber-Black, 1999). For example, a child may be told of a family secret at a point in her life when she is particularly vulnerable, such as just prior to her wedding or just before moving away from home. In one situation, a mother on her deathbed told her 65-year-old son that he had half-brothers from his father's subsequent marriage. Revealing this secret started the son on a cross-country search for the siblings he had never known. Revealing family secrets in conjunction with a developmental milestone can create problems for the recipient in later years. While there may be no perfect time to reveal family secrets, it seems most appropriate to avoid developmental milestones because of the potential consequences for the person entrusted with the secret.

Cutoffs *Cutoffs* are behaviors by individuals that isolate them from other members of their family of origin. Usually, cutoffs attempt to "develop a happier, more productive life in one's own nuclear family" (Berg-Cross, 1988, p. 83). As such, they represent a defense that allows individuals to put prior family problems, unresolved feelings, and turmoil behind them. Cutoffs create new boundaries in the family that may be either physical or emotional. However, both essentially stop or severely restrict communication between the individual and other family members. While it is tempting to see cutoffs as a problem affecting various family members, they can also be viewed as a strength. For example, individuals often employ cutoffs as a tool to achieve growth and to ensure that relationships that marred the family of origin do not intrude on the new nuclear family. Typically, cutoffs are used in families characterized by either high levels of anxiety or excessive emotional dependence. By cutting oneself off from certain family members, the individual avoids game playing and getting re-involved (Berg-Cross, 1988). Unfortunately, families may pass cutoffs from one generation to another as family connections evolve into a we–they dichotomy. Cutoffs also occur because of parental reactions to such things as one's choice of a spouse. For example, in some interracial couples cutoffs are employed to avoid racially motivated disapproval from one or both sets of parents (O'Neal, Brown, & Abadie, 1997).

Cutting oneself off from family members is both emotionally and practically difficult. Family rituals, such as holidays spent together, make it difficult to follow through on decisions not to stay connected with other family members. In addition, there are often family pressures that seek to prevent cutoffs.

THEORY IN ACTION | Cutoffs

Ben and his brother Gerald really never got along while they were growing up. More than 10 years apart, they often had little in common as far as interests went, and their interactions increasingly became strained. While Ben decided that he needed to distance himself from his brother, carrying out the plan was very difficult. Their mother often tried to plan family outings and reunions in an attempt to hold the family together. When the two brothers (now grown) managed to re-enact their long-festering antagonism toward each other, the mother would cry and use guilt to force them to interact. When the mother died, most contact between Ben and Gerald ended. Even family rituals involving marriage, sickness, or death failed to reunite the brothers.

Generally speaking, younger family members are those most likely to employ cutoffs. Most parents find it nearly impossible to cut off their children, though the opposite is not true. Other interpersonal resources available to the individual also affect cutoffs. For example, cutting off your only living parent is harder because there is no one to replace this person in your life. However, the presence of a second parent can make the cutoff more comfortable. Cutoffs are not limited to one point in life and can occur at almost any time. Teenagers who run away from home are often acting to enforce an emotional cutoff that has already occurred. Those who divorce are often just adding physical distance to the emotional distance that has existed for some time. Of course, divorce also means a detachment from other people besides the ex-spouse. This includes in-laws and mutual friends. Divorce often results in a loss of connection of more than 40 percent of the network of friends and family that existed before this event (Rands, 1986). These losses are likely to include one's former in-laws, married friends, and anyone whose primary allegiance is to the other partner. The problem is compounded when the divorce involves older couples (Goodman, 1992). This is one reason why the risk of mental health problems associated with divorces in later life exceeds that of younger divorced people (Chiriboga, 1982; Wallerstein, 1986).

Repairing a cutoff is a difficult task. The longer the disconnection has lasted, the more difficult it is to restore the relationship. Reconstruction requires a time commitment by both parties and a determination not to repeat past interactional patterns. On the other hand, not all cutoffs should be repaired. Those arising from sexual or physical abuse often continue because the survivor must maintain a focus on the future, not the past. The emotional damage caused by the parental behavior makes it necessary for the child to end interactions with the offender. Cutoffs may also be a sign of strength when the goal is to avoid contact with those who systematically sabotage the other person (see Highlight 5.1).

The dilemma of cutoffs is that they are only partially successful. While they do provide distance between the two parties, the emotional needs for closeness and relationships often remain strong. Consequently, these needs may find their way into other relationships, such as with a spouse or children, with even greater intensity (Carter & McGoldrick, 1999). This may then lead to additional cutoffs or distancing in these relationships.

ASSESSMENT TECHNIQUES AND TOOLS

Over the past several decades, a variety of family assessment tools and techniques have been developed. These methods are helpful in many different ways and gather information useful for understanding the family. Corcoran (2002) and others provide some excellent reasons for employing family assessment measures. These include the following:

Highlight 5.1 Cutoff as a Sign of Strength

Sylvia was the oldest and most attractive of two sisters from a family wracked by divorce, drug abuse, and continual turmoil. Sylvia made a practice of trying to steal her younger sister's (Gladys) male friends and had been quite successful for several years. The precipitating event occurred when Gladys discovered that Sylvia was engaged in an affair with Gladys's fiancé. From that point on, Gladys refused all contact with her sister because she felt she could no longer trust her.

1. Providing information about items that cannot be easily observed, such as feelings and attitudes
2. Helping the practitioner identify particular areas needing attention
3. Helping monitor a family's progress
4. Motivating clients by showing the progress they have made
5. Demonstrating effectiveness of specific interventions
6. Providing concrete evidence for third-party payers and others

This section identifies seven different types of instruments and techniques that a family practitioner can use in assessment. These include genograms, ecomaps, self-reports, observation, family histories, and the social network map and grid.

Genograms

Genograms show connections between generations within a family (Hartman, 1978). They are pictorial representations of the family over time and include such important events as births, deaths, marriage, divorce, and remarriage. The genogram is a collaborative effort by the practitioner and family and uses common rules for depicting different aspects of the family life. For instance, we use boxes to show male family members while using circles for women. We illustrate marriages as a straight horizontal line between the two partners while an additional line that bisects the marital line shows divorce. We also list dates of most events on the genogram. When a death occurs, we show this with both a date and an "X" through the box or circle representing the person who has died. Dotted lines indicate family members who are living together. Dashed lines show adoption. At the same time, there are no limitations on symbols a practitioner or family might select. Figure 5.2 shows a simple three-generation genogram. Although we cannot capture all information on a genogram, a great deal of information can be presented. For example, it can be determined from this genogram that both of the great-grandparents are still living. However, the absence of a dotted line between them shows they are not living together. Willie, his wife Matty, and her brother Martin live together, while Matty's sister Sarah is deceased. The dashed line linking Aracella with her parents shows that she is an adopted child as was her mother, Matty. Unlike her own parents, Matty has only the one adopted child. As can be seen on the genogram, a horizontal line shows a marital or other permanent relationship. Thus, Matty's daughter, Aracella, has a partner, Tricia, a fact recognized by the line connecting them. Keep in mind that a genogram will reflect both sides of the family, while this example shows just one.

Genograms can provide information on family patterns existing across two or more generations, such as early marriages, frequent divorces, or premature deaths of family members. At the same time, working with family members to create a genogram has other advantages. First, it helps family members be involved in their own change effort. It can also be educational as family members discover patterns or simply missing pieces of the puzzle. The genogram is a helpful assessment tool for the family practitioner.

Figure 5.2 Family Genogram

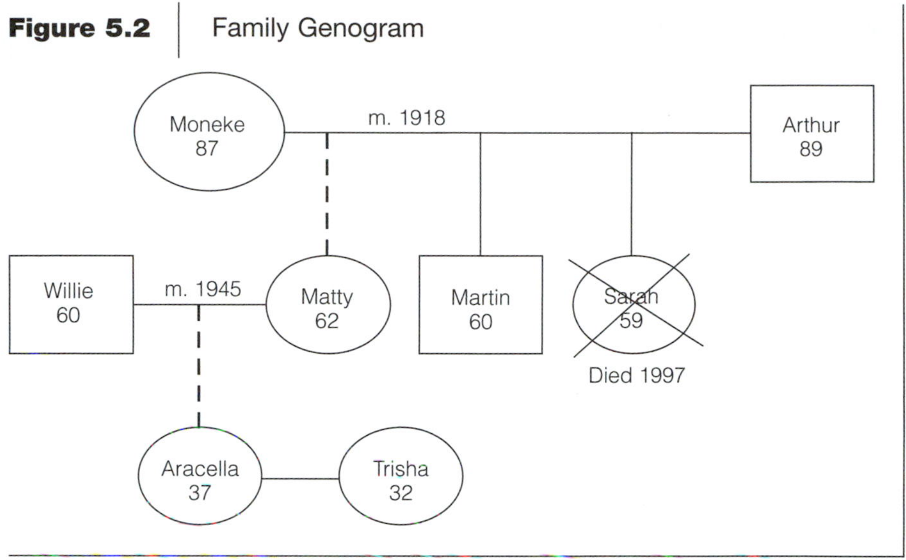

Ecomaps

Another assessment tool highlighted by Hartman (1978) is the *ecomap*. While the genogram shows the family from a genealogical perspective, the ecomap depicts a family's ecological system, which includes such things as relationships with other systems: families, churches, schools, social organizations, and social welfare agencies. Ecomaps also can display the absence of ties to other systems, identify stressful relationships, and show family strengths and resources. Ecomaps can be exceedingly complex or relatively simple, depending upon the number and type of relationships that family members have with the larger environment. Figure 5.3 shows a typical ecomap.

Like genograms, ecomaps use some common symbols. Different types of lines show the strength and quality of relationships, for example, solid lines for strong, dotted lines for weak, and zigzag lines for stressful or problematic relationships. Arrows on the lines show the direction in which resources flow. By *resources,* we mean such things as love, companionship, money, positive feelings, and so on. Thus, both Garth and Jillian have strong relationships with their work, and both find work a very positive part of their lives. They also have strong positive relationships with each other. Garth, however, has several troubled relationships. He has cutoffs from both his brother and his ex-wife and a strained relationship with his sister-in-law. As indicated by the connections between sports and family members, this is an important aspect of the lives of both Garth and his stepson, Jon. Jillian finds her church an important resource. Jillian is supporting her mother, who resides in a nursing home; hence, the direction of the flow of resources. This ecomap may seem complex, but a careful review of each relationship paints an interesting picture of how family members relate to one another and to the external environment.

Figure 5.3 | Ecomap

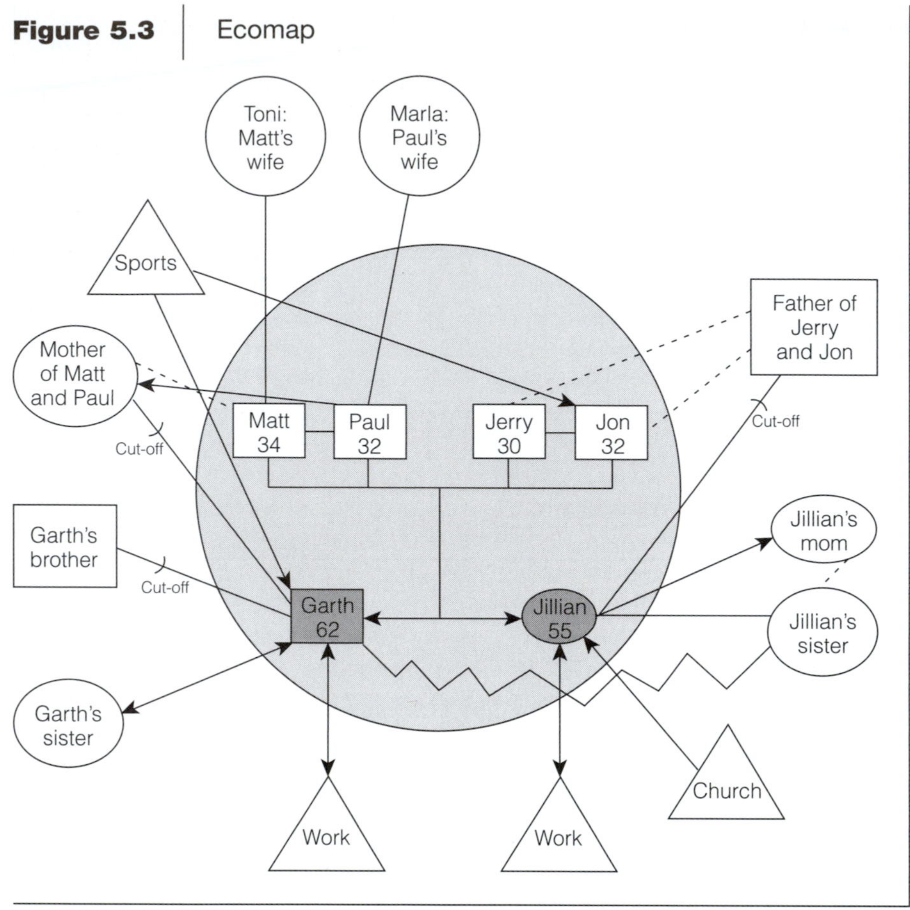

Self-Reports

By definition, self-reports refer to information provided by family members. They may range from informal reports of weekly activities to more detailed accountings of specific behaviors. They may also include some types of standardized questionnaires, such as those asking family members to rate their level of satisfaction with aspects of the family life. We can use some instruments, such as the Myers-Briggs Type Indicator, to help family members understand their own and other members' preferred ways of operating. This instrument reflects, for example, the preferences that people bring to making sense of their world. Some people approach situations from a logical perspective and make decisions only after careful thought. The Myers-Briggs calls this a *thinking* approach. Others are much more likely to make decisions from a feeling perspective, using all of their senses. Logic is less important in the decision-making processes of those who rely on *feeling*. At the same time, people also perceive events differently. Those who rely on *sensing* can be differentiated from those who use *intuition* to understand new experiences. Finally, the Myers-Briggs helps identify those who approach the world from two different directions. *Judging* people tend to make quicker decisions, while *perceiving* individuals often analyze situations before making any firm decisions. The Myers-Briggs is one of the most commonly used instruments among family practitioners (Boughner et al., 1994).

Other instruments are available that allow family members to provide information useful to the practitioner. These include The Dyadic Adjustment Scale (Spanier, 1999), which can help determine marital adjustment, and the Revised Conflict Tactics Scales (Straus et al., 1996), which assesses various dimensions of family violence. Likewise, the Child Behavior Checklist (CBCL) (Achenbach, 1991) can help provide data on the recent functioning of a child, while the Trauma Symptom Checklist for Children (Briere, 1996) is useful for children ages 8 through 15 who may have experienced child abuse.

Faiver et al. (2001) provide a list of inventories that are helpful in assessing the role of spirituality in clients' lives. Like one's way of making decisions and experiencing the world, the individual's spiritual life can be an important factor in a variety of situations. People with strong religious and spiritual aspects of their lives are likely to turn to this resource in tough times. How well some family members weather unexpected life disasters and disappointments can vary with the strength of their spiritual/religious resources. At the same time, major differences between partners around the issue of spirituality or religious beliefs/practices can be a painful source of conflict.

Corcoran (2002) provides some useful guidelines for using self-report instruments. These include attention to where the measure will be completed, whether the practitioner needs to be present, how the measure's purpose will be explained, what should be done when one or more family members have difficulty completing the instrument, and what the practitioner looks for when reviewing the completed self-report.

Observation

The practitioner's observation of a family can be a solid source of information and can augment self-reports provided by family members. Observation begins as soon as the family begins to address the reasons for seeking help. Brock and Barnard (1999) provide a helpful series of perspectives in this regard (see Highlight 5.2).

Similarly, home visits may allow the practitioner to observe aspects of the family that may otherwise not be visible. This might include such things as proximity of services, such as public transportation, recreational facilities, and schools. Location and condition of the family's housing may provide information about economic status and highlight the presence of environmental stresses, such as crime or gangs. At the same time, the way they maintain the home may give clues to a variety of things. A family with sufficient resources whose home is poorly maintained may suggest possible depression or apathy among one or more members (Collins et al., 1999). It may also suggest that

Highlight 5.2 Observational Considerations

1. Which family member is considered the identified patient?
2. Which member talks first?
3. Do any family members talk for others?
4. Do members interrupt each other?
5. What alliances among members are observable?
6. Who seems to be making decisions for the family?
7. Are family members' descriptions of events contradictory?
8. What is the energy level of individual members?
9. What nonverbal behaviors are observed?

family caretakers do not consider this area of their lives a priority. A sign in one family's home expressed this thought quite clearly: "The graveyards are full of women who kept their houses spotless."

Since the goal of observation is to attain objective information on the family, many social workers rely on rating scales to help them in systematically compiling observations. One such scale is the McMaster Model of Family Functioning used to detect how well a family performs in three areas: basic tasks (providing shelter, food, and so on), developmental tasks (dealing with typical family challenges, pregnancy, empty-nest, and so on), and hazardous tasks (managing crisis situations–death, illness, loss of job). The McMaster instrument is useful for assessing how well the family carries out critical and typical functions (Goldenberg & Goldenberg, 2002).

It is always wise to recall that cultural differences may affect a family's behavior and that the social worker's observations may reflect these differences. As Collins and colleagues note, "Some cultures have extended family living with them, and others find it disrespectful for certain family members to be in the same room" (p. 129). Recognizing these differences can help keep the practitioner from drawing the wrong conclusion.

Family Histories

Taking a family history has been a common method of assessing a family's functioning. Family histories gather information that will help the social worker better understand the family's background and possibly suggest approaches that may be employed to help the family. Unfortunately, family histories represent how family members perceive the family and do not necessarily provide an accurate picture. As Berg (1994) notes, the family "history is the client's construction, it is not made up of true or false statements, and with each retelling the story becomes more real to the client" (p. 43). This is a point echoed by Goldenberg and Goldenberg (2002), who note that family members should each share their own individual perspective in order for the practitioner to get a more complete view of how each views the family. Berg recommends that the practitioner accept the client's history but always view it as tentative. Genograms, as we have discussed previously, can be part of taking a family history, as we intend them to portray a particular segment of the family's life.

While social workers often gather a family history at the start of the practitioner-family relationship, this is not always necessary or appropriate. Family members may be too sensitive about the history to discuss it until later sessions. Reluctance to discuss can, in fact, be a key to the central issues of concern. In some approaches to family practice, history taking is downplayed. In the structural model, it is the current situation of the family that is of concern, not its history. Yet, as Kilpatrick and Holland (1999) observe, "It is also very realistic to assume that the current structure is based on a family history" (p. 104). As Minuchin and Nicholls (1993) note, " . . . we can listen to stories and deduce a family's systems of coalitions and balances, or we can look at behavior and infer the stories that support these behaviors" (p. 43). In other words, a family's history may be directly connected with the present situation either by creating the interactional patterns that are currently dysfunctional or by establishing structures and stories that inhibit family members' ability to adapt. Either way, the family's history becomes an important factor in their current structure and functioning. This would suggest that at least a cursory review of family history may help introduce the family to the practitioner even if the theory in use does not include history as an important component of the helping process.

Social Network Map and Grid

Tracy and Whittaker (1990) provide yet another tool for assessing family functioning, the Social Network Map and Grid. The purpose of this tool is to identify the relationships that support individual family members, including the kind, frequency, and reliability of the relationships (Thomlison, 2002). It is constructed using the format shown in Figures 5.4 and 5.5. Steps in the process include asking family members to name each person in their social network and placing the names in the appropriate sections of the pie chart. Once this information is complete, the practitioner employs the grid to describe the nature of the support provided by each named person.

Once family members have named all individuals in their social network, the next task is to complete the Social Network Grid. This grid allows an evaluation of the quality and quantity of support provided by those named in the map. Once completed, the Social Network Map and Grid can help identify familial resources and pinpoint where such resources are lacking. Families without adequate relationships are more likely to have difficulty coping with traumatic life events and other challenges and crises. Over time, we could employ the map and grid as a measure of the extent to which family resources are strengthened.

Figure 5.4 | Social Network Map

Source: Tracy and Whittaker, 1990.

CAVEATS

Thomlison (2002) provides a helpful set of caveats about the use of various family assessment measures. She notes that practitioners or agencies can misuse instruments. This can occur because of confusion about the instrument's purpose and limitations. A second concern is insufficient ability of the practitioner who has not been trained or is inexperienced in its use. A third problem lies in the instrument's degree of validity and reliability. In an ideal world, we would know both the reliability and validity of an instrument, thereby increasing its potential value as a data-gathering tool.

A fourth caveat is associated with using the wrong instrument. This may come about because the practitioner is unfamiliar with the correct instrument and simply uses a tool that is either handy or otherwise routinely available. Finally, the practitioner or agency may use instruments inappropriately so that any data gleaned may be idiosyncratic and thus not "amenable to quantification" (p. 72). We obtain the best results by using multiple instruments or measures that have proven reliability and validity and are carefully selected for the specific task at hand.

Finally, it is also important to inform family members about the need to accurately complete instruments. If family members are haphazard in their attention to the instrument or are not honest in what they record, the results

Figure 5.5 | Social Network Grid

Instructions: Use the first column of the grid to record the name of each person listed on the Social Network Map. For each person listed, ask the family member to describe the kind of support provided (concrete, emotional, information/advice), the degree to which an individual is critical of the family member, the direction of help provided to and/or provided by the family member, the degree of closeness perceived by the family member, and the frequency of contact and length of the relationship.

Name	Areas of Life	Concrete Support	Emotional Support	Information/ Advice	Critical of your activities?	Direction of help provided?	Closeness	How often do you see them?	How long have you known them?
	1. Household 2. Other family 3. Work/school 4. Organizations 5. Other friends 6. Neighbors 7. Professionals 8. Other	1. Hardly ever 2. Sometimes 3. Almost always	1. Hardly ever 2. Sometimes 3. Almost always	1. Hardly ever 2. Sometimes 3. Almost always	1. Hardly ever 2. Sometimes 3. Almost always	1. Goes both ways. 2. You to them. 3. They to you.	1. Not very close. 2. Sort of close. 3. Very close.	0. Does not see. 1. Few times per year. 2. Monthly 3. Weekly 4. Daily	1. Less than 1 year. 2. 1–5 years. 3. More than 5 years

Source: Tracy and Whittaker, 1990.

are likely to be compromised. Once instrument data is analyzed, the social worker should share the results with the family, emphasizing both strengths and challenges that were identified in the analysis. This reinforces for the family the importance of being honest and careful when completing instruments. It also offers the family the opportunity to react to the data generated, further assisting the social worker in understanding family dynamics.

Planning

CHAPTER 6

© Nancy Sheehan/PhotoEdit

INTRODUCTION

Planning, as the third phase in the structure of practice, is based on the assessment jointly completed by the social worker and family. In this chapter, we will explore in detail the planning process and the two major activities that occur during this phase, goal setting and contracting. We will also look at some of the ethnic and cultural factors that influence the planning process.

PLANNING

The purpose of the *planning* process is to establish goals that will help the family in dealing with challenges they have identified. Planning is typically an involved process characterized by several things. First, planning is directed by the client and family and not imposed by the practitioner. This recognizes that family members may have differing priorities and notions of which challenges facing them are most important. We should also note that families may be more receptive to planning for change when they are in crisis. This is important to remember as client motivation is a positive factor in bringing about change (Collins et al., 1999).

Second, planning incorporates strengths discovered in the assessment phase and involves the development of different possible goals. This step is then followed by a process that ultimately winnows down to a set of agreed-upon goals. The goals, which may entail many steps, must also be viewed in the context of both obstacles and strengths. Overcoming the former requires full use of the latter.

Like assessment, planning is subject to change as new information becomes available. In addition, planning done when a family is in crisis may need to be updated when the crisis is past. Similarly, a goal that the family achieves may result in the evolution of a new goal. The complexity of family life plus the multiple connections to external systems contribute to the tentativeness of any planning. Janzen and Harris (1997, p. 64) argue that practitioners must maintain an "investigative stance" throughout the process of assessment, planning, and intervention. This helps ensure that their understanding of the family remains as complete as possible. As Gehart and Tuttle (2003) suggest, "Plans often need to be modified because of outside factors, unanticipated events, or unrealistic expectations" (p. 2).

Often, plans are not only useful but required. Third-party payers, such as insurance and managed care companies, expect the practitioner to provide an intervention or treatment plan. Without such a document, the practitioner may not get paid. Plans are also useful for training purposes and valuable for supervisors helping new practitioners with their responsibilities.

Planning can be viewed as both a long-term and short-term activity. As Haley (1976) suggests, we can plan for both individual sessions or contacts with the family and also identify goals and activities that cover the entire practitioner-family change efforts. Planning for individual sessions has the benefit of focusing all of the social worker's energies on the family's situation and helps provide direction and structure to the helping process.

Client and Family Directed Planning

Ownership of the challenges, problems, and resources identified in the assessment phase always remains with the client and family. This means that all the way through the process, the family has a major role in planning with the social worker. As indicated, goal priorities should be set with the family, not imposed upon them. At the same time, social workers must take into account ethical concerns that arise while helping the family establish goals. For example, the practitioner may need to protect a family member endangered because of the sexual predations of another member, regardless of whether the family thinks this is important.

Strengths-Focused Planning

Families have many strengths that they bring to their work with the social worker. Even the most stressed-out and disorganized families have various strengths that must be considered in the planning process. These strengths may include informal resources not yet utilized, financial resources, commitment to the well-being of all family members, past success at overcoming barriers, resiliency in response to catastrophes, aspirations about the future, and positive attitudes toward hardship, among many others.

Saleebey (1997, p. 51–52) categorizes strengths as falling into several categories. First are the things that "people have learned about themselves, others, and their world" as they have gone through life. A second category includes "personal qualities, traits, and virtues that people possess." These might include "a sense of humor, creativity, loyalty, insight, independence, spirituality, moral imagination, and patience to name a few" (Wolin & Wolin, 1993).

A third category is the knowledge that individuals have learned through their life experiences. For example, one individual may have learned how to deal with confusing situations without getting upset. Another may have developed a capacity to connect emotionally with other people or to accept individual differences. The knowledge attained may be self-knowledge as well as better understandings of those around them.

A fourth category comprises the talents that people develop, such as telling jokes, playing an instrument, or skill in arts and crafts. Other talents may include the ability to repair automobiles, to write poetry, or to do pottery. Often these abilities are not evident to the practitioner and may even have been neglected over the years.

A fifth category includes the "cultural and personal stories and lore" that help people survive difficult life situations (Saleebey, 1997, p. 51). A grandmother may relate a philosophy of life that has allowed her to overcome the adversity associated with the deaths of both of her sons. A father, for example, may have learned a perspective that leads to positive attitudes about difficult tasks based on poems and stories shared by his parents ("I can't is a sluggard, too lazy to work, from duty he shrinks, all his tasks he does shirk"). Other stories may be of family members who overcame great odds to accomplish something.

A sixth category is pride, a characteristic of individuals who have overcome misfortune and regard themselves as "different." Proud individuals have shown themselves that they can make changes in their lives and have developed a sense of self as a doer.

The last category of strength is community, a term that encompasses not only the physical environment but the individuals and organizations that exist within the community.

THEORY IN ACTION | Community Strength

In the well-known case of Elizabeth Smart, a young Salt Lake City teenager who was kidnapped from her home and remained missing for nine months, the community responded to Elizabeth's disappearance by conducting massive searches, distributing missing person flyers, and comforting the family. The community's response, combined with the spiritual/religious resources of the family, helped them remain optimistic despite the passage of time. Eventually, members of the community located Elizabeth and her captors and reported them to the police.

Finding family strengths requires both observation and probing. Asking families how they have weathered past crises may give clues to latent strengths useful in planning. Having families list and describe the kinds and quality of support they receive from informal resource systems is another mechanism of discovery. Asking about aspirations may give useful information about how the family approaches the future, while asking them about past good times may elicit additional keys.

Families will usually share their strengths if social workers display an interest in attending to these characteristics. On the other hand, focusing solely on problems is likely to encourage a deficit mode of thinking and acting by both family and practitioner. By searching for strengths, the social worker is also stimulating the family to refocus their perspective away from what is wrong to what is right. This can help uncover strengths the family members have ignored or have not used recently.

Another method of focusing on strengths is to ask the family to describe times when things were better. This may be a point where both spouses paid more attention to one another or when the family seemed to function better.

This helps family members recall that they have had multiple times when they were happier or got their needs met more directly. It also gives the social worker an opportunity to highlight the positive behaviors of family members that contributed to the "good times." These can be incorporated into the intervention plan.

Another technique is to ask family members to identify positive characteristics they see in the other members. The social worker might ask the family to list the "gifts" that each person brings to the family. This recognizes how each person has attributes that help the family in its functioning. A spouse whose partner describes her as "pretty" may be verbalizing a characteristic the spouse has not heard for some time. Another partner who works so much that she has no time for other family members might be described as "a good provider" or "generous." In this way, even behaviors seen as problematic can have a positive side.

The social worker can also reinforce the competence of the family in such areas as problem solving, crisis management, or handling other life events. This highlights strengths that the family may have ignored or overlooked when struggling with other issues (Brown & Brown, 2002).

Family Members with Differing Priorities

We have hinted that family members may have different priorities. In practice, it is common for different members to have varying priorities or even divergent ideas about what changes are needed. Some may even disagree with the need for change. This arises from the fact that all are individuals with their own needs and wishes. One partner, for example, may see the relationship as needing repair while the other believes it is too late for this. An abusive partner or one with a publicly undisclosed problem such as drug use may be reluctant to have this behavior described to the social worker and would rather focus on less personal topics. Likewise, children are likely to have one set of goals and their parents another.

Part of the social worker's task is clearly to identify these goals and help the family decide which ones to pursue. Perhaps there is room for compromise so that one set of goals benefiting the entire family will be selected. Or maybe the family will try to work on two goals simultaneously. Another option is to alternate goals so that one gets priority the first month and another gets addressed the next month.

It is also possible that one family member will refuse to participate in the planning and goalsetting stage. This may occur because she believes the social worker will side with other members or because she has secrets that she is unwilling to discuss. While participation of all appropriate members is usually desirable, some social workers have developed strategies for overcoming these impediments. For example, the practitioner may contact the missing member by phone and enlist his participation while allowing him to remain outside of the family sessions. Thus, we may ask a missing spouse to help the attending spouse by engaging in certain behaviors in the home (Treadway, 1989). By not feeling pressured to attend sessions, the missing partner may be comfortable enough to help the family attain its goals. Sometimes, the missing partner may eventually want to be part of the sessions.

Prioritization in Planning

Prioritization is deciding what should be done first. Sometimes this is obvious—a homeless family needs shelter and food before counseling. Similarly, we must protect a suicidal family member before we can undertake long-range goals. A family facing multiple challenges will still need to establish goals that have higher priority and those that have less. Factors that we should take into account in prioritization include "the annoyance value of the problem to the family, the danger, the potential for success, the probable cost of working on an issue in terms of time, money, energy and other resources, and the likelihood that the new patterns will be maintained" (Kinney et al., 1991, p. 89).

Some problems facing a family may be vexing but not particularly important in and of themselves. The spouse who engages in such heinous behavior as leaving the toilet seat up, putting the toilet paper on the roll incorrectly, and squeezing the toothpaste container from the top is annoying. The consequences to the family, however, are less than would occur with a philandering or unfaithful spouse or one who sold drugs. This is an example of how annoying behavior may not be as high a priority to change as others.

In a family, a goal that reduces danger to individual members or the family as a whole obviously has greater priority than goals that simply improve the quality of life. For example, reducing and eliminating physical or sexual violence within the family has more importance than ensuring that a 17-year-old son obeys curfew.

Goals with higher probability of success will probably get higher priority, everything else being equal. The reason for selecting more easily achievable goals is to build confidence and hope in the family that things will improve. Demoralized families need to know that change is possible and to feel they have the power to achieve.

Some goals will take greater resources of time, energy, money, and cooperation than others. That does not mean they should not get priority, but it does mean that these factors must be considered and discussed with the family before they set priorities. The goals of one family member to return to high school, earn a GED, go on to college, and become a pharmacist are going to involve a great deal of time, energy, and money. Compare this with a family member who wants to return to college and complete her senior year. One goal is readily achievable in a relatively short period of time, while the other will take years to reach. Later in this chapter we will look at both long- and short-term goals.

Finally, we need to consider the likelihood that the family will maintain the desired changes. Families can more easily maintain change if the environment contains reinforcers and offers fewer opportunities for a relapse. A couple with sexual difficulties who learn to express their needs better may find their love life improving and a concomitant increase in mutual enjoyment. This is a change that is more likely to continue because of the inherent reinforcement that occurs. On the other hand, a behavior change that lacks such structured or built-in reinforcers is less likely to continue. Think of the adolescent male involved in a drug culture, all of whose friends are dealers or users or both. Such an environment offers much less promise of permanent change.

Develop Possible Plans

To the extent possible, plans should be based on the family's strengths, including informal support networks. As we have shown in Chapter 1, planning may involve the social worker in a variety of roles ranging from advocate, counselor, educator, case manager, and broker, and so on. It is the nature of the goals that will determine which roles are required and when the social worker will play them.

Several factors limit the actual range of possible plans, among which are family priorities and resources. Family priorities are important for at least two reasons. First, plans that address the family's most pressing concerns are more likely to elicit cooperation and enthusiasm. Second, plans that build upon already existing resources may be perceived as more likely to succeed.

It is important that plans be appropriate to meet family needs. For example, one plan may be to provide concrete services such as housing or arranging for food stamps or emergency health care of family members. Another may involve making referrals to appropriate agencies that provide services the practitioner or agency cannot. A third might be practitioner-provided family counseling, either alone or in combination with family members receiving individual counseling. A complicated case involving child welfare issues may require the creation of a case management plan in which the practitioner helps monitor and evaluate the effectiveness of services that others provide. Sometimes, advocacy may be needed to ensure that family members receive the benefits to which they are entitled or to break a bureaucratic bottleneck delaying timely services.

At the same time, some plans are less likely to be adopted. Consider, for example, the practitioner who has identified challenges facing the family that the family is not yet ready to tackle. Plans that only reflect the practitioner's assessment of challenges and not the family's are less likely to be adopted. As Worden (1994) so cogently notes, "Do not get ahead of the family; address the members' chief concerns first" (p. 129).

Evaluate Plans and Assess Obstacles

Even families in disarray can help evaluate various plans and sort out those about which they feel most positive. The social worker may help the family identify strengths and limitations, plus the obstacles they may encounter with specific goals. Obstacles might include lack of resources, family members who may try to sabotage change, fears about how others will react, and lack of confidence about how to accomplish the goals. A family may reject a goal because they are not emotionally ready to tackle a particular challenge at this time. Obstacle recognition is important because it allows the social worker and family to identify possible ways to overcome the barrier. By discussing obstacles, the family may come to recognize these barriers are surmountable. Even if the obstacle is formidable, discussing it allows family members to be fully aware of what must be done. Occasionally, an obstacle may appear so imposing that the plan is set aside for the time being. We may reconsider these plans later if the situation warrants.

THEORY IN ACTION | Dealing with Obstacles

FAMILY PRACTITIONER: We have agreed that the best plan of action is to help John get into a treatment program. What kinds of difficulties might affect this plan?

FATHER: Well, I am worried about the money for the program. What if my insurance doesn't cover it?

FAMILY PRACTITIONER: There are many programs in town that don't take insurance. However, before we deal with a problem we don't know we have, it would be best to find out the information right away. How can you find this information?

FATHER: Well, I can call my insurance company and see what they provide.

FAMILY PRACTITIONER: Yes, and also we can contact those residential treatment centers you and John have picked out and ask about the financial obligations for getting John into a program. Do you think you could also handle that, maybe with John's help?

JOHN: I would be willing to call a few of the treatment places. I almost did that once myself, but then I didn't.

FAMILY PRACTITIONER: I think taking part in working through your treatment is very important for you John. How are you feeling about that, Dad?

FATHER: I guess that would be all right. Now that John has agreed to get treatment, I don't want him to be overstressed.

Selecting a Plan

Selecting a plan involves choosing with the family the interventions that show the greatest promise of working and address specific family concerns. Planning may require a certain amount of negotiation as different family members seek to have their own needs addressed first.

GOAL SETTING

Setting goals is the ultimate purpose of planning. In the planning process we have focused on the challenges facing the family and the strengths and resources available to tackle the work ahead. To decide appropriate goals, the process is a collaborative effort by the practitioner and family. This may mean asking family members certain questions. "What do you hope to accomplish through our work together?" "Have you thought about how you might accomplish these goals?" Such questions begin to help the family think about what it is they want and realize that work will be required to achieve their goals. Brown and Brown (2002) suggest that one way of helping a family is to externalize the problem. Suggesting that the problem is outside of the family can help reduce the tendency to focus on a single family member. An example of externalizing the problem is referring to a family difficulty "as the 'noncooperation' problem" in which the parents' attempts to nag a child into doing homework results in even less homework being completed (p. 107). While casting this problem as belonging to the parents or the child would be easier, by externalizing it the practitioner may have more success eliciting the cooperation of family members in making needed changes. Collins et al. (1999), Berg, (1994), and others provide recommendations for establishing goals with families:

- Ensure that goals are concrete and specific. Goals must be measurable. A goal of "do more together" is too vague to be useful. An alternative might be "I would like to go out to dinner with you at least once a week."
- Select goals that have the highest priority with family members. Goals must be important to the family.
- Assist family members to negotiate with one another regarding specific changes they would like to see.
- Ask family members to validate the changes others expect of them. This involves asking each family member whether what the other wants of them is understandable and reasonable.
- Recognize the abilities and strengths of family members. One way of doing this is to reframe the family problem as a strength. For example, the mother who questions her adolescent son about where he is going and with whom is displaying a valid interest in the child's welfare even as it may seem intrusive to the child.
- Use the goal setting process "to obtain a commitment from the family" (Collins et al., 1999, p. 140).
- Describe goals in terms of how intrafamily interactions will change. What will be different in the family if change occurs?
- Establish goals that they can reasonably achieve.
- Break large goals into smaller components that they can more quickly achieve. For example, "applying to community college" is more easily achieved than "earning a college degree," even though the latter may be the ultimate goal.

- State goals in terms of what will *be* instead of what will *not be,* for example, "Modesto will place her dirty clothes in the hamper" instead of "Modesto will quit leaving her room a mess." Goals stated in the positive are less blame-oriented.
- Goals should emphasize the fact that change will require the family and practitioner to work hard together to overcome the barriers. This has the advantage of reframing the problem as a challenge to be overcome rather than one caused by a lack of effort by the family.
- Select goals that the family believes are important even if they are different from the practitioner's. "Starting where the client is" represents an important tool in social work practice.
- Goals should specify what the practitioner is going to do to help the family achieve a specific goal. For example, "the social worker will provide the family with the names and numbers of three agencies offering free tutoring for children."
- Goals should include a schedule that identifies how long the practitioner and family will be working together. Sometimes third-party payers mandate the length of this period.
- Goals should consider available resources.
- Goals should include a focus on interactional change in which family members agree to undertake different behaviors in their interactions with other members. Gurman and Knudson (1978) highlight the importance of reciprocal goals by noting that the behavior of one family member directly affects the actions of other members. They also recognize that family problems are, in fact, problems of interaction and not the result of individual psychopathology.

In the next section we will look at goals from several perspectives. This will include differentiating between short-term and long-term goals, using partialization to manage large challenges, working with both family and individual goals, and instilling hope. Some practitioners call goals *objectives,* but the terminology is less important than whether the goals meet the criteria just noted.

Long-Term Goals

It is difficult to establish an exact timeline that differentiates long-term from short-term goals. At the same time, the planning process previously described allowed for the importance of setting priorities. Thus, we can start with the assumption that goals deemed less emergent will be considered long-term while those having higher priority will be defined as short-term. *Long-term goals* typically focus on "(a) addressing long-term issues, (b) solidifying gains, (c) strategies for handling future issues, and (d) referrals" (Gehart & Tuttle, 2003, p. 7).

Short-Term Goals

Short-term goals will be the immediate focus of the family and social worker. This means that these goals will be broken down into specific tasks that family members and the practitioner must complete. Breaking goals down into inherent tasks is necessary because by themselves, goals remain desired ends without providing specific direction for anyone. Often, families enunciate goals in the negative in that they want a child to stop engaging in temper tantrums or they seek a reduction in the number of fights occurring between adult members. However, restating the goal in terms of positive outcomes is generally better. For example, consider the goal of reducing the triangulation occurring between Frances, her mom, and stepfather. Certainly, the goal is appropriate to improving the functioning of the family, but we need to rephrase it in the positive. Thus, we might word the goal as follows: Strengthen the dyad relationship of Frances's mother and stepfather. While positive in emphasis, the goal is still very broad. Our next step is to identify the tasks associated with this goal. We may need to complete, for example, each of the following tasks:

- Help each parent understand the concepts of boundaries and triangulation.
- Help each parent to understand common dynamics of blended families.
- Identify and practice new responses to Frances's triangulation behavior.

Ideally, we can measure each objective in some fashion. This is important because lack of clarity on the front end will lead to problematic evaluation on the back end. A goal that states, "Frances and her family will get along better" really leaves the social worker little to work with and less to evaluate. A good goal will specify the activity or behavior that is to occur, whether by the social worker or family. Built into the goal may be an implicit or explicit identification of when the change is to occur. If the schedule is implicit, it may coincide with the number of sessions and may be incorporated into a contract (to be discussed later). If explicit, the schedule may become part of the goal.

Small Steps toward Success Wanting wholesale change to occur in the challenges they face is common for families. At the same time, these challenges may be so enormous that there is realistically little chance of all of them being dealt with at once. While the assessment phase may have identified what seems like a large challenge, a key to planning is to reduce the size of the problem by partializing it. *Partialization* is a technique that breaks down problems into manageable components that can be tackled. We might ask a family that finds one child's behavior unacceptable to identify a single behavior that they would like to see the child change. The advantage of breaking the problem down is that it allows us to begin making progress in what may initially look like a quagmire. It also can serve to convince the family that change is possible, albeit in small increments. The child who begins to respect curfew and returns home at an acceptable hour is making an important small step in the movement toward success. Family goals concerning improved school performance, lessened drug use, or other desired changes will be dealt with in time.

One of the reasons for breaking goals down into activities or tasks is to help create a pattern that leads to success. For example, if the blended family described previously learns about issues of boundaries and triangulation, they are likely to understand better what is happening to their family relationships. Likewise, if they understand some of the challenges facing blended families, this may help prepare them for the new responses they will need to learn to bring about change in their family. Having completed one visible step or task gives the family a sense of hope about future changes.

Individual and Family Goals

It is wholly understandable that individual members of a family may come with divergent goals. Frances may like the control she has over the family by her ability to triangulate her parent and stepparent. The parents, on the other hand, are more likely to want this situation to stop and to improve their marital relationship. Adolescents coming to the practitioner may want help to loosen their parents' grip on their lives and to allow them greater freedom. Parents may want the practitioner to help them control their wayward teenager. Ultimately, the family must agree on what goals have priority. The following are some potential goals for families:

- Strengthen the parental dyad in handling issues related to discipline.
- Establish clear expectations and appropriate consequences (positive and negative).
- Help teenagers to learn more effective ways to express their needs for independence.
- Reduce self-blaming behaviors.
- Help reestablish the relationship between siblings.
- Assist family in developing strategies to reduce the intrusiveness of grandparents.
- Help the family express grief and their sense of loss resulting from a death in the family.
- Improving teenagers' performance in school.
- Assist family members in developing a support network external to the family.
- Help parents to identify joint activities they can pursue after the children leave for college
- Help parents show greater interest in their spouse's hobbies.
- Identify specific ways in which spouses can assist each other in carrying out family responsibilities.

As is evident, family goals may reflect desired ends that focus on the parental dyad, deal with child-rearing techniques, improve family communication, and eliminate identified problems. In proposing goals, practitioners are exploring with the family what they see as ways to resolve various challenges enumerated by family members. Family members may accept, reject, or suggest modifications in the goals, and this is appropriate.

Sometimes family members state different goals that, under scrutiny, are really very similar. For example, Micah may want his partner Thakura to spend less time in front of the TV, while Thakura wishes Micah would join her at weekly church services. Both goals have one thing in common: namely, spending more time together. The social worker can help the partners recognize the commonality of their desires and help them come up with a mutually acceptable goal.

When Goals Are Different

In selecting goals to work on, some level of agreement among family members is essential. If you are unable to help the family agree on at least one goal, providing much assistance to family members would be nearly impossible. In such situations, we may need to postpone work with the family.

An even more challenging problem for the practitioner occurs when one or more family members have goals that they have not shared. Such secret agendas may sabotage the intervention process. A partner, for example, who participates in family counseling while simultaneously carrying on an affair outside the marriage, is not committed to change. Similarly, a partner who has already decided to leave the relationship may be using the family practitioner to support his or her private agenda.

At other times, differences may be less troublesome. Consider a family who is court-ordered to see the practitioner or another who must receive counseling as required by a child protective service agency. While the partners may be less than enthusiastic about being coerced into seeking help, we still may help them to try, if only to achieve the goal of keeping their children. Though they may be initially resistant to the effort, there is potential for finding a common goal toward which they can work.

Planning Process Responsibility

As we have tried to emphasize previously, the planning process and goal selection is a joint process between family and practitioner. The family must have some level of commitment to the goals if there is to be much hope for change. Simultaneously, the social worker must be reasonably comfortable with the family's plans and goals. A family that seeks a goal the practitioner cannot ethically support can expect to be turned down as a client.

Instilling Hope

Hope for change is an important component of much of our work with families. If families expect to fail, if they believe that nothing will get better, they will likely act on those perceptions. Part of the social worker's work is aimed at instilling hope. Worden (1994) suggests the practitioner "is responsible for promoting an atmosphere conducive to change" (p. 55). We accomplish this through forming a therapeutic alliance with the family and clearly expressing a mutual responsibility for making change happen. The social worker supports hope through leading, "supporting, questioning, challenging, or provoking the family" (p. 55). Another way of providing hope is to help the family identify times in the past when interactions were more positive. This helps the family to place their current situation in perspective and avoids a focus on the failures and misery of the present (Brown & Brown, 2002).

THEORY IN ACTION | Supporting Hope

KAREN: I don't know how we will be able to accomplish all this, dealing with the drug use and our problems as a couple.

FAMILY PRACTITIONER: Many of your issues may be because of the drug use. With even a small change in that direction, your relationship as a couple can change. How you cannot move forward on these goals and this plan is really the question. Is there an alternative to improving things?

KAREN: No, I want things to be better, I just hope they can move forward like you said.

FAMILY PRACTITIONER: With that hope and some hard work, things will change for the better.

CONTRACTING

A *contract* is an agreement that we establish with the family. Generally, a contract will describe activities planned for the intervention phase, list goals and tasks to be accomplished, and identify who will do what. Contracts may be oral, written, or, more frequently, implied. By implied we mean that although no specific discussion of a contract has occurred, both the practitioner and family understand what is going to happen.

Contracts have several advantages (Halley, Kopp, & Austin, 1998; Johnson, 1998; Kirst-Ashman & Hull, 2002). First, they reduce the possibility of misunderstandings between the family and the social worker. Second, they help to document individual responsibilities and may specify time frames, such as the number of sessions. Third, contracts, especially written ones, underscore the fact that the relationship between the family and social worker is one of equality and that both parties share responsibility for the outcome. This can be an empowering factor for some families. Fourth, contacts help stimulate family members to action rather than simply expecting the practitioner to create change. Fifth, a contract may be especially helpful for "disorganized or forgetful" families because it reminds them of what they agreed to (Johnson, 1998, p. 316). Contracts may also be helpful in spurring family members to action both by focusing on specific problems needing resolution and energizing the family (Atwood, 1992). A contract can help reduce some of the stress and tension family members may experience at the start of the professional relationship. Contracts may be especially useful when partners or teenagers and parents "are at loggerheads, angry and resentful . . . [as contracts] provide an opportunity for a family to take stock and to break through vicious circles of retribution and unreason" (Harper-Dorton & Herbert, 1999, p. 180). Teenagers may find contracts empowering because they place their needs on the same level of importance as those of their parents. The process of negotiating a contract can be helpful to the extent that it shows participants a different means of bringing about change (Brock & Barnard, 1999). Finally, contracts can serve as a record of goals and plans useful for monitoring and assessing intervention outcomes.

Like planning, contracting can include plans for the overall practitioner-family activity as well as for individual sessions. *Overall contracts* may include items such as goals, family strengths, meeting times and places, length and number of sessions, listing of participants, a description of such things as the presence of observers, taping of sessions, and, of course, fees (Nichols & Schwartz, 2001). *Sessional contracts* may include a contract not to commit suicide between this session and the next or to engage in some specific behavior, such as applying for a job.

A final use of the term *contracting* relates to specific agreements that family members make in the context of the intervention. For example, one partner might agree to spend an extra hour per evening with the other partner. Or, a parent may agree to make daily contact with the school system to follow a child's progress. This type of *good faith* contracting has no strings attached in the sense that it is not contingent on the actions or behavior of any other person. An alternate form is the *contingency contract* in which individual family members agree to engage in a behavior contingent upon other family members behaving in a specific way. Thus, a parent may agree to take the child to a favorite movie in exchange for the child completing all homework assignments for the week. This *quid pro quo* is based on a clear understanding between the parties about what behavior is wanted from one and what the other will provide if the behavior is forthcoming.

It is important to note that these contracts are not legal documents but rather reflect both parties' commitment to the change process. Equally important, we may change these contracts as needed based upon the agreement of practitioner and family. At the same time, some aspects of the contract, especially if written, do offer a potential bit of help to the social worker. For example, a contract that explains the practitioner's duty to warn, mandatory reporting requirements for child or adult abuse, limits to confidentiality, and fee arrangements may be useful if a serious dispute between social worker and family ends up in court.

Involvement of All Family Members

As we have noted frequently, all aspects of the family–practitioner interaction should be mutual and involve as many family members as possible. This is also true of contracts because the advantages apply to all family members. Even children can be a party to a contract with the added benefit that it helps give them a sense of involvement and importance in what they otherwise might perceive as an adult activity. Since contracts capture goals and plans, they reflect things that all family members should already have accepted. Involving as many family members as possible in the planning stages is culturally appropriate. For example, in some cultures, including many Native American societies, family well-being is a corporate responsibility in that all members share the task of ensuring the family is healthy and stable.

Contracts, regardless of type, should have several common characteristics (Collins et al., 1999). First, the social worker and family negotiate contracts. No one imposes them upon the family. Second, contracts should use words that all family members can understand, including children. Third, whenever possible, the practitioner should get at least an oral commitment to the contract. Fourth, practitioners and families should review and revise contracts periodically and as needed.

Contracts may cover many topics, ranging from who will attend or participate in sessions, when we will hold sessions, what goals will be worked on, and what kinds of activities are likely to be involved. Activities might include between-session assignments, participation in outside groups, or others deemed appropriate to goal achievement. Other topics of a contract may include a schedule for renegotiating contract terms, and anything else that both practitioner and family members think is appropriate (Hanna & Brown, 1999).

It is the social worker's responsibility for bringing up the topic of contracting and discussing it with family members. Once agreed to, the contact "makes the family and [practitioner] accountable to one another" (Collins et al., 1999, p. 142). It is critical that all parties enter a contact with little or no coercion. While some clients may have less freedom than others about whether they will enter a contact (such as children or court-ordered individuals), the goal is to maximize the sense of voluntary involvement.

THEORY IN ACTION | Contracting

FAMILY PRACTITIONER: I think an important step for us to take as a family and practitioner is to establish a contract regarding what we have talked about and what we will do.

MS. STOLE: What kind of a contract?

FAMILY PRACTITIONER: One like you might make in other circumstances. Let's start by talking about what would be in the contract. What things do you remember that we have all agreed to?

MS. STOLE: Well, we agreed to when we would meet and what kinds of goals we wanted to have.

FAMILY PRACTITIONER: Those are exactly the types of things that would go into our contract. We would be saying that we are going to accomplish these goals together as a family with the help of a social worker.

Like plans for the future, contracts are best stated in terms of positive behaviors and actions instead of the avoidance of negative items. One way that we can achieve this is to ask family members to list the behaviors or actions they would like to see more of from the other members. We can follow this step by asking each person to share with the others the list he or she has prepared. Family members can then gauge or rate each item as to how easy it would be to do what the others want. A process of negotiation may follow, with members agreeing to behaviors of relatively equal weight. We should also structure contracts with reinforcements for members who follow the rules. Keep in mind that some family members (such as children) may need more frequent reinforcement. Thus, a contingency contract with weekly rewards may be difficult or impossible for some members. Initially, structuring in rewards following individual behaviors is preferable to waiting until the end of some predetermined time.

While we have emphasized the desirability of stating contracts in the positive, there are exceptions. Sometimes, as Gehart and Tuttle (2003) note, writing contacts in terms of positive behaviors is simply not possible. Falloon (1991) states that in some situations, "a contract may be made that concerns setting specific limits on undesirable behavior" (p. 84).

The social worker and family may need to renegotiate the contract from time to time as new information becomes available or the family's needs change. If the family fails to achieve goals within a reasonable period or if one or more members actively or passively refuse to work on their goals, this may suggest the need to rethink the contract. If the schedule adopted initially appears to have been too ambitious, we can adjust this easily. Renegotiating the contract can be a positive experience to the extent that it empowers family members "to know that they are able to change the conditions of the contract if they so desire" (Brown & Brown, 2002, p. 108).

Written Contracts

Written contacts can describe global agreements between the social worker and family, such as goals, strengths, sessions, and so on. We can also use them for specific purposes, such as contingency contracts between partners or between adults and children. One real advantage of written contacts is that they essentially publicize the good intentions and plans of the individual to both family members and the practitioner. This tends to increase one's level of commitment, much like telling your friends you are going on a diet. People are more likely to follow publicly stated intentions than those they never share with others (This also applies to politicians). Highlight 6.1 shows a sample written contract for the Mendoza family.

Verbal Contracts

Often a family-change effort begins when the family members make a commitment to the social worker to engage in new behaviors, follow recommendations, or otherwise show a willingness to participate fully in the helping

Highlight 6.1 | Written Contract

Contract between Jose and Marita Mendoza

We, Jose, Marita, and Martine Mendoza have agreed to develop better ways of relating to one another and our children. To accomplish this goal, we will each change our respective behaviors toward each other and our children. We agree to make the changes listed below:

Jose

1. Be home for dinner at 6:30 or call ahead of time if this is not possible.
2. Ask Marita to accompany me to line-dancing lessons each week.
3. Ask Marita about her day at the plant.
4. Refrain from reading the paper during meals.

Marita

1. Ask Jose about his day at the office.
2. Plan with Jose one evening per week together.
3. Accompany Jose to line-dancing lessons.
4. Ask Jose to accompany me to church.

Martine

1. Show Mom my homework as soon as I get home.
2. Complete homework before calling friends.

We agree to maintain a record of our progress with respect to rules. If one of us does not follow any rule, we agree to discuss this together and at our next session with the social worker.

Signed: ____________________ ____________________ ____________________

Jose Marita Martine

relationship. This willingness occurs only after the practitioner has gained the family's confidence. This is usually followed by a clear verbal agreement regarding goals, activities, and responsibilities that form the basis of the remaining work together. We may use a verbal contract when the family is uncomfortable or unwilling to enter into a written contract. The disadvantage of verbal contracts is the possibility of misunderstandings, forgetting details, or simply deciding to ignore specific portions of the agreement.

EVALUATION PLAN

Evaluation is an important component of family practice and may focus on several topics. Obviously, one of the most important is the outcome of the change effort undertaken by the family and social worker. Thus, we should be concerned about whether the family's situation is improving as perceived by family members or other stakeholders. We may also be interested in assessing the quality of the relationship between practitioner and family or the family's perception of the pace and method of the work (Shebib, 2003). We should develop an evaluation plan as part of the planning and goalsetting process.

A common shortcoming of many family practice texts is the lack of information on evaluation and creating an evaluation plan. Too often, they have introduced and discussed theories without paying any attention to how social workers are to assess the success or failure of their interventions with families. This is unfortunate because it is critical to develop an evaluation plan in order to assess success of the practitioner's efforts to help the family. An evaluation plan requires the establishment of unambiguous goals that we can measure in some fashion. The less concrete and clear the goals, the more difficult it will be to decide if they have been achieved.

In addition, the plan must also identify the sources of information that will be used to assess progress. For example, will the source be largely self-reports provided by members of the family? Self-reports may include verbal statements, completion of a questionnaire, or charting of behaviors, among others. Some social workers find it helpful to develop a questionnaire that reflects identified goals. We can use such an instrument both to chart progress and assess outcomes.

Sometimes, others outside of the family do the assessment of goal achievement. For example, the family may be mandated to seek help from the social worker. Thus, outside systems such as the courts, school, or another agency may be heavily invested in determining changes the family has made.

In an ideal world, the practitioner would have a source of data about family functioning that describes the status before intervention. For example, it would be very helpful to know that the family erupted in angry outbursts an average of three times per week. We might like to know how often the adult partners miscommunicated with each other or how often the husband retreated to his "cave" rather than deal with difficult issues. Since these types of information are usually not available, it is important that the social worker and family establish some sort of a baseline regarding the frequency of specific behaviors identified for change. This may occur by using various scales measuring levels of family functioning, such as the North Carolina Family Assessment Scale (Reed-Ashcraft, Kirk, & Fraser, 2001) or similar instruments. By using these assessment instruments in the beginning stage of work with a family, the social worker can re-employ them later to help determine what, if any, changes have occurred.

Ultimately, the goal is to have a plan for evaluation that is appropriate to the particular case and that will allow us to know whether the family has reached its goals. Without adequate prior planning, ending up without a basis for assessing success or failure other than practitioner or family opinions is easy.

THEORY IN ACTION | An Evaluation Plan

Consider the hypothetical Adams family. The school referred the family for help because of several unusual incidents that occurred at school. Assessment reveals a family struggling with several challenges:

- The bizarre behavior of Grandpa Adams who lives with them but spends all of his time in the basement muttering to himself and experimenting with explosives
- Mr. Adams' recurrent hallucinations about seeing a hand scurry across the floor of their house, perhaps resulting from a prior brain tumor
- The need for housing after the latest experiment of Grandpa Adams resulted in the destruction of their home
- Mrs. Adams inability to control the children's troublesome behavior in school

Following the assessment phase, an appropriate intervention plan is needed that is designed in cooperation with both Mr. and Mrs. Adams and the two children. The plan has the following components:

- The social worker will contact the city housing authority to determine whether they have any space available in their emergency housing facility. This will be accomplished by the end of the day.
- Mrs. Adams will contact her cousin to see if the family might be able to move in with them on a temporary basis. This will be accomplished by the end of the day.
- The social worker will refer Mr. Adams' father for evaluation by a psychiatrist specializing in work with the elderly. The referral will be provided in the next 3 days.
- Mr. Adams will have a complete medical examination to explore the possibility of the recurrence of a brain tumor that produces visual hallucinations. Mr. Adams will make this appointment within 10 days.

- Mr. and Mrs. Adams will attend parenting classes sponsored by the local mental health center. These classes will begin on the first of the month and continue for 4 weeks.
- The parents will contact the children's teachers in order to identify and monitor the specific behaviors needing attention. The teachers will be asked to maintain a checklist and log of behavioral difficulties provided by the social worker. This will be accomplished within 10 days.
- Mr. and Mrs. Adams will complete six weekly meetings with the social worker to monitor progress. The children will be included in at least three of these meetings. These meetings will begin next week and continue as scheduled.
- Mr. and Mrs. Adams will be responsible for paying 20 percent of the costs of their sessions with the practitioner in accordance with their health insurance policy. This copayment is due after each session unless Mr. and Mrs. Adams and the social worker negotiate an alternative arrangement.

We have tried to convey in this intervention plan who will accomplish which tasks within what time frame. Each of the tasks identified in the plan can be easily monitored and evaluated, important considerations when selecting plans. Evaluating the success of these efforts is an important component of the structure of change. Chapter 8 will provide a more detailed look at evaluation and consider multiple ways of assessing outcomes of family intervention. We will also discuss advantages and disadvantages of different approaches.

ETHNIC AND CULTURAL CHALLENGES IN PLANNING AND GOAL SETTING

Ethnicity, racial, and cultural backgrounds of family members can have an impact on all aspects of the planning and goalsetting process. While the terms *ethnicity* and *culture* are often used interchangeably, the differences between the two are, in fact, quite significant. "Culture is the way of life of a group, an integrated way of thinking, believing, doing, and being in the world that is passed on from one generation to the next" (Samantrai, 2004, p. 31). Thus, a family's culture may influence such things as their values, customs, traditional ways of doing things, and patterns of communication, among many others. Culture becomes the window through which families view their world. Culture may influence whether we show emotion, how we treat other family members, and how we raise children. As Samantrai notes, one's culture is "an amalgam of the beliefs, values, norms, and so forth of their race, ethnicity, religion, geographic location, socioeconomic status, and any other characteristics they share with others that gives them a sense of peoplehood, and the beliefs, values, norms, and so forth of the dominant mainstream culture of the society in which they live" (p. 31).

Ethnicity, on the other hand, is a component that influences culture and is based on a shared system of "history, ancestry, and language usually tied to a place and time" (p. 31). Thus, ethnicity contributes to culture but is not synonymous with it. Another notion, *race,* is important because of its frequent association with ethnicity. Essentially a social construct rather than a biologic one, race is one factor in helping people develop a common identity. The single most important element of this is the shared physical characteristic.

These factors make establishing widely applicable protocols for work with diverse families difficult. For example, the fact that two families are both African American provides little information about them. One family, middle-class and well-educated, may have little in common with the other that just emigrated from Botswana. Similarly, an Asian American couple of Japanese ancestry may have few shared characteristics with another Asian couple from Samoa. In this section, we will discuss how variables such as culture, race, and ethnicity may affect the practitioner's planning work with families. Simultaneously, we want to emphasize the risks associated with making blanket assumptions about any family based solely on these factors.

First, it is important to emphasize that commonly accepted developmental theories that suggest individuals will become independent from their families are often inappropriate when applied to different cultures. Indeed, in many cultures separation or independence from one's family is neither desirable nor expected. Likewise, because each culture is unique, it may prove beneficial to ask family members whether they believe other members should be included in the assessment and planning sessions. This is particularly true of "African, Asian, Middle Eastern and Native people" (Shebib, 2003, p. 301). Likewise, assumptions of equality between males and females may prove problematic in cultures where traditional values govern gender roles. Even values like confidentiality can be put to the test when it is the family leader, not the individual couple, who makes decisions. This reflects cultural respect for elders and one's sense of responsibility to the entire family (Shebib, 2003).

Cultural differences also may affect the availability and types of resources for the family. For example, natural helping networks are common in some Asian communities. With African American families, we should explore the church as an important resource. Sometimes, it may prove helpful to involve their minister in sessions, depending upon the wishes of the family (Paniagua, 1998). Planning must consider resource availability.

One way the practitioner can begin to manage cultural or other differences is to ask family members to teach the practitioner about important aspects of their culture or ethnicity (Brown & Brown, 2002). This sends at least three messages to the family. The first is the fact that the social worker recognizes that ethnicity or culture may play a significant role in the family's life. The second is the social worker's openness to learning about the family. A third message is one of empowerment as the social worker demonstrates a belief that the family has knowledge that will be important in their work together. This is especially true when considering planning and goal setting because the practitioner does not want to suggest strategies that are culturally inappropriate.

Interracial Families

O'Neal, Brown, and Abadie (1997) have studied some of the particular problems experienced by families where the parents are from different racial groups. They note that while the typical family can probably count on support from their extended kin, this is often not true in mixed marriages. Because many kin groups object to the marriage, this resource is often missing at a point when the family is most in need. When this is the case, the social worker must help the family to find other resources.

Besides the ordinary problems faced by typical families, interracial couples experience the challenge of "creating a new family culture from two dissimilar cultures" while potentially holding "subtle, oftentimes unconscious, negative attitudes and behaviors pertaining to a residue of learned beliefs about a partner's racial/cultural group" (p. 16). These factors influence how interracial families perceive themselves and, of course, affect the planning process.

Interracial families may experience the clash of different norms and expectations regarding roles and behaviors. Family-centeredness of Asian families, for example, may be at odds with the expectation of privacy and individualism of western values (Brown & Brown, 2002). Similarly, the typical adolescent struggles for independence may be considered disrespectful to the Asian family, where the emphasis is on the family, not the individual. Cultural characteristics of one spouse, such as open expression of feeling, may be considered odd when compared with norms of the other spouse. Likewise, traditions of verbal openness in one culture may run into traditions of emotional distancing in another (Brown & Brown, 2002). Rituals, joyfully celebrated in one culture, may not even exist in the other. One consequence of these differences is that family members' goals may be completely incompatible without one member or another abandoning some aspect of their culture.

These differences between couples in interracial families, while perhaps initially attractive, may later serve as flashpoints when other problems arise. They may see differences as deliberate attacks on other family members who do not share the values and norms of the "different" member. Boundaries that delineate the family system may also be sources of difficulty. In some cultures, the boundaries around the family are quite diffuse and include members such as in-laws or other relatives. This may seem strange or off-putting to a spouse who sees the family in much narrower terms. As is evident, all these issues may complicate the social worker–family relationship and present challenges in planning and goal setting.

Asian American Families

Asian Americans, like many ethnic families, are much more likely than interracial families to have an extended family as an important resource. This fact often derives from cultural values related to the role of the individual versus the role of the family. "In Korean culture, the family as a whole, rather than an individual member, is the central unit of society" (Choi, 1997, p. 91). This is also a common pattern among other Asian cultures. As Fong (1997) says, the extended Chinese "family has . . . been the primary dispenser of social support. Each extended family has taken it upon itself to guarantee the welfare and good behavior of all family members" (p. 36). Likewise, many Chinese families consider the community as a major source of support. The same is true for Koreans, who are likely to see their churches as playing a major role as a social and educational center, especially for new immigrants (Choi, 1997). This means that the family social worker must be aware of how a family's ethnicity may affect planning, particularly as it involves connecting families with social support resources. As might be expected, recently arrived immigrants may not have as strong a support network as more established families.

Other Asian cultural traits that may affect the planning process are the tendency for males to underreport problems and for women to hide feelings and emotions. Goals that involve changing basic roles of the adults may cause conflicts within the context of a culture that supports traditional gender expectations.

Fong (1997) also points out that extended family members in Chinese families may serve as barriers, especially if goals of family practice violate established norms and traditions. In addition, some groups, such as Asians, may be hesitant to use resources "outside of their ethnic communities because of inaccessibility, inappropriateness, and unavailability" (p. 44). The Chinese characteristic of valuing the family above the individual may affect planning, depending upon the goals sought by family members.

Latino Families

Like many Asian families, Latino culture commonly considers the family unit as more important than the individual. Extended family structure is another characteristic Latinos share with many Asian groups. Some authors have identified *fatalism* as a Latino belief that can have a major impact on planning and goal setting. Fatalism is a belief that "one's destiny is set, and one must live up to that fate with as much courage, strength, and self-respect that one can muster" (Bridger et al., 1997, p. 144). Clearly, this philosophy must be considered and discussed with the family if the social worker is to be successful in engaging members in planning.

Pierce and Elisme (1997) note that family involvement in goal planning may be problematic for Haitian families because of "learned passivity as a coping mechanism" (p. 49). They note that Haitians have learned through generations that being nonassertive can be an effective technique for getting along with others. This reluctance to take a major role in goal setting will need the social worker's attention. On the other hand, Wilk (1986) describes Haitians as a people with strong survival skills that may prove useful in practice. Like several other ethnic groups, Haitians tend to have strong ties to Catholicism, and a long tradition of extended family connections. At the same time, Haitian immigrants may have greater needs to learn nonpunitive child-rearing techniques that are consistent with values in this country. Because of reluctance to use formal resource planning, efforts aimed at connecting Haitians to self-help or mutual-aid groups are strongly recommended.

Other factors that may be important in planning are Haitians' traditional explanation of physical illness as caused by disturbances in body temperature, while they see mental health concerns arising from supernatural influences (Charles, 1986). Haitians are likely to rely on their spiritual resources when times are bad, another family strength that must be considered in planning. Formal contracting with Haitians can prove helpful in motivating families to become more active in resolving their own problems.

Keep in mind that the term *Latino* covers a wide territory and that the only characteristic shared by a Puerto Rican family and a Columbian family may be physical. Despite being lumped together into the same *race,* these families are unlikely to share the same *culture.* Factors such as socioeconomic class, religion, and geography may be of much greater import than a shared race.

Native American Families

Native Americans' willingness to share resources is a strength that should be incorporated into the planning process. "Generosity, sharing, and giving are highly valued," according to Weaver and White (1997, p. 69) because to give to another enhances one's own stature and respect among others. The extended family is a valued component of traditional Native American life, and sharing scarce resources is the norm. This means that other relatives outside the immediate family may be helpful and should be considered in the planning process. In addition, "members of tribes/Nations may be able to get services or funding for services through their Nations," a point that may be useful when other resources are not available (p. 78).

Sometimes, Native American resources such as traditional healers may be incorporated into the planning process. The advantage of this is threefold. First, traditional approaches tend to view the entire family as the focus of intervention, a model that is holistic, comprehensive, and consistent with social work's emphasis on the family-in-environment (Red Horse, 1997). Second, it ensures that all appropriate resources will be taken into consideration. Finally, this is consistent with Native American values that downplay the role of any one family member as the "identified patient."

Decision making around goals is more likely to occur through consensus and cooperation. However, the social worker should be careful about assuming that family members are all in agreement with a plan or set of goals. This is because the traditional Native American value of noninterference may result in the family agreeing with a plan simply to avoid conflict. Because of the historical traumas associated with Native Americans in this country, the social worker should also be sensitive to the role that a sense of loss plays in the family's life.

African American Families

African American families tend to enjoy an extended kinship network in many ways similar to other groups described previously (Green, 1994). Historically, the extended family unit has often served as a means of survival and can be an important resource for African American families today (McGee, 1997). In addition, Ho (1987) has argued that planning with African Americans (particularly low income) can only work when the practitioner has taken into account extrafamilial systems because these "draw upon the entire community and external systems which influence the lives of African American families" (p. 142). The church may be one such external resource when working with African American families.

Effects on Contracting

Ethnicity and cultural differences can also influence contracting. Contracting assumes a large measure of equality between social worker and family, but it also assumes that all parties understand the meaning of a contract. Families from different cultural backgrounds may find the notion of a contract confusing or be suspicious of the intentions of authority figures such as the practitioner. Power differentials may need to be overcome before those accustomed to lower power feel they have an equal role in the process (Ewalt & Mokuau, 1996).

Cultural Competence in Planning

We cannot overstate the importance of cultural competence in the planning and other helping phases. The Bridgers and colleagues (1997) study of family preservation practitioners found that they "actually possess only a smattering of culturally specific knowledge about the various ethnic groups with whom they work" (p. 154). For example, most were not aware of the importance of religion or the extended family among African Americans. Moreover, many possessed information about this group that was inaccurate and inconsistent with research findings. A similar, but less comprehensive, lack of knowledge was displayed concerning Latinos and other ethnic groups. The absence of key knowledge about various ethnic and cultural groups makes it unlikely that social workers can use the full range of options in arriving at a useful plan and set of goals.

Culturally competent planning requires several things. First, it is important that social workers know enough about themselves to recognize such things as built-in biases, deeply held stereotypes about the best ways of doing things, and values about one's own culture. Few people, if any, exist who are free from biases, as these are a reality for all human beings. Each of us has issues that can influence our ability to work with families from different racial or cultural groups. We can become aware of these through introspection, studying our own heritage, and being sensitive to feedback from others.

We also have to know enough about the culture of our clients to be of assistance to them. While few of us will become familiar with all cultures, learning as much as possible about the groups with whom one works is important. In one part of the country this may mean learning a great deal about Lakota heritage, while in another the focus may be on understanding Jewish culture. While we cannot assume that a family will be a certain way because of their cultural or racial background, it does give us a starting point from which to test assumptions.

We also need to be sensitive to the wide within-group differences that exist. Although two families are Korean, believing that one composed of third-generation U.S. citizens is going to think, feel, or believe the same things as another composed of first-generation immigrants would be foolish. Factors such as degree of assimilation or acculturation, or even lightness or darkness of skin, may result in significant differences that will influence planning and other stages. This is true of all groups.

The fact that cross-cultural and intra-cultural differences are so common suggests a degree of caution in trying to use any single approach in family practice. Ultimately, it probably is best to approach cultural differences as hypotheses that will gain or lose support only after testing. By learning directly from one's clients, being open to new understanding of cultural experiences, and maintaining an inquisitive nature, the social worker is better equipped to handle cultural, ethnic, and racial differences within the context of planning and goal setting. It is also helpful to remember that all families, whatever their cultural characteristics, are more similar than different.

7 CHAPTER | Implementation

© Michael Newman/PhotoEdit

INTRODUCTION

One of the more challenging aspects of family practice is the plethora of models available as part of the interventive approach. In this text, we have given you an overview of the different theories and their concepts. Continuing along these lines, in this chapter we will now present the models from specific theories and the related skills and techniques. For example, under the cognitive/behavioral model, the theories of behavior, cognition, communication, and systems all form the basis of skill development. Unlike many texts, we are not suggesting one model fits all. The models presented in this chapter are the basis for many family interventions, and their methods are utilized in the implementation stage. While a practitioner might choose a particular model for implementation with a family, it is more than likely that you will use several models and their techniques (Nichols & Schwartz, 2001). Therefore, this chapter addresses the basic skills and techniques that we can operationalize under the models presented. We have attempted to identify those models and techniques that researchers and practitioners have found most effective. The movement to use critically tested approaches evolves from several factors that we will address in the next section.

EVIDENCED-BASED PRACTICE

Evidenced-based practice is a term that is used today by many theorists and family practitioners. In short, the term implies that the effectiveness of a practice should be demonstrated by research and that practitioners should use that research when selecting an intervention. Health insurance agencies (third-party payers) and other funding bodies have emphasized the importance of using approaches that work. Professional organizations, licensing boards, and the public demand that practitioners demonstrate competence and employ only those theories, models, and techniques considered appropriate. Several recent news stories have focused on practitioners alleged to have used approaches that research has not supported. Loss of one's license, public condemnation, and both civil and criminal sanctions can accompany such lapses.

All this suggests strongly that when practitioners consider using one or more of the many theories reported in the literature, they must be aware of prior research on the approaches' effectiveness. This is also true when we choose models and techniques that derive from the theory. However, it is not sufficient that a theory is supported by past research. We have an obligation to consider whether these theories, models, and techniques have proven successful with families similar to those with whom we are working. An approach that has worked with enmeshed families may not be as useful with families dealing with substance abuse of one of its members. Likewise, techniques successful with couples may be less effective with entire families. This means that practitioners must keep current in their review of the literature on family practice. Being aware of what studies have been done with which family issues is a first step. The second step is to carefully examine these studies to decide which ones meet the highest standards of quality.

The importance of reviewing the quality of research does not mean that practitioners should limit themselves only to cognitive/behavioral models because they have been the most closely researched. While authors and practitioners have paid greater attention to such models, Hubble, Duncan, and Miller (1999) suggest that many other theories and models have been researched and found effective. Familiarity with this research is crucial, as care in choosing appropriate theories, models, and techniques is an ethical obligation of the family practitioner.

In line with this perspective, the following section presents basic skills and techniques shown to have been effective in working with individuals and families. With few exceptions, these skills and techniques are applicable to many different models. It is also important to differentiate the terms *skills* and *techniques* as they are used in this chapter. For example, a skill is something that is inherently part of your practice, while a technique is part of a particular process with identified stages. We will identify these as such as they are presented.

BASIC SKILLS AND TECHNIQUES

Basic skills and techniques discussed in this section include active listening, reflection, strengthening, reframing, identifying problems, problem solving, role playing, and warmth, empathy, and honesty.

Active Listening

Active listening is a skill that is developed through the process of carefully listening to a client in a way that reflects your understanding of what they have said. Pillari (2002, p. 181) has suggested that practitioners engage in four primary subtasks when active listening occurs:

1. Observing and understanding the client's nonverbal messages, including posture, facial expressions, movement and tone of voice
2. Listening to and understanding the client's verbal messages
3. Listening to the whole person in the context of the social setting of his life
4. Doing what Egan (1999) calls "tough-minded listening"

Active listening is not always an easy thing to do. It takes practice, patience, and an interest in a client from an empathetic perspective. Sometimes, there are situations in which clients have difficulty expressing themselves congruently and the family practitioner's ability to engage in active listening is limited. For example, consider a case where a family practitioner is trying to learn how a homework assignment went for the family.

THEORY IN ACTION | **Active Listening Limited**

FAMILY PRACTITIONER: Ms. Green, this is the second time I've met with you and your son. Last week we discussed that one way of better relating together would be to set aside an evening for doing something together. How did that work out?

MS. GREEN (*shifts noticeably in her chair and frowns*): It was fine. We went to McDonald's and then to a movie. (*The son slides farther down in his chair and makes an angry face.*)

FAMILY PRACTITIONER: How was it for you, Tim?

TIM (*loud voice, still with an angry face*): Oh, great! Just great!

FAMILY PRACTITIONER: I hear you both saying it was fine, but the look on your faces seems to suggest otherwise. What is that about?

MS. GREEN: No, really it was fine. Just fine! (*smiles*)

TIM (*angry face*): What are you now? A mind reader?

As you can see from this interaction, being an active listener has not helped here. However, a continuation of active listening done with patience and empathy will begin to break down barriers.

Reflection

Reflection is a term used to denote a "technique in which the social worker clarifies and shows the client what his or her feelings are right now and encourages further expression and understanding of those feelings" (Barker, 1999, p. 404). This type of reflection can be both verbal and nonverbal. When we are dealing with reflection of verbal messages, we are summarizing what the clients have said and conveying to them that we have understood them. It is used to help both you and the family understand the content of what is being said. Pillari (2002) states that content is the cognitive aspect of the message. While cognitive aspects of discussions can be based on the content of a thought that deals with a situation or a person, there is also the content that is not being said but that we can recognize by facial expression, tone of voice, posture, or client movement. Pillari calls this the affective aspect of the information being given. In a situation with a family member where we are attempting to summarize or pull together with reflection what he is saying, we must consider the affective aspect. Okun (1992) believes that most feelings fall into the seven categories of anger, fear, uncertainty, sadness, happiness, strength, and weakness. Hepworth et al. (1997) note the following additional categories: confusion, anxiety, rejection, inadequacy, caring, loneliness, guilt, and depression. As family practitioners pick up on these feelings, they need to be reflected back so the family and/or family member can correct or expand on the message they are giving. Consider, for example, a case in which a young woman is trying to express to her family her feelings about having AIDS.

THEORY IN ACTION | Reflection

DAUGHTER: I am so confused. I don't know what I did wrong. I did have sex, but I always use protection. I'm not sure how it happened. It feels like God is trying to punish me. (*Voice trembles; she starts crying.*) I also don't want my family to hate me. I know they hate me from the way they look at me. (*Looks over at other family members.*)

FAMILY PRACTITIONER: You're feeling confused at how this happened, and frightened and sad about having the disease. You're scared because you think your family hates you because you are sick.

DAUGHTER: I really am frightened about being alone with this.

Strengthening

Strengthening describes a technique by which we reinforce the family's strengths and encourage them to use their own resources to create change. Saleebey (1997, pp. 54–56) sees this technique as having four steps:

1. Acknowledge pain.
2. Stimulate the discourse and narratives of resilience and strength.
3. Act in context: education, action, advocacy and linkage.
4. Move toward normalizing and capitalizing upon one's strengths.

By following these steps, the family practitioner provides a strengthening process for the family and/or family member. We can see these steps in the example of a mother and father who are trying to help their son with his drug addiction. The family practitioner at the end of this example is moving the parents away from the present problem and having them think of what they hope they can do. The focus now will be on how they can use the strengths they are showing right now in this present crisis to achieve the goals.

THEORY IN ACTION | Strengthening

FAMILY PRACTITIONER: I know you are feeling a great deal of pain over your son being arrested. You seem in anguish.

MOTHER: I feel like I don't know where to turn or what to do. I can't sleep, I can't eat, and I worry constantly about his being in jail.

FAMILY PRACTITIONER: I know you are frightened and confused. How is the situation with the attorney and having your son released to your custody?

FATHER: The attorney says he can get him out today. I just don't know how we're going to get through this. He has such a problem. The attorney says if we can get him into a program that then the judge may let him go on probation since this is his first offense. He needs to be in a program. We've been looking for one all day today.

FAMILY PRACTITIONER: It sounds to me like you are doing everything you can. You have a good lawyer who has some good ideas on how to handle the situation. I know of several possible programs I can connect you with to see if they have an opening. I must tell you that I am really impressed by the way you have taken control of the situation and are moving forward to help your son. This family has many strengths to keep going the way you are.

MOTHER: I know he will go into a program willingly. He is so scared in that detention center.

FAMILY PRACTITIONER: I know you want what is best for your son. I think you have the strengths you need not only to see him through this but to encourage him to reach his goals. What are your hopes for him?

Reframing

Reframing is a technique used to help a family see a situation in a different context. For example, a three year old pinches a new sibling, and the parents are concerned that the child is too aggressive. As the family practitioner, you could go along with this understanding by the parents or you could present it in a new light, such as this being normal behavior of a young child when a new sibling enters the home. Of course, before giving this reframe of the situation, you will want to be certain that it is accurate and is something that the family can believe. If the three year old had been acting out aggressively before the new sibling arrived, the parents may rightly reject this interpretation. On the other hand, if this is not a common occurrence for their child, then this may be the appropriate reframe. Reframes are generally used to "emphasize the positive and appealing aspects of the most disturbing communication" (Pillari, 2002, p. 355). A reframe can also move the focus of a family problem away from that person. For example, in the case on reframing, the family has identified a child as the problem. Now, whether the family agrees with the practitioner or not is up to them. But it does aid in making a point about how much time they spend together doing something they do not want to do and how they could put that time to better use.

THEORY IN ACTION | **Reframing**

MOTHER: We try and we try, but she never does anything we want her to. She has terrible grades, doesn't do her chores, and breaks her curfew constantly.

FATHER: My wife and I have taken to staying up at night till she gets in and standing over her while she does her homework and completes her chores.

FAMILY PRACTITIONER: I realize this is not the kind of time you would like to be spending with her, but it is interesting that this behavior causes all of you to spend so much time together. I'm wondering if that time could be better spent with some fun activities.

Identifying Problems

Before beginning the discussion about identifying problems, it is important to point out that identifying problems and coming from a strength's-based perspective are not contradictory techniques. From a strengthening perspective, we have not ignored the problems but framed them so that the goals for a healthy family life assume greater importance. As we go through the steps in helping a family identify their problems, it is important to remember that this is an appropriate technique in all interventions.

Identifying problems is a technique that requires more then simply repeating what the client is saying. Families will present their problems as they see them; however, as they talk they may further explore their view of the problem and it may take a new form. It is important for the family practitioner to help all clients identify what they see as the problem. For family members to be involved in the family intervention, it is important that we hear and understand them. Thus, a wife may see the problem as her husband who works long hours, and the husband may see the problem as his wife nagging at him when he is home. As they discuss and explore the problem with the family practitioner, they may come to see the problem as composed of different things. These might include their lack of mutual interests, the difference in priorities for the family, and/or the lack of lovemaking going on in the relationship. The initial complaints about working too hard and nagging may turn out to be the way they were acting out the actual problems within the family.

In identifying the problem, Hepworth et al. (1997) suggest that "the problem identified by clients typically involves a deficiency of something needed (e.g., health care, adequate income or housing, companionship, harmonious family relationships, self esteem) or an excess of something that they do not want (e.g., fear, guilt, temper outbursts, marital or parent–child conflict, or addiction)" (p. 205). For the family practitioner, the problem might be a combination of these situations that have a domino effect on one another. For example, the lack of health care may cause feelings of guilt in a parent because he does not have the means to take care of the child. This may take the form of depression that the family members identify initially as the problem. It is up to the family practitioner to help the family sort through the problems and prioritize what is most important.

Sometimes, the situation may be so confusing to family members that they are unable to articulate the basic underlying issues. Challenging families early in practice around their definition of the problem is not helpful. Through a series of questions, the family practitioner can begin to gain an understanding of how individual members view the problem. While these problems might differ, it is good for the family practitioner to try to bring these ideas together for one formulation. So, for example, a mother complains that her son does not listen to her and the son says that his mom is always yelling at him. The family practitioner might then structure this around the problem of communication between the mother and son. Hanna and Brown (1999, pp. 147–148) suggest the following questions to begin to elicit a formulation of the problem:

1. What brings you here?
2. What would be helpful for us to discuss?
3. Who first noticed the problem and how long ago was this?
4. What led you (or another person) to conclude that this was a problem?
5. Who else agrees or disagrees that this is the problem?
6. Who else (inside or outside the family) has an opinion about the problem?
7. Have you or anyone else thought of any other possibilities regarding what the problem might be?
8. Are there times when the problem isn't occurring? What is going on at those times?
9. What are the differences between times when the problem does and doesn't occur?
10. What will happen if things don't change?

Helping family members sort through these questions, both individually and as a family, supports the formulation of a mutual identification of the problem and the goals to be set in the intervention. Adding more questions that detail out the reasons family members have these problems aids you in understanding how differences in the view of the problem arose.

Problem Solving

Problem solving is a term that writers use as the name of a theory, a model of practice, and a technique. In this section, it is the description of problem solving as a technique that we will address. Often, a family lacks the skills needed to problem solve. They feel helpless and hopeless in the overwhelming burden of the issue, and even if they knew how to resolve a problem, they could not do so now. Problem solving is not just about the therapist applying the technique, but it is also about teaching clients to use the steps through explicit instructions and/or role modeling. Hepworth et al. (1997, p. 415) describe the following steps as part of the problem-solving process.

Acknowledge the Problem Before beginning to resolve any problem, the family must acknowledge a problem. As seen in identifying problems, not everyone in a family will agree on what the problem is or, sometimes, even think there is a problem. So to acknowledge a problem means that the family practitioner must bring together each person's concerns and provide a reasoning for what the problem is. It is also important to acknowledge that there is more than one problem.

Analyze the Problem and Identify the Needs of Participants This second part of the process is more difficult but also very important. Without understanding each person's point of view and needs, we cannot arrive at a solution to everyone's satisfaction. Even in circumstances where one solution cannot satisfy everyone, efforts need to gather as much information about a family member's needs as possible. Being able to help each person express his or her needs requires special skills on the part of the family practitioner. Hepworth et al. (1997, pp. 416–417) suggest the following steps in this process:

1. Explain that the most effective solution to a problem is the one that best meets the needs of everyone concerned.
2. Clarify that the needs of every person are important and that no one will be left out in the problem solving process. We will ask all persons in turn to identify their needs, and we will ask others to listen attentively and to try to understand, seeking clarification as needed.
3. Ask for a volunteer to write down needs as the family identifies them. If no one volunteers, you may request that a person serve as a recorder or do it yourself.
4. Ask each person in succession to identify his or her personal need, encouraging open discussion and requesting clarification when expressed needs are vague or confusing. Begin with the person who initially identified a problem. Ensure that needs are recorded, and have the recorder check with participants to ascertain that their needs are accurately worded and that none are omitted.

After each person has identified his or her needs, it is now time to bring the concerns together. You may accomplish this by doing the following:

1. Explain to the family that each of their needs and their definition of the problem affect all family members.
2. Repeat the needs that you have heard and have been recorded. Ask family members if they think any of the problems and needs are similar.
3. Help prioritize the problems and needs into a smaller number.

Employ Brainstorming to Generate Possible Solutions During this phase, the use of brainstorming is important to resolving the problem, as it gives the family the opportunity to share thoughts and ideas about what could be done. The family then is really a part of the process of resolving the problem. Brainstorming needs to be done in an open environment in order for the family to discuss all possible solutions. Encourage family members to refrain from criticism and interruption while this is occurring (Hepworth et al., 1997).

Evaluate Each Option, Considering the Needs of Each Participant Allowing for open discussion about the possible alternatives is an important step toward finding a possible solution. As each family member discusses the ideas, try to summarize the needs each solution might meet. Help the family narrow down the solutions to one so they might implement it. The selection needs to be based on the one that meets the most needs of all family members.

Implement the Option Selected Once an option is selected, it is now time to implement the solution. This will involve the participation of all the family members. Commonly, you may still have a family member who is not completely committed to the solution, and this is all right. Follow through on implementing the solution and observe whether the family member is attempting to work with the idea or sabotage it. If one or more members raise obstacles, then an open discussion in the family on how to handle these issues is critical.

Evaluate the Outcome of Problem-Solving Efforts The final step in the process is to evaluate the outcome of the solution the family selected. If this solution is working, then you can move to other issues that surfaced but were not chosen as the highest priority. If the solution did not work or does not meet the needs of thc family, then discussion around an alternative solution is very important. They then implement this and go through the same stages in the implementation and evaluation process.

Role Playing

Role playing is another technique that we use frequently in individual and family practice. J. L. Moreno developed role playing in the 1920s through the application of psychodrama (Barker, 1999). Role-playing allows family members to deal with issues within the safety of the family session. In role playing, the person takes on either her own persona or that of another person. She then can practice with the family practitioner or another family member ways to handle an upcoming situation. She may also play the role of another person with that individual to give her an idea of what the other person may be feeling. This technique has also been used with past issues to confront those individuals family members can no longer confront, such as those who may have died. There are five basic steps in this process:

1. Explain to the family member what a role play (behavioral rehearsal) is.
2. Encourage the family member to portray either himself or another person (depending upon the purpose of the role play) as accurately as he can.
3. Before the role play begins, ask the family member/s to think about what they are feeling during the role play. Help them focus in on their own interactions.

4. During the role play, family members may want to stop and think about the best way to handle the situation and change some of their comments.
5. Following the role play, help the family members discuss what occurred and how they felt about it. They may also want to discuss some alternatives to the approach they took.

Warmth, Empathy, and Honesty

Warmth, empathy, and honesty are skills that we have already discussed in Chapter 3; however, their importance is worth noting again, as these skills count for almost 30 percent of the effectiveness of an intervention. The family practitioner, in implementing these skills, must be comfortable with them. If the practitioner attempts to present these qualities without it being real, family members will know. You must examine yourself before displaying these skills. Are you feeling this way or are you playing a role? What is occurring that you do not feel this way toward that family or family member? Are there things in your own life that are affecting this? Examining these issues and being honest with yourself will create an atmosphere of caring and concern needed in every meeting with the family.

OVERARCHING MODELS

In this section of the implementation chapter, we will examine some overarching models produced based on particular theories discussed in Chapter 2. We will describe each of these models briefly, including the specific concepts underlying the model, the objectives of the model, intervention planning, and techniques. It is important to understand that the authors are not suggesting that you use any particular family practice approach. The most recent work done in family practice has generally included an integration of several models. This section is simply to provide an overview of basic concepts in different approaches.

Psychodynamic/Psychoanalytic

From a psychodynamic theory base, several different models of practice have been developed for working with families. The original psychodynamic models have led more recently to a model that hinges on "object relations," in which the primary focus is on the client's sense of self and past and present relationships with significant others (Borden, 2002). However, these models share some basic concepts regarding practice. While we will examine no one model specifically here, the following six concepts fit across most psychodynamic family practice models:

1. Issues in family of origin affect the present relationships within the family. In this context, the parents, who were raised in their own families, are

strongly influenced by what happened to them and the relationships they had with their parents, siblings, and extended family.

2. Individuals with unresolved issues from their family of origin often attempt to work through them within their present family relationships. For example, an unresolved issue between a woman and her parent over an attachment issue may surface again in the relationship between the woman and her own daughter.
3. Individuals are the focus of intervention within the context of a family session. This does not preclude the family as a whole being a focal point, but most of the work is done with individuals as it relates to their family of origin. For example, a woman with unresolved issues with her own mother may focus on these to work through them first personally and then interpersonally.
4. It is through insight into unconscious memories that partners can work through their own individual relationships. For example, a husband who has idealized his mother places this idealization onto his wife. The husband, through his work in psychodynamic family therapy, comes to realize that his mother is not the idealized figure he has in his mind. Thus, the pressure on the wife to live up to unrealistic expectations is changed.
5. When roles are not complementary in a family, disturbances occur. These disturbances often lead to the *scapegoating* of one family member. Scapegoating occurs when the family identifies one individual member as the cause of the family's problems. Scapegoating often occurs as a way to deflect attention from the parents' interpersonal difficulties. Scapegoats, as part of the family dynamics, will act in the manner attributed to them to pull focus off the real difficulties in the marriage.
6. In many cases, individual family members may need to be challenged by the practitioner to look further into their emotions and interactions so that insight may emerge. A family practitioner might challenge a nonverbal presentation of hopelessness although the family member denies feeling hopeless. These challenges allow for individuals to understand their past and see how their emotions are affecting their current family behavior.

Objectives According to Nichols and Schwartz (2001), "the goal of psychoanalytic family therapy is to free family members of unconscious restrictions so that they'll be able to interact with one another as whole, healthy persons" (p. 213). This goal is connected directly to the relationship all family members have to their families of origin and any subsequent unconscious thoughts or emotions as they pertain to the family of origin. From a psychodynamic perspective, the interpersonal relationship between the parents is a reflection of how they related to their own parents. Dysfunctional relationships then reflect the individual's own past traumas. They subsequently pass on these past traumas to their children, and the children's behavior reflects this. Through insight and interpretation, there is a strengthening of an individual's sense of self-worth. There is also a reduction in interpersonal conflict and an increase in more satisfying relationships (Goldenberg & Goldenberg, 1991).

Intervention Planning The process through which individuals can make these changes in their life begins with formation of the therapist–family member relationship. Through a direct focus on early childhood experiences with the parents, the family begins to change in its interaction and improve. Ackerman (1966) states that families are helped by learning to "accommodate to new experiences, to cultivate new levels of complementarity in family role relationships, to find avenues for the solution of conflict, to build a favorable self-image, to buttress critical forms of defense against anxiety and to provide support for further creative development" (pp. 90–91). For Ackerman, complementarity signifies the interpersonal pattern in communication where one individual harmoniously interacts with another individual. An example would be the case of a husband whose stability matches his wife's spontaneity. Both husband and wife are complementary in this manner.

Techniques The following are five techniques used in the psychodynamic/psychoanalytic model:

1. *Engaging the relationship* is a skill that is crucial to the psychodynamic family practitioner. While we have discussed this process in other sections of the book, it is important to highlight it here since this skill leads to a safe environment in which family members can discuss their conscious and unconscious "family of origin" issues.
2. *Listening* and *challenging empathetic response* are skills utilized in the psychodynamic family model to help family members feel heard and safe while allowing for emergence of emotions and feelings related to past experiences. Through challenging empathetic and honest response, the family practitioner can model those expressions so badly needed within the family.
3. *Interpretation* is a technique that helps a family and its members see how these past issues are affecting the family in the "here and now." Unlike early individual psychodynamic approaches that called for the therapist to listen with little response, the psychodynamic family model involves the active participation of the family practitioner. Honest presentation of self by the family practitioner and the interactive presence brings those same characteristics out in the family.
4. *Transference* is an occurrence in family practice that encourages the family member to interact with the family practitioner as if she were a figure from the past with whom the family member has unresolved issues. In the psychodynamic family model, family practitioners encourage transference so the family member can work through her "family of origin" issues with the practitioner.
5. *Encouraging the individuation of children* and *the building of self-worth for each family member* are techniques that enhance the growth of the family and produce the healthy relationships needed for a stable family life. As children become their own people and can interact with their parents as individuals, healthier relationships arise. The building of individual self-worth for all members encourages relationships that are honest and respectful of one another's needs.

Experiential

Models of family therapy related to communication theory (known also as experiential family therapy), were prominent during the 1960s and 1970s. Carl Whitaker and Virginia Satir were two of the best-known leaders in this field. Carl Whitaker was a psychiatrist trained in traditional psychoanalytic theory. He came to believe in the humanity of men and in their drive to self-fulfillment. His work with young schizophrenics and children led to his focus on family therapy. Satir was a social worker who focused much of her work on the communication patterns families employed as they sought to have their needs met. The experiential family model came as a result of the "phenomenological techniques (Gestalt therapy, psychodrama, client-centered therapy, the encounter group movement) so popular in the individual therapy approaches of the 1960s" (Goldenberg & Goldenberg, 1991, p. 115). Like their psychodynamic counterparts, experiential family practitioners are authentic, caring individuals who challenge and confront family member experiences. Unlike their psychodynamic counterparts, they focus on the "here and now" and do not spend time on past "family of origin" issues. There are five basic concepts underlying most models of the experiential family approach.

1. Interventions focus on the growth of the individual within the family context. Whitaker saw individuals from a self-actualizing perspective and believed individuals were always able to grow to their own potential. His concept of this within the family context was to focus on growth of family members in the "here and now" (within the therapy sessions) (Whitaker & Keith, 1981).
2. Openness and spontaneity rather than theory and technique are a major part of the experiential family approach. Experiential family models do not focus on theory and technique, believing that change occurs in the process of the relationship between the family practitioner and client. The family practitioner's role is to react honestly in the sessions and allow the family to respond in a way that provides information and forces the family to take responsibility and to take initiative for their own lives.
3. The experiential family model calls for the personal involvement of practitioners to be themselves and be open to the needs of the family. In this model, family practitioners grow from the experience and learn valuable information about themselves that they can take into sessions in a different way.
4. Experiential family practitioners believe in a positive humanity rather than a pessimistic point of view. They accept the person for who he is and believe in the positive outlook that the person was always striving to self-actualize.
5. The flexibility in family roles and rules is a strong underlying basis of experiential family treatment. By encouraging family members to be flexible in their roles and their rules, they challenge themselves to view the other side of a situation and be creative in the types of changes they make. An example of this might be when a family practitioner suggests that a child should interact with the father as if he (the child) were the father.

Through this process, the child begins to experience his father's role and it allows him to understand better the father's point of view.

Objective The objective of the experiential family model is to help the family achieve an opportunity for each member to self-actualize. Through family members taking part in their own growth, they are able to be their own creative selves. This growth takes precedence over reduction of symptoms. Thus, the experiential practitioner exposes the uniqueness of each family member and, through communication, helps the individual members grow to their fullest capacity. For example, we might ask a mother who worries about her daughter's safety to describe how her daughter must feel when the mother worries. Through this type of experience, the mother creatively thinks outside herself as if she were the daughter, which causes her to experience this concern from a new perspective and role.

Intervention Planning Whitaker (1977) describes four phases of treatment. The first is the pretreatment phase, when family practitioners establish themselves as the expert. This is also the period when we include the whole family in the therapeutic process. While family practitioners view themselves as expert, they still ask the family members to think creatively for themselves and to confront their own difficulties.

In the second phase of treatment, through empathetic confrontation and authenticity, the family is encouraged to look at themselves in a different way and to communicate these new emotions and feelings to one another. We see growth of family members as occurring from these interchanges.

In the third phase of treatment, the family is encouraged to continue their growth through their own actions, enabling the family practitioner to take a less active role. The final phase occurs as the family begins to separate from the therapist and learns the importance of "joy" in their own freeing experiences.

Techniques There are six techniques used in the experiential model:

1. We have discussed *I statements* in other sections of the text; however, for the experiential therapist, it is critical for both practitioners and family members to model the technique. By using "I" statements, the experiential practitioner and the family members reinforce the differences between themselves and begin the process of developing individuality for each family member. Toward the final stages in this process, the practitioner also encourages a "we" mind-set to unite the family as one.
2. We utilize *confrontation* and *challenge* to create an environment of creative thinking. For Whitaker, the more creative an individual is, the more progress she can accomplish. Whitaker's confrontations are often hard hitting and empathetic. Known for using the absurd, Whitaker would challenge a person's actions with reasons that did not make any sense. By doing so, he encourages family members to respond with authentic feelings they may have mislabeled. For example, a father who complains that

his son does not do his chores might be told that in order for him to feel better about the family, he needs to do the chores himself so he will not be angry.

3. *Family sculpturing* is a technique utilized by Satir. It was developed by Duhl, Kantor, and Duhl (1973). Designed to help the family view themselves from a physical perspective, family sculpturing directs family members to place individuals in the family in the position they see them. For example, a distant member might be placed at a distance from the rest of the family. Thus, all members are placed spatially in relationship to one another. For example, a mother who is very controlling of her husband and children might be placed in the center of the sculpture, attempting to hold on to all her family members. We would then ask the mother to express her feelings about being placed in this position.
4. Whitaker sees *co-therapy* as a necessity in doing experiential family practice. Co-therapy is viewed as a way to create more variability in the approach, to decrease the amount of practitioner pathology from intruding, and to allow the practitioner time to think (Whitaker & Keith, 1981).
5. *Redefining the symptom* is the technique in which we redefine a symptom to fit another meaning. Sometimes, redefining the symptom may be part of redefining who is at the core of the difficulties. The family may have singled out one person as the identified patient, but an experiential practitioner might attempt to include all in the pathology. For example, a woman who claims her husband never loved her because he has tried to kill her might be asked, "How can you say he doesn't love you? Why else would he want to kill you?" (Whitaker & Keith, 1981). These types of responses are inclusive of all members in the absurdity of the situation and enable family members to look at their own feelings behind their definition of the problem.
6. *Modeling communication* is a key technique and was very important to Satir. She would often demonstrate to parents how they need to respond to their children. She would also interact with parents in ways that she hoped the parents would interact with their own children. We can see an example of this in a case where she demonstrated to a father the best way to get his son's attention. She took the father's arm with both hands and showed how he should look his child in the eye and explain that he will not let him hurt himself or others. This type of modeling enabled Satir to change interactions in a meaningful way.

Structural

A leading theorist in structural family therapy was Salvadore Minuchin. Originally educated in psychoanalysis, Minuchin believed his approach to family practice "was founded on the immediacy of the present reality, was oriented to solving problems, and was above all contextual, referring to the social environment that is a part of and the setting for an event" (Aponte & VanDeusen, 1981, p. 310). Other concepts underlying this approach are as follows:

- The family serves as the basic unit for human systems (Brown & Christensen, 1999). In this regard, we see the family as its own organism, not one made up of many parts.
- Within the family system, there are subsystems that operate between members of the family. An example of a subsystem might be the parents, or it may be the children or simply an individual within the family. Subsystems can often cross generational lines, such as when a parent and a child are aligned against another parent.
- Families structure their system and subsystems through boundaries, alignment, and power, which serve as the demarcation of relationships and interactional patterns. For example, a family without boundaries would have family members who are intrusive in each other's personal business (like on the television series *Everybody Loves Raymond*). An alignment between a father and a son might give more power to the son than the mother because of his relationship with the father.
- The foundation of this model is that the family has to be understood in terms of the relationship between its parts (family members) (Aponte & VanDeusen, 1981).
- Changing the structure of the family creates change in a family. By this, we mean that changing the functions and interactions within the family may call for the changing of power relationships and alignments of family members with one another. An example is a family with a passive mother and a daughter who carries a more powerful role. When we give the mother more say in what happens in the family, the role of the oldest daughter will diminish, and the subsystems will be realigned.

Objective The overall goal of the structural family practitioner, according to Umbarger (1983), "should be the repositioning of individual family members within their primary and secondary subsystems, with an attendant opportunity to form new and healthier alliances and structures" (pp. 30–31). The objective then is tied to the movement of family members into their appropriate subsystems within the family, such as the parental subsystem and the child subsystem, and to develop healthy alliances within and among all subsystems. These types of changes then lead to organizational realignments within the family and modifications in the transactions and interactions between family members.

Intervention Planning The underlying belief in structural family therapy is that families who are in trouble have dysfunctional structures maintaining the problem. The process through which structural family therapists move is that of "joining" with a family, "accommodating" to their frame of reference, and "restructuring" the structures within the family (Nichols & Schwartz, 2001). This method encourages the therapist to share with the family those relationships which maintain a dysfunctional structure and then reframe and reinforce for them the new more healthy structures.

Techniques The following are nine techniques used in the structural family model:

1. *Staging* is the process by which the family practitioner has a treatment plan staged. This may mean you begin working with the entire family and then move to small family units or sometimes stage the seating of family members so they interact with one another as the rest of the family observes (Umbarger, 1983).
2. *Accommodation* is the process of joining with the family by displaying characteristics similar to the family. It also involves the family practitioner respecting the family's communication style, structure, and rules. For example, an accommodation might be done by a structural family practitioner who kids with the family as they come into the office because the family often does this with the practitioner.
3. *Tracking* is the following of the family's communication so that the family understands that we are hearing them. This may involve the family practitioner's communication style of questioning or feedback, or it may involve the restating of comments in a way that emphasizes what is being heard but not said. For example, a partner complains because the other partner spends too much time in the gym. The family practitioner's response might entail a comment that speaks to how the partners are not sharing time together in activities such as exercise.
4. *Enactment* is a technique that entails the family bringing a situation into the family therapy session that is occurring at home. The family is asked to demonstrate how this situation would occur, and the therapist maps out ways in which they could handle the situation differently. The family then practices this new way in the session.
5. *Unbalancing* is a technique a structural family practitioner might use to change an interaction in a family. He might, for example, side with a family member who is in a low power position to change the power structure within the family. For example, a daughter who has very little power in the family might gain power by the practitioner taking her side in an interaction.
6. *Reconstruction* occurs in a family after the presiding alignments have been challenged between family members and the family is attempting to restructure itself into a new organization. The structural family practitioner believes realigning different subsystems within the family helps this reconstruction.
7. *Alteration of sequences* occurs when the practitioner begins to maneuver the interactional sequences between family members into different ones. An example might be when a structural family practitioner encourages a husband who has little to say about child raising to discuss with his son the rules he wants in the family.
8. *Mimesis* is a technique by which the therapist joins with the family through imitating characteristics of family members or by sharing a personal story that is similar to the family's experience. This type of activity

brings the practitioner closer to the family through members identifying with specific behaviors. For example, a structural family practitioner might begin slapping his/her knee as an expression of identification with a mother who does the same.

9. *Family mapping* is the process by which the structural family practitioner maps out the schemas that the family is carrying out. She then uses the family's organizational structure to chart diagnostically the structures and transactions in the family. Lines and demarcations that show the differences between family members generally delineate this map. For example, consider a family where there is overinvolvement of one parent with a child against the father, as seen in this diagram.

The practitioner's goal is to reestablish the parental structure or dyad as a unit and place the child back into the typical family alignment. Thus, the outcome would appear as shown here.

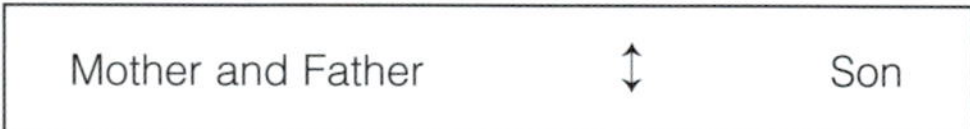

Cognitive/Behavioral

Models of cognitive-behavioral family practice range from basic behavioral or cognitive approaches to those that incorporate both. Recently, those models engaging in both theories have been most widely used. Family systems theory began to play a large part in the development of cognitive-behavioral methods around the 1980s (Nichols & Schwartz, 2001). Nichols and Schwartz (2001) note "that within this framework, family relationships, cognitions, emotions, and behavior are viewed as exerting mutual influence on one another, so that a cognitive inference can evoke emotion and behavior and emotion and behavior can likewise influence cognition" (p. 291).

While there are many different models of family therapy that incorporate cognitive-behavioral approaches, there are some general concepts underlying them all. Among the basic concepts of cognitive-behavioral family models are these:

- Situations within the family are based in the present time and not in past interactions. In this case, we would not ask the family about their family of origin, but we would discuss their present family life.
- Therapeutic models are based on the more conscious aspects of the personality. The implication here is that cognitive-behavioral aspects of a personality are generally conscious and not hidden in the unconscious.

- Communication is considered the most important feature of a good relationship (Gottman, Markman, & Notarius, 1977).
- Problems are believed to come from learned behaviors that are present in the current situation and surface in the cognitions employed by family members. For example, a child learns to manipulate his environment by throwing tantrums and does so in order to get what he wants. When family members decide what they are going to do as a family, they consider the child's feelings first to avoid the tantrums.
- The social exchange model is a basis for most couple and family relationships. In this model, a good relationship occurs when what one gives is balanced with what one gets (Thibaut & Kelley, 1959). For example, a wife who thinks of her husband when she shops by buying items he may need, may find herself feeling appreciated when the husband brings home flowers regularly.
- As family members come to understand their thoughts and family relationships, they will begin to engage in better communication and problem solving with each other (Schwebel & Fine, 1992).

Objectives In this section, we will specifically consider a cognitive-behavioral approach to family practice. This model "focuses on the underlying conditions, beliefs, and attributions that maintain the problem situation" and behaviors (Gehart & Tuttle, 2003). Nichols and Schwartz (2001) maintain that "the general goals of behavioral family therapy are to increase the rate of rewarding exchanges, to decrease aversive exchanges, and to teach communication and problem solving skills" (p. 297).

Intervention Planning There are many different approaches to cognitive-behavioral family therapy. The basic construct, however, involves the following process, according to Schwebel and Fine (1992):

1. *Rapport building* entails practitioners building their relationship with the family.
2. *Assessment of the family situation* occurs, in terms of feelings, thoughts, and behaviors.
3. *Personal application of concepts* is where the practitioner explains cognitive-behavioral family therapy to the family and they begin the process of identifying their own dysfunctional thoughts and behaviors.
4. *Preliminary cognitive change* occurs following Step 3 through the understanding the family has gained about their own thought processes. As they begin to think differently about things, they begin to communicate differently.
5. *Initiating behavioral change and assessing its impact* is the final step in the process. Different communication and behavior patterns within the family will cause feelings and emotions to change. We then assess or evaluate this and make appropriate modifications in the process to aid the family.

Techniques Six techniques are used in the cognitive/behavioral model:

1. *Shaping* is a term referring to the gradual increase in performance of a desired behavior. For example, a given behavior might include several subtasks that lead to the total behavior. Learning to ride a bike, for example, requires acquiring balance, peddling, and steering before one can safely ride. Reinforcements and/or punishments might be used to increase the likelihood of each subtask occurring until they achieve the whole behavior. For example, a mentally challenged adult who is learning to do his laundry is reinforced for gathering his laundry together, putting the clothes in a washer, putting in the detergent, and then pressing the buttons on the machine.
2. *Contingency contracting* refers to an agreement between two or more individuals, one of whom agrees to perform a desired behavior in exchange for some type of response from the other person. Becvar and Becvar (2003) note that contingency contracting is developed from a negotiated process with a specific reward for each person who carries out their end of the contract. The contract itself specifies the conditions under which the reinforcement will be given.
3. *Intermittent reinforcement* is a process of providing positive reinforcement on an irregular basis. This causes the desired behavior to be maintained with the anticipation of a reinforcement. The reinforcement is then given to maintain the behavior. For example, initially they may give a child a comic book every time a homework assignment is completed. Over time, the child would not receive the comic book each time but would receive it intermittently. This process would then encourage and maintain the homework behavior because of the expectation of a possible reinforcement.
4. *Psychoeducation* "involves teaching the cognitive-behavioral conceptualization of anxiety and its treatment" (Ginsburg & Schlossberg, 2002). In this process, the practitioner educates the family and its members about how anxiety can manifest itself and teaches strategies to family members on how to decrease this anxiety. For example, we might teach a person who chokes often due to emotional anxiety about why that is happening and how she can prevent it through specific strategies related to thoughts and the changing of the anxiety situations.
5. *Cognitive restructuring* is a technique utilized in most cognitive-behavioral situations. In this process, we help the family member to identify distorted thoughts. We then ask them to evaluate whether or not those thoughts are based in reality. Then the family member receives help in replacing negative thoughts with more realistic ones and thus more realistic behaviors (Ginsburg & Schlossberg, 2002).
6. *Problem solving* is a technique that we have addressed earlier in this chapter. It is important to recognize the important role that problem solving has in the cognitive-behavioral approach, as the process deals with the thoughts of the individual and how she can modify those thoughts through changes in thinking. For example, as a mother recognizes the problem she has with a child, she may think about all the ways she can

change that situation, pick one method she has thought of, and then attempt to make that change and evaluate its outcome. This all involves thought processes.

Postmodern

Postmodern models of family practice have developed over the last 15 years in response to older models of practitioners being seen as instrumental and patriarchal, with the therapist serving as the expert in the family's process. In postmodern models, the approach is established in conversation and mutual meaning making (Miller, Hubble, & Duncan, 1996). Two of the major models that come from postmodern thinking are solution-focused practice and narrative therapy. These models have developed enormous popularity over recent years, due in part to their brief structure and the mutual work of both the clients and the practitioner. While we will deal specifically with solution-focused therapy and narrative therapy, it is important to understand the underlying concepts of postmodern approaches. These include the following:

1. Postmodern models of family practice are a collaborative process between the practitioner and the family. By this we mean that the relationship between the social worker and the family is not hierarchical, and we give the family the information so that they can change their life in any way they want.
2. Treatment is focused on the future, where the family can still resolve issues, rather than on the past.
3. We assume that clients do want to change and that there are no underlying subconscious forces preventing this.
4. Language is the vehicle for change in that solution-focused practitioners believe that how we talk about a situation often determines its outcome. So, a family who talks negatively about how they cannot change things probably cannot change them. In contrast, one that talks about how positive things will be in the future will work toward those changes.
5. Clients have strengths and past successes that they can use to change their future. Social workers can usually locate times when the family successfully coped with challenges and developed strengths that can be used to overcome the current difficulties.

Objectives of Solution-Focused Therapy The objective of solution-focused family therapy is to provide a setting in which families can set goals and seek solutions to their issues. They do this through language as they self-identify problems. Why or how problems occurred is not part of the process. The focus is on how they will achieve the solution. "The goal is to expand understandings and possibilities" (Franklin & Jordan, 1999, p. 148).

Intervention Planning in Solution-Focused Therapy Generally, solution-focused family practice occurs over a brief treatment time frame, ranging from 6 to 12 weeks. During this time, we ask families several different questions that focus them on how they can be different from what they are now. Additionally, we ask families to carry out set tasks that can help move a situation along to where they would like it to be. The family and the social worker work in tandem to make the changes through concentration on conversational outcomes and planning for when there is no longer a problem.

Techniques for Solution-Focused Therapy The following are five techniques used in solution-focused therapy:

1. *Formula tasks* are assignments given to all clients. These are tasks that seem to produce more positive outcomes. An example of this, as cited by Nichols and Schwartz (2001, p. 376) is the one given in the first session that asks the family or family member to think about what happens in their lives that they would like to continue. This type of question pulls the person from thinking about the negative and into thinking about the positive. Tasks such as these are important techniques for moving the client forward in solution-focused family practice.
2. *Miracle questions* are those that help set goals for the solution-focused family practitioner and family. Generally, we ask the question "If you could wake up tomorrow with a miracle having happened, what would your life look like?" This type of question sets the tone for resolution of the difficulty and for thinking about how this change might take place.
3. *Exception questions* are those questions that ask not about the problem but about clients' lives when those problems did not exist. This again focuses attention on the positive aspects of the family's life and how their life would be without those problems.
4. *Scaling questions* are employed to signify change within any situation. A scaling question would be one in which we ask the family to measure on a scale where they are in relationship to a given situation. For example, we might ask a family member who is feeling discouraged to rank himself between 1 (being low) and 10 (being high) about how he feels today. If he were to say "5,", we may ask him to say where he thinks he will be in 3 months or how he was before the 5. In doing this, the practitioner is, from a positive perspective, encouraging the family member to see where he has come from and where he may be going.
5. *Coping questions* help the family consider ways in which they are coping with their current challenges. They help the family recognize the strengths they are employing in their current situation and may help uncover solutions that work at least part of the time. Thus, we may ask a family "What have you found helpful so far?" (De Jong & Berg, 2002, p. 235). Such techniques maximize client strengths and their sense of competence for confronting their problems.

Objectives of Narrative Therapy The objective of narrative therapy "is to help clients first understand the stories around which they have organized their lives and then to challenge and broaden them, thus creating new possibilities" (Kelly, 2002, p. 121). Clients are helped to do this by first viewing different aspects of their lives that do not have anything to do with those problems, aspects such as their skills, talents, and strengths. As they begin to see these different aspects, they begin to change the story they have created of their lives and bring into focus a more positive one.

Intervention Planning in Narrative Therapy The course of treatment generally follows three stages. These include the following, according to Nichols and Schwartz (2001):

1. The first stage is one in which the problem is seen as an externalizing force, one which has powerful effects on the individual and causes each person to create a negative story about themselves.
2. The second stage is where positive aspects of the self are found in instances of success, self-fulfillment, and times when their skills and strengths show through.
3. The third stage occurs when the person seeks out support for her new, more positive story by sharing it with others.

Techniques for Narrative Therapy Narrative therapists use many different types of techniques. Because the narrative model is one which challenges the idea that the person has a problem or problems that affect every aspect of their life, the main focus is on the cognitions they have about themselves and their "story." To get at these cognitions, individuals in a family are asked different types of questions:

1. *Deconstruction questions* or questions that aid the client in seeing that the problem is not him
2. *Opening space questions* or those that look for positive times when the problem did not control the client's life
3. *Preference questions* or questions in which clients are asked about times when the problem did not affect them and if this was good or bad
4. *Story development questions,* when a new story is gathered from the positive experiences without the problem
5. *Meaning questions* that challenge negative perceptions of self and emphasize positive perceptions (Nichols & Schwartz, 2001).

Additionally, in narrative therapy, techniques that involve the use of good listening skills are very important as is the use of externalization, which emphasizes moving the problem away from being part of the person.

While many of the models described in this chapter have set the basic path of family treatment for many years, new models of intervention, such as narrative therapy, have begun to be utilized in many family situations. These new models, like those before them, have provided a means for social workers to intervene and help families. The major models here have been shown to be effective in many different family situations.

8 CHAPTER Evaluation, Termination, and Follow-Up

© Tony Freeman/PhotoEdit

INTRODUCTION

Evaluation is a critical step in the structure of practice for several reasons. First, evaluating the effectiveness of our practice is an ethical responsibility of the social worker. If we are truly committed to aiding families, then we must be equally dedicated to determining whether our assistance to them has been helpful. Practicing without ensuring effectiveness is unethical. Professional accountability requires that we evaluate what we do (Harper-Dorton & Herbert, 1999).

Our continual need to learn is another reason for engaging in practice evaluation. To be effective with diverse cases and situations requires that we remain active learners. One of the best ways to learn is to gather information about the outcomes of what we do. If, for example, a particular theory or technique does not seem to help a family, it may mean it was the wrong choice for this group. Perhaps it will be more effective with different families under different circumstances. Without evaluation, we are unable to know what works with which clients experiencing what problems. Without this sort of information, we are left to practice in the dark, relying on information and approaches that may no longer be efficacious.

A third reason for evaluation is to allow for prompt adaptations where appropriate. If we are sensitive to, and gather feedback from, family members, we can consider mid-course corrections. Learning that a family found a particular recommendation difficult or impossible to carry out allows us to come up with more effective approaches or to modify the recommendation.

Evaluation also demonstrates changes that may be important for other stakeholders. The school, child protective service agencies, the courts, third-party payers (such as insurance companies), governmental agencies, and others may have an investment in the family changing in some way. Most agencies also want to know whether the services they offer are effective because it has a direct bearing on whether they should fund those services. Agency administrators may use evaluation data to make personnel decisions, allocate or reallocate resources, and plan for new services.

Of course, a fifth reason for using evaluation is its potential to show the family that they are making progress. Generally, awareness of success can fuel the family's motivation to continue. Success breeds success and tends to increase the family's commitment to further efforts (Thomlison, 2002).

Another good reason for employing evaluation is to ensure that "service conforms to acceptable methods of practice" (Kilpatrick & Holland, 1999, p. 94). Some agencies review case records to learn the extent to which practitioners have followed professional guidelines and acted according to organizational policies. These quality assurance approaches are used to help evaluate whether programs are achieving their desired ends.

Finally, evaluation helps us to know when it is most appropriate to terminate with a family. Evaluation helps identify what goals they have accomplished and which ones remain. It allows us to focus our efforts on the latter while celebrating the achievement of the former. It may also help identify when our interventions are not working or things are getting worse instead of better. Thus, evaluation is a crucial part of the helping process.

EVALUATION TOOLS

In Chapter 7, we discussed the importance of creating an evaluation plan that could be used to assess the effectiveness of our work with families. The major purpose of such a plan is to assure that we are positioned to carry out an evaluation at the appropriate point in the helping process. Fortunately, there are many instruments and scales that the family practitioner can use to conduct evaluations. We described some of these in Chapter 6, under assessment techniques and tools. This section will identify several others.

While evaluation is considered one step in the structure of practice, like assessment, it is actually an activity that continues throughout the family–social worker relationship. This continuity is important because of the many ways that things can change as we work with families. For example, initial assessments may prove inaccurate, and interventions may be ineffective. Only by conducting ongoing evaluations can we hope to respond appropriately to such changes.

Evaluation can also be a complex undertaking, depending upon how one defines success. Some practitioners would define success in terms of a couple remaining married or together even if some families would be better off divorced. Others might claim success if parenting behavior improves although the adult partners continue to have relationship problems.

We should also stress that evaluation is a joint process involving both the social worker and the family. The practitioner may need to take the lead in helping the family identify accomplishments and progress and can help by praising the hard work that went into making changes. However, as Bloom, Fischer, and Orme (1995) note, family members should be active participants in data gathering, assessment, and evaluation planning. In addition, Campbell (1988) has shown specific benefits that occur from involving clients in the evaluation process.

In the evaluation process, Collins et al. (1999) note that the social worker needs to focus on changes that occur at the "individual, parent–child, marital, and family system" levels (p. 196). Of these levels, changes in the family system have the most salience for practitioners. This is because individual behaviors can change without affecting the overall family situation, but changes in the family system generally reflect different behaviors by individuals. As such, family change holds the greatest promise for long-term continuation of therapeutic gains. This is important because, as Jacobson and Addis (1993) point out, many changes that occur in therapy do not continue for long afterward.

While it is possible to evaluate any number of aspects related to the practitioner–family relationship, we recommend that evaluation be selective and focus on a few specific goals. Because evaluation can be time consuming and sometimes complex, measuring a limited number of goals is better than a lengthy list. Since the process is a shared one with the family, evaluation efforts may be limited to what the family is willing to provide. For example, extensive logging or record keeping needed for some evaluations may be difficult or too time-consuming for family members. Likewise, completion of multiple instruments may impinge on other aspects of the social worker–family relationship. Measure a few things and do it well (Thomlison, 2002).

TRADITIONAL RESEARCH AND EVALUATION OF PRACTICE

We often refer to the practice evaluations used by family practitioners as *single-subject designs or single-subject research*. It differs from traditional research in that the focus is on measuring change in a specific single system, be it individual, family, or group. Typically, the social worker collects data on the single system at various points—prior to, during, and after intervention. While the purpose of traditional research is to build knowledge for wider dissemination, practice evaluation is really concerned more with knowing whether goals are being achieved. Traditional research requires substantial rigor, including random assignment of clients to control and treatment groups. This sometimes allows us to generalize our results to similar populations. Practice evaluation using single-subject designs rarely involves control groups or random assignment, and generalizability is usually not possible.

Similarly, traditional research places a premium on using well-validated instruments with demonstrable reliability, conditions that are critical to high-quality research. While the practitioner also should be using valid and reliable instruments, employing practice wisdom in creating and using measurement devices is permissible (Jordan & Franklin, 1995).

Single-subject evaluation of practice is much more likely to use clinical judgment of changes rather than rely on statistical tests. This reliance on visual comparisons of data is necessary because with single-subject designs we often cannot meet the assumptions underlying many statistical tests. Social workers are much more likely to use their own observations, self-reports from the family, and scores on rapid assessment instruments to detect whether and what kinds of changes have occurred. Rapid assessment instruments are relatively brief scales that we can use with many typical difficulties encountered in practice. We can use these instruments, of which more than 400 have been identified, with individuals, families, adults, and children and gather data on a myriad assortment of personal, social, and family problems (Fischer & Corcoran, 2000).

As a rule, single-subject designs are relatively inexpensive, and we can use them as an adjunct to individual sessions with families. Both clients and practitioners easily understand them, and results are available almost immediately. On the down side, we cannot generalize results to other groups, and both validity and reliability may be compromised. While the data acquired may help answer the question about whether the family is achieving its goals, they cannot add to the knowledge base of family practice (Yegidis, Weinbach, & Morrison-Rodriguez, 1999).

THEORY IN ACTION | Single-Subject Design Situation

The Carlton family had come into treatment due to the fear of the mother about her anger toward the children. While no physical abuse had transpired, the mother was concerned that her anger would prove too much for her, and she might become physically abusive. Some of the stress leading to the mother's anger stemmed from the long hours she spent working and caring for a physically disabled child after returning home from her part-time job. She admitted to being constantly tired and having a hard time keeping awake at work. Following an assessment by the social worker to gauge the risk of the family situation, the practitioner chose to use a scaling instrument to measure the mother's anger. The mother was asked to fill out the scale after work the day following the first visit to the family practitioner. Following this scale and measurement, the mother was given added supports for the care of her child, different ways of dealing with stress, and exercises to use at home when she began to become angry. The anger scale was given again three weeks into the intervention and following the sixth session (two sessions before termination). Each was done at the same time each day, following work. Results on the scale showed that the mother's anger was decreasing substantially as time went along in the treatment.

Tools for Evaluating Family Functioning

Family-functioning instruments are designed to provide the family's perception of how well they perform on particular dimensions. These self-report instruments often provide data on such things as the family's adaptability, cohesiveness, roles, rules, problem solving, affection-giving, and cooperativeness, among many others. Examples of such instruments include the Family Adaptability and Cohesion Evaluation Scale (FACES III) (Olson, Porter, & Ravee, 1985) and the Dyadic Adjustment Scale (Weiss & Perry, 1979). These instruments and the Marital Precounseling Inventory (Stuart & Stuart, 1972) also can be very useful for creating a baseline before beginning intervention. Thus, we can employ them as part of the assessment process. Following treatment, we may use the instruments again to measure changes that have occurred. Other instruments are also available for specific situations such as divorce counseling. These include the Divorce Adjustment Inventories (Brown et al., 1991).

The advantage of such instruments is the fact that they provide objective data on the family's functioning while sometimes eliciting information that might be withheld in an interview (Hanna & Brown, 1999). They may also reflect subjective impressions of change that are less observable by the practitioner or family. On the other hand, changes that we cannot observe are less likely to be clinically significant (Jordan & Franklin, 1995).

Tools for Evaluating the Social Worker–Family Relationship

The importance of the social worker–family relationship has been cited repeatedly as an extremely important contributor to the success or failure of family practice (Hubble et al., 1999). Thus, it is logical that we attempt to learn whether the therapeutic process is accomplishing its purpose. Process evaluations may focus on individual roles, communication style and patterns, and other factors that enhance or detract from the relationship between social worker and family. One real benefit of evaluating process is the ability to identify problems early in the relationship. As Hanna and Brown (1999) note, family members may be "evaluating the therapist with respect to trustworthiness, empathy, safety, helpfulness, and so on" (p. 264). While this type of feedback may be a bit scary initially because many practitioners will view it as potential criticism, getting past this fear is important. What we are seeking from families are their perceptions of what works for them, which communications are helpful and which are not, and what they need for us to assist them better. If family members do not experience the social worker as open to such information, they may become reluctant to share their concerns about specific activities or components of the therapeutic relationship. Reluctant clients may choose not to complete homework assignments, or to do them in a half-hearted manner. If they do not feel they can be honest with the social worker, the potential for problems increases.

A direct way of gaining thoughts about the helping process is to ask family members to rate their level of satisfaction with the overall social worker–family interactions. Seeking the family's perceptions can be as simple as asking them periodically about how they see the intervention progressing, with questions such as "Does what I've suggested make sense given your own experience as a member of this family?" or "Has there been anything I've said that has been particularly disturbing to you?" Some social workers ask the family to rate their level of comfort with particular plans or therapeutic activities (Hanna & Brown, 1999). We can ask such questions at any point in the social worker–family relationship. In addition, the social worker can display responsiveness and interest in the family's feedback when answering their questions. Consider a family member who asks the practitioner to clarify a confusing communication.

THEORY IN ACTION | Displaying Responsiveness and Interest in Feedback

MOTHER: Are you saying you think we shouldn't care about whether our children are home when they should be?

FAMILY PRACTITIONER: No, and I'm glad you asked what I meant. From time to time, communications can get a bit confusing, and I'm delighted you asked for clarification. What I meant was . . .

One real benefit of displaying openness to questions, challenges, and family doubts is the opportunity it presents to model the importance of listening carefully and seeking clarification of confusing messages. Another benefit is that it helps us identify changes in direction or approach that we may need in the helping process. A final benefit is that it helps prevent impasses that lead to premature termination when families become frustrated with what they perceive as an inability to communicate with the social worker.

Keep in mind that all questions or confusions may not be expressed verbally. Behavioral indicators of potential problems include such things as a failure to follow through on homework assignments, facial clues, and body posture. Negative responses to the social worker's suggestions, such as "Yeah, but that doesn't work for us" or "That can't work because . . ." are also a possible symptom. View these as opportunities to find alternative approaches or at least to hear why the family thinks something is a bad idea. Other indicators are the social worker's own reactions to things that occur during interactions with the family. Feelings of anger or other emotional reactions may suggest the practitioner has lost contact with the family and what they perceive as their needs.

THEORY IN ACTION | **Practitioner's Reaction**

FAMILY PRACTITIONER: I would like for you to share with me those things we have talked about today which have been helpful.

MS. OLSON: I don't think much that happened today was very helpful.

FAMILY PRACTITIONER: Well, let me share with you what I noticed and see whether we're on the same page.

Practitioners can take the opportunity to evaluate the professional–family relationship at almost any point in the process. It may be more important in the assessment and planning stage but can also be appropriate during interventions. It also can be used at any point where either the family or social worker is confused or when it appears that significant progress has slowed.

Tools for Practitioner Self-Evaluation

A normal goal of most, if not all, social workers is to be effective in their helping role. Often, evaluating one's own performance relies on some form of self-assessment. In this section, we will consider two such methods: use of a self-evaluation instrument and practitioner logs.

Practitioner Self-Evaluation Instrument Highlight 8.1 gives an example of a *practitioner self-evaluation instrument.* Self-assessment instruments such as

Highlight 8.1 | **The Practitioner Self-Evaluation Instrument**

Name of Family: ____________________ Date Completed: ____________________

A. List new skills employed while working with this family.

____

____

____

B. List new techniques or adaptations of techniques employed while working with this family.

____

____

____

C. List the particular problems or issues with which you were most effective.

____

____

____

D. List the particular problems or issues with which you were least effective.

____

____

____

E. List specific improvements you could have made in your work with this family.

____

____

____

this are designed to help social workers learn from each case and to consider what changes might be needed in similar family work. A thoughtful practitioner may consider these same questions without benefit of this specific form. The form may be most helpful for novice practitioners or to ensure consistency across multiple families.

Practitioner Logs Bloom et al. (1995) provide another tool for the social worker wishing to evaluate his or her own performance. *Practitioner logs* provide a structured method of recording information that relates directly to the family's goals. Suppose we are trying to help a family in which much of their communication with each other is critical and negative. We can design a prac-

Highlight 8.2 **Practitioner Log**

Date	Time	Description of Positive Communication	Comments

titioner log to record communication events that are positive in nature. Such a log might look like that in Highlight 8.2.

As the practitioner, you can collect data on what family members said plus provide a summary of your own reactions. For example, did you reinforce the family member who commented positively about another member? What led to the positive comment? The purpose of the practitioner log is to help in the self-evaluation process. Taping sessions with the family can also allow the social worker to compare log entries with actual recordings. While self-assessment can be an important tool for social workers, it cannot replace other evaluation foci, such as outcomes.

Tools for Evaluating Outcomes

Ultimately, it is the outcome of the intervention that is generally of most concern to both families and social workers. This is because changes in behavior are what families typically seek when they engage in a therapeutic relationship with a practitioner. While sometimes they will seek a change in another family member's attitude, it is usually a behavioral expression of the attitude that is most problematic. As a result, outcome evaluation is typically, but not exclusively, concerned with measuring changes in behavior. At the same time, we often couple behavioral-change measurements with other evaluation methods. Thomlison (2002) notes that measures used to evaluate family change are frequently of two types: individualized and standardized.

Individualized Instruments *Individualized measures* are created specifically for the family and often lack the psychometric strengths of standardized instruments. At the same time, they do have a direct relationship to the concerns facing the family. Thus, an instrument developed to measure the occurrence of behaviors the family has identified as problematic can be invaluable in charting progress on this dimension. This list can then be used to monitor change during the intervention and at the end of the social worker–family relationship. Essentially, this provides the family and practitioner with a baseline of data for assessing change. Another alternative is to have the family graph or chart the occurrence of specific behaviors that they observe. An example might be frequency of arguments, amount of time spent together, or number of positive interactions. Because the behaviors or areas listed are specific to the family, they tend to have an inherent value. This is in contrast to standardized instruments that are not tailor-made for any particular family.

Standardized Instruments *Standardized measures* usually have demonstrated validity and reliability and come in a variety of formats. For example, the rapid assessment instruments discussed earlier can be used to detect changes in family behaviors quickly. We can use a checklist of behaviors or a list of activities to measure whether a family is achieving its goals. By their simplicity, rapid assessment instruments lend themselves to regular use. Many are relatively short and scoring is generally quick. Thomlison (2002) recommends combining both individualized and standardized measures to more fully reflect the complexity of family functioning.

In the following sections, we will identify and describe several more commonly employed outcome evaluation approaches. These include self-reports, client logs, single-subject designs, content analysis designs, and goal attainment scaling.

Self-Reports Since self-reported problematic behavior is often the starting point for family–practitioner interaction, it is logical that it might be a useful measure for evaluation. For instance, families may report that they are having fewer negative interactions or that Donna is focusing more on her homework and less on Eric. They may suggest that the adults are spending more quality time together and are experiencing fewer fights or significant disagreements. Of course, they may also report no real change in the factors that caused them initially to seek help. Another difficulty is that self-reports require the family to carry out the charting with some degree of diligence. If the family gets bored or lax in recording their behaviors, the value of the self-report is diminished accordingly. One complication inherent in self-reports is that the actual charting of behavior is, in itself, an intervention because behavior watched is often behavior changed (Brown & Brown, 2002). To put it another way, we all tend to act differently when someone is watching us or when we watch ourselves. This is not necessarily a problem, but it does add another dimension to the question of what caused the family to change.

One method of attempting to assess change using self-reports is to ask families to rate their present situation or problem using a 1 to 10 point scale. We can use the resulting self-anchoring score to assess outcomes over time. Thus, a family that rates their present situation as a 5 provides data that can be used to measure changes occurring during and after intervention. If they later rate their situation as an 8, this shows some degree of progress.

Gottman (1999), whose research focused on couples, identified a list of 17 specific characteristics associated with a healthy marriage. These items, which range from emotional connectedness to sexuality to handling finances, provide a useful standardized measure that we can employ in a pre-post format.

Highlight 8.3

Self-Report Marital Satisfaction Scale

	High		Medium		Low
1. Degree to which we are emotionally connected	5	4	3	2	1
2. Degree to which we handle conflict successfully	5	4	3	2	1
3. Degree to which we trust each other	5	4	3	2	1
4. Level of satisfaction with our sexual relationship	5	4	3	2	1
5. Degree to which I feel respected by my partner	5	4	3	2	1
6. Extent to which we have similar values and beliefs	5	4	3	2	1
7. Extent to which we can talk openly about problems	5	4	3	2	1
8. Extent to which I feel my partner hears me	5	4	3	2	1
9. Degree to which we approach things as a team	5	4	3	2	1
10. Extent to which we have fun together	5	4	3	2	1
11. Level of satisfaction regarding handling of finances	5	4	3	2	1
12. Extent to which we agree on issues with children	5	4	3	2	1
13. Extent to which we share spiritual/religious views	5	4	3	2	1
14. Extent to which our relatives/in-laws are a problem	5	4	3	2	1

Source: Adapted from Gottman (1999), and Brown and Brown (2002).

Couples can use the list at the start of the intervention to identify potentially troubling aspects of their relationship and highlight subjects on which they wish to work. We can also use the list at the conclusion of the intervention to identify areas where changes have occurred. Highlight 8.3 contains a questionnaire reflecting some of Gottman's key items.

One of the largest drawbacks to the use of self-reports is the question of their accuracy and objectivity. Wanting to please the social worker may lead to overly optimistic reports, while a family's reluctance to terminate may contribute to the opposite. The subjective nature of people's perceptions is troublesome because one family member may report a change that other members have not seen. Self-reports are also subject to the vagaries of memory, particularly the tendency to recall recent events and to forget more distant events. Thus, a member may report recent positive events and feelings while ignoring the negative items that took place earlier in the week. Highlight 8.4 provides some guidelines that may prove useful when considering the selection and use of self-report inventories.

A variety of standardized measures are available to help family social workers. These include instruments that will assess issues such as family functioning, problems with children, marital or parenting problems, family violence, child maltreatment, substance abuse, and family and environmental stress, among others (Thomlison, 2002). Some instruments are designed to focus on particular problems, while others are multidimensional. Hudson

Highlight 8.4

Guidelines for Selecting and Using Self-Report Instruments

- Choose instruments measuring specific family functioning items rather than global behaviors. For example, information on spousal interaction is more useful than data on general problem-solving orientation.
- Use instruments with demonstrated validity for the population with which they will be employed. Be alert to instruments that have been normed only on white populations, as interpretations may be inappropriate with other groups.
- Combine sources of data from instruments with other evidence, such as observations by the practitioner or others, or additional outcome measures.
- Recognize that any instrument may miss salient aspects of a family's functioning.
- Ask family members to identify what still needs to happen for them to feel they have accomplished their goals.
- Have family members rate their level of change from the start to the end of the intervention. One end of the scale might be 5, which means significant change, while the other end is 0, suggesting no change. You can also ask them to use minus numbers to show things that have gotten worse than was initially the case.
- Ask family members to describe verbally how things are different now than they were at the start of the intervention. An appropriate question might be "Compare your interactions with your partner last September with those you are having now."
- Employ a scale developed in the assessment or planning phase to rate behavioral change. This tends to focus attention on the specific issues that originally brought the family to the social worker.
- Carefully review all measures before using them, even to the point of completing the instrument yourself. Look for readability levels, gender or cultural biases, or other characteristics that will limit the value of the instrument.
- Ensure that the family understands the reasons for using a particular instrument and what information will be gained by its use.
- After the measure is completed, give the family information on the results.

Source: Adapted from Hanna and Brown (1999) and Thomlison (2002).

(1992), for example, developed the Multi-Problem Screening Inventory (MPSI), which gathers data on more than 25 typical areas of family functioning. This measure provides a broad view of family problem areas. The MPSI can also be used to gather information on how parents see their relationships with children in the family and the extent of marital conflict.

Another useful measure is the Family Assessment Device (FAD) (Epstein, Baldwin, & Bishop, 1983). This instrument provides data on communication and problem-solving approaches used by the family as well as providing information on affective dimensions of family life. The FAD is useful for gathering information from families with teenage children and when we need an overall picture of family functioning. Sharlin and Shamai (2000) report on the usefulness of the FAD for quantitative evaluations of work with poor, unorganized families.

We can assess parenting skills using the Adult-Adolescent Inventory (Bavolek, 1984), which helps identify such factors as empathy, discipline, and the roles of both parents and adolescents. It is particularly useful when the initial presenting problem is behavior of an adolescent. For families with younger children, the Parental Bonding Instrument (Parker, Tupling, & Brown, 1979) provides data on how the child views the parents' behavior.

Instruments helpful for ferreting out violence and maltreatment in the family include the Conflict Tactics Scales (Straus & Gelles, 1990) and the Family Risk Scales (Magura, Silverman-Moses, & Jones, 1987). These risk assessment scales are sometimes used by child protective services to help determine the potential for family violence.

When the focus is on the impact of environmental and family stress, two other instruments may prove useful. The Family Coping Inventory (McCubbin et al., 1991) and the Family Hardiness Index (McCubbin, McCubbin, & Thompson, 1991) are both designed to provide data on how well the family manages the stresses they experience. The latter is particularly attuned to how well family members see themselves as managing stressful events.

Whenever possible, practitioners should use multiple measures when assessing family functioning. We can combine well-tested instruments with others designed specifically for a given family. By using more than one measure, the social worker is better able to overcome limitations of any single instrument or method. In addition, multiple instruments allow a much more comprehensive picture of the family than any single assessment measure provides (Jordan & Franklin, 1995).

It is not the intent of this chapter to provide an exhaustive list of potential instruments for measuring specific aspects of family life. Thomlison (2002) and Fischer and Corcoran (2000) provide a much more extensive list of useful evaluation measures.

Client Logs Besides using individualized and standardized rating scales or questionnaires, some practitioners employ logs to gather data on family functioning. *Client logs* are sometimes called "critical incident recordings" because they are often used to provide detail on important events happening in the family's life. We can design logs so that the clients enter data at preset times or only when a specific event occurs. For example, if we are interested in events that occur in the morning between 6:00 A.M. and 8:00 A.M., we would ask the client to record all events during this period. In other instances, we would ask the client to record only those events that were particularly important or related to the problem the family is having. Of course, families can also use logs to record positive events, such as time spent together or satisfying inter-

Highlight 8.5 | **Client Log**

Name ______________________ Date ______________

Time	Significant Event	Reactions
________	________________	____________
	________________	____________
	________________	____________
________	________________	____________
	________________	____________
________	________________	____________
	________________	____________
	________________	____________

actions. Moreover, logs can be designed to record antecedents and consequences of critical incidents to begin to understand what occurs before and after a particular behavior. Finally, adding a column to a log that allows the person to use a numerical rating to describe her reaction to the specific event is also possible. This might be useful for understanding what events the family experiences as most upsetting, depressing, or positive. For comparison purposes, we can ask each family member to maintain their own logs, thereby providing a rich source of data for the practitioner and family. A typical client log is provided in Highlight 8.5. While the client log shown here allows for recording only three events, we can extend the log as needed.

Single-System Designs

Single-system or *single-subject designs* are evaluation approaches that seek to determine changes that have occurred over time in the behaviors of client systems. The subject can be an individual, family, or, for that matter, a system of any size. The following section identifies several of these designs that can be used by social workers in their work with families. They include A-B, B, A-B-C, and multiple baseline designs.

A-B Designs *A-B designs* are quasi-experimental approaches to measuring change over time. They begin with a recording of the target behaviors at the start of the family–social worker relationship and end with a similar measurement at its conclusion. To be most useful, the baseline of behaviors must be of

Figure 8.1 | An A-B Design

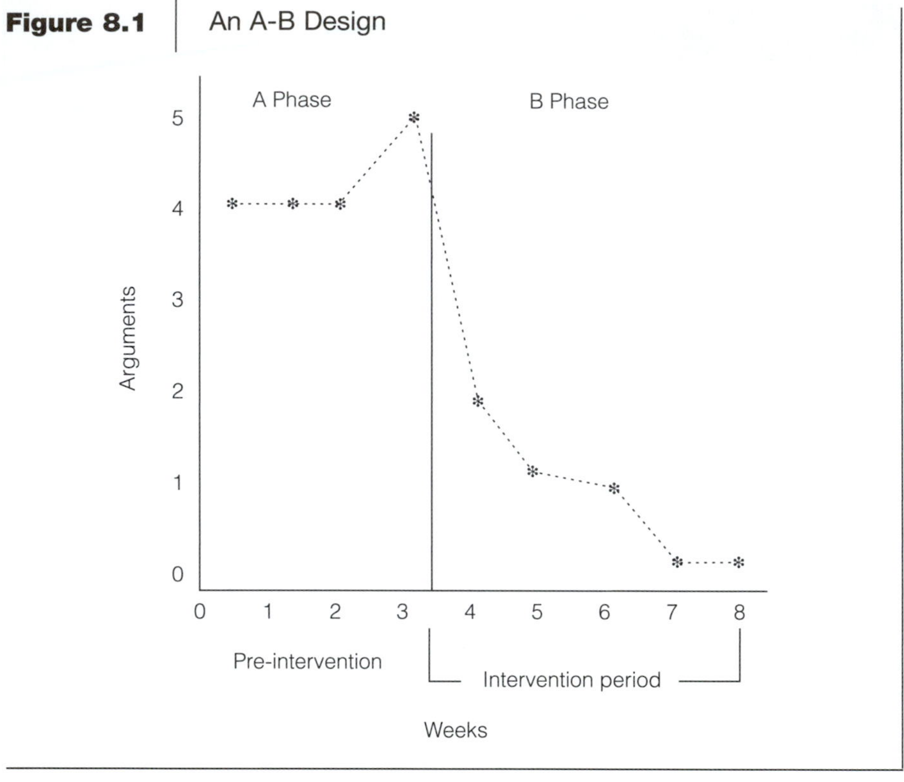

sufficient duration that the data patterns are reasonably stable. The baseline data can be in the form of self-reports, standardized or individualized instruments, or any other measurement system that is reasonably reliable and valid.

Sometimes the social worker will ask the family to record the frequency of a specific behavior that they wish to target. At other times, the practitioner uses assessment instruments in the first session to gain a snapshot in time of the family. In other situations, outside stakeholders may provide baseline data. This might occur, for example, when a child in the family is engaging in acting-out behavior in school.

To ensure the most stable baseline, it would be best to collect data over three or more occurrences. Unfortunately, this is often not possible (Royce & Thyer, 1996; Tripodi, 1994). Typically, neither families nor third-party payers are likely to agree to repeated baseline collection as this involves additional cost.

Whatever the number of baseline periods, it is the changes that occur between initial data collection and the end of the practitioner–family relationship that are usually seen as indicators of progress. Thus, a family might report frequent arguments at the start of therapy and report far fewer disputes after a two-month period of intervention. Such a model is shown in Figure 8.1. As is evident from the chart, arguments occurred about four times per week before the start of the intervention and dropped to zero during the last two weeks that the social worker helped the family members.

Figure 8.2 | B Design (No Pre-Existing Baseline)

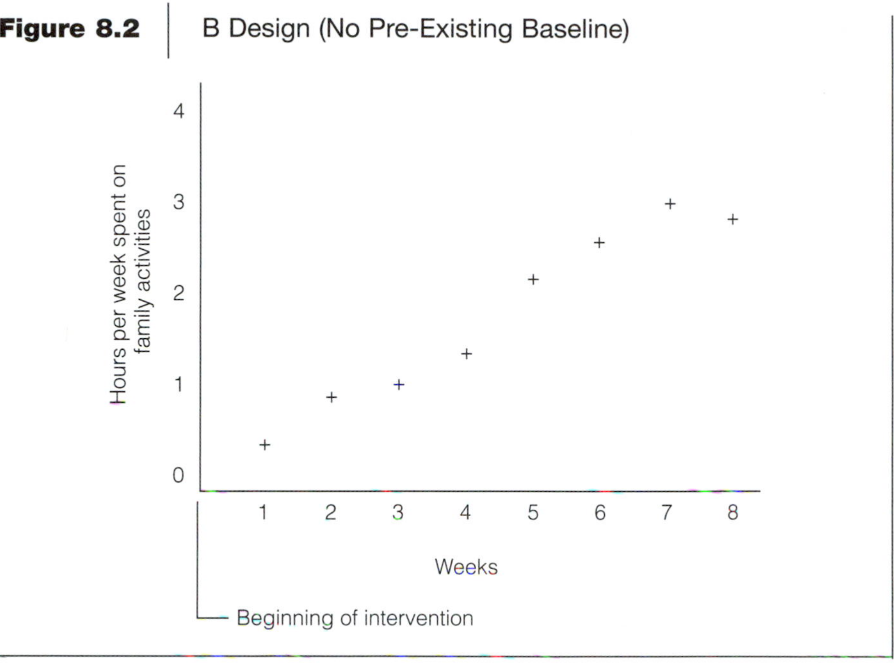

B Designs As suggested previously, in an ideal world, having a baseline showing occurrence of the target behavior before intervention began would be helpful. Often, this is not possible because few clients chart their behaviors before seeking assistance. Consequently, many baselines are constructed at the time of the first contact between practitioner and family. These are considered *B designs* because they lack a pre-intervention baseline. Figure 8.2 is an example of a B Design with a family that wanted more time together to engage in activities. The chart shows that the amount of time together increased over the eight-week period that the social worker and family worked together.

A-B-C Designs A variant of the A-B design is used in situations where we employ an additional intervention simultaneously with or later in the practitioner–family relationship. This might occur when a family member suffering from depression begins taking medication for this disorder. The result is an intervention with two treatments, family therapy and medication, both of which can influence the outcomes. To allow for such situations, the *A-B-C Design* is available. An example of this is seen in Figure 8.3. When we employ two or more interventions (in this case, family therapy and medication for a family member) together or sequentially, determining what is responsible for any change in behavior is difficult. Consequently, we should be careful when attempting to attribute outcomes to any single factor.

Multiple Baseline Designs *Multiple baseline designs* are simply variations of the previous designs that use baselines on more than one behavior. It is common for families and individual clients to have multiple goals they hope to

Figure 8.3 An A-B-C Design

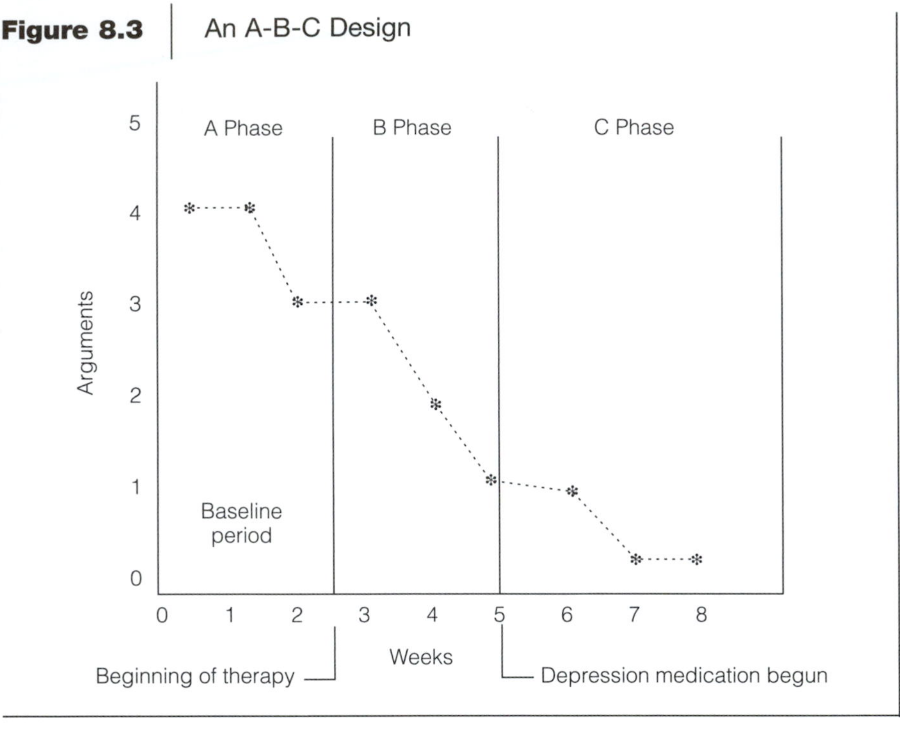

achieve through work with the social worker. For example, consider a family with three goals: reduced conflict between a parent and the oldest child; increased time spent on homework by children; and more time alone together for the parents. They can make progress on each goal and reflect this in an appropriate chart. Figure 8.4 shows how this might look. While the three behaviors measured in this figure might seem independent, in actuality, they may well be related. For example, if time spent arguing decreases, more time is available for children to spend on homework and for parents to spend time together. Also, if arguments are curtailed, children can probably focus more on their homework instead of worrying about a parent–child relationship. In many situations, changes in one area influence changes in others, with the result that behaviors become interdependent.

Content Analysis Designs *Content analysis* "involves searching for and counting key words, phrases, or concepts in communication" (Royse, 2004, p. 221). We may employ it, for instance, when we have recorded family sessions and when communications reflect important changes in family goals. Consider a family in which communications among members are frequently critical and negative and this is one of the presenting problems. We can compare recordings of early sessions with those from later sessions to learn the relative frequency of positive versus negative communications.

Figure 8.4 | B Design with Multiple Baselines

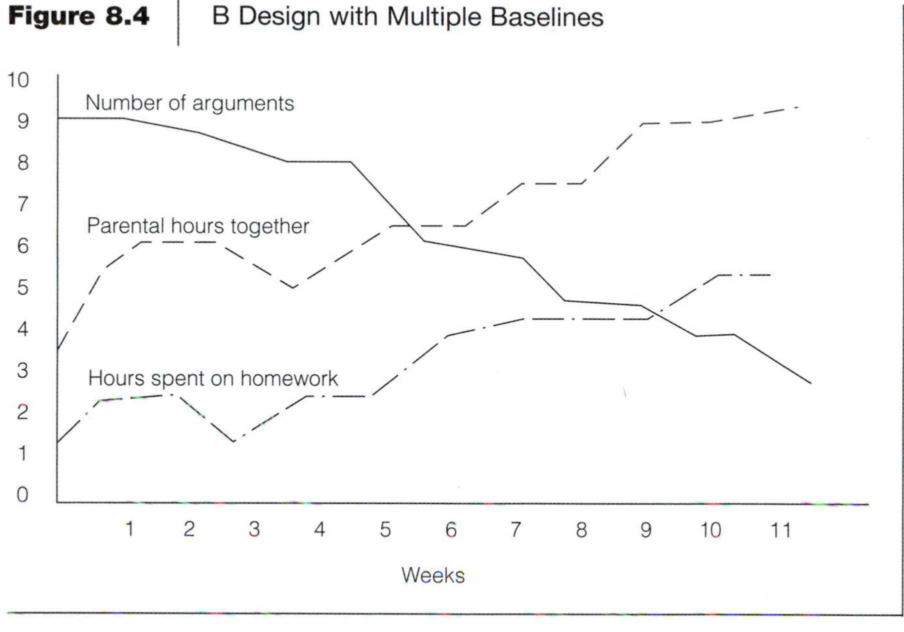

Content analysis is relatively easy to do and is unobtrusive. Simultaneously, it is subject to the same limitations as other single-subject designs, namely the inability to connect cause and effect (Royse, 2004). Content analysis is dependent largely on the ability of the listener to categorize communications properly.

Goal Attainment Scaling *Goal attainment scaling* is a means of assessing the extent to which the family has achieved a set of goals. It is based on the assumption that achievement of most goals can be laid out in a linear fashion, ranging from results that are much less than expected to those where the result is much more than expected. Goal attainment scaling follows a set of steps that includes the following:

1. State the goal clearly and in such a way that we can measure it.
2. Give each goal a weight that reflects its importance compared with the other goals. Goals that are most important have the highest value.
3. Identify the expected level of attainment for each goal. For example, if a family goal is to reduce the number of negative parent–child interactions, is the expected level no such interactions or is it okay if the number is cut by 75 percent? Perhaps the family would be satisfied if the number of negative interactions were reduced by 50 percent. Considering that parent–child arguments are really common, a goal of completely eliminating them may be unrealistic.
4. Identify other possible levels of attainment. These include those that are better than expected and those that are worse than expected.

Highlight 8.6 | **Goal Attainment Scaling**

Levels of Possible Outcomes	Goal 1	Goal 2
Least favorable outcome	Arguments continue/ worsen	Parents spend little/no additional time together
Expected outcome	Arguments reduced by 50 percent	Parents spend 50 percent more time together
Most favorable outcome	Arguments reduced by 75 percent	Parents spend 75 percent more time together

Highlight 8.6 shows a possible goal attainment scaling chart using two goals: reduction of arguments between parents and child and increased time for parents to be together. Here, the family's goal is to reduce parent–child arguments by one-half and to increase the time parents spend together by one-half.

Some authors have augmented the model in Highlight 8.6 by giving points for each of the possible outcomes. Thus, a least favorable outcome might be –2 while the most favorable would equal a +2. Additional outcomes can be identified, resulting in a series of steps. For example, the goal of more parental time together could have several gradations. Highlight 8.7 shows this alternative method of Goal Attainment Scaling.

A real benefit of goal attainment scaling is that it "forces us to select goals, and to monitor them" (Kinney et al., 1991, p. 90). If they are not making progress, a change in approach may be required, thus keeping the intervention plan current. Goal attainment scaling is a flexible tool that can be used with a variety of goals as long as the goals are measurable in some way.

Caveats in Evaluation

While we have stressed the importance of using evaluation as an integral part of the helping process, acknowledging some limitations and concerns is important. First, many social workers are not well-trained in the use of evaluation methodology and may be unaware of the availability of measurement instruments to assist their work. This reduces the likelihood that they will engage in the kind of systematic evaluation required. While social workers have a long-standing tradition of introspection and self-assessment, this is insufficient to satisfy the requirements of sound practice evaluation (Harper-Dorton & Herbert, 1999).

Second, many agencies and third-party payers do not provide funding to encourage evaluation, so the task falls solely on the practitioner. With little support for purchasing instruments or other family-appropriate measures, the burden may prove too difficult. Add to this the fact that many practitioners prefer to provide service and not worry about evaluation. Without institu-

Highlight 8.7

Alternative Goal Attainment Scaling

–2	–1	0	+1	+2
Time together is reduced by 50 percent	Time together is reduced by 25 percent	Starting Point	Time together is increased by 50 percent	Time together is increased by 100 percent

tional support (funding, technical expertise, and so on) to help practitioners, evaluation is likely to be ignored or done poorly.

A third concern is the potential threat inherent in doing evaluation. What if what we do does not work? What is the impact on our positions, programs, and agencies? These issues may surface when an agency suddenly decides to require evaluations without adequately preparing the staff for the effort. Outside evaluators brought in to conduct evaluations may be perceived as more threatening than internally generated and supported systems. Either way, practitioners must be clear about the purposes of evaluation and its impact on their professional lives.

A fourth problem occurs when evaluation does not receive ongoing support within the agency. The result may be half-hearted attempts at evaluation that result in "piecemeal and inconclusive" results (Harper-Dorton & Herbert, 1999). This leaves gaps in the information available to make policy decisions and impairs the practitioner's ability to prove efficacy.

A fifth limitation is inherent in drawing conclusions from evaluation results. For example, suppose the family reports significant change from the start of intervention to the end. Add to this that the goals identified early on have been achieved. While we would like to point to the intervention and our work with the family as the independent variable that produced the noted changes, this is simply not possible. There are a couple of reasons for our caution. For example, families spend a great deal more time outside the intervention than in it. This means that other factors may be causing the changes we are seeing or that, at the very least, these factors are interacting with our treatment, complicating any attempt at determining cause and effect. In addition, as we mentioned earlier, the process of actually monitoring behavior that occurs in most family interventions introduces an additional treatment methodology.

A sixth complication is that change may occur for reasons that have nothing to do with the intervention. For example, the problem child in the family may mature out of the behavior that caused the family to seek help. A family member begins to take medicine to treat a previously undiagnosed depression, and her changed mood positively impacts the entire family. Similarly, an unemployed caregiver experiencing several problems gets a job and begins to respond differently to other family members. In practice, many factors can contribute to the change of behavior noted in families, making it preferable to err on the side of caution when attributing causation.

Finally, during evaluation we may find that efforts to help clients have resulted in unintended consequences. For example, a couple decides to get a divorce, a goal neither the family nor practitioner anticipated. Family members may wind up with more problems than they started with as new stressful areas of their lives are uncovered. Family violence may erupt because the abuser is threatened by the changes occurring in his relationship with his wife and kids.

Ultimately, there is ample evidence that families can and do change for the positive through the help of social workers. However, we cannot ignore the possibility of iatrogenic outcomes, and the practitioner should be aware of such possibilities.

Ethnic and Cultural Challenges in Evaluation

It should be obvious by now that ethnic and cultural challenges are present throughout the structure of practice. In this section, we will look at how these factors may impinge on our efforts to evaluate practice.

One reason we have stressed the importance of involving the family in every aspect of the process relates to issues of cultural and ethnic sensitivity. Populations that have often been discriminated against and not included in planning that affects them are particularly susceptible to suspicion about the social worker's motives. One way to show the practitioner's commitment to full involvement with the family is to consult with them at each step of the process, including evaluation. This empowers the family to take responsibility for their own well-being with assistance from the social worker.

Another complexity in evaluation occurs when we use standardized scales that were not normed on nor designed for diverse groups. This means that the results of such scales are always subject to the question of whether they are valid measures for people of color. Attempts to interpret such measures usually result in comparing respondents of color to white respondents with all of the inaccuracies that implies (Royse, 2004). Ideally, the practitioner will need to find standardized instruments that have been developed on more than just white people.

Yegidis et al. (1999, p. 207) list three such instruments:

1. *Acculturation Rating Scale for Mexican Americans-II* by Cuellar, Arnold, and Maldanado (1995). This scale assesses degree of acculturation for Mexican-American populations.
2. *Hispanic Stress Inventory* by Cervantes, Padilla, and Salgado de Snyder (1991). This instrument measures psychological stress experienced by Hispanic immigrants.
3. *TEMAS (Tell-Me-A-Story)* by Constantino, Malgady, and Rogler (1992). This scale is a thematic apperception test modified for use with African American and Hispanic children.

Note that there are often large differences within the same group that may confound the use of even ethnic-sensitive instruments. For example, not all

Hispanic immigrants are alike, even if some have shared language and cultural elements. Likewise, Cuban immigrants to the United States are likely to have experienced different stresses and life events than those arriving from Colombia.

Not only should instruments used be culturally appropriate but they should also be understandable for clients lacking language skills in English. This applies to both written and oral interview questions that we give to clients. It some cases, it may be necessary to use interpreters to help family members understand what we are requesting.

Instruments and other measures should be gender neutral and not biased toward or against any group. Review such documents beforehand with an eye to spotting inappropriately worded questions or limited-response options that may not apply with your family. This also applies to situations where we ask clients to provide information on their ethnicity. Family members should be able to select a combination of groups rather than be forced to list an identification with only one.

While we are not able to generalize about evaluation findings based on single cases, we can note whether families from different cultural or ethnic groups achieved similar outcomes. Dissimilar results or levels of satisfaction might suggest the need to gather additional data to explore why these differences occurred.

TERMINATION

Termination is the final stage of the practice process for the family practitioner and the family. Termination begins when you first greet the family in the first session. There is no helping relationship designed to go on forever. Your responsibility is to help the family reach the point where their goals have been met and their skills for dealing with issues enhanced. In your initial session with the family when you first begin problem identification, you will have begun assessing the time needed to resolve the family issues. As you move into planning and contracting, you will actually set a specific schedule for completing your work with the family. Along the way, you need to remind the family of that time frame and encourage them to meet it.

THEORY IN ACTION | Reminding Clients of Termination

FAMILY PRACTITIONER: I think that as a family, you are working very hard right now to resolve these issues and you've made a lot of progress. It is important to remember that our day to evaluate our work together is in three weeks. This is when we planned to accomplish our goals and end our sessions.

MOTHER: I didn't realize it was coming up so quickly.

FAMILY PRACTITIONER: That is still plenty of time to complete your goals if we continue to work as hard as we have.

MOTHER: What if we are not ready?

FAMILY PRACTITIONER: We can talk about that situation if it happens, but I believe we can finish by then. It will be up to us to decide when we evaluate our goals.

By expressing to the family your encouragement and belief in them, you are giving them an opportunity to achieve those goals on the time schedule you set together. Does this mean if they do not meet the goals that you will end the relationship anyway? Not necessarily. Nevertheless, setting a specific time to evaluate these goals gives the family more time to plan for termination.

Reactions to Termination

There are different types of situations in which termination may occur. Remembering that each type has its own set of issues is important, and these need to be dealt with if possible. There are also common factors as well for any termination situation. Hellenbrand (1987) has suggested that the client's emotional reaction at termination is related to the duration of contact, the intensity of the relationship, whether termination was part of a planned or unplanned process, the client's strengths and support, whether they accomplished goals, and whether the client will continue receiving services from another worker. This many factors makes it difficult to know how a client will react to ending the helping relationship.

Sometimes there may be joy and even pride in the termination. The family feels good about what they have accomplished and stronger about other situations they may need to deal with in the future. They will have met goals, and the process of termination will have been handled appropriately. In other cases, there may be feelings of anger, rejection, sadness, and fear. Many of these negative feelings concern emotional attachments and dependency issues. These can occur not only on the part of the family but also on the part of the practitioner. When you begin working with a family, you may find that you are the first person who has ever treated them with concern, warmth, or empathy. This fact can lead many people to become too attached to you as someone who cares about them and will always be there.

While you do have their best interests at heart, issues that arise from termination situations can lead to feelings of rejection and anger. Some families may have experienced painful separations in their lives, and because they have placed so much trust in you, this can feel like abandonment to them. You may begin to see these feelings in the following ways: (1) regression to earlier issues that appeared resolved, (2) becoming too dependent on the family practitioner (for example, calling you every day), (3) the introduction of new problems by the family, and (4) finding a substitute for the worker (perhaps making an appointment with a new family practitioner). In cases such as these, it is important to sit down with the family and/or family members and examine these feelings and the reasons behind them.

THEORY IN ACTION | Dealing with Termination

MOTHER: I guess we will need to find someone else to help us now. We really didn't accomplish anything in here. I feel like you did not do the best you could have.

FAMILY PRACTITIONER: Let's talk about that. When we discussed ending the sessions a few weeks ago, that was with the knowledge that you had met your goals and you were feeling positive about the future. I wonder what has happened to change your mind.

MOTHER: I am not sure, but it just seems like we are ending too soon and I don't think we have reached our goals. Jeremy has been breaking his curfews, and we seem to be fighting more.

FAMILY PRACTITIONER: Sometimes when a helping relationship is about to end, families can experience feelings of anger and rejection. This may begin to reappear in the manner of old problems resurfacing and/or feelings of needing to find someone else to work with. Before we change our minds about what we believed we had accomplished a few weeks ago, let's talk about what you are feeling about ending the family sessions.

In other cases, the idea of termination from the helping process may bring on several fears on the part of the client. If in the past they have felt rejected, they may begin to pull away from the relationship suddenly and end the helping process before it is time. Families may start not showing up for their final appointments, and they may or may not call to reschedule. In situations like this, having the same type of honest conversation is important. Doing this in person would be best, but it can also be done over the phone if necessary.

THEORY IN ACTION | Dealing with Termination

FAMILY PRACTITIONER *(phone call):* Hello, Marion. This is Janet Lilly. I was calling to see if things were all right, since you missed your meeting with me yesterday.

FATHER: Yes, things are just fine. I just forgot and I have been so busy. I am not sure we need to meet any more, especially since we have worked so many things out.

FAMILY PRACTITIONER: I feel very good about what you have accomplished also. However, I know when we talked a week ago about setting a time for our ending the sessions, you seemed very open to doing that.

FATHER: I guess we just thought we didn't need to come back.

FAMILY PRACTITIONER: I think it would be good to meet a few more times as we planned, just to go over the things you have accomplished and to talk about the future and the skills you have to deal with other issues.

FATHER: I guess we could come in. We said we would.

Emotional reactions do not occur for the family alone. Social workers also have reactions to the ending of a helping process. There may be feelings of guilt over a family not reaching their goals or ending early because they are not making the kind of progress they had hoped for. There might also be feelings of guilt if it is the social worker who has to leave. At times, there may be feelings of ambivalence. The family practitioner may not have gotten as connected to the family as hoped or might not have liked the family or some of its family members. Endings like these need to be worked through as much as those where there are negative feelings. Even if we do not care for a family, we need to find a way to be able to work with them, and part of that way is to examine where our feelings are coming from.

Like clients, we may also feel angry or abandoned. If we have not resolved some of our own issues from the past or if the family reminds us of our own family, then we can become just as emotionally stressed as the family. In situations such as this, we should examine our own feelings and try to discern where they are coming from. Often, it is good for social workers to have their own counselor to speak to so these issues do not affect clients. The best situation, however, is to not let it get to this point. Good social workers work on their own issues before they meet families or are able to recognize when something seems different with a family and they need to seek out support. For families, it is important before they reach termination to have prepared them for this process, to help them become aware of their responses to you, and to alert yourself if there seem to be unusual feelings on the part of family members.

Types of Termination

There are two categories of termination that need attention. These include those that are mutually planned by both the social worker and the client, and those that are unplanned. Each has its own unique features and challenges.

Mutually Planned Termination The most successful termination is one that we have planned, where clients have met their goals and feel good about their situation, and when the evaluation results are positive. This is what most social workers strive to achieve. By setting a planned time for sessions to end, the social worker is giving the family "a light at the end of the tunnel." Family members generally will work toward this outcome if they believe in themselves and/or see themselves accomplishing their goals. During this type of termination, there is less likelihood that there will be difficulties arising from emotional reactions (Hess & Hess, 1994).

Unplanned Termination *Unplanned termination* might occur for many reasons. It may be because the family did not see any progress being made or things may have gotten worse. Sometimes, just the discussion of a forthcoming termination will lead the family to avoid the separation by leaving first. Whatever the situation, we need to try to process through termination. It is the family practitioner's responsibility to follow through and make contact with the family. While we may never know why the family chose an unplanned termination, it is still important to try to work through the event. Encouraging the family to come back in to meet with you is an appropriate step. Shulman (1999) believes we must give clients every opportunity to work through termination. Once we have the opportunity to speak with the family, engaging them in an open discussion about their reasons for terminating and their feelings behind those reasons will help us decide whether there is anything that can be done to help the family continue their work with us or with another person. In those situations where the family is not willing to discuss the unplanned termination, we will need to respect their right to make those decisions.

Other unplanned terminations may occur because the social worker is leaving. While generally there are opportunities to deal with termination before the practitioner leaves, sometimes there are not. Either way, the family may feel rejected because the social worker is leaving them suddenly while their work was not yet finished. Being sensitive to this situation can help the family to understand that you are not doing this because of them but that there are other factors affecting your decision. In cases like this, it is important to help the family through this process by dealing with termination issues and arranging for further services, if appropriate. Referring the family to another practitioner needs to be done very sensitively. The most successful transfers to another practitioner generally occur through the process of having that person involved in your final few sessions with the family. With the permission of the family, a new social worker can spend time getting to know the family, hearing about their accomplishments and better understanding the goals they are seeking. Most families appreciate this opportunity and find it less threatening to meet with a new person while you are still there.

Tasks in Termination

Generally speaking, there are several tasks associated with termination. One of the most important is stabilizing the changes that have occurred. Toseland and Rivas (1998) suggest seven things that workers can do to help with stabilization:

1. *Ensure that the situation the client is working on is realistic.* This begins at the beginning when the family is trying to identify problems and set goals. Setting a goal that is unrealistic with a family will never allow them

to be ready for termination. Making sure that we take the family's situation into account when goals are set will alleviate pressures from the implementation and termination processes.

2. *Empower clients to see their strengths.* When families recognize their strengths, they can begin to believe they will overcome their issues. The process of termination becomes less difficult if they are aware of their strengths and what they are capable of doing on their own.
3. *Move the understanding of the situation past that incident and onto differing situations.* It is important when working with families to draw similarities between a situation they may have just handled and other situations they may encounter. Families who can identify the skills that helped them in one situation and then translate that into other situations will be more effective in stabilizing change over time.
4. *Use natural consequences.* When families experience the natural consequences of their actions, they are better able to handle other difficult situations. Trying to protect a family from a natural consequence can create insecurity and a belief that they cannot handle their own situations. By dealing with natural consequences, families learn to use their different skills.
5. *Consider follow-up sessions.* Follow-up sessions allow the family to make their own decisions and try out their new skills without feeling completely alone. Follow-up meetings might be done once a month for a few months, or they might be done every other month for six months. The length of the time between follow-up sessions can be determined during termination. Having the family involved in this decision is helpful as it gives them further control in their lives.
6. *Work with the environment to extend the success they have had into other areas.* If you are working with a family who is dealing with issues regarding their son at school, involving the school in the family's efforts is important (with permission). In this way, the school can become a part of the success the family achieves and will respond in a positive manner to the family.
7. *Plan with clients for future problems by teaching them problem solving.* When you teach families problem-solving skills, you are giving them an opportunity to take care of themselves and future issues they may encounter.

Many tasks can be completed during termination, but several are more critical than others. To give the family the best opportunity to terminate in a healthy manner, Collins et al. (1999, pp.188–191) suggest the following:

1. *Recital.* When family members are given the opportunity to talk about what the family practice process has been about and to talk about the changes and challenges they have experienced, they are reinforcing themselves and what they have accomplished. A way to lead them in this discussion might be to ask them what they felt good about and what they might change about the process.

2. *Inducing awareness of change.* By the time a family finishes their sessions, they are well aware of the changes they have made. However it is always important to reinforce these changes by conveying to them your own awareness of what they have accomplished. This is more than simply showing support. Conveying this type of awareness calls for sincere comments and examples of the change.
3. *Consolidating gains.* Like a component of stabilizing change, talking about the future and how the family will use their new skills to cope in other situations moves the family practice process beyond what has been done to what will happen. Being able to identify situations where these new skills will be effective gives the family greater self-confidence.
4. *Providing feedback to the family social worker.* Providing feedback to the social worker aids the family in understanding how important they are in the process. It also gives the practitioner the opportunity to learn and understand the best possible approaches for families.
5. *Preparing family to handle future problems.* We should not only be talking with the family about other situations they might be dealing with but also about any obstacles they see as possibly hindering the family's success in the area in which they have been working. Helping families plan ahead for issues and have some ideas as to how to handle them gives the family the self-confidence to do just that.

FOLLOW-UP

Although *follow-up* may not be done with every family, sometimes this can be a critical step to helping the family maintain their changes. Follow-up or booster sessions, as defined by Kanfer and Schefft (1988), provide an opportunity for the family to discuss any issues that may have emerged since termination. The fact that the family is coming in to meet with the social worker can remind them of their success and enhance those things they have been doing. The difficulty with this process may be seen in the barriers that emerge in attempting to put the sessions together (Kirst-Ashman & Hull, 2002). Some reasons for these barriers can stem from the client, such as the reluctance to return to the practice process and feeling as if they are maintaining their accomplishments, so therefore they do not need follow-up. The social worker may have too busy a schedule, or the agency may not support these types of sessions. However, follow-up can be a vital part of the practice process, and efforts to meet with the family need to be made, if possible.

9 CHAPTER Interventions with Select Family Situations

© Photodisc/Royalty-Free/Getty Images

INTRODUCTION

This chapter describes interventions with families whose situations may be particularly challenging for the family social worker. Some of these challenges arise from characteristics of the family itself (for example, single parents and stepfamilies). Still others derive from broader societal issues, such as oppression, discrimination, and prejudice experienced by certain families (for example, gay and lesbian families). Among the topics addressed are family interventions with each of the following: older adults, gay and lesbian families, families living in poverty, single parents, and those with disabilities. Of particular interest are families that have experienced systematic prejudice, discrimination, restrictions, deprivation, devaluation, or exploitation. These factors often reduce access to services, prevent families from fully enjoying rights accorded other families, and result in other barriers to a fufilling life. Because of the frequency with which we encounter such families, social workers must be familiar with their special needs.

FAMILY INTERVENTION AND OLDER ADULTS

Older adults provide multiple challenges for family practitioners for several reasons. First, we live in a society that habitually celebrates youth and denigrates its more senior members. This shows up in several ways. For example, we often encounter negative attitudes toward older adults having sexual relations based on some preconceived notion that such behavior is the purview of the young. Second, older adults generally experience diminished capacity to engage in some physical activities, and others suffer losses of basic functions such as hearing or cognitive ability. Third, many of our attitudes toward older adults suggest that they are no longer socially useful, are prone to illness, and are otherwise nonproductive members of society (Janzen & Harris, 1997).

The aging process itself conjures up troublesome images of declining abilities and the end of life, neither of which is comfortable for family members. As aging family members reduce their involvement in certain activities and roles, they may experience declining satisfaction with their lives. The existence of a significant other with whom one has a strong relationship can counter this tendency. Similarly, retirement can produce a diminished sense of self-importance for those whose existence was substantially related to their work life. Reduced income may reduce one's sense of independence and exacerbate the need to rely on one's own children. The combination of physical, psychological, and social losses can be devastating for some older adults.

Older Couples

Being part of an older couple may have many ramifications. Sometimes, these impacts can be substantial. In addition, variables such as the family's ethnicity or culture may compound the typical challenges. For example, elderly black families are likely to enjoy much less income than their white counterparts.

Cultural expectations may result in such families taking "relatives and/or non relatives—particularly children and younger persons—into their households"" (Beaver, 1990, p. 224). The positive impacts of such arrangements are well-known: strengthening of black families and sharing of resources. The negative consequences may be evident in relationship problems and financial difficulty, both of which can affect the black family.

THEORY IN ACTION | Older Couple

Mr. and Mrs. Conley had retired three years ago. Between their social security and retirement funds from the railroad, they were able to get by. Then, in June of that year their daughter died in a car accident. As she had been a single mother with three children, there was no place else for the children to go except to a foster home, and the Conleys would not allow that. Now the couple and the three children are living in a two-bedroom apartment. Getting by was no longer possible with the expense of the three children, so Mr. Conley went back to work as a doorman at a nearby apartment building. Even with those funds, they are still struggling to get by.

The social worker can assist by helping such families locate appropriate resources, plan for potential future events (such as long-term care, advanced directives, and a will), and provide concrete services needed by the family (Beaver, 1990). Recommended strategies include careful listening and ethnic-sensitive assessment and intervention. In particular, we should explore the influence of social factors on the family's situation. Because of the history of past injustices, emphasizing the mutuality of assessment, planning, and goal setting is important. This helps the family recognize the social worker's commitment to the client. Since environmental factors often play a significant role in the family's situation, the social worker's willingness to intervene in the environment is also important. This means ensuring that resource referrals are relevant and advocating for the family with appropriate social service systems. In too many situations, black families find the assistance provided by practitioners inappropriate or unhelpful, resulting in a tendency to terminate the relationship prematurely.

Another challenge faced by the social worker is the absence of substantive information and adequate theories about the aging process experienced by African Americans (Beaver, 1990). It becomes even more important for the practitioner to explore with the couple intergenerational strengths and stresses, availability of community resources, and other factors that will help clarify the couple's needs. Beaver recommends that practitioners be "sensitive, respectful, and understanding" and provide interventions that are "culturally and ethnically specific" (p. 235).

Another difficult situation can arise with the death of a partner. When one member of an older couple dies, the practitioner should be sensitive to the risks faced by the surviving member. Losses arising from the death of a loved one, especially coupled with a survivor's medical illness, can lead to suicide. Unfortunately, other family members may not be able to understand or recognize the warning signs that suggest the individual is considering taking his or her life. Passing off the despondency of the survivor as a normal grief reaction is easy. Highlight 9.1 describes such a situation.

One role for the social worker in such situations is to screen for potential suicide. Another is to provide or arrange for services that will strengthen the surviving spouse's sense of purpose. Warning signs include threats to kill oneself, prior efforts to do so, changes in personality, significant recent losses, alcoholism, and health problems. The ability to carry out the suicide is also a major consideration practitioners must take into account. While predicting suicide is not an exact science by any means, we should take a confluence of these warning signs seriously. A depressed individual experiencing significant health problems who has a weapon available is a greater risk than one who feels the future is still positive and lacks the ready means for suicide.

Even if the risk of suicide is small, the practitioner should still be sensitive to the realities of bereavement and grief. Responses to loss may vary from individual to individual, but past research has illustrated the tasks and stages that

Highlight 9.1 | **Suicide of the Older Adult**

With the death of Martina, his wife of 45 years, Reuben experienced mixed emotions. Martina had been ill with cancer for over a year and had lingered for longer than anyone had expected. As in life, Reuben was at her side throughout her illness, providing care, comfort, and love. When she finally died, Reuben was grief-stricken on the one hand but also glad her suffering had ended. The hospice worker who had tended the family at the end was concerned about Reuben because she knew how close the couple had been in life. In the days immediately preceding the funeral, she shared her worry with the couple's two sons. Both assured her that their father was a very strong individual and would bounce back from this devastating loss. Following the funeral service, Reuben and his sons returned to the family home, where the latter made sure that Reuben had what he needed for the next few days. After a visual inventory of the refrigerator, the sons realized that Reuben was almost out of several items. They fixed and ate lunch and made a grocery list of needed foods. Following lunch, the two sons went grocery shopping. Reuben said he was too tired to join them and would wait for their return. When the sons returned home an hour later, Reuben was dead from a self-inflicted gunshot wound. Without Martina, Reuben no longer felt a reason to live and, absent a sense of purpose, ended his life.

the bereaved is likely to encounter. The social worker should be familiar with the stages of loss plus the ways that individual clients may handle their grief reactions. We should anticipate anger, denial, and despair and help the individual recognize and adjust to each of these reactions. Spiritual and religious values of the survivor should be considered. Some survivors may be relieved their loved one's suffering is over and look forward to a future together after death. Others may see death as a permanent end to their relationship with the deceased. Religious traditions often include perspectives on such matters, and it is helpful to explore with the client his or her spiritual beliefs. For example, in Jewish families the ritual of mourning "does not formally begin until after the burial" (Herz & Rosen, 1982, p. 383). Sitting *shiva* is followed by other events that serve to demark specific times in the mourning ritual and provide opportunities for the family to reconnect with each other.

The social worker also should be alert to clients who have not finished the work of mourning after a significant passage of time. While some individuals may appear to get stuck in one stage, others may show an absence of mourning to deny the event's reality. In both cases, this is an indicator that additional help is required.

Fortunately, according to Umberson (1996), the death of one parent tends to result in adult children providing greater support to the surviving parent. This includes increased contact between the two generations and greater emotional support, conditions that tend to exist at least until the immediate crisis has passed.

Other issues that might require assistance of a social worker include the decision by an elderly couple to divorce after a lengthy marital relationship. Such endings carry all of the trauma and difficulties that divorce causes at other ages, but now the children are grown. While the social worker can help couples work through the details surrounding the divorce, we may also need to work with the adult children, many of whom will find their parents' decision illogical. "Why, after 35 years of marriage, are you getting a divorce?" As with marriages at other life stages, divorce can occur for many reasons. Sometimes the partner seeking the divorce does so for unsound reasons, and in other situations the divorce is logical. We show an example of the former in Highlight 9.2.

The truth is that divorce of their parents poses problems for the adult children as well as for the separating couple. Children who saw their parents as a solid couple may be perplexed by the decision. The event can challenge their sense of solidity within their own marriages. Should the divorced parent begin to date and even marry again, this may provoke additional adjustments. Occasionally, this may force the adult children to reassess their definition of who is a family member.

Families with Older Members

Working with the family requires that the social worker recognize how the changes mentioned in the last section affect older members. These changes, coupled with intergenerational issues involving roles, communications, and

Highlight 9.2 Divorce for the Wrong Reason

The Sedgwicks had been married for 52 years, and throughout the years, religious differences between them had been tolerable, if not always pleasant. Alma Sedgwick was a devout Mormon who attended services each week while Ed Sedgwick did not believe in organized religion. When Alma's mobility decreased, elders from her church would make Sunday visits to their home, at which time Ed would go for a walk. This simple system worked for many years until both Ed and Alma went to live in a long-term care facility. Having lost much of his mobility too, Ed was now essentially restricted to their apartment. This meant he could no longer avoid the emissaries from the church who came to visit Alma. Frustrated with his new situation, Ed confided to his oldest daughter Maria that he wanted a divorce from Alma. He said it was the only way to avoid listening to the elders, a situation he could no longer tolerate. Maria, thinking quickly, decided to intervene. She told Ed, a life-long Democrat, that then-President Ronald Reagan had signed a law prohibiting divorce for couples married longer than 50 years. Ed fumed about the nerve of this Republican president and reiterated why he always remained a Democrat. In the end, Alma and Ed lived together until Ed died, and divorce was never mentioned again.

---

expectations, can produce crises in many families. Part of the social worker's task is to define accurately the problem presented by the family.

If adult children care for parents in their own home, this can be another source of difficulty. Communication and relationship difficulties that have existed in the past do not disappear simply because the two generations are colocated. In practice, they may become exacerbated as concerns about dependence/interdependence and role expectations arise. The practitioner may help the family by providing opportunities to talk about issues without allowing these to become openings for venting long-festering anger and resentment. If the level of relationship has deteriorated over the years, it may be impossible to resolve. Such situations may preclude attempts to have parents and children live together in the former's later years or even to involve the children in the planning process.

Adult children may need assistance to deal with their new roles vis-à-vis their parents. While some practitioners have used the term "role reversal" to describe these changes, others argue that this is a misnomer. As Spark and Brody (1970) observed more than a quarter-century ago, "There can be no true role reversal and no second childhood. The specific instrumental help given by an adult child to his older parent cannot be equated with psychological relationship. In feeling, though the adult child may be old himself, he remains in the relationship of child to parent. He does not become parent to his parent. The behavior of a brain-damaged regressed old person may appear child-like but he is not a child. Half a century or more of adulthood cannot be wiped out" (p. 206). Simultaneously, meeting the needs of their own children as well as those of an older parent can stretch the ability of adult children beyond capacity.

In addition, formerly independent, older adult family members may need to come to terms with their need for a greater measure of dependence on others. This is difficult when older parents have been self-reliant throughout their lives. Enforced dependency is likely to be an uncomfortable and unfamiliar role.

At the same time, adult caregivers may need help taking on this role. While actual role reversal may not occur, it is certainly true that the roles of both the adult child and parent will change. As we have seen, when one older adult spouse dies, coming to depend more heavily on the couple's children is common for the surviving spouse. When this occurs, the adult children frequently are simultaneously coping with the needs of their own children, a situation that produces the term *sandwich generation.* By being "sandwiched" between the needs of their children and their parents, such families may feel overcome or overextended. These dual responsibilities may affect the family's financial resources and tax their ability to respond emotionally to the needs of both generations. Feeling stressed and anxious is not a recipe for successfully weathering this life crisis.

THEORY IN ACTION | **Sandwich Generation**

Alan, age 50, has been married for 25 years and has two children attending the local state college. Since his father's death last May, Alan's mother has been staying in his home. As Alan owns a three-bedroom home, his mother has taken over one of the children's rooms. No longer able to drive, she makes lists every day of things she needs for Alan or his wife to get for her after they return home from work. With the children coming home for the holidays, the home will be crowded, and Alan's mother resents the attention taken away from her. Alan feels torn in many different directions and cannot seem to make anyone happy.

Other factors may also enter into the emotional life of parents and adult children. For example, the loss of friendships, job-related identity, and death or illness of other family members may result in a sense of mourning and sadness for the older family members. Too often, adult children underestimate how much loss their parents experience. Loss of the ability to drive a car, for example, impairs significantly one's sense of independence and freedom. Not understanding the license's significance to their parents, many adult children will see the decision to give up one's driver's license as highly logical.

If the adult child and the parent reside together, other challenges await. For example, conflicts over the best way to do things—cook, clean, and raise children—are events with the potential to cause problems. There may even be disputes over who will do what. The older adult parent may resist categorization as a built-in babysitter and look forward to the freedom from expectations that characterized earlier years (Armour, 1995). Other aging parents may insist on paying for everything—food, lodging, and so on—which may precipitate arguments with adult children who find this financial assistance patronizing. Simultaneously, the aging parent's increased dependency and need may stress relationships between the younger couple. It is always possible that the older adult parent's presence will contribute to the formation of triangles as family members seek support for their respective points of view. In the Franks family, the dispute became so heated that Marvin, the husband, demanded that his 85-year-old mother-in-law move out or else he would leave, ending a 30-year marriage. However, when his wife, Gladys, acceded to her husband's demands, the resulting situation caused major conflict with her own sisters, who did not understand how Gladys could be so heartless. The result was a long-standing estrangement among members of Gladys' family.

Sometimes, the need to care for aging parents creates other kinds of friction among the adult children. One sibling may feel the other is not making adequate efforts to help in the care of a parent. An adult child who is making a significant financial contribution to the care of the parent may grow resentful toward siblings who are not contributing to these costs. It is common for the person contributing the most effort and money to become a martyr over the added responsibilities. Such an attitude sows the seeds for bad feelings and anger in some families. In other cases, existing rivalries among adult children can show up when it comes time to decide parental care.

THEORY IN ACTION | Sibling Rivalry

Two sisters, Lucinda and Melinda, agreed initially that the oldest sister, Lucinda, would take responsibility for their mother, who they viewed as no longer capable of independent living. They moved the mother across the country, and she resided in Lucinda's home for several years. During this time, Melinda sent Lucinda money to help offset the costs of caring for their mother. While Lucinda complained constantly about the burden she had accepted, she also insisted that this arrangement was best for their mother. Later, it became obvious that the arrangement had its drawbacks. Lucinda was gone 12 hours per day working two jobs and was charging her mother for such things as cable television, utilities, and food. When their mother was clearly unhappy with the arrangement, the youngest sister, Melinda, planned to have their mother live with her. Despite repeated discussions among the two sisters,

Lucinda did not support the idea of allowing Melinda to assume this responsibility. Finally, in collusion with the mother, Melinda arranged for her mother to come for a short visit. During the "temporary" visit, Melinda helped her mother enter a semi-assisted living facility and took financial responsibility for providing for her mother's care. The mother, it appeared, was still capable of living with a large degree of independence. Moreover, even with a limited income, she was now able to have sufficient resources to go on periodic shopping trips with Melinda. While the living situation for the mother was improved, it was sibling rivalry that drove the struggle over where their mother should live as much as parental needs.

It should be clear by now that both the aging parent and the adult children who decide to live together will experience some degree of stress. Nevertheless, such arrangements can be enormously successful, with benefits for all involved. Children may benefit from having a closer relationship with grandparents and may get to spend more time with them than would otherwise be possible. Umberson (1992) and Freeberg and Stein (1996) noted that adult children often receive emotional support from aging parents. This is particularly true of African American and Mexican American families. In ways similar to the extended-family model that was more prevalent in the past century, generations living together can provide strengths that neither could experience alone. This can include financial assistance, child care, and help with various household activities. The potential for benefit is significant even if disputes do occur. Wilcoxon (1991) identified some roles that grandparents may play that can have positive outcomes for the family. We discuss these briefly in Highlight 9.3.

Resolving family disputes is a challenge for the social worker. The first consideration must always be the needs of the older adult parent, with help for the family's struggle coming after we resolve the former. Thus, we must help the family to see the need to plan for the parent as taking precedence. The social worker can be helpful in getting the family to attend to this. In addition, the social worker can help the family deal with the inevitable stresses and strains associated with adding a "new" family member. This is especially true when the spousal dyad is sufficiently solid.

However, a potential source of difficulty occurs when an elderly parent is added to an already weak marital dyad. While a strong spousal relationship can usually adapt to the changes and challenges arising from the inclusion of one spouse's parent in the family, this is not as true for damaged relationships. In such instances, neither the elderly parent's needs nor the spousal relationship is likely to be effectively addressed. If one spouse perceives the addition of the parent as another burden he or she must carry, it is likely to engender resentment and anger. While such situations are certainly not hopeless, they do represent significant challenges for the family and social worker.

Highlight 9.3 Grandparenting Roles

Historian	Grandparents can help transmit the family history to children. This can include religious, cultural, and ethnic traditions, including those no longer maintained by the family. It can also give the children a sense of perspective on their family's past.
Role Model	The grandparents can model a variety of positive behaviors, including handling of conflict, making decisions based on values, and taking responsibility for one's actions. The grandparent may also transmit or reinforce values such as the importance of education.
Wise Mentor	Grandparents may become the confidants of children who feel reluctant to bring certain issues to their own parents. This can have both positive and negative effects on the family.
Wizard	To children, grandparents can provide a delightful source of stories, sometimes including those parents would not want shared. Nevertheless, stories about a parent's childhood transgressions may help humanize a parent seen as somehow perfect.
Nurturer	In times of crisis, the grandparent may be helpful as a support person for both children and grandchildren. They may be more approachable than the children's own parents.

Nursing Home Placement

The decision to place a family member in a nursing or extended-care facility also presents challenges with which the family may need assistance. It is, in fact, quite common for adult children to feel remorse, guilt, and anxiety over the decision to place a parent in a care facility. These feelings may arise from a sense of obligation to the parent or from regret and embarrassment at not being able to care for the parent in the adult child's home. Thus, part of the social worker's job may involve helping the family address these underlying issues. Sometimes, they exhibit the feelings associated with placement in roundabout ways. Consider, for example, a couple worried about whether the wife's father is functioning adequately in an assisted-living facility. On the one hand, the family's fear and anxiety may be legitimately related to the father's physical and mental abilities and the amount and quality of care provided by the facility. On the other hand, it is just as possible that those emotions arise from the couple's discomfort about the need to place the father in such a facility in the first place.

Another family situation where the social worker may be involved occurs when one member of a couple is placed in a nursing home. The spouse remaining outside the facility faces a variety of strains. These may include financial losses, increased dependency on one's adult children, guilt about having placed one's spouse, a sense of loss or grief, and having to make unfamiliar decisions (Sidell, 2000). In addition, strains may occur in the relationship with the spouse in the care facility. These can include spousal anger about the placement, demands to be taken home, and adjustments to role changes. Communication can become distorted and one's general satisfaction with life diminished because of the placement. Existing marital conflict can be exacerbated. Equally troubling is the adjustment the spouse still living in the community must make to the situation. Unlike a death, the fact that one's spouse lives in a nursing home brings no closure to a difficult situation (MacKenzie & McLean, 1992).

The community-dwelling spouse may experience a loss of closeness to the other spouse, a decline in communication, and a sense that the marriage has ended (Bartlett, 1993; Gladstone, 1995). As might be expected with any loss, one spouse may feel guilt and anger over why this event occurred. There is often the added difficulty of negotiating a new environment in which care for one's spouse is now in the hands of strangers. Others outside the marital dyad may question why the placement was necessary and why the remaining spouse could not have provided care for the other. The social worker can help these clients through several mechanisms. These include a careful analysis of what factors will increase the spouse's degree of marital happiness and assistance in locating and using resources and community supports. The latter includes both social and spiritual supports that are important factors contributing to the satisfaction level of community-residing spouses (Sidell, 2000).

FAMILY INTERVENTION WITH GAY AND LESBIAN FAMILIES

Gay and lesbian families experience essentially the same problems and issues as other families but also have the added burden of dealing with societal prejudice and institutionalized discrimination. As we have discussed earlier, no family exists independent from other social organizations, and the same is true for gay and lesbian families. While societal institutions and organizations may be useful resources for other families, they often create added difficulties for gay and lesbian families. Remembering that the social worker is one component of these societal institutions and that our interactions with gay and lesbian families may be tainted with the same biases and prejudices as others is important. Because of these reactions, "the homosexual's family's relationship with the community is tenuous" and "the very nature of the family itself is fragile with few traditional supports" (Ross, 1994, p. 161). Social workers must be keenly aware of their own personal, religious, spiritual, and other feelings and thoughts regarding these families. The time for such self-reflection is not when the family arrives for a session because awareness of one's own prejudices should be part of the learning process as we prepare for working in this arena. If social workers' own values will prevent them from helping these families, they should refer the families to competent and appropriate counselors who are not disabled by homophobic views. (Note: This section is written primarily for heterosexual practitioners who have limited experience with gay, lesbian, bisexual, and transgendered clients.)

Societal Barriers

A variety of societal barriers confront gay and lesbian families as they struggle with the challenges of surviving and prospering in an often homophobic environment. They often encounter attitudes and behaviors that suggest the family is engaging in immoral and inappropriate practices. While the same-sex couple may be adequately prepared for such beliefs, their children are another story. Kids may be chided for having two mothers or two fathers, or derided using language suggesting that they share their parents' sexual orientation. Eventually, both parents and children may come to internalize some of society's negative attitudes toward gay and lesbian individuals (Goldenberg & Goldenberg, 2002).

Society has a long history of efforts to change the orientation of gay and lesbian individuals. These efforts include punishment, defining the behavior as abnormal with its own psychiatric diagnostic category, use of electroshock and aversive therapy, surgical interventions, conversion therapy, and other "treatments." Today, neither research findings nor the American Psychiatric Association's *Diagnostic and Statistical Manual* of mental disorders identify being gay and lesbian as a mental illness. In addition, we have no clear indication about how or why a person's sexual orientation develops as it does. As a result, most social workers today focus on the specific family issues that brought the couple in for help and not on the couple's sexual orientation (Goldenberg & Goldenberg, 2000).

The families of origin of gay men and lesbians may also present a major source of anguish for their children. Families may engage in outright rejection of their child who comes out as gay or lesbian. They may take other steps, such as ignoring the adult child's partner or simply not inviting them to special events and holiday celebrations. Still other parents will attempt to set the adult child up with a person of the opposite sex with the goal of changing the individual's sexual orientation. Such actions end up driving a wedge between the parents and gay or lesbian child that will only grow larger over time. The long-term result is that the adult child loses an important resource in his or her life as family support disappears. Cutoffs are sometimes the way that one or both parties reach resolution of such impasses.

In addition, gay and lesbian families "often lack rituals to symbolize their relationship" (Brown & Brown, 2002, p. 250). For example, legal ceremonies such as weddings are not routinely available, nor are there showers or similar events that demarcate one's changed status. Even if the couple creates their own service or ritual, it is likely not to be as celebrated an event as a traditional wedding, usually because of the lack of familial support and participation. One task of the social worker may be to help the couple plan and create their own rituals if this is one of their goals.

Gay and lesbian families often have little or no legal protection of the sort routinely provided to traditional families. For example, in some states they are denied the right to adopt a child or serve as a foster parent, and they can be prevented from taking certain jobs, such as in child care and education. They are often the targets of violence, including both verbal abuse and physical assault (Herek, 1989). In many instances, they may lose custody of their own children if one parent dies. In such situations, the surviving partner is denied Social Security benefits and the right to participate in medical decisions affecting his or her partner. In response to this obvious discrimination, many communities and some states have adopted laws that protect the legal rights of gay and lesbian individuals. Most, however, do not accord gay and lesbian individuals all of the rights routinely available to heterosexual couples. Even a recent U.S. Supreme Court decision extending privacy rights to same-sex relationships and a Massachusetts Supreme Court ruling allowing gays and lesbians the right to marry are unlikely to provide equal protection to these couples.

Unlike other couples, gay and lesbian couples often face the issue of *coming out,* in which their sexual orientation becomes public knowledge. Because the consequences of self-identifying as gay or lesbian can be so severe, fear of being so identified can affect many aspects of the individual's life. The secretiveness that many gays and lesbians must engage in to protect themselves can complicate their ability to resolve common problems. Uncertainty about how one's parents will react may contribute to creation of a life facade in which relationships with a loved partner are denied or hidden for years. Sometimes, the emotional pain associated with coming out may be the underlying reason that the gay man or lesbian woman seeks help from the social worker. However, the identified symptoms may involve sleep disturbances, anxiety, or other interpersonal problems (Janzen & Harris, 1997).

Gay and Lesbian Couples

As should be clear, gay and lesbian families face a great deal more discrimination than is ever experienced by other couples, solely because of their sexual orientation. As with other groups that have experienced such treatment, it is not unusual for gay and lesbian families to wonder about the social worker's ability to be fair and accept them. When gay and lesbian couples seek assistance, social workers need to be comfortable with their own attitudes, values, and expectations about sexual orientation. This requires a degree of understanding about how gay and lesbian families differ from and share some similarities with heterosexual families. For example, in gay or lesbian families, there may or may not be any traditional role playing in which male/female roles are taken. On the other hand, gay and lesbian individuals are likely to be influenced by the same societal expectations as heterosexuals. Consequently, gay males may be struggling with the same challenge of being emotionally open and nurturing that faces straight males. Lesbian women may have adopted traditional female behaviors and interpersonal patterns that characterize women in male/female relationships. Thus, the social worker may need to help the partners adopt more effective and satisfying ways of relating to each other.

There are additional issues facing gay men and lesbian women that are less problematic for heterosexuals. For example, there tend to be fewer natural locations where one can meet other same-sex individuals. Not only can heterosexuals congregate in any number of locations to meet individuals of the opposite sex, but family and friends often help them in their quest for a relationship (Murphy, 1994). These options are significantly reduced for gays and lesbians seeking partners. Attempts by well-meaning parents or relatives to set the gay man or lesbian woman up with an opposite-sex date often ignore the fact that the individual already has a significant other. Such disrespect for or neglect of a person's boundaries is much less likely to occur with heterosexuals.

THEORY IN ACTION | A Difficult Situation in a Gay or Lesbian Relationship

Henry was staying at his parents' house for the holidays. His partner, Fred, had gone to his own parents for the weekend as Henry's parents would not accept their open relationship. During church services on Sunday morning, his mother introduced him to a young woman she had obviously planned to have meet him. His parents were constantly trying to set him up with women when he came to visit them. Henry decided this would be his last holiday with his parents.

Lesbian women are more likely to meet each other at feminist gatherings where friendships can occur, leading to longer relationships. Gay men are more likely to connect at gay bars that tend to be more common than bars that serve primarily women (Berger, 1990; Peplau et al., 1978).

Simultaneously, gay and lesbian couples may have significantly different life experiences than other couples or even each other. For example, Brown (1995) found a much higher rate of past sexual abuse among lesbian couples than among gay couples. Other differences also exist. Sexual activity levels are likely to be higher in gay than in lesbian couples, while the latter are more apt to have had fewer partners (Kurdek, 1995). Within the two types of couples, lesbians are more likely to have stronger affectional connections to one another and are less likely to engage in casual sex that might threaten the relationship (Blumstein & Schwartz, 1983). Lesbian couples tend to be relationship-centered with a great degree of commitment to equality between the partners. Both gay and lesbian couples are more likely to share household tasks than is true for heterosexual couples (Kurdek, 1995).

Same-sex couples tend to have shorter love relationships than is true for heterosexuals despite the fact that both groups are equally committed to lasting romantic relationships with their partners (Kurdek, 1995; Weinberg, Williams, & Pryor, 1994). In addition, gay unions are less likely to be monogamous, and both partners often accept this freedom as normal. This is not to say that jealousy cannot exist but just that the norms for sexual behavior are more flexible than among either lesbian or heterosexual couples.

Peplau, Veniegas, and Campbell (1996) compared heterosexual couples with gay and lesbian couples and found several similarities. For example, both same-sex and opposite-sex partners experience similar kinds of conflicts, and tend to be satisfied with their current situation. On the other hand, same-sex couples are less likely to have trouble ending a problematic relationship and are more likely to reject traditional divisions of labor in the management of their lives.

Besides the more typical problems that families may face, gay and lesbian families are likely to have specific issues that may need to be addressed. These might include issues related to coming out to others, rebuilding connections to their own parents, expected role behavior, accepting their sexual orientation, sexual exclusiveness, fear of AIDS, deciding whether to have children and how, dealing with discrimination and violence, transitioning from one life stage to another without adequate role models, arranging for such things as medical power of attorney, and learning to trust the social worker.

Franklin and Jordan (1999) and others identify several techniques that are helpful in working with same-sex couples. One of the first approaches is to learn how the clients refer to each other. For example, do they use the term *partner, significant other, lover,* or some other appellation? A second is to ask whether the couple lives together or apart. Contrary to popular belief, about 50 percent of same-sex couples live apart (Jay & Young, 1979), a pattern significantly different from heterosexual partners. This question is important because it may help clarify how much commitment the couple has to each other.

A third technique is to help the couple adjust to what has been called the "loss of heterosexual privilege" (Murphy, 1994, p. 13), which precludes them from enjoying the usual array of socially approved commitment markers such as wedding ceremonies and formal announcements of their union. At the same time, some couples will reject the notion of marriage as inherently patriarchal. Whatever the choices, the social worker will want to use the same language as the family members in discussing these topics.

A fourth recommendation is to explore with lesbian women their experience of sexual abuse and violence that can have a direct impact on various aspects of their self-identify and ability to form relationships. Brown's (1995) study, mentioned earlier, supports this suggestion.

A fifth approach is to look at the issue of coming out and its influence on the family. For example, one partner who comes out may create anxiety in the other who is not yet ready to take that step. The practitioner can help the couple strengthen and acknowledge their commitment to one another despite the coming-out decision of one partner. However, helping both members of the couple come out can contribute to healthier psychological adjustment (Murphy, 1989), and the social worker can help the couple in planning how and when to convey this information to family and friends. Ultimately, however, it is entirely the decision of the individuals involved whether they wish to self-disclose their sexual identities.

A sixth technique involves asking the couple to use journaling to record role expectations and identify major areas of disagreement about such things as decision making, distribution of tasks, and sexual needs. This is an important tool for exploring potential problem areas and learning how each partner perceives the situation.

A seventh suggestion for helping same-sex couples is to explore with them issues relating to children. This is important for a couple of reasons. First, many lesbian and gay families have children either from pre-existing relationships or through other means. Second, many same-sex couples want children but face a variety of legal, medical, financial, and social barriers (Patterson, 1994). They may need referral to legal or medical professionals to manage these issues while the social worker helps deal with social and emotional components of the decision-making process.

Couples with children may benefit from the support offered by community parent groups composed of other gay and lesbian couples. We can access information about such groups on the Internet through such organizations as We are Family, or Lesbian Parents Network for parents and Colage for children of gay and lesbian parents. At least one periodical, *Gay Parent Magazine*, is devoted specifically to this topic.

It is important that the social worker accept and value the couple as human beings seeking assistance with life challenges. Familiarity with gay and lesbian lifestyles is essential if the social worker is to understand the context within which these families exist. For example, the social worker must have a degree of comfort for discussing such things as sexual behavior between same-sex couples. Some authors have advocated that practitioners seek out personal and professional relationships with gay and lesbian individuals to help learn more about this group and increase one's level of comfort (Long, 1996).

The relatively wide spread of AIDS and HIV in the same-sex community requires a social worker who is sensitive to the importance of this disease for many gays and lesbians. For example, many same-sex couples will have lost a friend to the disease. Others may have or have had an afflicted partner. These experiences often lead to grief and a sense of loss as well as creating concerns about one's own sexual activities. The social worker may need to provide grief counseling to help clients resolve the feelings these deaths and illness have engendered. This is especially true if other typical support providers such as clergy and family are unsympathetic toward same-sex sexual orientation.

Other couples may have to face the possibility that one partner's acquisition of the disease is going to limit their relationship. Such illnesses have implications for emotional connections, income streams, and health and retirement benefits. Serodiscordant couples may need help discussing their situations. Unexpressed feelings and reactions to one person being HIV-positive while the other is negative often exist. Fear, anxiety, and anger are all common in such situations, and the social worker can see partners both individually and together to help them deal with these issues (Mattison & McWhirter, 1994). By getting these topics out on the table, the couple is better able to avoid the denial that will increase the risk of transmitting the disease. Of course, the HIV-negative partner may end up providing end-of-life care for the HIV-positive partner, with all the stresses, heartache, and disappointment that the slow death of a loved one entails. In this as in other instances, the social worker's knowledge of community support groups would be particularly helpful.

We also need a solid knowledge about sexual orientation to deal with the many myths regarding this topic. Social workers should know enough to refute each of them. Highlight 9.4 provides a list of common misunderstandings and myths about gay and lesbian individuals.

A sizeable body of knowledge exists on the experiences of children raised in same-sex families. These findings refute concerns that children in such homes experience deficits or become gay or lesbian at any greater rate than is true for heterosexual couples (Allen & Burrell, 1996). Children from same-sex families experience no more difficulties with identity, self-concept, and behavioral or peer problems, and are no more likely to be sexually abused.

Knowledge of community resources for gay and lesbian individuals and couples is important because these often become major sources of assistance to such families. Occasionally, gay men and lesbians have created families of choice with other community members, thereby replacing an unaccepting family of origin. In addition, knowing agencies or individuals that provide HIV or AIDS counseling may also prove useful if the social worker is not able to do this counseling. The social worker should be comfortable with issues of sexuality as these topics are at least as important in gay couples as in others.

While many gay or lesbian children are estranged from their parents because of the child's sexual orientation, it would be misleading to suggest that this is the norm. Savin-Williams and Esterberg (2000) note that "the gay child–heterosexual parent relationship, especially the child–mother relationship, is generally positive and satisfying" (p. 201). It is interesting that the mother is most often the parent to whom the gay man or lesbian woman comes out (Savin-Williams, 1998). An estimated 40 percent to 75 percent share their sexual orientation with their mother, while a lower percentage provide this information to their father. At the same time, many children who have come out to their families experienced harassment, either verbal or physical. Young women are the most likely to suffer physical assault, with the mother being the most common abuser. The fear of such reactions often drives many gay or lesbian children to withhold this information from one or both

Highlight 9.4 | Myths and Misunderstandings

1. *Same-sex orientation is caused by behavior and actions of parents.* Current research points more to biologic factors than to the behavior of one's parents. As Laird (1994) indicates: "In spite of efforts to blame certain stereotypical family constellations (e.g., the domineering, seductive mother and the passive, peripheral father), researchers were not able to link male or female homosexuality to any particular family form" (p. 120).
2. *Attraction to individuals of the same sex is simply a matter of preference.* There is strong evidence that one's sexual orientation is set at birth and is not easily changed (Bargh & Chartrand, 1999; LeVay & Hamer, 1994; Whitam, Diamond, & Martin, 1993).
3. *Gay and lesbian people are a threat to the safety of children.* Most pedophiles are heterosexual males, and there is almost no sexual abuse of children in same-sex homes. Gay and lesbian people pose no greater risk to children than is true of heterosexuals (Child Welfare League of America, 1995a; Jenny, Roesler, & Poyer, 1994).
4. *Children who grow up in a gay or lesbian family are likely to be gay themselves.* Children raised in same-sex homes are no more likely to become gay or lesbian than children raised in heterosexual homes. In fact, most homosexuals are raised by heterosexual families (Bailey et al., 1995).
5. *Gays and lesbians who work with children attempt to attract them to a same-sex life.* There is no evidence that gay men or lesbian women engage in proselytizing children with regard to sexual orientation. The research regarding causation does not support the idea that a person can be talked into or out of becoming homosexual (Morgan & Nerison, 1993).
6. *Gay men and lesbians are mentally ill.* Homosexuality was discarded as a mental illness many years ago and is no longer considered deviant by any of the major mental health organizations in the world (Barret & Logan, 2002).
7. *There is little in common between gay/lesbian and heterosexual families.* All families tend to face the same challenges, life tasks, and developmental issues, whatever the sexual orientation of the parents. Same-sex parents and families do have some different experiences because of discrimination and prejudice (Barret & Logan, 2002).

parents. Siblings tend to be supportive of their gay brother or lesbian sister, although it is still more likely that friends will be most accepting and helpful. Robinson, Walters, and Skeen (1989) found that about a quarter of parents had suspicions about their child's sexual orientation before the child's coming out to them.

Negative parental reactions do occur with some degree of frequency. This may be in the form of shock, grief, abuse, disbelief, condemnation, threats to withhold emotional or financial support, and demands that the child not share this information with anyone else in the family. Depending upon the age when the child comes out, parents may force the child to seek mental health counseling to treat the "deviance." Often, this reaction is the result of the parent having almost no exposure to homosexuality (Ben-Ari, 1995). Some parents will blame themselves for the child's sexual orientation, while others will wonder what they could have done differently that might have changed the outcome. Blaming other family or nonfamily members for causing this "calamity" is also common.

While parents may react negatively when the child first broaches the topic, there is evidence that greater acceptance on the part of the parent often follows this stage (Ben-Ari, 1995). Sometimes this is driven by parental anxiety that rejecting the child may result in a permanent disruption or loss of the parent–child relationship (Boxer, Cook, & Herdt, 1991). Social workers can help in this process by recommending written material that they can give to parents to help educate them about sexual orientation.

In the end, the task of the social worker working with a same-sex couple is similar to helping heterosexual couples. This entails helping "clients learn ways to deal with life problems that will promote greater satisfaction in individual and family functioning and in relations with others" (Janzen & Harris, 1997, p. 217).

FAMILY INTERVENTION WITH PEOPLE LIVING IN POVERTY

Poor families experience the same kinds of difficulties as do other families, with the addition of severe financial constraints. Poverty exacerbates problems in family functioning and often results in feelings of extreme distress (Shamai & Sharlin, 1996). This contributes to the family's sense of hopelessness and doubts about the potential success of any intervention. Sharlin and Shamai (1990) found that this sometimes led practitioners to join with the family in feeling that nothing is likely to change. In such situations, a "coalition of despair" is created that ultimately compromises the social worker's ability to help the family. When social workers no longer believe they can help families, it is entirely likely that families themselves will sense this. Families who lose hope and motivation are missing two important factors in successful outcomes (Shamai & Sharlin, 1996).

THEORY IN ACTION | Hopelessness

MR. ERIN: I don't know how we are going to be able to continue. I have no job, and without the money to support us, I am afraid we will be at the homeless shelter forever. I tried to find a job, but they all say I am either too old or do not have enough skills. We have our four grandchildren to care for, and living in that shelter is horrible on the children. I don't feel like I can find any way out.

First, it is important to make the judgment about whether extreme distress characterizes the family's situation. One way of making this assessment is to use the Families in Extreme Distress Scale (Sharlin & Shamai, 2000). The scale is basically a checklist completed by the social worker that helps enumerate the nature and type of problems experienced by the family. Categories include poverty, housing, health, couple functioning, parental functioning, children, substance abuse, antisocial behavior, and support systems. If a variety of problems emerge, the social worker can consider using one of several approaches to help prevent the tendency to become overwhelmed. One method is to work with a team of helpers so that the social worker is not feeling the entire burden of helping the family. This allows for one practitioner to assume the role of therapist while another operates as case manager. An additional method is for the social worker to seek feedback in either peer supervision or from one's own supervisor. The primary goal here is to provide a resource for the social worker to help offset the impact of the family's situation.

A third recommended approach is to plan for interagency collaboration that can bring to bear the resources of more than one service provider. Again, this expands the ability of the social worker to help the family overcome the multiple barriers they face.

Working directly with the family often means finding ways to enhance their motivation to change along with raising hope that change is possible. Techniques that empower families by highlighting and building on their strengths are positive steps in the right direction. It is important that clients recognize they have a variety of strengths that can be helpful in managing their situations. Sometimes the social worker may need to reframe some of the family's situation to identify these strengths. For example, a family experiencing multiple challenges may feel they have little or nothing going for them. The social worker, however, can help them understand that the very act of recognizing their problems and seeking help is an indication of one of the family's strengths. Sharlin and Shamai (2000) suggest that the practitioner can also use written messages with families. The messages are basic summaries of the family's situation coupled with recognition for their accomplishments. These serve to reinforce positive growth on the parents' part while also rewriting the story of their lives to emphasize strengths instead of deficits.

Families mired in poverty and in danger of losing all hope may lash out at the social worker or other agencies perceived as providing insufficient help or too many barriers to service. It is important that the social worker not become defensive in such situations and recognize the anger for what it is, namely a reaction to the frustrations facing the family. As long as the social worker does not personalize the family's anger, working with them is still possible. Helping the family focus on a specific problem may also help because the tendency to see all problems as intertwined and insurmountable is common.

Poor families generally do not lack income alone. Frequently, the lack of income is complicated by the absence of health insurance, homelessness or substandard living situations, and related issues. Helping families experiencing poverty and related economic deprivation often requires creative and prompt interventions. Lindsey (1997) suggests several specific approaches that can prove effective. These include meeting immediate needs first, which includes assistance in locating housing, temporary assistance with food, and emergency medical care, if needed. Families that are also homeless may need help maintaining parental roles in an environment that tends to undercut this aspect of family life. Families may need help learning to create and use a budget and to more effectively manage the resources they do have. To the extent that other problems are intertwined, specialized assistance may also be required. For example, the family living with a drug-abusing member may need help to assist this person into a treatment center. An abusive spouse may require involvement in an appropriate treatment program.

Poverty is not an equal opportunity affliction and affects people of color disproportionately. Williams (1990) and others have recommended several practitioner activities that we can use specifically to help people of color experiencing poverty. Their suggestions are likely just as reasonable for other poor families. They include getting the family connected with natural support systems in the environment, including "existing community groups (minority preferably) that are oriented to advocacy, socialization, parenting, education, job training, and so on" (p. 186). Finding and building a network of indigenous supports and the use of nontraditional resources may be helpful. This is consistent with studies by Edin and Lein (1997) and others that find those in poverty are more likely to use networks composed of kin to obtain goods and services (Rank, 2000). Werner (1999) has substantiated the benefits of relying on support from extended family members. He notes that repeated studies have shown how such care can produce resilient children able to withstand the influences of "chronic poverty, family discord, or parental psychopathology" (p. 143). Moreover, resilient children tend to recruit surrogate parents who may be older siblings, grandparents, teachers, or others. Sometimes, peers may play a similar role as a source of support. The role of spiritual and religious values as a positive influence in such situations has also been identified.

Even families that are just above the poverty line may become victims of events that are beyond their control. Losing a job, major illness and medical bills, and separation and divorce from a spouse all have the potential of turning the near poor into the poor. In some ways, both this group and the poor are just one paycheck away from a catastrophe. Anything that diminishes income or increases expenses can push these families over the edge. While poverty does not automatically mean that a family has other problems, this is often the case. Unemployment and lack of resources can quickly engender family stress, producing or exacerbating both intrapersonal and interpersonal strains.

Newman (1994) describes what happens when the slide into poverty begins for a previously financially secure family. Parental reactions to loss of a lifestyle may vary from initial bickering amid increasing stress and tension to more serious family breakdowns. If one wage earner is responsible for the income drop, self-recrimination, anger, and frustration are common. Some families attempt to maintain a facade of normality in such situations, but this typically lasts only as long as financial reserves hold out. During this period, family members may fabricate stories about employment, and all members of the family may get drawn into the charade. Symbols of success like homes and cars are retained as long as possible. The family may avoid bankruptcy through fear of losing face, but often this is inevitable. Foreclosures and repossession of goods not yet paid for threaten the family in other ways. Loss of transportation limits employment opportunities and impairs one's sense of freedom.

Emotionally, children in such homes may be drawn closer to parents but at the risk of role reversals in which parents depend on their children for the psychological strength to carry on. It is also problematic for adolescent children who should be moving in the direction of greater independence from parents. Late-adolescent children may decide to forego further schooling or at least to postpone it until the financial situation improves. Many will work and send money to their parents to help out. Financial support may move from children to parents instead of the other way around, with the result that children feel stressed and parents feel guilty. Parental fighting may affect both the parents and the children who are exposed to it. Divorce may result when the stresses and strains overwhelm the parents' emotional resources and resolve. Because the financial consequences of divorce affect women more than men, the net result may be another single mother joining the ranks of the poor.

As should be evident by now, effective practice with impoverished people will take interventions at the micro, mezzo, and macro levels, as the problems of poverty involve all three levels. Individual counseling approaches can assist but not replace larger social development activities. We will address some of the macro and policy issues relating to the family in some detail in Chapter 13.

The success of family intervention programs such as family preservation and the use of wrap-around services is due in part to their ability to address multiple problems confronting the system. These specialized programs will be discussed further in Chapter 11.

FAMILY INTERVENTION WITH SINGLE PARENTS

Single parents can fall into several categories, with very different consequences for each. They may include a mother who has never married, a mother or father who is separated or divorced, a lesbian woman, or other arrangements. As Coates (1999) notes, single teenage mothers face a potentially much bleaker future than professional or middle-class women who are single parents. In addition, most recent research on poverty indicates that single women head a large proportion of poor families. Their poverty is largely a consequence of reduced earning ability, absence of adequate day care, and insufficient financial help from absent fathers and government welfare systems (McLanahan & Garfinkle, 1989). In this section, we will look specifically at interventions with single-parent families including, but not restricted to, the poor.

Singlehood, especially because of divorce, is a relatively "temporary condition since 80% of men and 75% of women will remarry" (Hetherington, 1989, p. 537). Nevertheless, the period immediately following divorce is often a painful one for both children and parents. It is common to see complaints about emotional and physical maladies, dysfunctional family behavior, problems adjusting to new expectations, and other life changes. Doubts that one can manage everything are common, along with grief, confusion, and the task of planning for the future (Nichols, 1999). Though unhappiness, fighting, and stress may have characterized the immediate past, both adults and children will still experience the actual separation and divorce as traumatic. Rules that had previously governed one's behavior as part of a couple no longer seem to apply. Old friends may suddenly disappear, and one's own parents may be unhappy over the situation. The possibility of reunification leaves things in limbo so that getting on with life becomes more tentative.

Once they achieve a divorce, the opportunity for moving on becomes an obligation. Both "psychological work and a reorganization of the family system" are required (Nichols, 1999, p. 181). Neither friends, family, nor practitioners can shorten this period of mourning or lessen the pain associated with it. Moving on will likely not occur until the individual accepts the finality of the situation. The social worker can assist during this period by helping the person come to terms with the feelings of loss and emptiness while letting go of the past.

Typically, this rough period lasts for up to two years, with some lingering difficulties for individual family members. Nichols notes that "loss of access to the noncustodial parent (usually the father) is associated with problems in the children's adjustment to divorce, while loss of access to the children is associated with problems for fathers" (p. 183). Kruk (1994) found that noncustodial divorced fathers often experienced high levels of distress even several years after the end of the marriage. These fathers saw loss of involvement with their children as the most significant negative factor in their lives. He concludes that "fathers, who continue to comprise the majority of the noncustodial parent population, may thus be considered a highly at risk but less visible population in the context of divorce and its consequences" (p. 19). Indeed, Dudley and

Stone (2001) point out that noncustodial male parents are in danger of becoming obsolete as a consequence of factors that include societal barriers, stereotyping, and public policy. One role for social workers in similar situations is to help both parents maintain positive relationships with their children, no matter which one receives custody. Another role is to encourage parental cooperation to ensure that the divorce does not also destroy the parent–child relationship. Showing respect for the noncustodial parent's feelings of loss and emotional reactions to the divorce is also an appropriate activity. This may help counter the traditional male tendency to display an outward calm while inwardly struggling with grief and other normal reactions. "The clinical picture for fathers is most favorable if diminution of contact and disengagement can be prevented and if fathers are encouraged to continue a satisfying and unthreatened parental relationship with their children" (Kruk, 1994, p. 24).

Custodial parents are likely to experience their own difficulties. Mothers with sole custody report more depression from the overwhelming burden of taking care of the children without help. The social worker's role may be to encourage the parents to create some sort of civil relationship that will not further endanger anyone. They may need help designing rules and consistent approaches to typical childhood antics, such as attempts to triangulate the parents.

Although the two-year post-divorce period is a useful yardstick, it is not an infallible predictor of who will be okay and who will not. For example, boys show the greatest tendency to maintain maladaptive behavior after the two-year period. Thus, it is to be expected that assistance with parenting and improvement in parent–child relationships might be a fertile area for intervention. Assistance with such things as disciplinary repertoire and communication patterns between mothers and sons is also a likely area of need. As Hetherington (1989) notes, "Divorced mothers were ineffectual in their control attempts and gave many instructions with little follow-through. They tended to nag, natter, and complain and were often involved in angry, escalating coercive cycles with their sons. Spontaneous negative 'start-ups,' that is negative behavior initiated following neutral or positive behavior by the other person, were twice as likely to occur between mothers and sons in divorced families as in nondivorced families" (p. 5). The intensity and duration of such occurrences tended to overshadow positive interactions and expressions of caring and warmth.

In such families, it is common for both sons and daughters to achieve a greater degree of equality, power, and independence than in intact families. They are also less likely to have appropriate supervision and expressed parental interest in their comings and goings. Once a stepfamily is formed, some of these dynamics will change though conflicts are likely to continue. Interestingly, once the stepfamily is formed, daughters may begin to have more difficult interactions with their mother while the sons' struggles with the mother tend to end.

Mothers frequently struggle with the multiple demands placed on single parents. The stresses may create resentment among some parents toward children they perceive both as burdens and as barriers to other life changes, such as a remarriage. Other mothers will become overly protective. Usually, however, the mother assumes the burden of trying to provide a safe, healthy, and positive environment for her children (Weiss, 1994). This may extend to routinely placing the children's needs ahead of her own, an area that may need attention if it becomes extreme. Many mothers will worry about whether the decision to divorce has caused permanent damage to children and are somewhat reassured when the children function normally.

The absence of one parent from the home may allow the remaining parent and children to become closer. This can be a two-edged sword. On the one hand, in lacking another adult to talk to, the parent may share developmentally inappropriate feelings and reactions with children. On the other hand, this sharing gives the parent an outlet for expressing feelings while drawing children and parent closer together (Weiss, 1994). Children can begin to assume greater responsibility for maintaining the family environment and have an increased sense of involvement in family decisions.

Some parents can switch from being a partner to being a parent when they believe the situation warrants. If, for example, a child balks at doing something the parent requests, he or she may assume that there is room for negotiation. The parent, on the other hand, must become more assertive and assume the parental role to ensure that the child does as asked. Sometimes this need to shift between roles is confusing for both parent and child.

Following a divorce, children may be especially attuned to parental conflicts over a variety of things, including money. This, however, need not be a major problem, and parents can be encouraged to refrain from sharing all the gory details, especially if sharing upsets their children. The tendency to treat children like small adults can have the unintended consequence of creating role reversals. This might occur when the child demands to know when the parent will be returning home or warns the parent not to drink and drive. It can also occur when one child tries to assume adult control over a sibling without either the parent's encouragement or the sibling's agreement. Such events can be problematic (Weiss, 1994).

FAMILY INTERVENTION WITH STEPFAMILIES

Ihinger-Tallman and Pasley (1987) summarize some ways in which remarriage to someone with children differs from one's first marriage. First, there is immediately a new family with members who have not had sufficient time and opportunity to get to know, let alone like, one another. Second, there is the potential for generational confusion in which a stepmother, for example, might have trouble playing a parental role with a stepchild near her own age. This is often the case when the new wife is much younger than her husband. A third challenge arises from the involvement of former in-laws, who can threaten the new couple's privacy and have a claim on the affections of their grandchildren. A fourth difference is that confusion of roles is much more likely, and ambiguity is the norm. Another difference arises from mixed loyalties and allegiances. For example, one or both stepparents may wonder who is responsible for managing money and who will discipline whom. It is expected that a parent might favor one's own children over those of the spouse in matters of affection, time, and money. A sixth difference is the presence of emotional residue (baggage) from the previous marriage. Past problems can interfere with a partner's ability to trust the new spouse. Finally, the new partnership has some unwilling participants who did not necessarily vote to join the group.

As is evident, blending two families is not an easy chore. Often, blending families means children must move away from old friends and lose continuity in other institutions, such as school and recreational organizations. They may react to these changes with a mixture of feelings, but anger and resentment are very common. They may not understand why their parent remarried, although they will ultimately be the beneficiaries of a more structured and dependable existence (Nichols, 1999). Attempts by one parent to supplant the birth parent's role are likely to be met with hostility and verbal rebukes. Understandably, the child is now facing several issues. First is the fact that the new parent is taking up the time and emotional attention of the birth parent. Second, there is the possible loss of the flexibility and freedom that have characterized life in a single-parent household. Third, there are not the longstanding emotional ties that undergird a birth parent's efforts to discipline a child.

Social workers can help stepparents recognize these factors and suggest a go-slow approach in which the biological parent handles disciplinary chores. Only after a closer emotional connection exists between stepparent and stepchild should the role of the former be increased. During this period of adjustment, it is important for the couple to strengthen and cement their own relationship, which can otherwise become a casualty to the wars with children. Indeed, Cissna, Cox, and Bocher (1994) state that "the first task of a newly formed stepfamily is to establish the solidarity of the marriage relationship in the minds of the stepchildren" (p. 264). Absent the children's acceptance of the marriage, stepparent attempts to assume greater authority over them is probably futile. Social workers can help by explaining to parents that their marriage must come first in the priorities of this new arrangement. This must in turn be communicated clearly to the children.

Of course, parents must devote the time together to strategize on the best ways to strengthen the dyad and eventually the family unit. Support groups for stepparents can be of assistance in anticipating and managing typical challenges arising in the new family structure. More formal assistance can come in the form of training to prepare stepparents in the areas of child management, partner support and communication, and problem solving (Rutter, 1999, p. 178). Ultimately, it is rarely possible for the bond between stepparents to be stronger than that between parent and child. New stepparents need to expect this and recognize that it does not represent a threat or challenge to their relationship with one another.

Although 80 percent of stepchildren show few or no behavioral problems, this is not true for all such children (Rutter, 1999). While children who are younger when the remarriage occurs seem to have less difficulty with the new entity, the early years of remarriage and establishment of a stepfamily are sometimes particularly difficult for early adolescents. Children from age 9 to about 15 are less likely to enter into the new family emotionally, resisting anything that seems to threaten their newfound independence. Even intensive efforts by stepparents may not be successful in gaining their stepchildren's affection. Disputes between stepdaughters and stepfathers are common. For a variety of reasons, this lack of a rapprochement continues for many stepfamilies.

Stepmothers, of course, may also face significant challenges to their new role, in part because of the social expectation that they will take major responsibility for raising the children. This can place the stepmother in a very difficult position at a time when the stepchildren are not prepared to accept a replacement parent. Encouraging the biological father to take a greater role in disciplining his children rather than expecting the stepmother to shoulder this burden is a logical social worker activity.

Recommendations during this period vary. With stepfathers, it is better to encourage the stepfather to work on relationship building with the stepchildren, provide support for the biological mother, and later to assume a more authoritative role. With stepmothers, the task may be to encourage the biological father to assume the lead in rearing and disciplining his own children. In blended families, the biological parents should take major responsibility for their own children and allow the other parent to work on establishing a relationship with stepchildren before assuming disciplinary responsibilities.

In some families, helping siblings who find the transitions are threatening their relationships with each other also may be necessary. In other families, the relationship among siblings may become too enmeshed and dependent upon each other, apparently in reaction to the uncertainty of events occurring in their lives. Parents may need assistance in dealing with this situation and with rivalries between stepsiblings.

While the trials and tribulations of stepfamilies are legend (sometimes mostly), many positive features characterize them (Rutter, 1999). "Children acquire multiple role models, they get a chance to see their parents happier with other people than they were with each other. They learn how to be flexible" (p. 177). Children can learn increased responsibility for themselves and for younger siblings. They also have an opportunity to build stronger relationships with their own siblings. As Hetherington and Stanley-Hagan (2000) point out, "If close parent–child relationships and authoritative parenting can be sustained, children are better adjusted in divorced or remarried families than in conflict-ridden first-marriage families" (p. 184). Moreover, there is increasing evidence that children who do experience significant adjustment problems following divorce are reacting less to the transition and more to previously existing difficulties. The same may be true for parents (Simons, Johnson, & Lorenz, 1996). Cherlin et al. (1991) suggest that when children's adjustment before divorce is controlled, the actual occurrence of adjustment problems following divorce is much lower.

Most remarried couples have a strong desire to make the new marriage work. Despite the best of intentions, however, 60 percent of such couples divorce (Hetherington & Stanley-Hagan, 2000). Moreover, the divorce is likely to come sooner rather than later, especially when stepchildren are involved. According to Tzeng and Mare (1995), divorce rates for families with stepchildren are 50 percent higher than those where there are no stepchildren. These figures suggest that for at least some stepfamilies, multiple transitions will confront them and exacerbate the already problematic nature of divorce.

FAMILY INTERVENTION AND FAMILIES WITH DISABILITIES

Managing the multiple challenges of creating and raising a family is a Herculean chore. It requires substantial commitment by all family members, particularly the parents. Families composed of one or more individuals with a disability typically have an added layer of responsibility with which to contend. When we use the term *disability,* we are including both children and adults whose mental or physical condition limits their ability to fulfill some life responsibilities. These responsibilities can include "caring for oneself, performing manual tasks, walking, seeing, hearing, speaking, breathing, learning, and working" (Equal Employment Opportunity Commission [EEOC], 1991, p. I-27). Disabilities can be permanent or temporary. We are also including anyone who is perceived as part of the family, whether related by blood or marriage. This definition includes the son who uses a wheelchair, the sister with a brain injury limiting her ability to process information, the mother with a mental disorder, the father who is unemployed after falling off a ladder at work, and the grandfather suffering from dementia and being cared for by his daughter.

Parents may need help adjusting to the fact that their child has been born with a disability. Parental reactions to this event can range from anxiety to guilt to anger to depression. Some parents may worry about whether they can care for a child born with a disability. Others may privately wish the child had not lived and feel the guilt associated with this reaction. Some may experience anger and denial and may require assistance working through the stages of loss that frequently accompany the birth of a disabled child (Buscaglia, 1983). Parents often have strong feelings at the time of birth and afterward, all of which may be appropriate areas for social worker intervention. Parental reactions may differ depending upon whether the disability is visible, such as a missing limb, or is not as noticeable, such as a hearing deficit. They may combine self-pity with self-recrimination over real or imagined transgressions that parents think may have contributed to the birth child's disability. Religious and spiritual values may play a role in that some parents may fear the child's birth is punishment from God.

Rolland (1990) has noted that sometimes families know in advance that they will be dealing with a person experiencing a disability. This can lead to what he calls "anticipatory loss" (p. 229) in which parents begin the mourning process even before the event occurs. This can also lead to families trying to behave as if nothing will change despite the obvious potential for such transitions. In these cases, the social worker may need to help the family consider different ways of adapting and suggest that change may now be needed in order for successful adaptation to occur. Patterson and Garwick (1994) point out that "disability can and usually does have a significant impact on a family's identity, usually challenging an old identity and calling for something new" (p. 293). It is also possible that a disability can worsen and lead to greater limitations and even death. Rolland highlights the problem when he states, "A family must learn to live 'in limbo' and grieve for the ambiguities they must endure over the long term. A family's efforts to resist acceptance of chronicity may express their wish to elude living with threatened loss or 'death over their shoulder.' Coping with threatened loss for an indeterminate period makes it much harder for a family to define present and future structural and emotional boundaries. Helping families establish functional patterns early promotes later coping and adaptation to loss" (p. 234). If a disability becomes terminal, social workers "can function as a guide for families, helping them gently relinquish their prior hopes for cure, initiate a humane plan for palliative care, and instill hope by developing a pathway for the experience of death. Their task is to join with the family at a time when members are preoccupied with thoughts of a final separation" (pp. 234–235).

Other challenges can trouble the new parent of a child with a disability. For example, a sense of chronic sorrow may prevent parents from dealing with the challenges that caring for such a child brings. Parents may need help figuring out how to explain the child's impairment to their other children, relatives, and/or friends. Still other parents will feel ashamed that they did not produce a "normal" child. Social workers can help some family members grapple with their initial reactions of denial or pretense that there really is nothing seriously wrong with the child. For example, Sloman, Springer, and Vachon (1993) cite an example of "parents who are reluctant to place their learning-disabled, retarded, or autistic child in a special program because they cannot acknowledge the full extent of their child's difficulties. An unresolved mourning process around the birth of a deaf child can contribute to dysfunctional communication that persists over several generations" (p. 172).

Similarly, parents may need to consider the realistic costs in time and money that caring for the child will entail. All members of the family will experience the increased burden in some fashion or another. Social workers can also aid parents by helping them learn new and more effective techniques for working with a special-needs child. Some parents will turn a blind eye to the difficulties involved in this care, pretending that these do not faze them at all. Eventually, these parents will also have to deal with their feelings about having a child with a disability. Recognizing that the parents are using defense mechanisms to cope with the stress they are experiencing is important for the social worker (Buscaglia, 1983). Several writers (Buscaglia, 1983; Mackelprang & Salsgiver, 1999) have provided some useful information about how a social worker may assist parents of a child born with disabilities. We describe some of these in Highlight 9.5.

Highlight 9.5

Social Worker Communications with Family Members of a Child with a Disability

1. Feelings of guilt and shame are normal reactions, and there is nothing wrong with the parent who feels this way.
2. Protecting oneself from dealing with the pain of this birth by denying or wishing things were different is typical and not evidence of a flight from reality.
3. It is not unusual to experience shock or disbelief about the birth of a child with disabilities. Few people expect to give birth to a child who is different in such a significant way.
4. Initial feelings of helplessness and powerlessness to change the situation are okay. It is normal to have such reactions.
5. Feeling sorry for oneself and mourning the fact that the child has a disability is not unusual in such situations.
6. Worrying about whether one can cope with the demands that such a child will undoubtedly place on a family is healthy. It can help prepare parents to realistically look at what will be required.
7. Wondering what a parent did wrong that produced a disabled child is common. We all want to understand why things happen, and looking at one's own contribution to the situation is healthy.
8. Feeling overwhelmed by the new responsibilities of caring for such a child is realistic. Few parents are initially prepared for the additional burdens a child with a disability places on the family.
9. Resentment toward the work involved and sorrow over the loss of free time is to be expected. Even anger toward one's spouse is not usual.
10. Fearing for the future safety and happiness of a child with a disability is typical and a sign that the family is beginning to realistically assess what the future holds.
11. Adjusting to life with a disabled child will be a continuous endeavor, and it is expected that parents may have to grapple periodically with their reactions and feelings.
12. Using a strengths perspective toward the person with a disability is preferable to a continuous focus on the limitations he or she experiences.

Families caring for a member with a disability often face multiple challenges beyond those of other families. Some of these are easy to anticipate. For example, a child with cerebral palsy will undoubtedly need additional attention from the parents and perhaps from siblings as well. The grandfather with dementia will need careful supervision because of his tendency to become confused and lost. A family member with a mental illness may need assistance remembering to take medication, requiring behavioral cues from other members. A temporarily injured father will need assistance to move about because of impaired mobility. These needs will place both physical and emotional demands on families, depending on the type of disability, and the family members may require support to handle these additional expectations. A social worker can be of help by providing accurate information to the family about potential special needs of a disabled family member.

Obviously, parents of a child with disabilities may need to rely on resources beyond those under their own control. To the extent that the family requires the assistance of community agencies, they may encounter other hurdles. For example, trying to meet a specific need of the client without regard for whether the services provided can or will satisfy all needs is common for agencies. Lack of cooperation among the different agencies can make coordination of treatment components difficult (Jemerin & Philips, 1988). At the same time, the parents may have to fight for the child's rights with agencies, schools, and other societal institutions. For the family, living with a disability tends to be more expensive, at least in terms of health care, remediation, and support services. For many families, it will also be their first encounter with discrimination and the limitations imposed by a nonaccessible world.

Social worker roles might include providing assertiveness training for parents and, if appropriate, the person with the disability. The purpose of such training is to help families advocate for themselves with unresponsive agencies. Another role might be that of an advocate when the family requires services that are not being provided. As a broker, the social worker can connect families with a parent support group in the community. Initiating such a group is another possibility. Since parents with disabled family members often have many unmet needs, the social worker can take responsibility for surveying the family to identify those services the family finds most pressing (Brown, Bayer, & Brown, 1992). Assessing with the family what life skills the person with the disability needs to develop and helping arrange for these are often social work roles.

Parents may require assistance in recognizing that their adult child with a disability needs greater independence. Sometimes, the parents may even resist planning for such an eventuality. A social worker can work with the family to assess the child's potential for self-sufficiency realistically and to help structure a plan that will accomplish this goal. Parents may also need assistance in coming to grips with issues of sexuality, love, and marriage that affect their child in late adolescence and early adulthood. They may require specialized counseling services if the social worker does not feel sufficiently comfortable with or prepared for providing this help.

On a macro level, there is also a role for the practitioner to support and lobby for increased community awareness of the needs of those with disabilities. While we have made significant progress since passage of the Americans with Disabilities Act, much work remains. There are public buildings that are legally required to be accessible to those with disabilities but remain unavailable because a governmental body has refused to comply with the law. There also are organizations and agencies that choose to ignore the needs of people with disabilities. Respite-care services that allow the parents of those with disabilities the opportunity to take time off from their parental roles are not always available where needed. A social worker can assist families in finding such services and can work with other professionals to create such resources where they do not exist.

We would be remiss if we did not note the challenges facing the person who has the disability. Saetersdal (1997) highlights some of these issues. "Loneliness seems to be the lot of many disabled people" (p. 434). Those with disabilities have difficulties "establishing and renewing their social network on a deeper, personal level." People experiencing developmental and other chronic disabilities, for example, often have a network composed of family members, others with disabilities, and agency staff. The network tends to be much smaller than is true for other people in society.

Buscaglia (1983) does an excellent job of identifying some common experiences of disabled family members. For example, frustration is always a risk when the individual struggles with new physical or mental challenges. An adult who must learn to try to walk again after suffering a brain injury is likely to experience frustration and anger over slow progress toward achieving a skill that was previously second nature. Having a disability may expose a family member to rejection, discrimination, and stereotyping in society. Ignorance and prejudice may lead well-meaning individuals to say or do the wrong thing, thereby making the life of the disabled person that much more difficult. Depending upon the nature of the disability, the reactions of others may be problematic. A significant and obvious facial or other physical deformity may elicit discomfort and avoidance from people, while other disabilities are essentially invisible to the outside world.

Sometimes the person with a disability will suffer pain and discomfort because of the infirmity. For those who have ever used crutches or been in a cast, it is easy to recall the uncomfortable nature of the rehabilitation period. For a person with a permanent disability, such unpleasantness may last a lifetime. Emotional pain may result when the person with a disability experiences the reactions of others. It should be clear that the social worker can play a role in working with the individual who has a disability. Activities might include counseling, empowerment, advocacy, brokering, or any others that are responsive to client needs. Commonly, the social worker will need to work in concert with other professionals providing service to the person with a disability.

A family member with a disability engenders a variety of issues that the family and the individual must both address. The social worker can help the family meet the special needs and challenges they will face while also assisting the person with the disability. At the same time, families with disabled members are likely to experience most of the same problems as other families and will need similar assistance.

10 CHAPTER

Additional Interventions with Select Family Situations

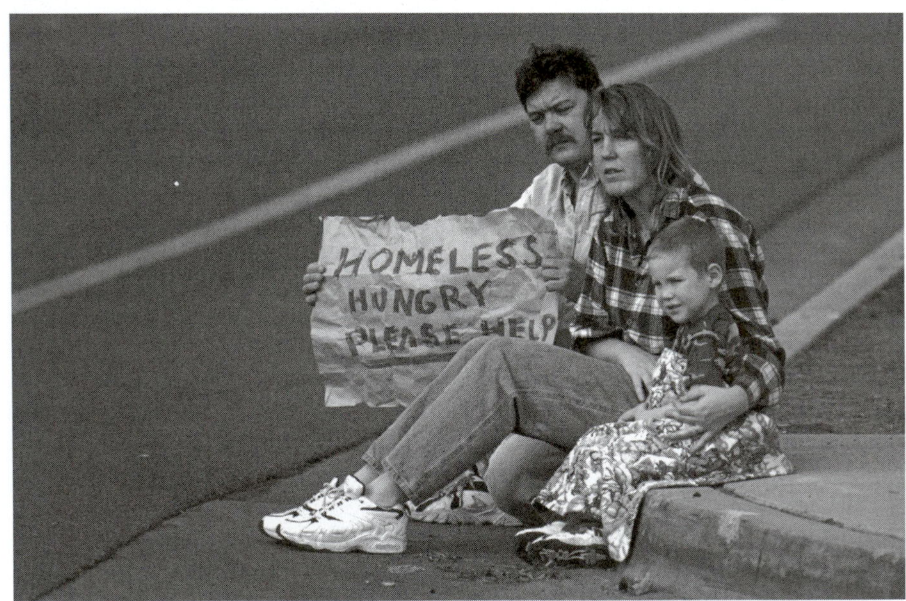

© Tony Freeman/PhotoEdit

INTRODUCTION

Chapter 9 described interventions with several challenging family situations social workers are likely to encounter in practice. This chapter continues this focus with particular attention to four common but equally complex family problems: divorce, multi-barrier families, death in the family, and mental illness. As in the preceding chapter, social workers must both understand the dynamics of such situations and possess knowledge and skills that will help the families.

DIVORCING/SEPARATING FAMILIES

In the United States, 50 percent of first marriages (Cherlin, 1992) and 60 percent of second marriages (Emery, 1998) are likely to end in divorce. Additionally, divorce will affect close to 40 percent of all children before they reach age 18 (Bumpass, 1984). These numbers make it imperative that social workers know how to work with these families and the many children needing services.

While some research suggests that adjustment to separation and divorce can become easier over time (Wallerstein & Johnston, 1990), additional research indicates that both parents and children can suffer dramatically through this process (Wallerstein, 1989). At the same time, Cherlin, Chase-Lansdale, and McRae (1998) have studied families of divorce who displayed dysfunctional behaviors. They concluded that problems were often present before the separation or divorce, suggesting that family dysfunction following divorce is not necessarily related to the divorce itself. With this idea in mind, it seems best to try to reach those families with these problems before divorce takes place. It is also important to remember that a surprising number of children who did not have a good situation while their parents were married are in better situations following the divorce. They experience lower stress and less exposure to their parents' emotional strains. In short, although divorce is usually traumatic, it does not automatically produce dysfunctions in those experiencing it. Moreover, in certain circumstances it may have a salutatory influence for some family members. In the next section, we consider these issues in more detail.

Over the years, researchers have identified several different behavioral problems resulting from separation or divorce. These include internalized effects and externalized effects. *Internalized effects* are those that occur within the person and might include depression, anger, and fear. These internalizations have been found most often in girls from divorcing family situations. Boys, on the other hand, are more likely to show *externalized effects* and act out their feelings through behavior problems or delinquency (Videon, 2002). Regardless of primary effect, all children need to go through a series of tasks following their parents' divorce. Wallerstein (1983) has identified these tasks as follows: (1) Recognize the marital disruption. This involves the child coming to understand the realities of the divorce situation. (2) Begin to readjust to a normal life and activities. In this step, the child resumes his or her school responsibilities and addresses the changes that have occurred in the family life. (3) Deal with feelings of rejection by the absent parent; typically, this involves establishing new relationships with one's parents or others. (4) Forgive the parents; forgiving helps reduce some of the child's anger arising from the losses that divorce creates. (5) Accept and adjust to the post-divorce lifestyle (pp. 265–302). This step may involve adapting to a different lifestyle and changes in environment, among others. These stages are important for the emotional adjustment of the child and may take several years to complete.

Of course, children are not the only ones who have to navigate the changes divorce produces; divorcing partners face their own challenges. Pam (1998) notes that there are several different stages that a partner in a marriage goes through following a divorce. She bases the following on the most common path of divorce, that of an acrimonious divorce wanted by only one partner.

STAGES	
PARTNER WHO LEFT RELATIONSHIP	REJECTED PARTNER
1. Shock	1. Alienation
2. Breakup	2. Grief/rage
3. The love entitlement quest	3. Courting the rejecter
4. Looking back/mourning	4. Distancing
5. Disentanglement	5. Indifference

As you can gather from these lists, the path through divorce is not an easy one for either person. Both partners face their own set of stages with the ultimate goal of surviving and functioning effectively in their own worlds. Social workers can be of help to partners as they negotiate these new challenges. First, it is important to acknowledge that providing support to a couple going through a divorce can be very difficult. Attempting to do this with both spouses in the room makes it twice as difficult. To balance these different stages, it is often appropriate for the social worker to work with each individual separately at times. While this approach is useful, there is always a risk that one ex-spouse will take what we say in the individual sessions out of context and share it with the other ex-spouse. That is why it is so critical to work with the couple together as much as possible.

So far we have identified the stages and challenges that children and partners go through as they adapt to a divorce. Families themselves, as basic human systems, go through their own stages of divorce. Garfield (1982) suggests that the following stages are important for the process of divorce to go smoothly for a family:

1. *Coming to terms with loss and acceptance by spouses.* This stage often involves great sadness and anxiety about the future for all participants. If spouses can recognize and accept the sense of loss rather than battle against it, the outcome will probably be healthier for everyone.
2. *Taking on of new roles and responsibilities.* Here we are talking about basic tasks such as assuming complete responsibility for child care, income

production, managing finances, and making decisions without the input of the spouse. These are often tasks that they shared before the divorce or perhaps were previously handled by the other spouse.

3. *Forming different relationships with others in the family's life.* This stage can involve adapting to one's changed status with in-laws, grandparents, and mutual friends. Sometimes it means ending relationships that are too painful to maintain or losing connections with people who were closer to the other spouse.
4. *Establishing a different and more adjusted relationship between ex-spouses.* Overcoming the hurt, anger, and other feelings associated with the divorce process is necessary if the ex-spouses are to have any kind of relationship. Too often, this stage is not completed satisfactorily, and the ex-spouses have either no relationship at all or one characterized by antipathy and hatred.

When you take into account the stages children, parents, and families generally undertake to reach the other side of divorce, it can be a devastating process. Yet Wallerstein (1989), in her longitudinal studies of divorced families, has found that individuals can be enormously resilient in this process. The level of success in weathering the divorce depends upon several factors. These include the relationship of the parents during the process, the gender of the parent who had custody, and the ability of the parents to place their children back in a consistent, structured, loving environment. One way to help facilitate a positive outcome is to help the family anticipate and cope with post-divorce issues.

Post-Divorce Issues

Following a separation and/or divorce, several issues commonly emerge for the family. These include the following:

Child Custody Arrangements These are among the hardest issues that a divorcing family can face. Very often, both parents want custody or they want to share custody when that may be neither possible because of geographic issues nor appropriate. Often, courts give the mother custody of the children with the father having visitation rights. Yet, fathers more and more are gaining custody of their children. In the United States, approximately one-fifth of all children living in single-parent homes are with their fathers. Of the fathers who win custody, most are in the upper economic class and often win because they can prove the mother is unfit (Emery, 1988). The strain of the loss of children from a daily life can be devastating to the noncustodial parent. Sometimes, this parent can become more isolated from the child as a reaction to the stress of the loss. Dudley and Stone (2001) summarize the particular difficulties faced by non-custodial fathers by noting that they typically have higher suicide rates than divorced women. "Fathers who are able to maintain a positive relationship with their children after divorce have been found to report lower levels of depression, anxiety, and stress" (p. 248).

Psychological Stress Stress is a key issue following divorce. This psychological stress affects all members of the family as can be noted by the stages through which family members go. Feelings of loss, betrayal, guilt (especially in younger children who may believe they caused the divorce), and depression are all emotions that children and/or adults may experience.

Visitation Problems These often arise due to the custody arrangement made for the children and the relationship of the ex-spouses. Children can often be used as the messenger between ex-spouses and become pawns in continuing angry exchanges. Changes in visitation, the amount of visitation, and the location of the visitation are all factors that play a significant role in the well-being of the children and the relationship of the ex-spouses.

Financial Changes These occur in every divorce situation as the expenses of maintaining two households are always greater than the cost of one. For the parent with sole custody (generally this has been the mother in our society), the cost can be astronomical. This includes the cost of child care where they may not have needed it before and the cost of living with new responsibilities that no one shares. Other changes may involve the cost of alimony and child support that were not a part of the marital life. These expenses, plus the former partners' income level, seriously affect the standard of living.

Social Changes These occur for both parents and children as they try to adjust to a new life. This might include a new school and neighborhood for children, or it may mean the loss of friends who knew the spouses as a couple. Very often, friends are torn between who to see and support so they tend to remove themselves from the situation. Family changes can also occur as extended family members feel pulled toward one side or another. Acrimonious feelings about this type of situation can also keep the children isolated from their extended families.

THEORY IN ACTION | Divorcing Family Situation

The Evans family was court ordered into counseling following an unsuccessful attempt by the divorce counselor at the family court center. The Evans had been married approximately 12 years and had two children, ages 9 and 10. Mr. Evans had initiated the divorce, following what he called an unhappy marriage. He had recently become involved with another woman who spent time with the children when they came to visit. Mr. Evans wanted custody of the children, as he felt he could offer them a more stable environment. Mrs. Evans appeared lost in the process, claiming they had had an ideal marriage up until the time the new woman came into her husband's life. The Evans could not resolve their differences over custody and visitation, financial obligations, and responsibility for the breakup. As the family began counseling, it became clear that each of the parents used the children to find out information about the other. Additionally, visitation was not very successful because the bad relationship between the parents was showing up in their children's behavior, such as acting out at school and the inability to keep their grades up.

Intervention

Social workers can play many different roles when working with families undergoing a divorce. These include predivorce counselor, divorce mediator, and/or a postdivorce counselor. These roles have very different meanings and responsibilities. When you work as a *counselor* with a couple over separation and divorce issues, some of the same work you would typically do with a family is put aside. Generally, couples who recognize their marriage is in trouble and those who come to recognize difficulties through family therapy will try to work this out separately from the rest of the family. They do this to avoid involving the children in the process. While we may deal with some issues as a family, others will require separate sessions for the parents. Coming to a decision about whether to separate or divorce is often a difficult one for couples. While one person may want out of the marriage, the emotional factors may keep him or her tied into it. Staying married in an unhealthy situation is not necessarily the best thing to do, and the social worker/counselor must be prepared to work with these issues as they arise.

The role of *divorce mediator* or *divorce counselor* is not new, although it was less accepted in the early '70s and before. Prior to the 1970s, many members of the counseling professions viewed divorce as a nonalternative (Goldenberg & Goldenberg, 2002). Now, divorce counseling and mediation are major roles played by many social workers. The mediator attempts to address the issues that arise through divorce, such as custody, parental agreements regarding the children, the relationship between the spouses, and sometimes property settlements. Salts (1985) notes three stages of divorce counseling. These include (1) predivorce decision-making stage, when we help couples look at what is the best choice for them; (2) restructuring stage, where both individuals are encouraged to reaffirm or accept the divorce; and (3) postdivorce recovery stage, where each person in the divorce begins to take on his own individuality. In each stage, the divorce counselor/mediator needs good preparation for conflict resolution and the handling of emotional issues that arise.

In *postdivorce counseling*, help may be offered for the children and/or the adults. Sometimes this may be done as a family and at other times individually. Groups for children and adults experiencing separation and divorce have also been found effective. Helping members of different families connect to others who are going through the same process can be a normalizing experience. Often, these are short-term groups that allow for individuals to express their feelings and receive feedback from others. One of the major issues, as we have mentioned before, is for ex-spouses to work out the angry feelings between them, as well as the psychological issues. Generally speaking, the healthier the relationship between the divorced parents, the healthier the child.

Cultural Issues in Divorce

It is important to recognize that not all cultures react in the same way to divorce. African-Americans and Hispanics have been found to have a higher divorce rate than their Caucasian counterparts (Martin & Bumpass, 1989). We have not necessarily understood the reason for this difference. While low-income families are more likely to divorce, this difference between cultures is apparent across all income levels. Additionally, as social workers, we need to be culturally sensitive to what involvement families want us to have. Are they open to outside support or would they rather be left to making their own decisions and taking their own counsel? By exploring such issues with the family, social workers are more likely to be culturally sensitive and culturally competent.

MULTI-BARRIER FAMILIES

This section of the chapter discusses the complex situations facing *multi-barrier families*. While giving a definition of who these families are is important, it is not necessarily easy. Known as *multi-problem families* for many years, the term has changed since the 1980s to be inclusive of more than just a definition based on problems. While many of these families are poor, disorganized, and have multiple problems, this terminology does little to convey the extreme complexity of the issue. Sharlin and Shamai (2000) do an excellent job in pointing out that we are really talking about families in extreme distress (FED). These families generally suffer from economic deprivation and experience many problems caused by a myriad of complex issues, including but not limited to health, behavioral, social, and psychological adjustment. Following is an example of a family in extreme distress.

THEORY IN ACTION | Family in Extreme Distress

Mary, age 30, and Andy, age 40, have been married for 3 years. They have two children, Susan, age 11, and Carol, age 9. Andy and Mary have lived together on and off for the last 10 years. Pregnant with their first child at 19, Mary has worked at a variety of jobs over the last 11 years. She has been a table server, exotic dancer, cashier, and wash girl in a local salon. Andy, having never finished high school, has generally not held a job for more than 2 months. Alcoholic and with little hope for the future, Andy spends much of his time sitting home with the kids and playing cards when he has the money. During the last 3 years, Mary and Andy have gone through a series of difficulties, beginning with Susan's use of alcohol and Carol's elective mutism. Wanting to help their children, they have tried to get to appointments across town even though they do not own a car. In the last year, they have suffered severe losses in their lives, beginning with Andy's mother, who died in a car crash, and Mary's sister, who died of breast cancer. Lately, they have been struggling with many different issues regarding Carol and school. Although she attends many of her speech appointments and receives some counseling services, her mutism has gotten worse. The week before coming in to see Carol's counselor, Andy was hospitalized following a biking accident. They have no insurance.

As you read this situation, it is easy to feel overwhelmed and to wonder where you would begin to help this family. So many issues are affecting them that giving one a higher priority than another is not easy. That is why it is always important to start where the client is.

Basic Approaches

Social workers have tried many different types of approaches with families in extreme distress, and Geismar and La Sorte (1964) categorize several of these. These include the following, as outlined by Sharlin and Shamai (2000):

1. The *intensive casework approach* is based on conventional techniques used in social casework, sometimes allied with a more assertive approach such as frequent home visits. A casework approach includes diagnosis and treatment of the entire family by the social worker, as well as coordination of various other available services. A psychodynamic orientation dominated most of the intensive casework done up to the end of the 1960s, because of the education that most social workers had acquired (Kaplan, 1984).
2. The *case conference approach* is based on presenting a case by various workers from a formally assembled group. The group presents its diagnosis and treatment plan and assigns responsibility for the treatment to one or more workers within one or more agencies. Without one designated person to organize the plan, this approach has not been very effective for distressed families. It has, however, been widely used among social workers when intervening with difficult and hard-to-reach families. With this approach, the range of problems can be so overwhelming that it pushes the social worker to delegate intervention tasks rather than taking into account the family's special character, which calls for one person to take charge in helping the family to get organized (Geismar & La Sorte, 1964).
3. The *multi-service approach* involves the consolidation of treatments administered by different organizations in various areas of specialization, while a totally separate organization is responsible for the coordination of the treatment approaches (Geismar & La Sorte, 1964). Due to the discrepancy between services that may require clients to perform numerous and often conflicting tasks, this approach may have an overwhelmingly negative impact on the family. We should note that coordinating treatments does not guarantee supervision of all the details that make up a treatment approach.

4. The *community development approach* refers to programs that aim to strengthen the entire community as a context for the individual family unit. These programs include a variety of services, such as full-day and after-school child care, parents' groups, and support groups to prevent adolescents from becoming involved in delinquency and drug abuse. It is important to note that many social service programs developed in the 1960s involved the community development approach.
5. Other approaches incorporate the community development approach while taking into account the individual family. Accordingly, a volunteer to guide the family or a professional who works together with the parents (especially the mothers) is sent by the community service agency to individual families as needed. (pp. 19–20)

These differing approaches to working with families in extreme distress all have their benefits and weaknesses. The approach most recently taken with these families has been one of strengthening and empowering the family within their own home environment. Often called *family preservation,* this approach has been found effective in recent research related to working with families with child protection issues (Sharlin & Shamai, 2000). Sundelin and Hansson (2000) report on an intensive family therapy (IFT) program used to change family functioning in distressed families. The program was based on day-long intervention for one month by a staff of psychologists, psychiatrists, social workers, preschool teachers, and schoolteachers, among others. The initial results show a change toward a better family environment and higher family functioning.

Many different areas must be considered in working with what Kilpatrick and Holland (1999) refer to as Level I families. These are families whose basic needs for survival are not being met. Basic needs in this case include such things as food, shelter, or other nurturing and protective resources. When examining these issues, it is easy to see why the areas of financial resources, a sense of hope, leadership skills, problem-solving skills, and emotional nurturance play such important roles.

Financial Resources We see financial resources as one of the major difficulties faced by families in extreme distress. While not the only issue by far, this component has a significant impact on all other areas. Without the financial resources available to create changes and foster hope, the less likely the family will be able to pull themselves out of this difficult situation. They live from day to day on what resources they can obtain, with very little time or money to keep themselves going. While some families have multiple problems without being poor and others are poor but without multiple problems, the two do go hand in hand often. Families so caught up in meeting the daily needs of their members have little opportunity for problem solving other than what can be done on a day-by-day basis to survive. The fact that we live in a society where one's material goods, sadly, are associated with the one's value as a human being does little to offset this issue.

Sense of Hope In order for an individual or family to move forward, there must be some belief that there is something that can be seen in the future. The lack of hope in the future has strong ties to the family's inability to make a difference in their lives. To have a sense of hope, you need to have the skill to set a goal and know you can accomplish it. With families unable to cope with anything more than meeting their basic needs, few longer term goals can be set. A father, worrying daily about whether his family will have a home, has little time to plan for more education or even hope for a better future.

Leadership Skills Along with issues in finances and hope are those skills and abilities that individual family members bring into a situation. The parents and their own leadership skills affect the well-being of the family. In many ways, these types of family situations create a domino effect. As the financial resources dwindle and individuals are forced to focus only on survival, hope diminishes. Simultaneously, the skills the family members may have had now are consumed by the impact of poverty and overwhelming needs of the other family members. While many individuals do have leadership skills, many others who have lived in a generation of hopelessness do not.

Problem-Solving Skills One of the earliest signs of a family in extreme distress will be their lack of ability to do problem solving. Unlike many of us who understand the process of looking at a situation, considering all alternatives, and selecting a way to resolve the issue, the family who is unable to problem solve experiences even more difficulties in their lives. The ability to problem solve is about more than the skills; it is also about being able to take pride in yourself as you accomplish goals and resolve situations. It is about having hope that circumstances can change no matter what the present holds. For distressed families, having hope is very difficult.

Supportive Environment A supportive environment that allows for its members to grow and succeed is another important part of family life. A supportive environment helps individuals establish objectives, support decisions, and succeed in their goals and dreams. When people have others who stand beside them and take care of many things for them, it is possible to move ahead, to have an opportunity to accomplish goals, and to have hope for the future. In situations where those same people cannot support themselves, there is little prospect of their strengths alone moving them past their present situation.

Emotional Nurturance Belief in yourself comes in part from others believing in you. Those individuals who can provide warm and caring emotional support give you hope and free your time to move forward. We are all aware of those family conditions where there was little food or financial resources, yet a parent's love moved individuals forward in spite of the difficulties. The importance of having others to provide emotional nurturance is often reflected in both professional literature and in biography.

Intervention

In bringing about change in these family situations, the families and the social worker must be open to providing some basic skills as part of ongoing service. One of the most important is those skills learned in problem solving. Teaching problem solving regarding basic needs to a family will help. However, for the family to have the opportunity to problem solve and succeed, they must select some long-term goals beyond basic survival needs.

It is also necessary to begin in these families by focusing on their strengths and resources. Without recognizing their strengths, family members are handicapped in their ability to make substantial change. This is as important for the social worker as it is for the family. Social workers need to be able to see the family's strengths to believe that they can instill hope in the family and to work with them to create change.

Working with the family in their own home has proven to be a helpful intervention. It gives the social worker the opportunity to view the family in their own surroundings and to pick up on their strengths. The family is generally more relaxed in this situation and will be more able to share some of their ideas with the worker. It also gives the practitioner an idea of how the family feels about their situation and the amount of hope they have. Focusing the family's work on immediate needs is necessary. However, there are many areas where the social worker's involvement can help the family learn to plan and communicate with one another in a way that accomplishes other tasks.

Working with the family structure by reinforcing the parents and their roles as family leaders helps create change. Having parents take more responsibility for decisions regarding their children enables the parents to structure a healthy environment for everyone. Additionally, involving other systems to support the family in an intensive concentrated manner has shown to be very effective in creating changes.

DEATH WITHIN THE FAMILY

The face of death in the family has changed a great deal within the last century. At the beginning of the 20th century, 30 percent of all deaths were of children 10 and under, and 30 percent were of adults over the age of 60 (National Center for Health Statistics, 1996). The new advances in medicine and technology have now made these figures very different. At the start of the 21st century, only 1 percent of deaths are children under the age of 10, and nearly 80 percent of deaths are of those over the age of 60 (Hoyert, Kochanek, & Murphy, 1999). The family's experience of death has become more about the loss of the elderly related to chronic illnesses than about sudden loss of the young.

Death of a loved one within the family can have a significant impact on all family members. The experience of this loss will differ with the age of the person and the type of relationship. The reaction of the family to the death will also be affected by whether it is a sudden death, such as in an accident, or a long, drawn-out illness. Loss of a family member predicates a crisis within the family. With the loss comes the loss of family roles and changes in the rules and systems within the family. The family practitioner will need to recognize that along with grief will be a new structure in which roles and rules change.

Stages of Grief

Bowlby (1980) notes four different stages in the grieving process. These include numbing, yearning and searching, disorganization, and resolution.

Numbing is a defensive process in which the individual prepares for the mourning period (Genovese, 1992). An example of this would be a woman who, at the loss of her husband, moves through the period of funeral preparation in a controlled and thoughtful manner without displaying mourning symptoms. During the numbing phase, family members experience a process by which they mount their resources and strengths in order to meet the upcoming experience.

Yearning and searching is where there is a deep aching for the individual who has died. As Genovese (1992) points out, there is a constant conflict with the realization that the person is gone and the deep craving for being reunited. This period of time is a constant moving in and out of mourning. At times, its resolution may be too difficult for the person to bear. For example, a woman whose mother has recently died cannot move beyond the yearning and searching stage because she has issues she wishes to resolve with her mother but cannot do so because of the death. In cases like this, it is sometimes important for the family member to write a letter to the deceased or to spend some time talking to the deceased as if she were there.

Disorganization is the phase at which depression emerges and along with it disorganization in thinking and behavior. Since many family members' roles were dependent on the role of the lost individual, there is a significant process by which the mourning family members suffer through letting go. During this period, "the mourner may feel lost and disconnected" (Genovese, 1992) and unable to function within her world. An example is the mother who has lost a young child and cannot think clearly at work or even make it to work. She does not take care of herself, and her whole time is spent crying and wishing for her own death.

Resolution is the period in which the mourning process begins to complete itself. Although the person will not go back to the way she was (the impact of loss affects the person's view of their own life), she does begin to resolve some depression and disorganization in her life. Genovese (1992) and Parkes and Weiss (1983) suggest that we view the process of resolution as containing three tasks:

1. *Intellectual recognition and explanation of the loss.* This is a task where family members come to terms with the recognition of the death and the development of an explanation for the loss. Without being able to explain the death, the person will continue to be hypervigilant about new losses.

2. *Emotional acceptance.* This is a task that focuses the family members on not continuing to be overwhelmed by the pain and loss. In this process, members review the thoughts and memories and begin to move forward in their thinking.
3. *Formation of a new identity.* In this task, individuals begin to recreate themselves around their current reality and not necessarily in connection with the person they have lost. Individuals begin to view their life with some meaning and start to create a new world without the deceased.

Children can face these stages of mourning differently. Cituk, Graves, and Prout (1999) define these children's stages as follows:

1. *Denial.* This is common in young children who do not understand death is final. It may be expressed in the young by the statement that the loved one did not actually die and is coming back. A young child may be pretending death did not occur because the grief is too much to feel.
2. *Fear.* A child who has lost a loved one through death will face two specific fears: abandonment and death of self or others who are emotionally close. Often inappropriate comments from others such as "be brave," "be extra good for mommy," or "now you are the man of the family" increase these fears and may suppress the child's grief. In older children, this fear may be expressed as panic or confusion about who will take care of them. They may take on characteristics of the deceased or idealize the deceased. They may also try emotionally to replace the deceased with a substitute trying to cope with the fear and pain of abandonment.
3. *Anger.* Children who feel abandoned by the loved one usually experience intense anger. This anger is often directed at the survivors or at themselves. Children's anger upsets adults and is often expressed in destructive ways.
4. *Guilt.* The younger the child, the more likely he or she is to think that anything that happens in the world is his or her fault. What child has not wished at some time that a parent would die? The older the child, the more the guilt can be relieved by giving the child permission to have positive and negative feelings about the deceased. (p. 394).

Intervention

The immediate reaction to this kind of loss comes in the form of grief. While many people can move through the grieving process on their own, others will become stuck in the process. Working with families who have suffered a loss requires the social worker to begin with a concentrated effort to help move the family members through the grieving process. The "goal of grief counseling is to develop the ability to express both joy at having known the deceased and sadness at the loss" (Thomlison, 2002, p. 145).

Social workers need to be aware that the more open a family is to their grieving, the better off they will be in adjusting to the changes affecting them. Death is an experience of the living as much as for the deceased. Assessing the issues of loss within a family right away is an important task for the social worker. Family members may not identify the loss as the problem but may concentrate on other issues. Encountering a family whose issues began to emerge several months after the death of a close family member is common in practice situations.

With the death of a family member, issues regarding relationships, belonging, and closeness will emerge (Brock & Barnard, 1999). Family members may seek to cope with the loss of a family member through their relationship with others in the family. Unresolved grief can take many forms, and its impact on individual family members may be to try to cope with it in a way that causes additional problems.

THEORY IN ACTION | **Unresolved Grief**

The Johnson family arrives at the clinic 10 minutes before the session. All family members are present except the husband, Joe, who decided he did not need help. While many issues are occurring in the family, the one that continues to surface is the issue over the 16-year-old son's drinking. In discussing the situation, the son at one point responds that "I don't do anything differently than Dad does. He drinks every night." When asked about the use of alcohol in the home, the mother describes her husband as having "begun to drink too much" following the death of his mother 9 months ago.

Paul (1967) has called the process of the practitioner helping clients deal with unresolved loss *operational mourning*. This is a time when the social worker will want to speak directly and not hesitate to examine the importance of the loss. Family members may be defended against speaking about the loss, and this is an area the social worker will need to look at carefully and help move the family past (Brock & Barnard, 1999). In moving through this process of grief counseling, the practitioner will need to be sensitive to family members' needs and aware of the relationship the deceased had with each member. Social workers will help the family work through resolution by direct, honest discussion, helping members to answer the "why" question and assisting in the creation of a family whose role and rules can now adapt to the loss (Genovese, 1992).

MENTAL ILLNESS WITHIN THE FAMILY

The study of schizophrenia and family systems began in the 1950s. As part of the work with young schizophrenics, theorists such as Bateson, Minuchin, and Haley began to examine the relationship between the family and mental illness. There have been contradicting opinions over time as to whether the family's interactions with the young schizophrenic caused the illness or the illness caused dysfunctions in the family. During the 1950s, researchers found a correlation between mental illness and family deterioration (Pasamanick, 1959) as well as higher incidence of mental illness in individuals from stressful families (Harvey & Bray, 1991). Today, dysfunctional families and mental illness are not blamed on one another as there are too many factors that affect this complex situation. They are, however, viewed as interacting factors that influence each other in complex ways. In other words, families can affect the mental health of the individual and mental illness can affect the functioning of the family.

One of the more interesting findings regarding mental illness and families stems from research done on high expressed emotion (EE) families. Brown, Birley, and Wing (1972) found that in families where high emotions were expressed, there was more of a likelihood of relapse in an ill member of the family. They defined EE families with two particular concepts: expression of criticism and hostility, and emotional overinvolvement (Janzen & Harris, 1997). In emotional involvement, we see the family as too intrusive in the patient's life, trying to protect him or her from the illness. We see this as just as dysfunctional as the criticizing family.

Helping a family cope with the mental illness of a member is another role for the social worker. Nichols and Schwartz (2001) note that the goal of family treatment in working with the mentally ill hinges upon maximizing the coping abilities of ill or dysfunctional clients. Goldstein et al. (1978) designed a model in the '70s that concentrated on the family working to reduce their stressful relationships with the client and simultaneously reducing conflict around the person. Of the multiple approaches that have been tried with this population, the one that may be the most effective is the *psychoeducational family approach* (Anderson, Reiss, & Hogarty, 1986).

Psychoeducational family therapy is a method that does not try to find a reason for or a cure for the illness. It focuses on informing the family about the illness, involving them from the first step in the diagnosis of the illness, and in helping the family learn to cope in a functioning way with the member experiencing mental illness. "Psychoeducators seek to establish a collaborative partnership in which family members feel supported and empowered to deal with the patient" (Nichols & Schwartz, 2002, p. 333) This method also sends the message that the family is not alone in the process and will have aid along the way. It is believed that as the family's stress over the illness is decreased, the patient will respond more effectively.

Franklin and Jordan (1999) note that the use of psychoeducation has increased because of (1) changes in health care economics (which promote the more cost-efficient method of group treatment over individual treatment), (2) studies showing the increased psychological and social benefits of "like members" (other families who have a mentally ill relation) getting together to provide support, and (3) new theories of mental illness that illuminate the social, environmental, and biological influences (e.g., biopsychosocial models) while reducing "family blaming" theories (e.g., psychoanalytic and family systems theories) (Corcoran & Vandiver, 1996; Johnson, 1987; McFarlane, 1991).

Psychoeducational family treatment begins with a strengths perspective that believes that the family is competent to handle the situation. Generally, this treatment is handled over a brief period with many families involved, so there is a connection between families with the same issues. The focus of treatment is on "social and community support, social skills, and family therapy" (Franklin & Jordan, 1999). It also aids in the development of community and system resources, so the family can work through a particular issue with someone. Work in improving expressed emotions is also done with the family. As is evident below, a family can be engaged in many different things throughout the session.

THEORY IN ACTION | Family Dealing with Multiple Intervention Needs

The Montovo family arrived at the in-patient hospital on family night and was met by the social worker providing support that evening. The Montovos had hospitalized their 19-year-old son, Ed, for an overdose a few days before. He had been diagnosed with drug abuse and had been placed on medication and suicide watch. Ed had a long history of drug use, and this was his third overdose. The family had been in treatment with Ed over the last few years but always ended up feeling they were to blame for Ed's problems and did not believe their own issues were being addressed.

This evening the social worker asked the Montovo family (mother, father, and brother Sid, age 16) to sit in with a group of other families to gather information regarding issues surrounding drug use. With their agreement and an understanding of confidentiality issues of being in a group, the family joined the others. When the Montovos entered the room, three other families were present. Each family had a member who abused drugs. One other family had a daughter who had overdosed just before being admitted. The practitioner explained again the purpose of the session and talked about confidentiality issues. The weekly sessions were to last for six weeks, and the program for them had been carefully laid out.

Each family member was handed an outline of the sessions over the next few weeks and asked if they had any questions. They explained the psychoeducational family approach and discussed the objectives of the intervention. The social worker began the first session with a presentation about drug abuse and the many issues that affected the person with the illness. Additionally, there was a discussion of what a family experiences when they have a loved one who is addicted. It was during this period that Mr. Montovo could talk about his feelings about the overdose and how helpless he felt. The father of the young woman who had also overdosed started talking about having similar feelings and looking for a way to protect her. This led to a broader discussion of how difficult changing someone was if that person did not want to be changed. When the group ended for the evening, the Montovos felt they had a better understanding of their son's illness and felt there were others who also related to their situation.

Psychoeducational family treatment is an effective way for members of a family to cope with a mental illness. It is also an effective way for those who are ill to receive support from their family. These special family circumstances have a significant impact on all family members, and understanding the approaches that work the best represents a good starting point for resolving the issues.

Specialized Family Interventions

CHAPTER 11

© Photodisc/Royalty-Free/Getty Images

INTRODUCTION

This chapter will focus on four family intervention approaches that have emerged in the past couple of decades. These include family preservation, wraparound services, extended family support programs, and multiple family group interventions. Each has as its goal assistance to families who are at risk and shares similar methods, and all may be used together to provide comprehensive services to families. They are covered here for three reasons. First, social workers may be employed in programs using these approaches and should have a beginning knowledge of the philosophy and methods utilized. Second, even social workers employed outside these programs will need to be aware of their existence because they may serve as a resource for the practitioner. Finally, these programs may refer clients to a social worker for assistance in addition to that provided by their own practitioners.

FAMILY PRESERVATION

Family preservation is a name given to both a philosophy of practice with families as well as to specific models and programs. In general, the philosophy behind family preservation is that families must be preserved if at all possible. A model of family preservation describes the conditions under which children may be maintained in their homes with an adequate degree of safety. If the child's safety cannot reasonably be assured, placing the child outside the home is appropriate. Schuerman, Rzepnicki, and Littell (1994) describe the perspective that drives family preservation as a belief that "in the absence of serious contraindications, children are better off in their homes of origin than anyplace else and a belief that children are harmed by foster placement. The belief that children belong in their own homes comes out of child development research and is based at least in part on evidence of a special bond between children and mothers" (p. 5). At the same, Schuerman and colleagues question whether this perspective is accurate and raised doubts about whether the term *family preservation* is clearly enough defined to allow such programs to be evaluated.

It is important to distinguish between family preservation programs and family support programs. The former are time limited and intensive, designed to restore "adequate family functioning, reduce the risk of harm to the children, and thereby avert the need for imminent removal of children from their homes" (Samantrai, 2004, p. 133). In short, "family preservation programs are intended to remove the risk rather than the child from the home" (p. 135).

Family support programs, on the other hand, are designed to "increase the strength and stability of families and prevent child and family problems from escalating to the point of crisis where out-of-home placement may have to be considered" (p. 133). Time limits are generally not imposed, and families may make use of family support services as long as they need them. Several assumptions underlie family preservation and characterize programs operating under this model. They are listed in Highlight 11.1. These programs both model and teach skills to families that are designed to help them become more effective

Highlight 11.1 **Family Preservation Assumptions**

- Family preservation services are offered in situations where a child's removal from the family is imminent. Time limits are often used by states to help define *imminent.*
- Decisions about who receives services are made after careful screening to ensure that only those most in need are served. As a consequence, caseloads are small.
- Families require services that are responsive to their needs. This may entail direct contact with the family from 5–20 hours per week.
- Services must be available when needed. This means prompt assessment and 24-hour-a-day availability.
- Services are offered to families within their own homes.
- Safety of all family members and of the community is a primary concern.
- Raising children in their own families is preferable to other alternatives.
- Families are considered partners rather than recipients of service.
- Families are doing the best they can within existing circumstances.
- Families are presumed to be able to change their behaviors.
- Barriers to service must be removed to assist families.
- Services are time limited, often lasting four to eight weeks.
- Treatment objectives are limited and objectives are specific and measurable.
- Services are based on the family's strengths.
- No single clinical model predominates; practitioners use whatever works.

Source: Adapted from Alfano et al., 1990; Bridger et al., 1997; Brock and Barnard, 1999; Levine and Sallee, 1999; and Samantrai, 2004.

and ultimately to avoid out-of-home placements such as foster care. They are also designed to help reestablish families whose children are already in care and to support at-risk adoptive families. A wide variety of services are offered by practitioners in family preservation programs. They include parent and life skills training, marital counseling, communication building, behavioral management skills, self-management of moods and/or behavior, safety planning, relapse prevention, direct service, advocacy, school interventions, and referral to other resources.

A Brief History of Family Preservation

Family preservation programs began to emerge in the early 1970s, when foster care programs were being criticized for keeping families and children apart unnecessarily. They focused on maintaining children in their own homes whenever possible by providing a variety of resources. While traditional child welfare services had a child-centered focus with protection of the child as the primary concern, family preservation was family centered. Family preservation did not ignore the issue of protecting the child but saw children as better off in their own homes whenever possible. Arguments in favor of family preservation services include the fact that it reduces the need for homefinding and training of foster parents, reduces the risk of child injury and death, allows staff to concentrate on families most at risk, and is cost effective.

Homebuilders, one of the best known family preservation programs, began in 1974 in the state of Washington. It was quickly followed by scores of programs using the Homebuilders approach or some variation on the theme. Both private and public agencies adopted the model in some fashion.

In 1980, Congress passed the Adoption Assistance and Child Welfare Act, which led to a dramatic expansion of programs built on the Homebuilders model. This law required that states make reasonable efforts to prevent or end the removal of children from their homes and to take active steps to allow children in foster care to return home. The law specifically identified family preservation services as a critical means for satisfying the requirement of "reasonable efforts." The new law also signaled a major shift in thinking about helping families. As a consequence, many private foundations also began funding family preservation programs and services. Supported by the 1993 passage of the Family Preservation and Support Act, interest in family preservation programs increased dramatically as one state after another selected this model of service delivery. According to the General Accounting Office, almost all 50 states had either created or expanded such programs as of 1997 (USGAO, 1997). The Homebuilders model, in particular, was adopted by 33 states (Cole & Duva, 1990; Kinney et al., 1991; McGowan, 1990).

Along the way, family preservation became a popular concept, spawning its own journal (*Family Preservation Journal*) and various institutes and programs providing consultation and training for practitioners. At least one graduate school of social work adopted family preservation as its primary concentration, and an industry grew up focused on this approach to family practice.

Social Worker Activities

Social workers employed in family preservation programs help families assess their strengths and problems and provide a wide variety of services to assist them. This includes giving families the knowledge and skill needed to achieve mutually agreed-upon goals. Termination begins almost immediately because of the short duration of services provided, and aftercare or follow-up is a very important component of family preservation. During the time a family is receiving service, the social worker is available 24 hours a day and will spend several hours a day with a family. Practitioners are familiar with multiple approaches to helping families but also recognize the role that *concrete services* play in improving the quality of life. Concrete services might include providing the family with a deposit for a better apartment in a safer neighborhood, assisting with household tasks that are overwhelming the parents, or arranging for medical or dental services.

Families may be assisted in locating child care or employment training programs. Social workers may also provide financial counseling, do counseling to improve relationships between the parents, teach disciplinary techniques, and arrange for clothing and food. For families where removal of the child has already taken place and reunification is the goal, social workers may oversee parent–child visits, provide transportation, attend court appearances with the family, and monitor services being provided by other agencies. Counseling services provided as part of family preservation can include crisis intervention, advocacy, individual and group counseling, and drug/alcohol treatment (Schuerman et al., 1994).

Social workers engage in a variety of activities to overcome the hurdles families in these programs face. Some families benefit from learning how to structure their time and routines to better meet the needs of all members. Social workers help others learn how to solve problems using the process of identifying obstacles, generating options, planning, and carrying out agreed-upon activities. Some parents may be given homework assignments related to achieving their goals, while others will work on practicing skills such as relaxation and assertiveness (Schuerman et al., 1994).

The theories used by social workers working in family preservation are the same as in other avenues of practice. Practitioners using behavioral and cognitive-behavioral theories engage in reinforcement, modeling, role playing, behavioral rehearsal, systematic desensitization, and teaching parents cognitive self-control. Other social workers will use techniques such as encouraging catharsis, exploration of past life experiences, and analysis of transference drawn from psychodynamic/psychoanalytic theory. Sculpting may be used with some families, along with helping them better understand family roles, rules, and process, techniques drawn from communication theory and systems theory (Schuerman et al., 1994).

Research on Family Preservation's Effectiveness

Early research on the effectiveness of family preservation services raised questions about whether it was superior to traditional services typically offered by child welfare agencies. Littell and Schuerman (1995), in a review of existing research on the effectiveness of family preservation and reunification programs, concluded "that family preservation programs have very modest effects on family and child functioning. Researchers have found few significant differences between program and comparison groups in levels of child and family functioning after services have been provided and the results of available studies are conflicting" (pp. 19–20). A subsequent study of family preservation programs in three states—Kentucky, New Jersey, and Tennessee—conducted by Westat (2002) summarized findings by noting that "we are unable to conclude that the family preservation programs in these three states achieve the objective of reducing placement of children in foster care" (p. 2).

Kirk (2002) has critiqued the research by Westat, holding that flaws in the project led to the findings of no difference between treatment and experimental groups. He argues that "there is a growing body of evidence that [intensive family preservation services] works, in that it is more effective than traditional services in preventing out-of-home placements of children in high-risk families" (Note 6).

Other research supports the use of family preservation programs for preventing out-of-home placement in high-risk families if the services provided strictly adhere to the standards of the Homebuilders program (Blythe & Jayaratne, 2002; Heneghan, Horwitz, & Leventhal, 1996; Kirk, 2002; NCDSS, 2001). Lewis, Walton, and Fraser (1995), in a study of Utah families, found that 77.2 percent of children whose families received services following reunification were still with their birth parents after one year. This compared to only 49.1 percent of children in the control group. Family preservation advocates point out that children in foster care die from abuse at twice the rate of children in the general population (United States Department of Health and Human Services, 2001). They also point out that the rate of sexual abuse in foster care is several times as high as in the general population (NCCPR, 2003). Others (Schuerman et al., 1994) point out that children who are abused in their own home and left there are abused 10 times as often as children in foster care. Cheung, Leung, and Alpert (1997) raise a concern that past research on family preservation outcomes "have not presented a systematic framework with clinical guidelines for practitioners" (p. 19). Walton and Denby (1997), in their review of 71 child welfare agencies in the United States, point out that the decision to begin family preservation services is based on an assessment that a child is at imminent risk of being removed from the home. They suggest that this criteria is "fraught with problems. First, the difficulties associated with predicting imminent risk were noted. Second, who determines imminent risk was identified as a significant factor," and "third, there was a great deal of vagueness and imprecision associated with decision making . . ." (p. 67). What is clear is that there is hearty debate in the field about whether family preservation is as effective as touted. Practitioners and researchers duel with statistics and criticisms of each other's work, and each side has adherents strongly committed to their positions.

Current Practices

While federal legislation and policies have consistently supported family preservation services, more recently several changes have begun to erode the effectiveness of such programs. For example, the 1997 Adoption and Safe Families Act (ASFA) appears to have shifted the emphasis away from keeping families together and on to termination of parental rights and adoption. The goal of the ASFA was to bring about permanency for children and to do so within specific time limits. This goal, while laudable, increased the pressure on state protective service agencies to come up with permanent plans for each child in their care. This resulted in less time and effort being devoted to reunification and family preservation.

In addition, many states have or are facing economic downturns that have stretched budgets and led to reduced funding for most, if not all, state programs. As money became less prevalent, state agencies reduced funding for family preservation programs, which, by design, served limited numbers of families. The mid 1990s also saw an increase in the number of child welfare cases involving substance abuse. These family situations tended to be more problematic and required increased services.

This confluence of events has had several consequences for family preservation programs. First, caseloads in many state agencies have become unmanageable, leading to staff turnover and greater risks to children. Second, attempts to modify such programs to stretch state dollars often mean that the models of practice originally adopted to provide effective services have been modified to the point where they can no longer achieve the quality indicators associated with programs such as Homebuilders. In addition, early research questioning the effectiveness of family preservation as a theory and intervention undermined efforts to build these programs, ultimately leading many states to drift away from the model.

WRAPAROUND SERVICES

Wraparound services is a term used to describe efforts to prevent out-of-home placement and promote unification of families by providing multi-need or multiple barrier "families with whatever community services they need" to achieve these goals (Downs, Costin, & McFadden, 1996, p. 24). Wraparound services are employed in a number of practice venues, particularly within the public sector, either alone or in conjunction with other efforts to assist families and children. For example, O'Malley (2003) and Chenven and Brady (2003) report on its use with severely disturbed children and their families. Ward and Bosek (2002) describe the use of wraparound services for adolescents and adults with developmental disabilities who are engaging in inappropriate or offensive sexual behavior. Wraparound services have been employed in schools for students with behavioral difficulties and to prevent the out-of-home placement of children (Maluccio, Ainsworth, & Thoburn, 2000). One benefit of its use in the school setting is the opportunity for involving all school personnel in planning both for services and for aftercare.

Services that might be wrapped around a family include "parent education, supportive counseling, help with housing and employment, drug treatment and others" based upon what the family requires. For some families, this might include kinship care, post-adoption services, day treatment, or respite care. Sometimes referred to as the "circle of caring," the goal of wraparound services is to ensure an integrated package of services rather than a discontinuous collection of agency programs (Downs et al., 1996, pp. 24–25).

Several things tend to characterize wraparound services, regardless of where they are used. First, services are designed to meet the specific needs of the individual and family. Second, practitioners work collaboratively with the family in designing the individualized intervention plan. Third, there is an

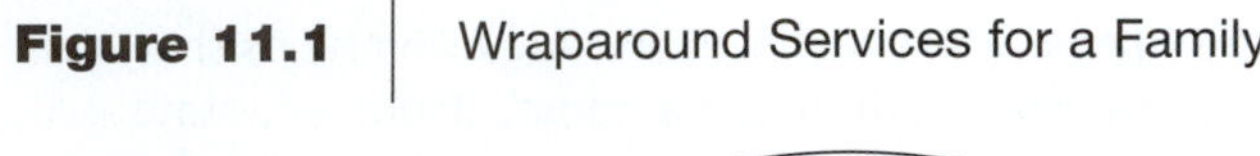

Figure 11.1 | Wraparound Services for a Family

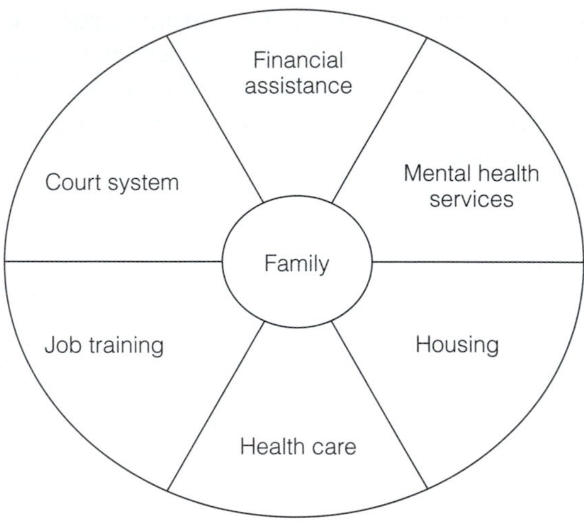

assumption that practitioners should "never give up" on a family due to the fact that such families often experience failure and rejection by other agencies and services. Fourth, flexibility in adapting plans and the ability to develop new services are characteristic of wraparound service providers. Fifth, wraparound programs incorporate a team approach using the services of all appropriate resources. This might include mental health, child welfare, vocational rehabilitation, juvenile justice, parents, and any other community service available. Sixth, a single coordinator performs the role of case manager and takes responsibility for creating a service team by joining together with all of the other people who are already involved with the family. The goal is to ensure that every available resource is used to keep the family together. Seventh, like family preservation, wraparound services adhere to the strengths model and use creative approaches to helping families resolve their difficulties (Downs et al., 1996; Mather & Lager, 2000). Eighth, wraparound services are intended to empower the family and provide them with a sense of control over their lives by involving them fully in the assessment, planning, implementation, and evaluation phases (Huffine, 2002). Ninth, services are expected to be culturally competent, and tenth, services make maximum use of natural (informal) and formal resource systems (Burns et al., 2000; Grundle, 2002). Figure 11.1 suggests how wraparound services are focused on the needs of the family.

Wraparound services are designed to avoid the criticism that many programs place "children in existing, but possibly inappropriate, service systems, requiring the child and family to conform to what is already in place" (Christian-Michaels, 1995, p. 59). Specific wraparound service programs have been implemented to help ensure agency collaboration, engage families early in the process, and reform traditional agency-focused interventions. Cook-Morales (2002) argues that the five Cs are important components of wraparound services: communication, cooperation, coordination, collaboration, and consultation.

Myaard et al. (2000) studied the outcomes of wraparound services for severely disturbed adolescents who were in danger of being placed in long-term residential care. They found immediate improvement in behavior that continued over time. Laveman (2000) reported the value of wraparound services in conjunction with "systems theory, solution focused therapy" with adolescents whose behavior placed them at-risk (p. 1). Similar observations were made by Borduin, Heiblum, Jones, and Grabe (2000), who described the role of wraparound services in addition to family and multi-systemic therapy to deal with antisocial behavior of adolescents. Seybold (2002) found significant reductions in externalized behavior disorders symptoms for youth in the Milwaukee wraparound program.

Success using wraparound services for juvenile offenders has been reported by Kamradt and Meyers (1999), Morrison-Velasco (2002), and Clark et al. (1998). It has also proven effective with incarcerated adult females preparing for their reintegration into the community (Bednar, 2001).

The use of wraparound services with suicidal adolescents has been described by Dollinger (1998) and Eber and Nelson (1997) note that it was effective in a school setting for children with emotional and behavioral difficulties. Based on the latter's findings, wraparound services helped children avoid more restrictive academic settings, reduced hospital days, and prevented out-of-home placement.

LaVigna et al. (2002) discuss the effectiveness of community-based wraparound services for people with developmental disabilities, demonstrating both cost savings and the ability to employ the least restrictive settings in their care. Brown and Hill (1996) also found success and significantly lower costs with a wraparound program in Canada. Skiba and Nichols (2000) examined research on wraparound services and concluded that it is a promising approach to delivering services to children and adolescents with severe emotional and behavioral problems. They also found that it often allows children to be maintained in less restrictive settings.

Csokasy (1998), in an *ex post facto* study using a quasi-experimental design, evaluated the effectiveness of wraparound care for severely disturbed adolescents. He found that children involved in the program were residing in less restrictive settings and experienced significantly lower rates of psychiatric hospitalization. Findings also reflected improvements in the behavior of the children and functioning of the parents/caregivers and family. Participants were also very satisfied with the program.

Evenson and his colleagues (1998) studied the success of a program that combines wraparound services with intensive case management for substance abusers. Findings demonstrated consistently positive results that increased in conjunction with the length of time participants spent in the program.

For children already in out-of-home placements, wraparound services improved outcomes, including both stability of placement and development of permanency plans, while also enhancing the emotional and behavioral adjustment of the children (Clark et al., 1996).

EXTENDED FAMILY SUPPORT PROGRAMS (KINSHIP CARE)

Extended family support programs (kinship care) are designed to provide short-term services and assistance to members of the extended family who are caring for related children outside of the child's own home. *Kinship care* is another term used for such models that ensure that children receive care from other family members while avoiding placement into foster care or other out-of-home institutions. Kinship care differs from traditional care by relatives because the relationship is formalized, and there is involvement of social service agencies in the placement. Kinship care has become a much more common form of placement for children in the child welfare system over the past 20 years (Grogan-Kaylor, 2000). The importance of kinship care arrangements can be seen in the context of a declining number of foster homes. The 10-year period from 1985 to 1994 witnessed a decline in foster homes from 147,000 to 125,000 (Child Welfare League of America, 1995b). This drop in available homes is just one of several factors driving the increased use of kinship care (Grogan-Kaylor, 2000). Court decisions that expanded the rights of relatives to receive financial assistance when caring for a child were a major impetus, as were federal laws mandating the least-restrictive setting for out-of-home placements. In addition, the need to provide care for children that reflected their cultural heritage was also a factor, as was the Indian Child Welfare Act of 1978, which discouraged the out-of-home placement of Native American children in non-Indian homes. Berrick, Barth, and Needell (1994) and Altstein and McRoy (2000) describe kinship care as a type of family preservation in that children remain in the home of relatives rather than placed with strangers.

Like family preservation programs and wraparound services, these efforts are designed to utilize all available resources on behalf of the caregivers. This may include concrete resources such as money, food or furniture, advocacy, referral to other community services, and social/emotional support to help them cope with their new responsibilities. Unlike the other programs, there is no presumption that a child is in danger, and the situation is not automatically considered emergent. However, there are many situations where an extended family caregiver is left with the children unexpectedly. An example appears in Highlight 11.2.

Although Rosa's kinship care involved her sister's children, this is certainly not the only extended family arrangement in use. According to the 2000 Census, about 6 million children are being cared for by siblings, grandparents, and other members of the extended family. However, only a portion of these

Highlight 11.2 | **Extended Family Support Example**

Rosa is the 38-year-old sister of Dannette, a mother of three children under the age of 12. Dannette struggled with substance abuse for several years, going in and out of treatment programs. One day, she dropped her kids off at the babysitter and never returned. The babysitter called the Department of Family Services and reported the situation, leading to the children's temporary placement in foster care. Dannette wrote eight months later, saying that she was starting a new life and could not care for the kids. Rosa, who was single, was asked about her willingness to take in her niece and nephews, and she agreed to do so.

The sudden nature of her new responsibilities caught Rosa by surprise. With no children of her own and a full-time job, she knew she would need help. The Department of Family Services offered to provide services through their Extended Family Support Program. To start with, Rosa needed assistance in finding a larger apartment as her one-bedroom flat was no longer adequate. She also needed additional bedroom furniture, bedding, and clothing for the children. Most importantly, she needed help learning how to raise three small children and support for doing so. The agency agreed to work with Rosa for the first six months to help in the transition.

placements are formal arrangements. Kinship placements are now the fastest-growing segment of child welfare placements (Gleeson & Craig, 1994). Figure 11.2 gives an indication of kinship care provided by grandparents, either by themselves or in concert with one or more of the grandchild's parents. Approximately 2.1 million children are living only with their grandparents.

Research on Kinship Care

Placement of children with relatives has many potential benefits, although it is not without drawbacks. As might be expected, placement with relatives often reduces the emotional trauma associated with out-of-home placement (Shlonsky & Berrick, 2001). Kinship placements tend to mean fewer moves for children and reduce the likelihood that the child will re-enter foster care or end up in group care. The risk of the child being maltreated appears to be lower in kinship placements (Zuravin, Benedict, & Somerfield, 1997). Children placed in the homes of relatives are also more likely to be placed with their siblings (Duerr-Berrick, Barth, & Needell, 1994). Chipungu et al. (1998) found that children in extended family placements have better health, both mental and physical, than those placed with nonkin. They also fare as well behaviorally and academically as those in traditional care (Altstein & McRoy, 2000).

Figure 11.2 | Grandparents Providing Kinship Care

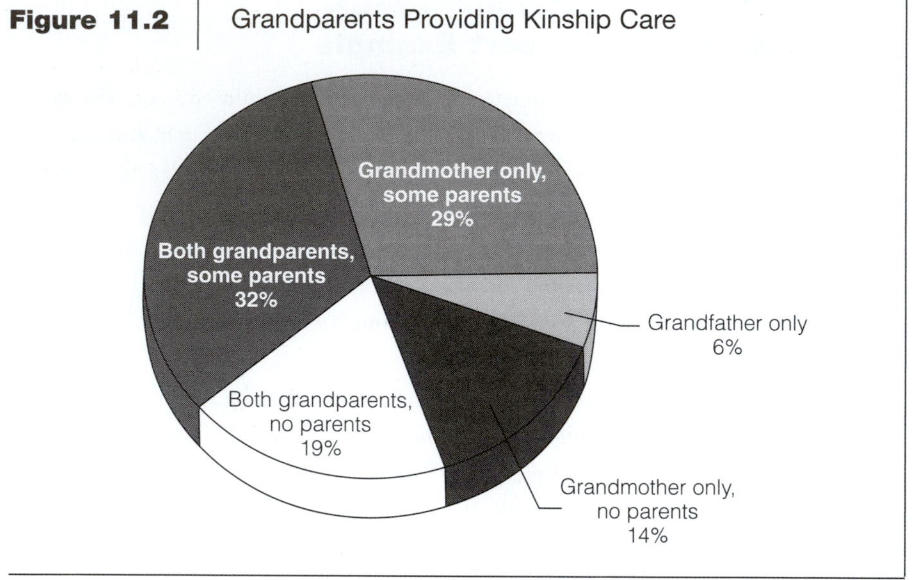

Source: U.S. Census Bureau, 2000; Generations United, 2003.

At the same time, kinship care is associated with slower reunification with the child's parents (Barth & Berry, 1994). In addition, many children cared for by relatives are not provided medical or mental health services when needed (Dubowitz et al., 1994; Dubowitz, Feigelman, & Zuravin, 1993). Moreover, Hollander (2002), summarizing results from the 1995 National Survey of Family Growth, indicates that women who spend any time living in either kinship care or regular foster homes have an increased chance of "engaging in high-risk sexual behaviors" (p. 55). They are also more likely to have more than three sexual partners during their lifetime and to become pregnant earlier. It is clear that kinship care does not protect a child from some long-term consequences.

Children who enter kinship care are more likely to have been neglected than abused and to have come from low-income mother-only or father-only homes (Grogan-Kaylor, 2000). As a consequence, this often means that potential relative placements are also likely to be low income. In fact, Berrick, et al. (1994) found that kinship foster parents tend to be older, African American, and with lower income levels than nonkin foster parents. Many have major economic, health, or other concerns of their own, and a large number are single. This has implications for the kinds and amount of support, both financial and emotional, that families may require (Hawkins & Bland, 2002).

In addition, Berrick et al. (1994) raised doubts that potential kinship families were satisfactorily screened by the placing agencies. Gleeson (1995) also found that children in foster care with relatives tend to receive fewer services than children placed in the home of nonkin. Chipungu et al. (1998) noted that kin caregivers also receive fewer services, including training and respite care. This is particularly significant when over 40 percent of children living with kin do not receive food stamps or Medicaid, for which they are clearly eligible (Ehrle, Green, & Clark, 2001).

When available, supportive services provided to extended-family placements have been shown to have several benefits. For example, Hawkins and Bland (2002), in a study of kinship care in Texas, found that marginal placements that might have disrupted without support were able to be sustained. In addition, the satisfaction level of caregivers was high.

Social Worker Services

As has been suggested, social workers in extended-family support programs can provide a variety of services for caregivers. These might include locating money to pay for needed items; linking the caregiver up with resources such as food banks; arranging for legal services for items such as guardianship papers; finding ongoing financial support; providing transportation for errands such as shopping or attending support group meetings; helping find money for meals and clothing; and arranging housekeeping services, home repairs and modifications and paying related costs (Generations United, 2003). Other services range from case management to formal training and include crisis management and referrals to other agencies (Hawkins & Bland, 2002).

Current Situation

Kinship care arrangements are becoming more popular as a means of avoiding placement into the regular foster care system. Programs are in place throughout the United States and England, although not all offer the same degree of services to the caregivers. The National Family Caregiver Support Program (NFCSP), a program of U.S. Department of Health and Human Services Administration on Aging, offers a variety of services to help support grandparents and relatives aged 60 and over who are providing kinship care. Unfortunately, state and federal policies do not uniformly recognize the enormous contributions that kin caregivers are providing. While some states find ways to help pay for kinship care, others do not (Hegar & Scannapieco, 2000). The failure of practitioners to assist extended-family caregivers in receiving services to which they are entitled continues to be a problem. At the same time, there is still a need for research to demonstrate the benefits and limitations of kinship care (Shlonsky & Berrick, 2001). Knowing in what ways children do best in which type of homes would be helpful information for social workers and policy makers.

MULTIPLE FAMILY GROUPS

A *multiple family group* involves two or more families meeting together in the same room with the family practitioner (Stone, McKay, & Stoops, 1996). Thorngren and Kleist (2002) refer to multiple family group therapy as an "interpersonal/postmodern approach." They recommend that practitioners receive training in both family and group therapy to be most effective and be flexible with a good sense of humor.

The multiple family group model has been used in the United States, England, China, and New Zealand for a wide variety of situations. For example, in the past, multiple family groups were used directly with alcoholics and in peer support groups like Al-Anon, designed for the relatives of individuals with substance abuse problems. Multiple family interventions have been used in work with psychiatric populations, particularly families of patients suffering from schizophrenia. They have also been used with dialysis patients and their families to involve everyone in monitoring the patient's condition. They have also been employed with families of disaster victims (O'Shea & Phelps 1985). In some cases, the family group has been managed like a workshop, with primarily an educational focus dedicated to helping family members better understand the client's illness and to describe available interventions.

Those invited to participate in multi-family groups differ depending upon the purpose of the group. Some social workers prefer to involve everyone in the family, including those not present in the home. Others invite just the immediate family members. Interestingly, some family groups exclude the client and are open only to other family members. Gonzalez, Steinglass, and Reiss (1989), for example, found "the multiple-family format proved a safe, generally de-intensified forum for the airing of long-unspoken feelings within individual families. The presence of other families (both patients and nonpatients) who share similar feelings and perspectives, tended to dilute the often harshly self-critical attitudes found within individual families" (p. 72). If the client needs a network to rely on to avoid relapse or to ensure compliance with treatments, the family group will be focused on creating a support group.

Other social workers have used family groups as an orientation to individual family therapy by sharing expectations, answering questions, and helping families decide whether to participate. Family group interventions have been utilized in both inpatient and outpatient settings. Corey and Corey (2002) report the use of multiple family groups with adolescents and note that families help each other in a number of ways, including pointing out strengths and encouraging changes in individual and family behavior. At the same time, they note that "families may 'hear' one another easier than they 'hear' the therapist" (p. 320). Much like other groups, family groups benefit from members' sharing of experiences, and the value is mutual.

An important consideration in multiple family groups is the issue of confidentiality. Creation of trust requires that families be confident that information they share will not find its way out of the group. Similarly, rules for interacting may need to be established to ensure each party has an opportunity to talk and to be listened to. Sessions are structured to be time limited in many cases, with at least two hours per week set aside.

Several principles underlie the use of multi-family groups by the family practitioner (O'Shea & Phelps 1985). These are outlined in Highlight 11.3.

Most recent research on the use of multiple family groups has reported positive findings regarding its effectiveness. However, in the past the model has

Highlight 11.3

Principles Underlying Multi-Family Groups

- The multiple family group is a microcosm of the larger social and cultural context by virtue of the fact that several ages, family roles, phases of psychosocial development, and stages of the marital-family life cycle are embodied simultaneously by the participants. As such, it more accurately reflects the social/cultural context and provides more qualitatively varied opportunities for learning, adaptation, and growth than does group therapy.
- Developmental history is encompassed in the here and now by virtue of the presence of family members representing multiple generations. This prompts participants to reenact past events or to understand them differently.
- Multi-family groups provide multiple opportunities for participants to modify boundaries by fostering cohesiveness and differentiation within families through inter-family competition and by promoting alliances among members of different families based on symptomatic status, age, and family role.
- The presence of two or more patients with the same problem diffuses the stigma associated with being a symptom bearer, and the presence of two or more family households dilutes the contamination effects of having a symptomatic person in the family.
- The therapist's interventions in multi-family group therapy are public, enhancing the likelihood that clinical changes will be more stable and will generalize to other behaviors or participants, as well as promoting adherence to a treatment regimen.
- The multiple family group can directly modify family norms and values and challenge family myths.

Source: O'Shea and Phelps (1985 p. 569).

been criticized for a variety of perceived shortcomings. For example, O'Shea and Phelps (1985) concluded that multi-family groups were "underused, conceptually underdeveloped, and poorly differentiated from other treatment approaches" (p. 554). As a blending of group therapy and family therapy, the authors point out that the approach appears attractive to some practitioners but remained inaccessible to most others. Multi-family groups have been criticized for other reasons. These include loose definitions of what constitutes a multiple family group and a failure to identify specific clinical techniques for use with this population. On the other hand, the latter criticism is less compelling in light of practitioners' tendency to use various techniques drawn from different theoretical approaches.

On the positive side, several studies have found that multiple family groups helped produce a sense of mutual support, allowed sharing of both dissimilar and similar experiences, encouraged clients and family members to share feelings, reduced isolation of all participants, and taught groups how to problem solve. Treatment techniques, however, vary from practitioner to practitioner. For example, in some groups, the social worker provides advice, suggestions, and information, while in others the group is charged with working out things by themselves. In some cases, the group is an adjunct to other interventions, while in others it is used by itself as a psychoeducational activity.

One of the most recent studies on multiple family groups was completed by McFarlane et al. (1995), who worked with families of clients with schizophrenia. They summarized the results of their findings with this observation:

> [M]ultifamily groups, combined with family psycho-education and maintenance medication, significantly reduce risk for relapse over an extended period, and suggested that longer-term outcome may derive more from the multifamily group component than from psychoeducation. It also indicated, in its short-term outcome, the advantages of family psychoeducation compared to treatments that lack that intervention approach. The significant main effect for relapse in psychoeducational, multifamily groups, compared to a higher rate in single-family application of the same therapeutic model, indicates that there is a factor or constellation of factors present in the larger social context of these family groups that supports remission in schizophrenic patients in ways that add to the therapeutic effects of psychoeducation itself." (p. 137)

Quinn, VanDyke, and Kurth (2002) reported on the successful use of multiple family groups for first-time juvenile offenders. The groups focused on helping families and offenders identify ways to prevent recidivism and promote family well-being. Improvements in parenting, youth life, and communication skills were reported. McKay and her colleagues (2002) found similar results when using multiple family groups with families of children with conduct and oppositional behavioral difficulties. An earlier study by McKay et al. (1999) also demonstrated that the method was effective in reducing dropout rates for therapy as well as decreasing incidents of hyperactivity, learning difficulties, and impulsivity.

Mullen, Murray, and Happell (2002) also found multiple family group interventions helpful with families of patients experiencing their first psychotic episode, a perspective echoed earlier by Gleeson and colleagues (1999). Dyck et al. (2002) noted that the method was successful in reducing psychiatric hospitalization for patients with schizophrenia. Previous research by Dyck et al. (2000) found that those participating in multiple family groups experienced significantly fewer negative systems compared with patients receiving standard care.

The use of multiple family groups has also been tested successfully with families of children with disabilities. Findings indicate an increased sense of empowerment and belonging among family members and reduced feelings of isolation (Saks, 1999). McDonnell and others (2003) were one of the few groups of researchers to find no benefit to using multiple family groups with caregivers of outpatients suffering from schizophrenia or other psychotic disorders.

Most of the available evidence points to the effectiveness of multiple group interventions with a number of different client groups ranging from those with moderate to severe physical and mental disabilities. Specific targeted populations included adolescents with behavioral disorders, substance abusers, individuals with schizophrenia and other psychoses, spouses and family members of substance abusers, patients with end-stage renal failure, and cancer survivors (Behr, 1996; Branch, 1996; Brennan, 1995; McFarlane, 1997; Ostroff, & Steinglass, 1996; Valentine, 1996). It has been employed in schools, hospitals, inpatient and outpatient mental health facilities, and in the community. Practitioners have employed it alone or in concert with other intervention modalities, and it shows promise in a number of different venues.

12 CHAPTER Commuity Focus on Families*

© David Young-Wolff/PhotoEdit

INTRODUCTION

Up to this point, we have identified specific practice theories and methods that we can employ when working with families. However, providing direct services to a family is not the only role for a social worker. Earlier we introduced the broker role in which the social worker links families with resources of various kinds. The broker role reflects the reality that, as we said in earlier chapters, the family exists within its environment. That environment may offer few or many resources. For most families, the community comprises a large component of the overall environment. Resources in the community often mean the difference between a family meeting and not meeting its own needs. Social workers must be aware of the many ways in which a community can provide resources and, in particular, understand which ones may be of most value to any given family.

This chapter looks at several ways that the community can be of assistance to families. We also consider some institutional deficiencies that present obstacles to families. The chapter discusses the federal government's role in sustaining families, in addition to special programs offered by community schools and educational facilities and by employers. Social workers must recognize how such programs may benefit families and be alert to the need to create and expand such programs.

IMPORTANCE OF THE COMMUNITY

In a community, individuals gather together with common needs and shared objectives. At the center of many communities are similarly held values and beliefs. They share a history: stories and memories that represent mutual struggles and victories developing their characters. Communities nurture children; it is where they grow and find role models to imitate. Communities carry a context of meaning that provides the environment where individuals become families, and families become communities. There is a sense of connectedness. By providing programs and services designed to support individual members and family systems, we similarly enhance the well-being of a community. When we provide family support services within the context of a community, we create opportunities for members to develop the traits that are essential to our national character and our commitment to others (Bellah et al., 1985).

While it is true that neighborhood, regions, and localities define some communities, many are not restricted by geographical boundaries. There are ethnic, racial, religious, social, employment, political, and educational communities, each with their own stories. There are also urban, rural, national, international, and global communities. These are the environments where families interact and nurture their members. In these communities, families share their fears and establish hope. Within the context of larger communities,

*This chapter was specially written for this text by Rosemarie Hunter, PhD. Dr. Hunter is BSW Field Director at the University of Utah College of Social Work.

individuals make the connections that define and sustain us as a society (Bellah et al., 1985).

Increasingly, comprehensive community-based family support programs are being established in both rural and urban areas to encourage positive family functioning. The primary goal of these family-friendly services and programs is to provide resources and supports that enable the family unit to maintain and address the needs of individual members. Social workers can use their knowledge of such resources to assist families grappling with specific challenges. They can also help create resources in those communities that have none.

Family support programs can be found in a variety of social institutions, schools, religious institutions, and community-based programs, and with employers. For example, to meet the needs of families in urban areas, many school districts are keeping school buildings open for extended hours. Before- and after-school programs have co-located and integrated education, health, job-training, and recreation services to recreate school settings as community centers. Similarly, religious institutions in many cities offer a full continuum of family supports and social services. In the workplace, many companies include families and the community in their mission statements. Flexible work hours, job-sharing, child care, elder care, and health care benefits are examples of family support services offered by employers. Federal, state, and local agencies provide programs focused on the prevention, education, and treatment of issues that interfere with healthy family functioning. Community-based support programs provide avenues for families to engage in ongoing community participation and relationship building. Through both structured and grassroots efforts, community-based programs offer a wide range of youth and adult recreation programs, information and education services, and cultural experiences (Schor & Gorski, 1995).

Beyond providing for individual members and families, delivering services in the context of naturally existing communities enhances the benefits to communities. If communities can offer services and programs within safe environments, individuals are more likely to be drawn to these communities. These are the communities where they will raise and care for their families. Similarly, schools that offer comprehensive programs often receive additional funding and the loyalty of community stakeholders. Finally, companies that provide family-friendly environments experience positive results with employee satisfaction and experience cost savings.

THEORY IN ACTION | Community-Based Support Program

Neighbors Helping Neighbors is a community-based support program begun in the 1990s by a private individual to aid elderly individuals in staying in their homes with the help of ongoing support from volunteers and with project renovations to keep their homes in good repair. These services are provided through the volunteer efforts of local community members and organizations.

HISTORICAL PERSPECTIVES

We can trace the current policies and programs providing family support services to relatively recent changes in our understanding of the challenges confronting families. Most of the early research trying to understand the needs of families was fundamentally linked to examining the issues of living in poverty. Vulnerable families often live in poverty, with minimal resources and complex life circumstances. Early theories maintained that poverty resulted from individual inadequacies. Researchers thought that a personal inability to function and adapt at the same level as the mainstream led to a subculture that, in turn, created the values and norms that enabled poverty to continue. As our understanding of the dynamics involved with living in poverty became more informed, we began to shift the responsibility of poverty from the individual to society. We began to understand that there was something about the way society distributed resources and power, and the availability and access to all, that significantly contributed to the complexity of the problems facing families (O'Conner, 2001).

Shifting the focus of the poverty debate from the individual to understanding the dynamics and barriers present in society led to redefining the causes of poverty and a greater understanding of what was needed to support families. Rather than focusing on the poor, research began to address the systemic and structural mechanisms that perpetuate the unequal distribution of power, resources, and opportunities. In addition, it provided an understanding about the convergence of politics and economics in shaping and sustaining these circumstances. This information became the foundation of developing social policy and programs that would support the family unit. Chapter 13 discusses some of these policy considerations in greater depth.

UNDERSTANDING BASIC FAMILY NEEDS

Resource deficiencies, or the lack of basic material needs, are some of the primary characteristics of families living in poverty. Lacking the basic resources necessary for life has a cumulative effect on families. For example, without having adequate food, shelter, and clothing, families experience problems with nutrition, growth and development, health, learning, and so on. Understanding that any group living without their basic needs would experience chronic hardships is not hard. Rather than holding the individual responsible, poverty was understood to be a result of the social condition in which people lived. From this research, movements such as the War on Poverty created programs that concentrated on specific kinds of services that could provide targeted support for vulnerable families. Head Start, neighborhood health centers, training initiatives, and community action programs are examples of programs aimed at changing the environment and circumstances in which the poor lived (Gilbert & Terrell, 2002).

While many family support services are intended for all members in society, it is understandable that the most vulnerable families are often those who live in poverty. You might be wondering: Who are the poor? What groups do

Highlight 12.1

Mother Teresa on Basic Family Needs

I will tell you a story. One night a man came to our house and told me, "There is a family with eight children. They have not eaten for days." I took some food with me and went. When I came to that family, I saw the faces of those little children disfigured by hunger. There was no sorrow or sadness in their faces, just the deep pain of hunger. I gave the rice to the mother. She divided the rice in two, and went out, carrying half the rice. When she came back, I asked her, "Where did you go?" She gave me this simple answer, "To my neighbors; they are hungry also!"

Source: Mother Teresa, 1997.

they represent? How widespread is poverty in the United States? In 2000, the overall poverty rate was 11.3 percent; this represents 31 million people. Sixteen percent of children lived in poverty (11.6 million children), and 21.6 percent of these children are under the age of 6. Of those aged 65 and older, 10.9 percent lived in poverty. In addition, 31.2 percent of those 85 and older experience the most severe poverty level of any group. Almost 25 percent of female heads of household are poor, while the rate of poverty for married couples is a much lower 5.2 percent. Black and Hispanic families headed by women account for 35 percent of the poor. The 2002 census reported that 7.7 percent of poor populations identified themselves as non-Hispanic white, while 21.2 percent said they were Hispanic. Twenty-one percent were African Americans, and Asian and Pacific Islanders accounted for 10.7 percent. The highest poor population was indigenous people, at 25.9 percent. Understanding which groups are at risk provides essential information for providing effective services. Federally supported family initiatives are aimed at addressing some of the major barriers affecting healthy family functioning (U.S. Department of Health and Human Services, 2004).

INSTITUTIONAL DEFICIENCIES

Once research and practice experience provided a better understanding of the complexity of problems families faced, government entities and other social institutions began developing programs focused on providing the necessary resources and services. The increased commitment of the government and community-based organizations saw a growth in institutional programs aimed specifically at providing resources to support the family unit. While well-intended, family support programs provided through formal institutional structures often present some specific challenges for families. Government institutions and social programs may function in ways that further create barriers for families (Gilbert & Terrell, 2002).

You may have your own experiences about trying to access information and services from a governmental program. If you are lacking for examples, imagine having to deal with the Internal Revenue Service regarding a tax return, or receiving a notice for jury duty. Indeed, something as simple as registering one's vehicle has been known to induce mild panic attacks. Similarly, resources and relief programs provided by state and federal bureaucracies are complex and difficult to negotiate. Inside these institutions, along with having limited resources and access, families often have limited power. Understanding the convergence of politics and economics in shaping and sustaining the unequal distribution of power and resources is fundamental to developing social policies that provide supports for families.

Besides the poverty research, studies in the 1970s began focusing on the developmental nature of children's experiences. Specifically, what a child experienced from birth to three years old could significantly influence the developmental outcome. We know now that children may be at risk before they are even born. Circumstances in prenatal development and genetic indicators have significant influence on development. Research findings from such programs as the Syracuse University Family Development Research Project, and the Yale University Child Study Center, contributed to the development of family support programs aimed at maternal and infant health and early intervention programs (Manalo & Meezan, 2000). For example, we began to understand that early interaction with an infant could affect the child's development of language and intelligence. At the same time, the ecological perspective proposed the theory that we must view individuals within their environment. It maintained that there is an interrelationship between the child, family, the community in which they live, and society at large (Bronfenbrenner, 1979). Family support programs began placing a greater emphasis on the early years of a child's life. Public health agencies provided resources focused on adequate nutrition and medical care, while programs such as Head Start and the Montessori preschools focused on early childhood developmental issues (Manalo & Meezan, 2000).

Meanwhile, the mental health system began redirecting its efforts from treatment to prevention. Primary prevention principles focused on building strengths and resources, providing education and life skills, and developing social networks and personal resources. The family support movement was an essential ingredient in supporting these efforts and moving the prevention agenda forward. Families could provide the support that individual members needed to deal with difficult life circumstances and general stress. In addition, providing family support can minimize children's risk factors and maximize their protective factors. By investing in families, we support both individual members and communities as a whole (Manalo & Meezan, 2000).

THE FAMILY SUPPORT MOVEMENT

Because families are members of communities, support services are best when provided within the context of community life. Through links to community resources, families can participate voluntarily and determine the needs of their members. Support services offered through the schools we attend, the companies we work for, and the communities in which we live, are indigenous elements of community life. Family support services enhance the quality of life for individual members and the community as a whole. Programs that focus on family strengths are well received, and their effectiveness is well documented. Comprehensive family support programs are directed toward strengthening the family unit and the community while preventing isolation and family dysfunction. These programs are an essential ingredient in promoting the healthy functioning of communities and assuring the well-being of children and families (Schor & Gorski, 1995).

The Family Support Movement has flourished through a confluence of events. State initiatives have encouraged development of programs and services supporting families. These programs are offered in school buildings, health centers, employment settings, and religious institutions. While providing family-oriented services was not a new notion, the Family Support Movement offered a new philosophy. The emphasis was on family strengths, rather than family problems. Families joined with other community stakeholders to develop common goals and shared solutions. No single social institution or agency could provide the collective wisdom and diversity that are found when community members work together. This demanded a new way of thinking. The Family Support Movement provided a new paradigm where the community itself would be transformed.

Consider the fable in Highlight 12.2 as an example of the paradigm shift that occurred. While at first it may appear that this fable has very little to do with the family support movement, it illustrates the need to see situations from a different perspective. Just as the stream could not understand giving itself up to the wind, many community stakeholders have difficulty relinquishing their power and control. In order for communities to work together, communal goals must take priority over individual goals. Similarly, just as the stream needed to develop trust and take a risk, without establishing trust between community residents and service providers, the collaborative process cannot work. In the fable, something as simplistic as a grain of sand understood the circumstances and provided a solution. The same can be found with the Family Support Movement. Sometimes the solutions are basic. Families have fundamental needs that we must address in order for them to provide a safe environment for their members. It is often family members themselves who best know the circumstances and have the solutions. The primary message from the fable is that the solution is found in working together.

The Family Support Movement supplied the vision for the development of many national programs and foundations aimed at supporting families and enhancing communities. One example is Family Support America (FSA), formerly known as the Family Resource Coalition of America, which focuses its funds and activities on empowering families and communities. Through networking and advocacy activities with both public and private agencies, FSA encourages community stakeholders and service providers to work together to provide an environment where families get what they need to succeed (Family Support America, 2002).

Highlight 12.2 The Tale of the Sands

A bubbling stream reached a desert, and found that it could not cross it.
The water was disappearing into the fine sand, faster and faster. The Stream said
Aloud, "I want to cross this desert, but I can see no way."
The voice of the Desert answered, in the hidden tongue of nature, saying,
"The Wind crosses the desert, and so can you."

"But whenever I try, I am absorbed into the sand; and even if I dash myself at the desert, I can only go a little distance."

The voice of the Desert said, "The Wind does not dash itself against the desert sand."

"But the Wind can fly, and I cannot."

"Allow yourself to be absorbed in the Wind."

The Stream protested that it did not want to lose its individuality in that
Way. If it did, it might not exist again.
Said the Voice, when the Wind absorbed moisture, it carried it over the
Desert, and then let it fall again like rain. The rain again became a river.
But how, asked the Stream, could it know that this was true?

"It is so, and you must believe it, or you will simply be sucked down by the sand to form, after several million years, a quagmire."

"But if that is so, will I be the same river that I am today?"

"You cannot in any case remain the same stream that you are today. The choice is not open to you; it only seems to be open. The Wind will carry your essence, the finer part of you. When you become a river again at the mountains beyond the sand, men may call you by a different name. . . ."

So the Stream crossed the desert by raising itself into the arms of the welcoming Wind, which gathered it slowly and carefully upward, and then let it down with gentle firmness, atop the mountains of a far-off land. "Now," said the Stream, "I have learned my true identity."

But it had a question, which it bubbled up as it sped along: "Why could I not reason this out on my own: Why did the Sands have to tell me? What would have happened if I had not listened to the Sands?"

Suddenly a small voice spoke to the Stream. It came from a grain of sand. "Only the Sands know, for they have seen it happen; moreover, they extend from the river to the mountain. They form the link, and they have their function to perform, as has everything. The way in which the stream of life is to carry itself on its journey is written in the Sands."

Source: Hendricks and Wills, 1975.

FSA (2002) established the family practice principles listed in Highlight 12.3 for communities to use as a guide in developing community-based family support centers and programs.

A FEDERAL RESPONSE

Federal family support policies and programs have an essential role in stabilizing and supporting families. While many individuals typically associate the Social Security Act with retirement, in actuality it encompasses social insurance, public assistance, and health and social services. Initially developed in 1935 as a response to the widespread and intense poverty brought on by the Great Depression, the Social Security Act continues to provide much of the federally funded support services for families. Through 21 different titles, Social Security authorizes a variety of social welfare programs to needy families, unemployed individuals, the disabled, the elderly, maternal and children's health needs, mental retardation, and block grants to states for children's health insurance and social services (Barusch, 2001). We discuss several of these programs in Chapter 13.

Highlight 12.3 Principles of Family Support Practice

- Staff and families work together in relationships based on equality and respect.
- Staff enhances families' capacity to support the growth and development of all family members—adults, youth, and children.
- Families are resources to their own members, to other families, to programs, and to communities.
- Programs affirm and strengthen families' cultural, racial, and linguistic identities and enhance their ability to function in a multicultural society.
- Programs are embedded in their communities and contribute to the community-building process.
- Programs advocate with families for services and systems that are fair, responsive, and accountable to the families served.
- Practitioners work with families to mobilize formal and informal resources to support family development.
- Programs are flexible and continually responsive to emerging family and community issues.
- Principles of family support are modeled in all program activities, including planning, governance, and administration.

Source: Family Support America, 2002.

Additional sources of funds for family initiatives can be found in the Departments of Health and Human Services, Education, Labor, Justice, Agriculture and Housing, and Urban Development. Federal legislation has directed funding to many initiatives designed to provide community support for families. These initiatives may be found providing service to families through many social institutions and community agencies. Goals 2000, Parent Information Resource Centers, and Family Preservation and Support Programs are a few examples of federal legislation focused on supporting families and enhancing community programs. For example, under the Family Preservation and Support Programs, the Omnibus Budget Reconciliation Act of 1993 provided federal funding specifically for the development of family support programs and centers (Manalo & Meezan, 2000).

As part of this legislation the Department of Health and Human Services defined family support services as the following:

> Community-based preventive activities designed to alleviate stress and promote parental competencies and behaviors that will increase the ability of families to successfully nurture their children; enable families to use other resources and opportunities available in the community; and create supportive networks to enhance child-rearing abilities of parents and help compensate for the increased social isolation and vulnerability of families. (U.S. Department of Health and Human Services, 1994, p. 9)

Several federally funded programs, such as the Model Cities and Community Action Programs, require the participation of community residents throughout the process. Because of federal legislation, communities have the necessary funding to develop community-based centers where families can gather to support each other. Family support centers may be found in schools, childcare settings, libraries, churches, synagogues, health clinics, and other community locations. Their philosophy is to provide services that build upon family strengths. They are designed to be a social setting and safe gathering place for community members of all ages and circumstances, and where family members act as resources for others.

Recently the federal response to families has expanded to included faith-based communities. Just as families are part of neighborhood, school, and work communities, many families participate in religious communities. Besides spiritual guidance and services, many religious institutions provide a variety of prevention, education, and treatment services. From informal support systems to complex organizations, faith-based communities are responding to the needs of families and communities by providing basic resources and counseling.

While several faith communities, such as Catholic Charities USA, Jewish Family Services, Lutheran Social Services, Salvation Army, and others, have historically provided social welfare services, the numbers of these programs have grown considerably in the last decade. The "charitable choice" provision of the Welfare Reform Act in 1996 authorized state systems to contract with faith-based organizations to provide social services. This is a significant philosophical shift. Under Temporary Assistance for Needy Families, many churches are providing programs that include prevention, education, and treatment, provided they do not actively pursue converting clients or discriminate against nonmembers.

THEORY IN ACTION | Faith-Based Community Program

Interfaith Community Services, located in a western United States community, is a program in which 12 churches (different denominations) offer homeless shelter to 5 to 6 families a week. Each church shares a week's responsibility for the families in providing shelter and additional services. Some of the additional services that the community program provides is help in finding employment and housing within the 12-week recovery process.

SCHOOL-BASED FAMILY SUPPORT PROGRAMS

Another venue for offering family-supportive services is the school. In fact, some of the most exciting family-friendly social policy perspectives to emerge in recent years are the school–community initiatives. There is a growing recognition that no single institution can address all the needs and conditions of children. An active and engaged community includes parents, neighborhood leaders, religious institutions, community organizations, service providers, and local governments. All community members play an enormous role in supporting the well-being of families (Melaville, 1998).

The importance of school-based family support programs was underscored by Moore and Vandivere (2000), who surveyed families of school-aged children across the nation. Their report concluded that more than one in five children in the United States lives in a stressful family environment. They define the criteria for stressful family environments as the existence of two or more of the following six stressors: (1) the inability to pay bills, (2) inability to obtain food, (3) uncertainty about health care, (4) parent or child in poor health, (5) a physical or learning disability, and (6) a mental health condition. After analyzing the data, the authors concluded that children living in stressful family environments are nearly twice as likely as other children to exhibit a decrease in school participation and performance. In addition, these same children are four times as likely to show an increase in behavioral and emotional problems.

Even without stressful family environments, schools are often structured settings that produce their own set of stressors. Can you remember a time in your own education when you were particularly uncomfortable or under a lot of stress at school? Maybe the circumstances involved a difficult subject, teacher, or fellow student; perhaps involvement with a particular sport or activity; or maybe it was a social situation. For a moment, try to remember the circumstances and details of the event. How old were you? Where did you live at the time? What did you look like? Think about what your life was like then and pay attention to how you felt. Perhaps you have a current example, such as the anxiety you experience trying to prepare for a midterm or even just getting through this chapter. In any event, remember that many adults enter school settings today and carry with them their experiences and feelings from past events associated with schools. Some adults may avoid these settings because these experiences and associations are negative. Still others who may not have completed their education feel alienated and out of place in the academic environment. Supporting families from the school setting involves an understanding of the institutional barriers and a new paradigm for defining school communities.

Dryfoos (1998) describes a model for *full-service schools* that includes goals broad enough to address the issues of a stressful environment, while assuring equality, equity, and adequacy. Full-service schools, sometimes called *community schools,* redefine the boundaries of education to include the entire community. The model includes an assessment of children's needs as family needs, understanding that family needs are multidimensional and complex. Consequently, the response must also be multidimensional and comprehensive. Full-service community schools offer a wide array of services, such as health care, mental health, employment services, childcare, adult education, parenting classes, recreation, and cultural events. Most of these services are available to families in or near the school building and are open to all members of the community, not just families with school-age children.

While initially full-service schools began co-locating health and social services at the school site, it quickly became evident that comprehensive, collaborative assessments and integrated methods of delivery were necessary to address the needs of all community members. Dryfoos (1998) calls the result, a *seamless* institution that provides the maximum responsiveness to community members and accessibility for those families who are most in need of support services.

Besides educators and family members, local community leaders have an important role to play in establishing school sites as community support centers. By identifying resources and providing links to existing services, community leaders take an active role in creating family-friendly schools and communities (Obiakor et al., 2002).

In order for schools to maximize resources and minimize duplication of services, all participants need to gather a comprehensive assessment of the existing resources and the community environment. Banks and McGee-Banks (1997) developed the following questions as a guide for assessing existing community programs and services, and to aid in identifying the gaps present in needed services for families:

- Are there any drama, musical, dance, or art groups in the community?
- Is there a senior-citizen group or public library, or a cooperative extension service in the community?

- Are employment services such as the state employment securing department available in the community?
- Are civil rights organizations such as the Urban League, Anti-Defamation League, or NAACP active in the community?
- What is the procedure for referring people to the Salvation Army, Goodwill Industries, or the state Department of Public Assistance for emergency assistance for housing, food, and clothing?
- Does the community have a mental-health center, family counseling center, or crisis clinic?
- Are programs and activities for youth, such as Boys and Girls Clubs, Campfire, Boy Scouts, Girl Scouts, YMCA, and the YWCA, available for students?

When viewing the school as a community, the focus is on the needs of the members of the community rather than on single individuals. In a community school model, the principal, teachers, parents, students, and community stakeholders are valued members, and each is an integral part of the community functioning. As a community identity emerges, the educational goals become less individual and more collective. The school as a community is a system that is constantly providing for its members. Community members are motivated and committed to the process through a shared agenda and ownership (Sergiovanni, 1992).

Beyond a shared vision, effective school–community partnerships require establishing a well-developed infrastructure that provides leadership, decision making, problem solving, resource building, accountability, and relationship building. Detailed, well-defined plans and task assignments are essential ingredients in successful collaborations. While the initial collaboration may begin at any level, with any stakeholder, keeping neighborhood residents involved in the process and sharing in the power is crucial. Effective changes are made by the participation of residents who have a personal stake in the decisions and outcomes. As a result, while community schools share the same goals, they may look very different in the ways in which they identify and meet the needs of each community. There are wide variations in service delivery and design methods. In addition to community diversity, these variations often reflect the range of funding sources available (School Mental Health Project, 2003)

As communities struggle to address the needs of families in an environment of shrinking resources, *university engagement* and *community partnership* models have emerged as successful methods of addressing these complex challenges. American communities are facing widespread concern regarding the future. Through competing economic and political interests, new national priorities arise while others disappear. Government family support programs have introduced time limits and a greater emphasis on individual responsibility. Following September 11, 2001, new national priorities are focused on homeland security and the threat of terrorism. These growing concerns compete for the same government funding that provides a substantial portion of family support programs and services. Older industrial cities around the country that already experience long-standing problems of poverty, unemployment, inadequate housing, and middle-class flight feel the effects of global and economic pressures even more intensely.

Americans have often viewed education as the great equalizer. This social institution enabled immigrants to acculturate and gain some form of equity in the system. Higher education provided a vehicle for the United States to develop and eventually compete globally. The Community Partnership Act of 1992 and the U.S. Department of Housing and Urban Development (HUD) established Community Outreach Partnership Centers (COPC). Since its implementation, 143 institutions of higher education have received federal seed money to establish university–community partnerships. While contributing much-needed services to local communities, these COPC centers have provided essential knowledge about what defines university–community partnerships and how to sustain these relationships (U.S. Department of Housing and Urban Development, 2002).

In 2000, the Association for Community–Higher Education Partnerships, consisting of a group of COPC grant recipients, was established to provide knowledge, support, and advocacy that would further promote university–community collaboration. Embracing the same goals of the Family Support Movement, COPC partnerships emphasize reciprocal goals, equal partners, and the importance of establishing good relationships. From the beginning, families must be part of the process. They must be involved with identifying the needs, establishing the goals, setting priorities, and creating solutions (U.S. Department of Housing and Urban Development, 2002).

The following Theory in Action contains a few examples of community partnerships that developed with the participation of families and other community stakeholders. Their focus is to provide community-based family support programs while contributing to overall community revitalization. They provide strong evidence that successful community-based programs require the participation of all members. Similarly, personal ownership in the process is essential to the outcome.

THEORY IN ACTION | University–Community Partnerships

The University of Pennsylvania (Penn)

Originally started as the Charity School of Philadelphia by Benjamin Franklin in 1740, Penn has always had a strong mission of community service. Beyond its Ivy League status, Penn is a significant local employer for the West Philadelphia community and, simultaneously, is dependent upon the local community for its survival. The growing crime and poverty rate in the surrounding neighborhoods supplied Penn with an immediate self-interest for developing initiatives that would stabilize the community and provide much-needed support for families. Penn has developed multiple community revitalization projects focusing on schools, housing, economic stimulation, employment, and safety. This major research university has also established itself as a major economic contributor. Penn has invested approximately 200 million dollars into the community, generating new jobs, businesses, and improved education and housing. The university is committed to hiring local businesses and providing incentives for minority and women contractors. Additionally, Penn's involvement has attracted other economic interests to the area, providing additional jobs for community residents (Maurrasse, 2001).

Illinois Institute of Technology (IIT)

Located near Chicago, IIT administration and faculty acknowledged the growing economic, educational, and digital divide in their surrounding neighborhoods as unacceptable and reaffirmed a commitment to the community as their mission. IIT is found in the Bronzeville area, which is home to more than 16,000 students in 28 public schools. The population experiences a high incidence of economic and educational challenges. In one area, 51 percent of the population did not complete high school, while in another 55 percent did not have high school degrees. Understanding how these circumstances have a direct effect on IIT is not difficult. While IIT has always had a strong mission and track record of public service, it refocused that commitment in 1998. President Lew Collens, in his letter to the Department of Housing and Urban Development, stated, "IIT's Board of Trustees recently adopted new university priorities that included reaffirmation of the university's goal to be a full partner in the transformation of Bronzeville" (Wenger et al., 2001).

Through the Paul V. Galvin Library at IIT, the institution provides a community-accepted meeting place that offers educational and technologically focused programs for adults. They conducted surveys and focus groups with area residents and public school educators to identify their greatest needs. In addition, IIT partners with the area public schools, providing training and technology to public school teachers. Training teachers created a widespread multilevel means of influencing the economic and educational gap in the community. By supporting the public school system, IIT could spread their services to larger numbers throughout the community, thereby having a greater effect. They knew these services would have a direct impact on children in the area schools. The library continues as a location with community identity. It provides community members with training methods and activities that allow them to have full access to information available through libraries in an environment that exposes families to education and system resources (Wenger et al., 2001).

The Twomey Center for Peace through Justice

Another example of a grassroots community partnership aimed at supporting families can be found at The Twomey Center for Peace through Justice. The center, located at Loyola University in New Orleans, has an emphasis on social justice and is home to many innovative family-friendly programs. Founded in 1947, the center addresses issues ranging from the death penalty and civil rights in Central America, to homelessness, hunger, and housing programs. The Center's Urban Partners Program (UPP) connects Loyola faculty and staff as a resource to community leaders. These relationships have led to the development of a computer school located in a public housing development. This program provides adult education and job training during the day, and an after-school study skills program with tutoring and homework assistance for youth. Other examples include a public school-based conflict resolution program known as Resolving Conflict Creatively (RCCP), and the Crescent City Farmers Market, a university–community, grassroots economic enterprise (Loyola University, 2002).

The Crescent City Farmers Market is an example of successful partnership with family farmers, commercial fishers, restaurant chefs, public housing residents, consumers, and Loyola University. It began as a grassroots effort that eventually led to the development of the Economic Institute at Loyola. At the start of this program, Louisiana was suffering the effects of an oil-related recession, and shrinking economic opportunities were fueling growth in violent crimes, homelessness, and poverty. In New Orleans, food is part of the culture. It provides a common language for individuals of different groups to come together. The university's faculty worked with community residents to identify everyone who came to mind, whatever their differences, that might support the establishment of a new farmers' market in downtown New Orleans. The list included chefs, business leaders, farmers, downtown residents, public housing residents, city hall officials, health and nutrition advocates, public social service representatives, county cooperative extension agents, community gardeners, and members of the medical community. Over a five-year period, a new commercial infrastructure for farmers developed. The community was extremely needy for an economic enterprise that worked. The involvement of many facets of the community population developed ownership and gave a human face to both agriculture and the university (McCarthy, 2001).

EMPLOYER-BASED FAMILY SUPPORT PROGRAMS

Increasingly, employers are introducing family-friendly employment policies that allow families to balance their priorities while maintaining their employment and benefits. Job-sharing, flex time, telecommuting, on-site or subsidized elder and childcare services, low-interest loans, community-based services, and family resources and referral services are some of the ways that companies provide support to families. In the next section, we provide an example of job-sharing that offered the best solution for one employer and two families.

Flexible Work-Family Options

Individuals today face decisions of how to care for families and maintain their employment. Besides pregnancy and childcare issues, many families are caring for elderly parents and family members with disabilities and mental health issues. Even when individuals can afford to manage on a part-time salary, their decisions are further complicated by the potential loss of health care and retirement benefits. Increasingly, companies are looking for ways to retain and support quality employees while they deal with life circumstances. Highlight 12.4 shows one example of how employers are responding to the needs of families by providing more flexible schedules and shared responsibilities.

North Carolina took the idea of job-sharing seriously. In January 2003, the North Carolina State Legislature passed a law to further support educators who are interested in job-sharing. School districts there can now provide part-time teachers with full health care and retirement benefits to encourage creative job-sharing options (Blair, 2003).

Job-sharing is only one example of the ways in which employers are supporting families. Morgan and Tucker (1991) provide many more examples in the book, *Companies Who Care*. Morgan and Tucker include more than 100 examples of companies that provide family support services, including subsidies for child and elder care, referral and resource services, low-interest loans, flexible work schedules, and paid maternity or paternity leave.

Following the passage of the Family Medical Leave Act (FMLA) of 1993, many more companies can be added to the list. This federal legislation ensures that employees can take up to 12 weeks of unpaid leave in a 12-month period to care for a newborn or a sick family member, without the threat of losing their jobs. The FMLA benefit applies to companies that have a minimum of 50 employees. In fact, FMLA is broad in its protection and includes birth; adoption; foster-care placement; care for a sick child, spouse, or parent; or an employee's serious health condition (Williams, 1998). While FMLA does not provide paid leave, several companies have taken the next step and offer subsidized leave as an additional benefit to recruit and retain quality individuals.

A Closer Look at Costs and Benefits As a social worker, you may be wondering why companies would offer such support. After all, what is in it for

Highlight 12.4 | Job-Sharing

When Renette Stinson, a kindergarten teacher at Mounds Park Academy in St. Paul, Minnesota, learned she was pregnant with her first child, she planned to take several months' maternity leave, then return to work full time. But her principal, who didn't want to hire a long-term substitute, had a better idea. Stinson's twin sister, Renee Wright, had applied for a part-time teaching job there, and the administrator suggested that they share a classroom, both working a little more than part time, with full-time benefits. Fifteen years later, the sisters are still sharing a job, and they've inspired copycat set-ups at the school.

Source: Blair, 2003, p. 11. Reprinted by permission.

them? Family support policies initially were a response to the increasing numbers of women entering the workforce. However, human resource specialists are proving that such services increase productivity and assist companies in attracting and retaining quality employees regardless of gender. While measuring an individual's productivity accurately is often difficult, observing specific behaviors that affect their performance is possible. For example, employee tardiness, turnover, and absenteeism are behaviors that result in significant costs to companies every year. Losses of production, recruiting, and training are time consuming and costly activities for employers. Providing family support programs that address the needs of families is more cost effective and reduces the overall cost to the employer. To many families, these types of benefits are more of a consideration than the salary. The truth is that this philosophy is good for families and, simultaneously, good for company profits (Conrad, 1995).

Some companies are focusing on ways to strengthen the community rather than just providing on-site services and benefits. The American Business Collaboration for Quality Dependent Care (ABC) is a consortium of 22 companies, including Amoco, IBM, Mobil, Xerox, Kodak, and others. Included in the mission of ABC is to create and improve child care, after-school care, and elder care in the communities where the programs operate. Instead of providing large subsidies to employees for family care services, ABC invested those funds into child development training and professional development for existing care providers located in the surrounding areas. The goal is to improve child care, after-school, and elder care services by supporting and training caregivers. By supporting the programs and services in the communities in which they exist, the consortium hopes to strengthen the community for all members, not just their employees. These are the communities where companies and their employees reside. A commitment to strengthen communities provides a better quality of life for all members (Hammonds, 1997).

During 2002, the Society for Human Resource Managers conducted a survey of 551 human-resource professionals, which indicated that 24 percent of the participating companies were offering job-sharing. In addition, 33 percent of companies provided some alternative workday schedule or compressed time. This involved working 40 hours weekly but in an alternative format, such as four 10-hour days. Even more popular was some form of telecommuting. Thirty-seven percent of the companies offered employees the option of working from home via a computer. Finally, at 64 percent, flex time was clearly the most company-supported alternative work method. With flextime benefits, employees can maintain their own work hours. Besides having more variety than the traditional 9 to 5 schedule, employees can also take off for appointments or other commitments and make up their hours on a different day (Cain, 2003).

Dealing with Issues of Diversity Just as employers support families through the benefits they offer, several companies support families by the protection they offer. Many companies and universities, including Adolph Coors

Co., Walt Disney Co., IBM, Microsoft, Sun Microsystems, Stanford, Harvard, University of Iowa, University of Minnesota, Brown University, and others, provide nondiscrimination policies based on sexual orientation. Some companies recognize that policies are not enough, and many of these same companies extend fringe benefits to partners, whatever their gender. Still others understand that the issues of discrimination are complex and deeply ingrained. As a response, employers are offering, and sometimes requiring, diversity training. Increasingly, employers are taking efforts to nurture and strengthen the work environment. Sun Microsystems and Knight-Ridder are examples of two companies that have taken a proactive stance. By conducting ongoing employee training programs related to minority issues and oppressed populations, they give employees an opportunity to learn about and explore their differences in a safe and respectful environment (Van Wormer, Wells & Boes, 2000).

A Corporate Commitment to Families

The corporate response to families has an extensive and rich history. Affluent companies across the nation have long participated in addressing the needs of community and families. In fact, in the years following World War II, contributions from private industry are credited with accomplishments such as the national expansion of the library system, the discovery of the polio vaccine, public broadcasting services, the Model Cities program, and Head Start, to name a few. Private foundations continue to provide billions of dollars aimed at addressing the needs of families. Approximately 47,000 foundations annually award an estimated 23 billion corporate dollars today. In recent years, the primary focus of private foundations has been directed toward the elementary and secondary education systems, health care, and social services. Corporate leaders, such as Andrew Carnegie, John D. Rockefeller, Henry Ford, Robert Wood Johnson, and Annie E. Casey, initially recognized for their accomplishments in the private sector and their immense fortunes, displayed a devotion to public service that continues today through the ongoing work of private foundations (Gilbert & Terrell, 2000).

In the future, social workers will increasingly find a combination of public and private services targeted at families. Some will come from the corporate world, others from governmental agencies, and still others from religious and secular organizations. Staying abreast of these resources will allow the social worker to connect families with those services that best meet their needs. In addition, awareness of the multiple ways in which communities can help families grow and prosper has another benefit. Social workers can serve as advocates for establishing programs that assist families in meeting their needs. They can also be active in the policy arena, supporting better services for families of all kinds.

Families and Social Policy*

CHAPTER 13

© Michael Newman/PhotoEdit

INTRODUCTION

The most vulnerable families and children are those who live in poverty and experience multiple environmental risks. Policies that guide services to these families are for the most part related to welfare and child welfare. This chapter summarizes major policies related to these families and offers guidance for practice. The chapter's intent is twofold. The first goal is to help social workers recognize some of the most critical resources available to families and the limitations of those programs. A second goal is to underscore the importance of advocacy for family-responsive social policies and programs, a key role for social workers.

PUBLIC ASSISTANCE

While families can be classified in a variety of ways, public assistance (welfare) programs define social policies that affect families living in economic poverty. The unique needs of this population make understanding social policy regarding public assistance programs, and the underlying attitudes that fostered the development of such policies, vital to successful practice with these families.

Assistance for families in economic poverty is channeled through a complex web of programs, policies, and services. In this section, we discuss one such program, Temporary Assistance to Needy Families (TANF), which delivers the bulk of cash assistance to families living in poverty. The attitudes underlying the formation of this program are explored as a means of understanding the culture surrounding current practice with families in the program. Finally, we suggest some implications for practice through a checklist of areas recommended for consideration when working with families affected by these public assistance programs and policies.

A Brief History

Creation of AFDC Providing a "safety net" for families (and especially children) who live in poverty was an element of social policy in the United States transported by the colonists from their experiences in England. Rooted in a communal sense of fundamental responsibility to care for the poor, these safety nets have been continuously provided by various combinations of government agencies, church groups, and nonprofit organizations.

Understanding current social policies that have shaped the TANF program requires knowledge of its predecessor, Aid to Families with Dependent Children (AFDC). "Originally called Aid to Dependent Children (ADC), the AFDC program was part of the Social Security Act of 1935 and was designed to provide support for children by dispensing aid to their mothers" (Karger & Stoesz, 2002, p. 277). The word "families" was added in 1962 to highlight the

*This chapter was specially written for this text by Adrian Popa and Mary Beth Vogel-Ferguson, doctoral candidates at the University of Utah College of Social Work.

family unit. AFDC, as well as most public assistance programs of the day, was a means-tested program that provided a certain amount of cash assistance based on household need. This meant that any family who met the means test was entitled to the assistance. The goal was to make sure no family fell below a basic survival level.

AFDC was in many ways a very controversial program. Some criticisms were based on flaws within the program structure; other concerns were rooted in societal views and myths regarding the people receiving assistance. Structural issues were addressed over time. One example was an attempt in some states to expand services to include not only single-parent families (generally headed by single mothers) but two-parent families where one parent was unemployed. This new program was called Aid to Families with Dependent Children—Unemployed Parent (AFDC-UP). Another structural issue was the difference between what a family could receive while on assistance and what the potential take-home income was if the head of the household was working. Because of inadequate support services, it was financially advantageous for a single parent to remain on assistance rather than seek employment. Work did not pay. There were few incentives for participants to improve their skills through either education or training.

Moving Forward While AFDC was originally established as an income maintenance program, the Jobs Opportunity and Basic Skills (JOBS) program, part of the Family Support Act (FSA) of 1988, shifted the focus to mandatory work and training. These structural changes responded to both the need to improve program services as well as general perceptions about people receiving pubic assistance.

The early 1990s was a transition period in many states. One often-forgotten element of the FSA (1988) was the provision for states to receive waivers from AFDC policy to pilot new programs. The limitations of AFDC led to innovations aimed at repairing its structural deficits and responding to public perceptions about welfare recipients. Some of these programs served as models for the sweeping changes that were about to come.

The "End of Welfare As We Know It": PRWORA On August 22, 1996, President Bill Clinton fulfilled his 1992 campaign promise to "end welfare as we know it" by signing the Personal Responsibility and Work Opportunity Reconciliation Act of 1996 (PRWORA, HR 3734). PRWORA was one of the most important pieces of welfare legislation to emerge since the Social Security Act of 1935. It fundamentally changed the social welfare system by replacing AFDC, JOBS, and the Emergency Assistance Program with the TANF program (Karger & Stoesz, 2002, p. 279). PRWORA replaced the individual entitlement program with the TANF block grant, which provides family assistance funds to the states. TANF's emphasis is on the transitional nature of assistance and the importance of reducing welfare dependence through employment and other goals. Public cash assistance would no longer be a benefit to which the poor were entitled; it had to be earned. "PRWORA provided the capstone to policy initiatives undertaken in many states to modify AFDC under federal waivers" (Committee for Economic Development, 2000, p. 1). The Department of Health and Human Services administers the TANF block grant program, which provides states with up to $16.5 billion each year (as of September 2002) (USGAO, 2002, p. 4).

The sweeping philosophical changes introduced by the TANF program outlined a new way of viewing public social policy. The four purposes of TANF include the following:

1. Provide assistance to needy families so children can remain in their own homes or in the home of a relative
2. End dependence of needy families on government benefits by promoting job preparedness, work, and marriage
3. Prevent and reduce the incidence of out-of-wedlock births
4. Encourage the formation and maintenance of two-parent families

These four purposes are concretely supported by changes to major structural elements of the program. These changes are as follows:

- *Time Limits.* States may use TANF funds to assist families for up to 60 months. States may choose to set a shorter time limit and can make exceptions for up to 20 percent of the caseload.
- *Work Participation.* States are required to have at least a given percentage of program participants engaged in work activities in order to receive their full block grant. The percentage increased each year, from 25 percent in 1997 to 50 percent in 2002.
- *Sanctions.* Because this is no longer an entitlement program, families who do not participate in the program to a satisfactory degree are sanctioned; that is, their grant amount is reduced or completely withheld until they are again participating in the program at an acceptable level. States are also allowed to reduce or eliminate assistance if a participant does not cooperate with efforts to secure child support.
- *Family Cap.* PRWORA allows states to initiate family caps, meaning that families who have more children after beginning cash assistance would not receive a larger grant to cover the new child.
- *Marriage Support and Reduction of Out-of-Wedlock Pregnancy Funding.* States are allowed and encouraged to use a portion of TANF funds to support programs that encourage marriage, support the formation of two-parent families, and strive to reduce the incidence of out-of-wedlock pregnancies.
- *Immigrants.* All immigrants arriving in the United States after August 22, 1996 are ineligible to receive any means-tested, federally funded public benefits until they have been here for five years.

As the first authorization period of the TANF block grant came to an end in September 2002, proponents of the program were more than pleased with the results. Case loads had been reduced by more than 50 percent. More former recipients had left the rolls due to employment. Skeptics wondered if reduced case loads really meant that people were moving out of poverty. There were concerns as to whether the jobs being attained were really sufficient for sustaining a family and what impact these changes might have on the children who comprise more than two-thirds of all TANF recipients.

Welfare Reauthorization When the original TANF block grant funding expired in September 2002, and was presented for reauthorization, it was clear that no changes to the core elements of work first, time limits, and sanctions had been made. Yet, the House and Senate were unable to come to agreement on other basic elements of the program, and reauthorization was postponed several times. Funding remained at original levels to sustain programming through this period. While there was general agreement regarding funding levels, major areas of debate between the House and the Senate focused on (1) the number of hours of work and work-related activities to be required for all participants, (2) what can be considered "countable" activities toward participation and how long a participant can engage in such activities, and (3) the amount of money authorized for childcare assistance. While there were some significant areas of disagreement, it is clear the new "welfare-to-work" view (verses ending poverty) of social welfare policy introduced by PRWORA remains.

The sweeping nature of the changes in the basic nature of American welfare policy has led to much discussion as to society's responsibility to the poor. The discussion around the reauthorization period again raised the issue of whether TANF was contributing to the reduction of poverty or was simply a way of removing the poor from the welfare rolls and forcing them into employment. The focus of TANF has clearly shifted public cash assistance programs from the focus on a safety net for the poor to temporarily assisting families on their way to self-sufficiency through employment. This new reality forms the cultural framework surrounding practice with poor families today.

Public Assistance Policy and Attitudes toward the Poor

The changes codified in the passage of PRWORA, and specifically TANF, represent a major shift in the relationship between government and families facing economic hardships. This shift represents broad societal attitudes toward those who receive public assistance. Given these attitudes, there is still much debate over what should be the primary focus or goal of public assistance, what policies should be used to meet these goals, and to what degree government should attempt to influence shifts in family structure to achieve these goals.

Social Attitudes and Public Assistance

General attitudes toward public assistance programs and those who receive aid vacillate over time and can vary widely depending on the individual circumstances of a recipient. The evolution of public assistance programs in the United States both reflects and is shaped by the attitudes of the general public toward those who receive such aid. For example, in the United States most programs use means tests as the primary eligibility criteria. This is in contrast to some European countries, where universal services are available.

Many of the attitudes expressed in the form of current legislation were also present through the AFDC years. Then as now, there were many who believed the myths about public assistance recipients. These beliefs included ideas such as these:

- Welfare recipients are lazy and choose not to work; the poor do not apply themselves and lack the desire to better themselves.
- Welfare "moms" just keep having more kids to get a bigger check.
- Most women on welfare are minorities.
- Most welfare recipients are out to cheat the system.
- Welfare programs get in the way of marriage as women can become financially dependent on the state and do not need a husband.
- Welfare costs are a huge part of our federal budget—welfare recipients suck money out of the system and give nothing back.
- If welfare recipients would only get married, they would not be poor.
- If welfare recipients would just get a job, they would not be poor.

There is much statistical as well as anecdotal information that disproves each of these myths, either somewhat or completely. Unfortunately, the facts have done little to change general perceptions in society. These attitudes have influenced policy changes from AFDC to the present. One of the most significant and detrimental effects of these myths is the message they send to recipients of cash assistance. Many of them come to believe the negative messages, further undermining often shaky self-esteem.

A recent study of former public cash assistance recipients reveals the multiple sources of such messages. Several respondents spoke of people shaming them in the checkout line because their basket did not contain the type of food the person thought should be purchased with food stamps. One respondent had a state case worker suggest she get an abortion because she did not believe the client should be having more children while on public assistance. Study respondents as well as community advocates were outraged when a state legislator publicly commented that "those women just get beat up so they can receive more money from the government" (Taylor, Barusch, & Vogel-Ferguson, 2002). These scenarios reflect a societal view that does not go unnoticed by those receiving assistance.

TANF: What Is the Goal?

The primary purpose of public assistance programs prior to PRWORA was to provide a safety net to catch families sliding down the economic scale into poverty. Regardless of structural changes, the preference of many advocates for the poor was for poverty reduction to remain the central focus of public assistance policy. However, this perspective has not prevailed. Promoters of the new policy acknowledge, "Currently, there is a campaign by the detractors to make TANF an anti-poverty and career development program. The TANF goal was not to lift families out of poverty, but to move families from welfare to work. The TANF program is not a promise to move the working poor up the career ladder, but to help the non-working poor get to the first rung of the ladder by obtaining a job" (Anderson, 2001). While the distinction between these two perspectives may seem small, it is particularly relevant to one group—immigrants.

"An estimated 27% of poor children are immigrants or the children of immigrants, and the nation cannot implement an effective anti-poverty strategy that excludes this group" (Greenberg, 2001). Those who support the idea of TANF as an anti-poverty program likely agree with this statement, while those who view it as more employment related question the statement's relevance because some immigrants are not legally able to work in the United States and thus, by definition, could not participate in the public assistance program.

As TANF neared reauthorization, proponents often quoted statistics citing reduced caseloads, increased employment, and reductions in out-of-wedlock pregnancies as indicators of this program's success. Indeed, these are the markers now being used to judge the success of this new type of public assistance program.

Policies for Reaching the Goal

The title "Personal Responsibility and Work Opportunity Reconciliation Act" reveals the policy view that individuals are personally responsible for their own well-being. The Committee for Economic Development "endorses PRWORA's mandate to replace a public assistance program that often discourages personal responsibility and employment with one whose central premise is that most assistance recipients *can* and *should* work" (CED, 2000, p. 1). The implication is clear: In the past, recipients have been discouraged from taking personal responsibility for the well-being of themselves and their families. Therefore, government needs to make shifting this responsibility back to the family a priority.

Because there is still a core belief that many recipients of public assistance are intentionally choosing not to better their situation, consequences for failure to "participate" (as defined by TANF policy) were written into the legislation. The result is a policy environment where the prevailing belief is that government's major challenge is to persuade low-income individuals to make more-responsible work and family decisions. Toward this end, state TANF programs rely heavily on financial penalties and incentives to motivate desired changes in behavior.

"Implicit in TANF's emphasis on persuasion is the assumption that welfare recipients have deficient family values and attitudes and that welfare policies can and should change these values and attitudes" (Mauldon et al., 2002, p. 2). Yet, there are concerns that other factors may be influencing a person's ability to participate. "Sanction policies may have spurred work participation, but they have also resulted in termination of assistance to families with the most serious employment barriers, often without basic protection in place" (Greenberg, 2001).

Research reveals that people with health problems are leaving the system due to noncompliance at a faster rate than those without health issues (USGAO, 2002, p. 5). This raises the question of whether the person was choosing not to comply or whether the health barrier made compliance difficult, if not impossible. There is a strong, documented relationship between mental illness and welfare receipt, in that mental illness clearly makes a parent less likely to work and, accordingly, more likely to receive welfare. "The very symptoms associated with mental health problems, such as loss of concentration, fatigue, and irritability, may make it difficult to function in a work environment" (Rosman, McCarthy, & Woolverton, 2001, p. 4).

This issue is especially prevalent among minorities as "racial and ethnic minorities collectively experience a greater disability burden from mental illness than do whites. This higher level of burden stems from minorities receiving less care and poorer quality of care, rather than from their illnesses being inherently more severe or prevalent in the community" (Rosman, 2001, p. 4). While higher sanction rates make it appear that minorities are less willing to participate in work and move toward self-sufficiency, other factors are likely more significant than simple unwillingness.

People with mental health issues may have a difficult time complying with work requirements, are more likely to be sanctioned, hit the time limit, or simply leave the system unemployed. In the past, public assistance has served as a resource for people pursuing Social Security Income (SSI). In states where the length of time available for cash assistance or the work participation requirements are more stringent, the new regulations can pose a problem. TANF is primarily work focused, yet it is being accessed by people no longer able to work who have not yet been approved for SSI benefits. These situations challenge the assumption that all participants in the program *can* and *should* work. The fact that people who enter the system with some employment history, educational background, work skills, and an adequate level of mental and physical health are more likely to succeed makes it clear that these are the people for whom the system was designed.

Connecting Government and Family Formation

PRWORA highlights the connection between public assistance policy and family formation. Three of the four basic purposes of TANF relate to family structure. The policy supports (1) ending dependency on government programs through marriage, (2) preventing and reducing the incidence of out-of-wedlock pregnancies, and (3) encouraging the formation and maintenance of two-parent families. These types of family formation choices have generally been considered private matters, best left to the individuals involved. This would be especially true when all parties are of legal age. This focus of government policy on "preferred" family structures has caused some to ask what role government has in suggesting particular family structures as preferable for those most affected by this policy, a policy specifically for the poor.

Criticism of the AFDC program for containing disincentives to marriage may have contributed to this new emphasis. There is some research that indicates that children who grow up in families with both biological parents in a low-conflict situation generally fare better. "It appears that living with married, biological parents strengthens children's claims to the economic resources, love and affection, nurturing, and social capital of both parents, including access to the resources of both sets of extended family" (Ooms, 2002, p. 2). But there are those who would question the rationale for using a pro-marriage agenda in anti-poverty programs (Coontz, 2000). There are fears that any special incentives to marriage, especially when linked to financial gain, can increase choices to enter into high-conflict and possibly dangerous situations.

The fact that these ideals have been put in policy as goals challenges all those who, for whatever reason, do not fit these models. Do these standards present yet another way for the poor to have their lives controlled by forces beyond their influence? Research has found that women who have received public assistance, and those who have not, report similar attitudes toward marriage and child bearing. The differences come in the ability of each group to reach its goals. It would appear that interventions touting the benefits of marriage are not needed as much as services that might help women fulfill the (pro-marriage) aspirations they already hold (Mauldon et al., 2002, p. 3).

It is generally accepted that there have been and continue to be policy aspects that create disincentives to marriage. More time and study are needed to discover how best to support those who struggle both financially and in their efforts to provide a healthy family structure for themselves and their children.

Policy Implications in Practice

As outlined in Chapter 1, there are many roles a social worker may fill. When working with economically poor families, the realities of the requirements of and attitudes toward public assistance policy might need to be incorporated as part of the family's environment.

A study of former recipients of cash assistance was conducted with the intent of learning more about the experiences with the system. From their first-hand experiences, respondents were able to communicate powerfully their ideas on how people like themselves could be better served by the professional community. The following cases are from data gathered in this study and provide real-life examples of how public assistance policy and attitudes might affect work with families (Taylor et al., 2002).

THEORY IN ACTION | Time Limits

Sara had been bringing her severely depressed 12-year-old son Mark to counseling for the past 6 months. They were always on time and, on the rare occasion they had to miss a session, she called to reschedule. Sara, a single mother, had been job searching for months and finally was hired just as she came to the end of her eligibility for cash assistance. Unfortunately, there was a one-hour commute, and she worked the same hours as the clinic. Sara tried to ask to leave a little early to bring her son in for his appointments, but the boss was unwilling to cooperate. Sara called in sick a couple of days so she could make the appointment but had her job threatened if she called in again. Finally, she gave up trying to bring her son in for the therapy sessions. Two months later, she returned home from work to find that her son had hung himself in the family's living room.

Sara felt trapped. She was responsible for the physical *and* emotional needs of her son. She herself had been ill, on and off, for years, and she used up her months of eligibility during this time. Taking the job had been a difficult choice, but what else could she do? With no family in the area, she was totally responsible for herself and her son.

The imposition of time limits on cash assistance affects all families receiving this assistance. For some families, the imposition of a time limit on cash assistance has been a motivational tool moving them toward self-sufficiency. As one respondent said, "Losing my cash was the kick in the butt I needed to get a job. " For others, losing assistance is the pivotal event that moves the family into crisis. One respondent told how she lost her apartment and had to quit school when her time expired. Her car broke down a week later, and she had no transportation. Because of this her children had to move in with their father, who lived close to their school, because she was unable to transport them and provide for their basic needs. The downward spiral can happen very quickly.

In Maslow's hierarchy of needs, basic physiological needs come first. For a family who is about to lose their cash assistance, food, shelter, and other basic needs may be in jeopardy. A practitioner who is aware of this aspect of the family's environment can be prepared to assist with the immediate needs that will certainly occupy the client's mind. Because public cash assistance is no longer available, connecting with other community resources may be the only option.

THEORY IN ACTION | Slipping through the Cracks

John and his wife live with their five children. John has Tourette's syndrome, and doctors have documented that he is able to work but only for very short periods. When he found a job as a crossing guard, John was very happy because he was able to work about 20 hours a week in short intervals. The income did not put his application for SSI in jeopardy, but it did cause difficulties with his public assistance case. John had already come to the time limit for his months of public cash assistance, and, amazingly, the family was able to make ends meet during the school year. What John needed was an extension of his benefits through the summer. John was told that he was not working enough hours to be considered "participating." The worker had a hard time not believing that since John was working 20 hours, he could not work more hours if he really wanted. John knew from past experience that this was not possible and felt he was doing the best he could to support his family. He finally came to the attention of an advocate who was able to help him gather the proof needed, and together they challenged the agency. John received an extension based on his participation at his greatest possible level and was able to care for his family through the summer months.

Social workers need to be alert to cracks in the system and be ready to assist clients in navigating the challenges in a way that will keep the family moving forward. Often, state workers within the public assistance agencies are also carrying large case loads. It is difficult for them to give the time and attention needed to understand complicated policies and how they might apply to individual cases that do not fit the norm. Families with multiple barriers often must use resources from many places. Managing all of the various agency requirements, case reviews, verifications, and so on can be a full-time job. Even though PRWORA was established with the belief that most families could and should eventually become self-sufficient through work, there will always be those who will never truly be self-sufficient.

Social workers who work in areas where sustainable employment is difficult to find also face challenges connected with TANF policy. State participation rates (counted as the number of people in each state case load who are working or engaged in work activity at a minimal level) are the same for everyone. Very rural or highly urbanized states are no exception. This means that, for example, someone living in a small rural town is required to put in as much time seeking employment or working as someone in a more populated area with many more job opportunities. Current policy makes no provision for changes in the local or national economy or for variances in opportunities for education, training, and employment. PRWORA was introduced during a period of unprecedented economic growth. Jobs were plentiful in most areas. The recession of the early 21st century has created serious challenges for states trying to meet participation rates and families trying to meet work activity requirements.

THEORY IN ACTION | Multiple Agency Involvement

Heather and her four children, ages 2–13, were well known to many of the social service agencies. Heather left the children unsupervised and was consequently reported to child protective services a number of times. The 13 year old already had quite a history with the police. All the children were having trouble in school. Teachers, counselors, and principals had all made attempts to help the family. Heather's 8th-grade education and chronic depression made steady employment difficult. The work guidelines of her public assistance program required her to job search 30 hours a week to keep her cash assistance.

Her child protection worker required her to participate in parenting classes, counseling, and to be at home with the children whenever they were not in school. The 13 year old had court dates, community service hours, and regular counseling of his own. Heather was overwhelmed. Finally, one of her social workers was able to see the bigger picture and recognize that Heather's greatest skill had become keeping one step ahead of whichever agency was pushing her the hardest at the moment. This person called together Heather and representatives from each of the agencies involved with the family. This time of sharing of information and setting realistic goals made life better for everyone involved, especially Heather and her children.

As a social worker working with a family on a specific issue, it is often difficult to remember that there may be many other legitimate pulls on the client's time. The many tasks required of sometimes low-functioning, multiple-barriers families can be daunting. Taking the family-in-environment approach means knowing and understanding the other agencies with whom the family is involved. It also means asking yourself "How might what I am asking the client to do come in conflict with what is required by another agency?" Understanding the policies of other agencies is vital to this coordination of services.

Another hurdle for families involved with multiple agencies is the enormous amount of paperwork and time spent giving information to each agency. Multiple screenings, assessments, and what some describe as interrogations often contribute to the family's feelings of powerlessness. So many people are telling these families what they can and cannot do. Some families report feeling frustrated to the point of disengaging with a variety of agencies because the combination of requirements were simply overwhelming. Finding ways for social service agencies to share information and consolidate requirements would go far in reducing the stress on program participants. In an ideal world, there would be one plan for each family—an overarching plan that takes the needs of each member into consideration and helps reduce competing demands on fragile families that are already stretched in many other ways.

THEORY IN ACTION | Family Formation

Derrick and Susan have been together for two years. They have discussed marriage, but because both were in difficult previous marriages (Susan's involved severe domestic violence) they were moving forward slowly. Derrick has two children from his previous marriage. Susan has two children, ages 3 and 5. Derrick has been like a father to Susan's children and would like them to be a family.

Finances have been a struggle. Susan has worked on and off all her life even though she has only an 11th-grade education. She suffers from severe anxiety and depression and often loses jobs because her symptoms become worse and she cannot function for a while. She has been in counseling and it has helped. She also is on some medication now that really helps even out her moods. Susan has received cash assistance periodically as well, but the food stamps and Medicaid have been the vital resources for the family. Since Derrick moved in, things have been a little easier. Derrick is a hard worker but only brings home about $1100 per month, $500 of which goes to child support. Susan receives no child support as her ex-husband is in jail.

The problem is that Susan is pregnant. While she and Derrick are excited about having a child together and would like to marry, financially it seems impossible. The fact that Derrick is not the father of Susan's children meant that his income is not included in the calculation of her benefits. Once the baby comes, all his income (even the part that goes to child support) will be counted against not only the cash assistance but also the food stamps and Medicaid. Susan needs the Medicaid to cover her counseling and prescriptions as well as any of the children's needs. She will also have a new baby who will need regular medical care.

Susan's case worker looked over the situation. Her suggestion is for Susan and Derrick to split up their living arrangement. It is the only way for Susan to keep the benefits she needs. While this solution may seem drastic, current policy makes it difficult for couples like Susan and Derrick to support their family financially and create the family structure most supported by social norms. There are couples who have been together for years who are thinking about splitting up because the mother and children would be able to receive more help in this living situation. There is a conflict between a desire for parents of children to be married and living together, and an unwillingness to help such families, who are assumed to be able to make it on their own. This conflict of values is not lost on the families caught in the middle.

Social workers may struggle, as the families do, to understand these conflicting policies. Families are often aware of the gap between socially acceptable relationships and what they are able to experience in their own lives. Many seek the stability and security of having a partner, but many other factors must be considered. Couple counseling for those receiving public assistance needs to include realistic discussions on how decisions to live together or marry may affect family income, food stamps, and even access to the Medicaid that may be making the counseling possible.

CHILD WELFARE

Like public assistance programs, child welfare agencies, responsible for providing services to vulnerable children and families, are one of the most important public social services. Ideally, child welfare services should include a broad continuum of preventive and treatment services, such as child protective services, foster care, adoption, day care, emergency shelter services, intensive home-based-services, respite services, and others (American Public Welfare Association, 1990). Child welfare organizations are complex living, breathing, and evolving bureaucratic ecosystems that encounter countless challenges from a systemic synergy experienced within converging micro, mezzo, and macro arteries. The organization synergy and output is reflected through direct services, outcomes, and performance in response to administrative regulations, legislative representation, and numerous partnerships with private and nonprofit community organizations. Organizations experience not only diminishing resources and apathetic fiscal support but increasing expectations prompted by federal regulation (Adoption and Safe Families Act of 1997, P.L. 105-89) and current class action lawsuits *(Angela R. v. Clinton,* 1991; *David C. v. Leavitt,* 1993). At the same time, they must deal with concurring expectations to refine and improve the performance, outcomes, and efficiency of service delivery.

Social policy influences and is influenced by political struggles, barriers, limitations, and bureaucratic regulations. At the same time, organizational goals and decisions are influenced through lobbying, research, bargaining, and negotiation. Conflict is inevitable as divergent interests compete within the larger arena forging compromise as a last resort. This bureaucratic ecosystem is rooted and functions primarily within a political framework (Bolman & Deal, 1997). A political framework is structured around special interests and coalitions that routinely compete, bargain, negotiate, coerce, and compromise one another. Because not all players have the same amount of influence in the political process, power gaps occur.

Social workers need to understand the bureaucratic, political, and social systems that produce both beneficial and sometimes incomprehensible social policies. For example, once a law has been passed, it must be interpreted and structured through a process of rulemaking. This process is a dynamic one that also involves manipulation and influence initiated by political leaders, lobbyists, interest groups, researchers, expert witnesses, litigation, direct practitioners, and other influential bodies. As with policies aimed at the poor, the field of child welfare needs knowledgeable social workers who understand public policy and regulations that drive resource allocation and affect decisions. This knowledge is critical because these forces inevitably trickle down to indiscriminately impact service delivery with clients of all ages and ethnicities. To affect public policies and regulations, contribute to formal and informal rulemaking, and address and strengthen efficacy of regulations, social work practitioners need to become catalysts for innovation and policy making. With their experience delivering services, social workers are well positioned to reflect and represent critical strengths and limitations of existing and proposed policies. In the section that follows, we will examine how the process of enacting regulation and rulemaking can be influenced using the Adoption and Safe Families Act as an exemplar.

Adoption and Safe Families Act

In the years prior to enactment of the Adoption Assistance and Child Welfare Act (P.L. 96-272), public law and policy had been passive in advocating on behalf of children. This passivity reflected the fact that public attention and political interest were focused on a variety of other issues, including the legitimacy of the Vietnam War, Watergate hearings, and Nixon's resignation, along with the arms race between the United States and the former Soviet Union. Domestic programs, especially social programs advocating on behalf of youth, were minimal, underfunded, or nonexistent.

Beginning in the mid 1960s, several factors began to change this situation. There was a growing concern about the rights of the prisoner and the well-being of war veterans, women, and Native Americans, and finally a slight movement toward the rights of the child. One of the first landmark children's rights cases was the 1965 Supreme Court decision *In re Gault,* in which the court extended constitutional due process to children (Pine, 1986). Pine documented societal trends, such as increasing single-parent families, a dramatic increase in the incidence of divorce and out-of-wedlock births, and an increased interest in adoption as movements focusing attention on the treatment of children.

These dynamics, along with misrepresentations of the federal requirement for "reasonable efforts" to preserve and reunify families, exponentially increased the child protective caseloads. Agencies could not keep pace with the children entering the system and allowed children to remain in or return to unsafe homes. This, in turn, increased recidivism and the numbers of children in temporary foster care. This is reflected in the fact that the number of children in foster care rose from 270,000 at the end of 1985 to approximately 502,000 at the end of 1996 (U.S. House of Representatives Committee on Ways and Means, 1998).

In an attempt to address increasing social problems and neglect of certain populations, the Adoption Assistance and Child Welfare Act (P.L. 96-272) was enacted into law in 1980. This law hoped to respond to the growing problem of children lost in the system of state protection and foster care. The Act was also intended to reform the public child welfare systems by focusing on three components. The first component was increased accountability of the public child welfare system for the government and the families served. A second component was heightened emphasis on prevention of placement, reunification, or alternative permanent placements and a reallocation of existing funds to support this goal. The third component was creation of initiatives that would increase the adoption of children previously considered unadoptable. This component involved the provision of subsidies to individuals who would adopt these children and remove them from the child welfare system.

The law as implemented focused on preventative services, permanency planning, and further identification of appropriate services. This federal framework also set direction and parameters for the operation of state and local child welfare agencies and courts. The passage of P.L. 96-272 discouraged the dominant and excessive reliance on foster care placement and promoted greater use of services to assist and rehabilitate families, preventing out-of-home placements. It introduced the concept of permanency planning and incorporated specified time frames for decision making for children and families.

Despite the intentions of this Act, the needs and the complexity of problems facing families progressively escalated throughout the 1980s and early 1990s. The diversifying family dynamics were too complex to be addressed by diminishing services, community-based organizations, and innovations unreflective of current societal trends. The complexity of social problems was also the catalyst for increased foster care caseloads, placements, permanency, and systemic gridlock. Policymakers and administrators became more aware that in order to address the root causes of child abuse and neglect, additional efforts must be devoted to prevention and early intervention with children and families.

In 1993, Congress passed the Family Preservation and Support Services Program that increased the amount of available funding to states. The funds were designed to provide continuity in services addressing community-based family support opportunities, intensive family preservation, reunification, and adoption, as appropriate (U.S. DHHS, 2000). The Omnibus Budget Reconciliation Act of 1993 introducing Public Law 103-55 and Congressional amendments to Title IV-E created and extended the range of child and family services funded under Title IV-B to strengthen and support families and children in their homes and out-of-home care.

Congress passed the Multiethnic Placement Act (MEPA) (P.L. 103-382) in 1994 to address excessive lengths of stay in foster care experienced by children of minority heritage. This law also forbid the delay or denial of a foster or adoptive placement based on race, color, or national origin of the prospective foster parent, adoptive parent, or children involved. Confusion over the intent of MEPA resulted in changes to the law in 1996, followed by imposition of stricter penalties and corrective actions for any state violating sections of MEPA.

The passage of the Adoption and Safe Families Act of 1997 (P.L. 105-89) served as the capstone to previous attempts at reforming the child welfare field. The objectives of ASFA in 1997 was to provide states with the necessary tools and incentives to achieve the original goals of the original 1980 Public Law 96-272. The motivation behind ASFA was the dissatisfaction with the performance of state child welfare systems in achieving these goals for children and families. The law reflected bipartisan action to ensure that children's safety would be the overall concern of all child welfare decision making and to promote the adoption of children who cannot safely return to their own homes. Two goals were established: (1) to move children who are stranded in the child welfare system with no place to go, and (2) to change the experience of children who are currently entering the system.

ASFA established time limits for permanency and termination of parental rights in order to expedite safety, permanency, continuity of care, and individualized services (see Table 13.1). Additional mandates introduce the component of parental involvement in case planning and resolution, and increased accountability of service delivery. In addition, the law gave consideration about the level of staffing, training, and other principles to ensure high-quality service delivery.

The enacted bill amended the Social Security Act to revise procedures for foster care and adoption placements and provided incentive payments to states that increase adoptions from the foster care system. The process increases accountability by requiring states to develop plans to facilitate adoptions across state and county jurisdictions. It also authorizes DHHS to expand the number of state child welfare projects addressing kinship care (discussed in Chapter 11). Additional amendments to expand and authorize fiscal appropriations continue to provide for family preservation and support services, and health insurance coverage of adopted children with special needs.

History of Congressional Legislation

It is important to understand how any law is created and to recognize the multiple opportunities that exist for impacting legislation. The process that led to P.L. 105-89 is similar to that followed by many legislative proposals. A recap of the process is instructive for social workers who need to understand how a bill becomes law and how to become a player in the process.

Committee Meetings and Hearings Meetings and hearings on P.L. 105-89 held on Capitol Hill involved individuals, organizations, and interest groups presenting information, data, and expert testimony. Peter Pecora, researcher with The Casey Family Program, presented data and practice information on

Table 13.1 ASFA Required Time Periods

Requirement	Deadline	Starting Date
Case plan	60 days	Actual removal
Reasonable efforts to prevent removal	60 days	Actual removal
Six-month periodic review	6 months	Foster care entry
Permanency hearing	12 months	Foster care entry
Reasonable efforts to finalize permanency plan	12 months	Foster care entry
Mandatory termination petition filing	15 of the last 22 months	Foster care entry

Source: Baker, 2000.

Highlight 13.1 ASFA (P.L. 105-89): Five Key Principles

1. Safety is the paramount concern that must guide all child welfare services.
2. Foster care is temporary.
3. Permanency planning efforts should begin as soon as a child enters care.
4. The child welfare system must focus on results and accountability.
5. Innovative approaches are advocated.

family-based services (FBS). Evidence-based material from FBS programs presented a more-balanced approach in contrast to previous child rescue efforts. Program effectiveness was attributed to a reliance on monitoring systems that would track clear outcome-oriented approaches to delivery of FBS and address problems in administration, practice, service, and evaluation. The new methods would form innovative strategies to implement new polices.

The National Association of Social Workers (NASW) also presented testimony, noting that "service provision can only be effective when service providers have the necessary academic training, knowledge, skills, and experience." This training and experience enhances their capacity to address complex dynamics, align problem-solving interventions, and maximize positive outcomes for victims and their families. Numerous studies were presented in order to strengthen the value of social work training, as well as empirical research showing that few workers within family services have higher degrees required for the job capacity. The focus was placed on the premise that services provision cannot be enhanced when it is often provided by individuals who are not professionally trained social workers.

Social legislation analyst Dale Robinson testified about the scarcity of data available on adoption. The national data collected by the federal government's Department of Health and Human Services is gathered through the public child welfare system. Data showed that increasing numbers of children are in foster care and that a proportion of these children linger in the child welfare system and foster care. Children on adoption waitlists in the foster care system also tend to be disproportionately from minority groups. There was a clear need for increasing research, data collection, and tracking of trends in order to explain and anticipate increasingly complex challenges facing the child welfare system (96-H781-13, NO1).

The need for change was also underscored by testimony based on the experiences of representatives, administrators, line workers, and children. The overwhelming evidence was in favor of new laws that would address obvious systemic problems.

Committee Reports Following testimony, the legislative committee's report recommended the passage of the Adoption Promotion Act to promote the adoption of children in foster care. The report included provisions to clarify that states are not required, prior to placement of a child in foster care, to make reasonable efforts to preserve and reunify families if it is determined that reunification with the parent is not in the best interest of the child's health or safety. Best-interest-of-the-child cases require states to initiate proceedings to terminate parental rights for children under 10 years old who have been in foster care for 18 of the previous 24 months. These requirements are stimulated by incentive payments to states that increase adoptions from the foster care system.

Congressional Debate/Record The Congressional Record (Vol. 143, No. 54) documents the process of consideration of the bill (H.R. 867) to promote and speed up the adoption process of children who have been abused or neglected and languish in foster care. Debates were confined to the bill and did not exceed one hour in length. The passive attempts to move children out of foster care and the absence of incentives to states to do so were highlighted. Discussion focused on moving children from foster care to adoptions and establishing a positive incentive to reduce the foster care caseload. The goals, objectives, and provisions of the bill were clearly depicted throughout the debate, and the bill had solid bipartisan support.

Subsequent sessions continued to consider the bill (H.R. 867) in promoting the adoption of children in foster care. Additional support and urgency to pass a combination of reforms to change the child welfare system were presented.

During debate on the bill, crisis nurseries were also introduced as a means of providing respite and therapeutic services for families with young children and assisting parents toward self-sufficiency. Crisis nurseries were seen as another way to avert foster care or other out-of-home placement. Another proposed intervention was kinship care, in which relatives become caretakers in cases where parents cannot. There was concern that the United States had no national policy to address relative-care arrangements and that it was important to recognize relative-care arrangements as legitimate and appropriate placements for a family. These amendments were passed and remained on the record.

Highlight 13.2 Additional Provisions in ASFA That Promote Permanence

- Reasonable efforts toward permanence
- Continuation of the Family Preservation and Support Services Program
- Attention to geographic barriers to adoption
- Expanded health coverage for adopted children with special needs
- Notice and right to be heard for certain caregivers
- Continuing eligibility for federal adoption assistance
- Use of Federal Parent Locator Service
- Congressional encouragement of standby guardianship laws

Source: Adapted from Children's Defense Fund, 2003.

The Adoption and Safe Families Act was enacted in November 1997, and amended the 1980 Adoption Assistance and Child Welfare Act by enhancing and diversifying steps to promote safety and permanence for abused and neglected children.

Laws The law, as written, emphasizes the criteria for determining substantial conformity with Title IV-B and Title IV-E (45 CFR 1355.34), including the ability of states to meet national standards for collecting data relating to specific outcomes for children and families (see Highlight 13.3). Carefully defining what would be considered compliance with the law was important for states for at least two reasons. First, states are the bodies that ultimately would have to implement the law because the federal government does not have responsibility for actual provision of direct services. Second, states would be seeking federal funds to help pay for child welfare services and needed to know what would be required to access the grants. Highlight 13.3 identifies some of the criteria established by the law.

States were also allowed, in appropriate cases, to provide foster care and transitional independent living programs for children and adoption assistance for children with special needs. The federal government would also provide money in cases of abandonment of infants and young children in hospitals, and medical costs of treatment in cases of AIDS (42 USCS §1396).

Public Opinion on Bill Prior to drafting regulations for the recently enacted Adoption and Safe Families Act, the HHS Children's Bureau organized a number of focus groups representing multiple interests to explore implementation issues in the new law. Groups met with Children's Bureau staff in Washington, D.C., and with HHS regional office staff around the country (U.S. DHHS, 2000). Because the shift to outcomes monitoring represented an important

Highlight 13.3 Criteria Related to Outcomes

- State substantial conformity will be determined by its ability to substantially achieve child and family service outcomes.
- State level of achievement with regard to each outcome reflects the extent to which a state meets and implements specific standards.
- State conformity is based on performance of statewide indicators and outcomes.
- State Secretary has discretion to develop data indicators for specific outcomes to establish conformity and add, amend, or suspend statewide indicators when appropriate.
- State Secretary has discretion to adjust national standards as influenced by statewide indicators.

change in the way child welfare programs were held accountable, HHS engaged in numerous pilot tests with states to refine its approach. In addition to focus groups and pilot studies focusing on child and family reviews, opportunities were extended for written reactions to the new law. These opportunities allowed for suggestions about the most effective and efficient methods to implement the new law.

The final rules amend existing regulations by adding new requirements governing the review of state conformity with plans under Titles IV-B and IV-E of the Social Security Act. They also implement provisions and amendments of the 1994 MEPA (P.L. 103-382) and certain provisions of the Adoption and Safe Families Act. The final rule also sets forth regulations that clarify eligibility criteria that govern Title IV-E foster care eligibility reviews, which the Administration on Children, Youth, and Families conducts to ensure a state agency's compliance with statutory requirements. Finally, it made technical changes to the race and ethnicity data elements in the Adoption and Foster Care Analysis and Reporting System (AFCARS) (65 FR 4020).

Opportunities for influencing the final rule were extensive. These included a notice published in the Federal Register with a 90-day opportunity for public comment. There was also extensive consultation within the field of child welfare and multiple focus groups related to the child and family services reviews with representatives of state programs and national organizations. Personalized interviews and focus groups were conducted with both families and child advocates. Prior to final rule, state and federal teams conducted 12 pilot programs of child and family services reviews, and IV-E eligibility reviews that shaped further development and amendment of the regulation. Additional focus groups were held in Washington, D.C. and in the 10 federal regions to obtain input shortly after the enactment and implementation of the law.

Based upon public comments and feedback, there were some major changes and provisions of the final rule. One of the most important was the recognition that because state governments have responsibility for providing and delivering child welfare programs, they should also be given discretion and flexibility in designing programs and services that best fit the needs of the clients and community within their jurisdiction. The rule clarified that the role of the federal government is to create a common policy structure fiscally supporting child welfare programs, advocating research leading to evaluation and innovation, offering technical assistance, and largely holding states accountable to their outcomes. The final rule (65 FR 4020, 4078, Jan. 25, 2000) contributed the critical roles of technical assistance and accountability. In particular, it outlined the outcome-based child and family services review process that initiates federal government oversight of how well state child welfare programs are ensuring child safety, permanency, and well-being. It created a feedback channel between federal and state government, allowing for collaborative assistance and program improvement in addition to establishing accountability standards.

The final rule also strengthened the objectives while retaining focus on subjective analysis of quality in the intensive review process. National standards were developed defining how states would be rated on data indicators such as repeat maltreatment, length of time in foster care, and achievement of permanency through adoption or reunification. Another pertinent change was to balance the regulation through dissemination of technical and program assistance from the federal government, followed by increased state accountability with implication of penalties. This change provides states with resources and infrastructure to refine and improve state programs, explore and establish outcomes, and rectify limitations not in compliance with federal guidelines. Innovation, improvement, and outcomes are enforced through the provision of a penalty structure for noncompliance (U.S. DHHS, 2000).

Agency and Judicial Interpretation Once a federal law is passed and rules written to clarify legislative intent, it is up to states to actually implement the law. If states fail to follow the law and its regulations, a variety of consequences may follow. Christian (1999) describes how states have been given discretion under ASFA as to which state plan requirements they incorporate within state statute. Although direct laws are not required to implement many of ASFA's terms and conditions, those that affect court process and decision making require legislation in most states. As a result, many states have amended or added statutory provisions regarding timing of permanency hearings, judicial reasonable efforts determinations, and the requirement for proceeding to terminate parental rights. States also determined that some of the law required changes to administrative regulations, court rules, or internal agency policy, rather than state law.

To accommodate such needs, the law permitted a delayed effective date, to be determined by the Secretary of the U.S. Department of Health and Human Services. Subsequently, DHHS asked each state to identify which ASFA provisions required changes to state law. Every state certified that at least some of ASFA's requirements would require state legislation and requested a delayed effective date for those requirements. The need for states to pass legislation or create regulations in order to meet federal requirements offers yet another opportunity for social workers to engage in legislative advocacy seeking services that benefit families.

While there have been no judicial interpretations or analysis of the regulation, two recent landmark cases indicate how courts can interpret federal legislation and place additional pressure on states to provide effective services to families and children. *Angela R. v. Clinton* (1991) and *David C. v. Leavitt* (1993) have had a major impact in this area. *Angela R. v. Clinton* was a civil rights class action brought on behalf of abused and neglected children of Arkansas. The complaint cited numerous violations of federal and state law in the state's operation of protective services and foster care system. The plaintiff class consisted of a large number of children subjected to abuse and neglect reports received by the state's Department of Human Services (DHS). The defendants—Governor Bill Clinton and Director of DHS Terry Yammauchi—sought broad relief on behalf of the plaintiff class of children. The Governor appointed a panel of child welfare experts as consultants to hearings on child welfare issues across the state of Arkansas. A settlement was submitted and approved by the district court judge, who denied the state's motion to narrow the scope of the settlement in light of previous decisions. The defendants appealed to the Eighth Circuit, but the motion was denied and a date was set for trial. The State of Arkansas attempted to engage in multiple settlement negotiations prior to trial, finally introducing a yearly implementation plan that included outcome measures for determining sufficient progress toward standards. The district court approved the settlement and appointed the Center for the Study of Social Policy (CSSP) to monitor and annually assess compliance with the settlement agreement.

Subsequently, the state failed to meet these standards, leading to the resignation of agency administrators and the Standards Committee. The most current effort by state legislators in collaboration with DHS was to enact a bill resembling ASFA provisions, implementing annual independent evaluations, ongoing collaboration, and consultation of deficiencies, and to extend the settlement agreement for two years. This slow progression and postponement was possibly a result of incoming ASFA regulations.

The other court case, *David C. v. Leavitt* (1993), was a child welfare reform class action on behalf of state foster children and children reported as abused or neglected in the state of Utah. The National Center for Youth Law (NCYL) filed the complaint that led to proposals to reform Utah's child welfare system. A panel was appointed to monitor compliance with the settlement and to resolve disputes. In response to heightened negative attention and scrutiny of Utah's child welfare outcomes, the legislature expressed interest in passing two bills that initiate and support the systemic overhaul. As in *Angela R. v. Clinton,* enforcement in Utah continued to be problematic, requiring continued technical assistance, support, and close monitoring by NCYL. Plaintiffs filed multiple motions for continued monitoring of responsibilities and compliance with the settlement agreement. The plaintiffs were granted the motion to revise the Comprehensive Plan and to develop new mechanisms for monitoring compliance, correcting problems, and resolving disputes.

As is evident in the preceding material, policies affecting services to families and children do not function within a vacuum. Policies are themselves an outgrowth of manipulation and persuasion from multiple entities and interests, numerous constituents, and stakeholders. Those policies in turn must be implemented by agencies and organizations encountering their own political and systemic influences. The need for oversight for these agencies is clear, for without supervision, bureaucracies may fail to carry out the intent of laws and policies. The result can be feeble practitioner retention, directionless training, and diminished organizational commitment. Failure of states to provide adequate services for families and children can subject them to additional federal oversight, loss of funds, and penalties imposed by the court system. Finally, these failures have dramatic impacts on vulnerable families who should be able to rely on public social services to meet their needs. Neither families nor social workers benefit when the state falls short in responding to those needs. Families go without assistance, and social workers lose a vital resource for their own work with families.

Highlight 13.4 | **Family Legislation Landmarks**

1980	Adoption Assistance and Child Welfare Act (P.L. 96-272)
1993	Omnibus Reconciliation Act (P.L. 103-66)
1994	Multiethnic Placement Act (P.L. 103-382)
1996	Small Business Job Protection Act (P.L. 104-188)
1997	Adoption and Safe Families Act (P.L. 96-272)

As should be clear, the last quarter century has seen numerous attempts to improve the quality of services provided to families and children. Highlight 13.4 summarizes five major federal laws impacting families and, in particular, the child welfare system from 1980 to the present. What is evident is that regardless of the political party in power, new legislation relating to families can and does come into being. Social workers must be aware of new laws impacting families and be willing to share their expertise with policy makers at all stages of the policy-making process.

Trends and Directions

CHAPTER 14

© Photodisc/Royalty-Free/Getty Images

INTRODUCTION

Alex Haley, author of *Roots,* succinctly sums up the importance of the family in his observation that "in every conceivable manner, the family is link to our past, bridge to our future" (quoted in Lewis, 2004, p. 1). This text has highlighted both the past as well as the current state of family practice. Now we will turn to the future of social work practice with families. We do so with the humility that comes from recognizing that charting future trends in a field as vast as family practice is an undertaking replete with opportunities to be wrong. With that caveat in mind, this chapter will look at factors that are likely to influence our understanding of families as well as those that suggest future directions for our work with the family. The first section will look at how the family itself is changing and possible implications of such trends. The second section will consider ways that our efforts to assist families are likely to evolve. Along the way, we will identify some of the directions that family practice should consider taking. In these latter recommendations, we will also identify policy recommendations that have the potential for strengthening services to families.

THE FAMILY—CHANGING AND STABLE

Family Composition

Changes in family composition can be easily measured using data provided by the U.S. Census Bureau (Bryson & Casper, 1998). In 1940, families accounted for about 90 percent of all households, a number which declined to about 70 percent at the end of the 20th century. Nonfamily households, conversely, grew from 19 percent to 30 percent just in the past 30 years.

In 1970, 85 percent of children in the United States lived with two parents. A decade later the percentage had dropped to 80 percent, with 15 percent of children living with their mother as head of household (Brieland, Costin, & Atherton, 1980). Only 1.5 percent of families consisted of a child and father only. Now, fathers account for about 17 percent of one-parent households, a sizeable increase from 1970. Mothers who never married went from 33 percent to 41 percent over this same time frame. One-parent families have increased from 24 percent to 28 percent. It appears as though the most dramatic changes came between 1970 and 1990. Subsequently, the rate of change slowed, and dramatic fluctuations in the future are not expected.

The number of female-headed families with no spouse in the home increased by 133 percent, while the increase for male-headed families went up by over 213 percent, trends that appear to be continuing albeit at a slower pace. There is increasing evidence that many mothers and their children are living with or dependent upon relatives for housing and other support.

Nontraditional families in different varieties will continue to exist and expand, fueled by both social and economic forces. These forces include the increased requirements for further education that will keep family members in school longer and a trend toward later marriages (Coates, 1999). The combination of divorce, cohabitation, death of a spouse, and childbearing out of wedlock will expand the numbers of nontraditional units as will the growing acceptance of gay families.

The continued popularity of marriage is evident in the fact that stepfamilies are increasing at such a rate that at least one-third of all Americans will be part of a blended or reconstituted family at some point in their life. Divorce appears to be a constant although the rate is not increasing as it did from the mid 1950s to 1980.

Household Location

Household locations tended to grow in the South and in urban areas, and decline in traditional "rust-belt" areas of the Midwest and Northeast. In 1970, more than half of all households were located in the latter areas, declining to 43 percent by year 2000. At the same time, more families moved to urban areas, increasing from 69 percent to 80 percent over the past three decades.

A more disturbing trend is the increase in families with children that are homeless, a pattern that has changed dramatically over the past quarter-century (Lewit & Baker, 1996). Children in these families "have twice as many health problems, are more likely to go hungry, and have higher rates of developmental delay" along with other mental health and behavioral difficulties (p. 146). Homelessness tends to reflect family situations characterized by great poverty and single-parent families. Both of these factors are likely to increase in the near future.

Economic reasons may also change the living arrangements for elderly parents who find it necessary to move in with their children. This will, of course, have a major bearing on the emotional and financial resources of the children and grandchildren. It will also allow more grandchildren to benefit from the wisdom and company of their grandparents.

Family Demographics

Another trend that is likely to continue is the decision by young couples to delay marriage and to postpone having children. In addition, a much larger percentage of families have both adult members employed, a consequence of both economics and personal choice.

Age is also a significant factor in the future because within about 15 years, a quarter of the U.S. population will be 65 or older (NASW, 1993). This fact alone will place greater burdens on families as they serve as a resource for aging parents and grandparents (Zlotnik, 1995). The fact that more and more families will have caretaking responsibilities for older kin is exacerbated by health care policies that limit length of hospital stays, require more hands-on care by unprepared family members, and limit reimbursement for extended-care facilities.

At the same time, these changes in "longevity lead to the death of one spouse substantially before the other, creating a companionship crisis" (Coates, 1999, p. 210). Longer life spans also mean that families will increasingly seek new experiences and ways to meet their needs that are disconnected from the traditional focus on raising children. The use of the Internet to locate and connect with others sharing one's interests will be especially attractive for computer-literate parents and grandparents. Coates (1999) argues that interest and support groups will grow in importance, both for helping family members experiencing health problems as well as filling leisure time.

Employment, Economics, and Child Care

In 1970 only 30 percent of married mothers with preschool children were employed. That number has more than doubled along with an increased use of child care (Hofferth, 1996). The kind of child care provided for preschool children has shifted markedly with care provided by parents or relatives declining as more and more parents place children in childcare centers. Interestingly, the use of childcare centers has increased even though the number of women in the workforce has stabilized at about 60 percent. This suggests that many families believe their children can benefit from this experience, and it is likely that the use of child care, especially childcare centers, will remain a common thread over the next few years. On the other hand, major changes in tax structure allowing parents to write-off more of their childcare costs or increased subsidies for childcare facilities could increase the use of such facilities.

While the use of day care is becoming predictable, its availability is significantly uneven. Availability of child care as an option for parents is often a function of the child's age, parental hours of work, and the affluence of the community in which they live. Costs for child care have increased in concert with the trend away from care by a child's grandparents or other relatives. In some cases, the cost becomes a major burden affecting poverty-level families as well as others. Single-parent families expend 12 percent of their income on child care while poor families contribute 18 percent. By contrast, married-couple families spend only 7 percent on child care. (U.S. Department of Commerce, 1996, p. 2).

Another trend that may increase is that of two-income families. While the percentage of mothers with children below age 18 hovers around 65 percent, the United States is still far below other countries that have seen both parents working outside the home. Other countries have rates between 80 percent and 90 percent (Coates, 1999, p. 211). The impact of two-income families may be felt in several ways. First, both income producers will expect to have a say over decisions regarding spending money, relocation for employment, and other aspects of career planning. Another influence, according to Coates, is the disappearance of women from the community, where they have traditionally been active in volunteer activities and in roles such as shopping. This will have a profound impact on agencies and organizations that rely on volunteer assistance to perform their missions.

A third consequence of the number and percentage of women joining the workforce is the lessened need to marry in order to support oneself. Marriage's popularity will continue, but the economic factors driving it will likely be reduced.

There are also some major concerns on the horizon from an economic standpoint. The savings that families traditionally maintained in order to assist them in retirement have dropped dramatically from 7.9 percent of personal income in 1980 to 4.1 percent today. This shortfall in funds for retirement, coupled with better health and the social benefits of working, means that many people will not retire at the standard retirement age (Coates, 1999).

Effects of Ethnicity

There are some dramatic differences across various ethnic groups with respect to some of these changes. For example, about 25 percent of white female heads of family had never been married while the rate for African American females with children was 58 percent. The rate of poverty is also greater for people of color than for whites, a situation which will likely not change dramatically.

Stability of the Family

At the same time the institution of the family is changing, some aspects of family life have remained relatively stable over the past 25 years. In 1970, married couples with children composed about 26 percent of all households, a number that only dropped to 25 percent at the start of the 21st century. The average household size has not changed significantly either, moving from 2.63 to 2.64 people per unit. The percentage of families with no children under 18 was unchanged at 51 percent. In many respects, the family remains a flexible institution that can and does respond to changes in economic, social, and political life (Coates, 1999).

THE EVOLUTION OF FAMILY PRACTICE

Changes confronting families will have many implications for social work practice with families. In addition, research on the effectiveness of family practice will help social workers improve the theories, models, and techniques used with families. This is already happening in several areas. For example, the quickly evolving definitions of what a family is are changing the nature of what social workers are taught and what they do in practice. Definitions of *family* now in use take into account nuclear, extended, step, gay and lesbian, single-parent, and other family forms previously not considered as families.

It is entirely possible that the definition of *family* may broaden to include other configurations that we have not yet envisioned. These changed definitions have implications for the activities of social workers. As an example, Jones (2003) points out that there is increasing evidence "that generic intervention models are ineffective with stepfamilies" (p. 228). She suggests that attempts to understand and assist stepfamilies will require different theories than are currently in use. In addition, the increased numbers of stepfamilies as a result of divorce and other factors will force a reevaluation of the nuclear family as the norm in American society. Increased acceptance of stepfamilies as just one variation of family structure would likely lift some of the stigmatization associated with this family form. Moreover, stepfamilies tend to make greater use of mental health services simply because of the increased complexity of such unions (Zill & Schoenborn, 1991). The increased numbers of complex family arrangements coupled with an increased need for mental health services suggests that such services must change to address stepfamily issues.

Increased attention to spirituality and religious values has become a recent theme in the family practice literature. The evidence that spirituality plays a major role in the lives of individuals and families has been documented repeatedly (Canda & Furman, 1999; Faiver et al., 2001; Van Hook, Hugen, & Aguilar, 2001). Religion and spiritual values have the potential to enhance the health and coping ability of families. In addition to giving life a sense of meaning, these values provide important supports in times of need.

Traditionally, many social workers feared that delving into a family's religious or spiritual values might seem inappropriate or be perceived as proselytizing. In addition, some clients were unwilling to bring the topic up for fear that the practitioner would not honor them as important components in the client's life (Thayne, 1997). It is now apparent that a failure to explore the role, if any, played by a family's religion and spiritual beliefs is as shortsighted as failing to ask about the influence of one's job, degree of family support, or the availability of resources. It is anticipated that this attention to spirituality and religion in the lives of families will continue as the subject is identified as important in the training of social workers. At the same time, there will be more training of social workers in the creative and effective use of these value issues (Benningfield, 1998).

Goldenberg and Goldenberg (1999) identify four trends that they believe will influence family practice in this century. The first is the growth of "postmodern outlooks" in which the social worker's role becomes one of helping families recognize that the belief systems they maintain have both helped them and prevented them from fulfilling their lives. Rather than helping families discover the correct (right vs. wrong) ways of thinking or acting, the focus will be on expanding options for decision making and problem resolution. Solution-focused and narrative therapies both are forms of *social constructionist* approaches dedicated to the principle that social workers can help families best by hearing their story, working with them, and using a wider array of intervention techniques while supporting diversity and empowerment as key concepts in understanding human behavior.

A second trend is the enormous diversity change operating in the United States. Within a few years, about one-third of the population will be people of color (Jones, 1991). This is important when we realize that many theories and therapies were predominantly developed and evaluated on white individuals and families. Thus, there is likely to be major attention to incorporating diversity content in existing approaches as well as devising theories that are particularly effective with certain groups.

This will put greater pressure on social workers who "must try to understand the cultural backgrounds of their clients in their assessment or therapeutic or basic communication efforts to avoid misdiagnosing or mislabeling family behavior and, in the process, pathologizing ethnic minority families whose behavior is unfamiliar. At the same time, therapists must also be aware of their own cultural heritage and the inevitable influence of values, attitudes, and expressive styles on their own perceptions and outlooks" (Jones, 1991, p. 321). To be effective in a multicultural environment, social workers must become multicultural in outlook and action while learning about the specific cultures with which they will work.

Fine, Demo, and Allen (2000) also stress the need to extend and refine extant family theories with knowledge drawn from diverse family forms. They recommend research that looks at the intersections of diversity to better understand the experiences of different groups in society. Research might examine, for example, the intersection of race and sexual orientation to learn more about the consequences of being, say, Hispanic and lesbian. Likewise, learning more about what it is like to be a single mom with a disability could help better prepare social workers for working with individuals at that intersection. At the same time, there is a danger of overemphasizing differences without acknowledging the enormous commonality across families. The authors remind us that there is no one right way for families to exist or function. Instead, they urge social workers to recognize "that there are a multitude of healthy, adaptive, and successful ways for families to function" (p. 447).

Another area for future study and understanding is the topic of family process. We need to know more about how families actually operate, make decisions, and problem-solve, and to know how these processes are used by diverse family forms. Our understanding in this area is still relatively limited.

Gender-sensitive family practice will be demanded by an increasingly sophisticated clientele who are aware of the ways that society has supported a nonfeminist agenda that has often ignored the needs of women. Women are more likely to want and insist on gender equity within the family system, which has major implications for task distribution, child rearing, decision making, and role relationships.

Likewise, feminist perspectives on traditional theories are likely to encourage the development of new approaches that avoid paternalistic assumptions and roles. This will mean a reassessment of what a healthy family looks like while encouraging family relationships built on presumptions of equality and collaboration (Goldenberg & Goldenberg, 1999).

As gay and lesbian families increase their usage of family practice services, this will also influence the nature and quality of services provided. Social workers will find their own values and assumptions challenged, and many will need to grapple with their own heterosexism. In addition, effective practitioners will need to know a great deal more about the development of gay and lesbian identity in order to better understand their clients' life experiences.

Attempts to apply some traditional family concepts to gay and lesbian families may be doomed to failure. Lynch (2000) suggests, for example, that "lesbian and gay stepfamilies are unique family forms which must be investigated as such" (p. 81). While there are important similarities in strengths and challenges between gay and straight families, the differences are also critical and cannot be overlooked.

We also want to be sure that instruments we use for assessment are applicable to more than just heterosexual couples. For example, Means-Christensen, Snyder, and Negy (2003) have found that a specific instrument (Marital Satisfaction Inventory—Revised) appears equally useful for both same-gender couples and opposite-gender couples. To what extent is this true for other relationship measures? This remains an area for further research.

A third trend predicted by the Goldenbergs (1999) is the increased use of qualitative research methods that provide a more informative view of the inner workings of family life. They note that qualitative perspectives will help the social worker to better recognize "clinically significant criteria" for assisting families and to rely less on statistical significance that may or may not reflect improvement in the family's quality of life. The real value of qualitative approaches is the assistance it gives the social worker in understanding how families actually function and survive. Whether qualitative or quantitative, research on the family will continue to have major consequences for family scholars and practitioners. Knowing, for example, what constellation of family and biological factors are most likely to lead to specific problems such as substance abuse, violence, depression, or other mental health disorders would be an important contribution to the work of practitioners. Research that identifies which family theories are most useful for identified family problems or issues also would be an asset to social workers.

The Goldenbergs' fourth trend is the increased use of outcomes studies designed to measure the effectiveness of family therapy. This reflects several factors. First is the greater sophistication of social workers in the use of evaluation methodology, largely a consequence of academic training that has lately emphasized the importance of evaluating one's practice. A second factor is the emphasis put on outcomes by third-party payers demanding evidence of practice effectiveness. A third explanation is that more and more research is being published relating to practice efficacy, some of which finds its way into the repertoire of practitioners. The increasing evidence that family practice is effective has encouraged its use by social workers, psychologists, psychiatrists, and others. In the future it is likely that outcome assessment tools will become more sensitive and helpful, thereby assisting social workers in the evaluation of their practice. A desirable outcome would be learning which approaches are most useful with which family problems and populations (Goldenberg & Goldenberg, 1999).

Lebow (1995) agrees with many of the Goldenbergs' predictions and notes that both researchers and practitioners are getting more comfortable with each other. Researchers try to couch their results in terms of information that is useful to practitioners who, in turn, are paying more attention to research findings. A likely area for future research is on methods that sustain the changes that families make in therapy. Current research indicates that family changes do not continue indefinitely, and the family may need additional assistance after the passage of time.

It is also important to recognize how the vast differences among families can influence the work of the social worker. For example, common sense might tell us that a family that has been intact and stable until overwhelmed by events will be easier to restabilize than a chronically stressed family. Yet, we do not really know a lot about how much time and effort it takes to stabilize both types of families (Vosler, 1996). This is just one of many gaps in our knowledge about what works best for families.

Becvar and Becvar (2003) point out that the events of September 11, 2001, will likely impact family practice for the foreseeable future. For example, social workers will need to be well prepared to help families deal with losses arising from terrorist acts, military action, or similar events. Families will also need help dealing with issues of violence, particularly of a kind that cannot be predicted. An aging society will also require social workers to learn more about the legal and health care systems. In the latter case, questions about late-life concerns, medical power of attorney, advanced directives, and end-of-life decision making will become more important.

Another area of change that will prove helpful to social workers is related to the growing emphasis on internationalizing curricula so that students become familiar with the interconnectedness of nations and peoples. If this movement continues, it is likely that we can learn a great deal more about the ways that different cultures cope with family issues and situations. We might learn from refugees and others who have coped with similar traumas about the resiliency of children and adults. It also would be beneficial to know what specific factors seem to protect children raised in troubled families from growing into adults who exhibit problematic behaviors within their own families.

Future research should help social workers better understand the relative influence of biology and genetics within the eternal debate about nature versus nurture. Plomin and Asbury (2001) note that past research in behavioral genetics shows that inherited tendencies account for no more than 50 percent of the behaviors and disorders seen by marriage and family practitioners. The remainder appears to be a function of environmental influences. Additional research may allow us to identify what components of the environment have the greatest impact on human behavior. The combination of genetic and environmental influences is particularly acute in people experiencing marital and family problems. According to Beach (2003), those seeking help with such problems are also likely to have unipolar depressive disorders. The influence of biologic factors in depression might suggest to the social worker that the client would not benefit from marital or family therapy. To the contrary, after evaluating well-controlled outcome studies, Beach notes that many depressed patients do in fact benefit from both marital and parenting intervention. What is important is to accurately judge who will and who will not benefit. Future research will assist in this effort.

Because of the enormous emotional, social, and financial costs associated with divorce, a fruitful area for research is whether marriages can be strengthened through education or training. Carroll and Doherty (2003) point out that premarital prevention programs have led to immediate and short-term benefits in the areas of interpersonal skills and quality of relationships. In addition, the changes for participants far outweigh satisfaction levels for nonparticipants. However, the absence of long-term follow up does not allow us to know whether such changes are lasting, an important limitation. We do not know, for instance, whether participants are less likely to get a divorce, have serious marital or family problems, or experience other difficulties. Additional research in this area is crucial.

Service Delivery

Samantrai (2004) and others have discussed the need to move family services into the neighborhood and away from traditional agency-based arrangements. In some ways, the family preservation movement has emphasized a similar desire to make services available to families in their own homes.

A more recent development led largely by the George W. Bush administration is the idea of encouraging faith-based organizations to apply for and spend public funds on behalf of beneficial projects, including supporting families. Carole Thompson of the Annie E. Casey Foundation (2003a) highlighted the potential of such organizations recently: "We found that faith matters because of its power to promote personal transformation and its potential to strengthen family and community bonds. Because of the spiritual development they foster, communities of faith have been and will continue to be strong partners in our effort to promote family and community strengthening. We recognize the assets and gifts that faith communities bring to this work" (p. 1).

The idea of allowing faith-based organizations to use tax money has been controversial for several reasons. Some fear an erosion of the separation between church and state while others worry that religious organizations will use government funds to help proselytize potential converts. Still others are concerned that the limited amount of funds available will further stretch the resources of existing family and social service agencies that have relied on this resource in the past.

A major challenge facing the United States is how to ensure that families eligible for various state and federal programs receive the assistance they need. For example, 41 percent of families who qualify for food stamps are not getting them. Twelve percent of children are not covered by health insurance in spite of the CHIPS program, and another 21 percent have not been immunized against common diseases. Forty-eight percent of families eligible for Medicaid are not enrolled, and 85 percent of families eligible for federally subsidized child care do not participate (Annie E. Casey Foundation, 2003b). Social workers can serve as brokers to help families learn about these resources and also support efforts to strengthen services to families.

Policy Issues

Legal rights and privileges accorded to biological families are likely to be expanded to include other family constellations. Laws, especially state statutes, frequently favor biological families while being unfair to stepchildren (Mason & Mauldon, 1996). For example, stepparents have neither legal rights nor obligations to stepchildren and often have less standing than do foster parents. "They have no legal authority to discipline, authorize emergency medical treatment, or even sign a school report card" (Jones, 2003, p. 231). Should a child's biological parent die or divorce the stepparent, the relationship between stepchild and stepparent is automatically terminated in most states. These and other factors tend to place stepchildren and families at risk and increase their vulnerability (Jones, 2003). A future direction may be greater recognition of family ties based on psychological connections rather than solely on biological ones. Such a movement could also have major implications for the recognition of gay and lesbian relationships. Legal marriages of gay men and lesbian women are currently only possible in the Netherlands, Belgium, Canada, and Massacusetts. However, recent court decisions and initiatives in the United States may bring changes in this area.

In response to increased caregiving responsibilities for older family members, it is likely that both business and government will be pressured into supporting dependent care programs. While the Family and Medical Leave Act of 1993 has helped, more will be required to moderate the burdens of caring for the family's elder members. Similarly, it is anticipated that more families will consider and purchase long-term care insurance designed to cover the costs of a variety of elder care options. The burgeoning population of the elderly and the concerns of their adult children are already encouraging insurance companies to offer such policies.

At the same time, there is an ongoing need for childcare services that are flexible with respect to hours. Too many such services are not designed to coincide with the diverse work-hour needs of families. A corollary is expansion of after-school programs that reduce the numbers of latch-key children while providing appropriate activities and supervision (Sharlin & Shamai, 2000).

Zlotnik (1995) has highlighted several potential strategies that will help address the future caregiving responsibilities of families. First, she anticipates the need for more informal support networks composed of family members and friends, neighborhood and church programs. A second approach is the creation of allowances or payments to caregivers whose responsibilities preclude their participation in the work force. The third policy strategy is for existing social agencies ranging from hospitals to community centers to expand the types and range of services aimed at supporting family caregivers.

It is important to remember that "virtually every government policy at the federal, state, and local level affects families" (DiNitto & Gustavsson, 1999, p. 343). Thus there is a continuing need for social workers to be sensitive to the impact of policies on families. In many cases it is social workers who will be acutely aware of how proposed policies will affect families and who must actively involve themselves in the policy debate. DiNitto and Gustavsson note some of the policies areas with the greatest potential for affecting the quality of life of families. They include income maintenance policies; social insurance, which covers Social Security, unemployment, and Workers Compensation; public assistance such as Supplemental Security Income, Temporary Assistance to Needy Families, and General Assistance; child support enforcement policies; and income tax policies. In addition, policies dealing with nutrition, such as food stamps; Special Supplemental Nutrition Program for Women, Infants, and Children (WIC); and similar food programs for the elderly, are all areas that can facilitate or impede the family from having the resources to maintain a quality life.

Other policy arenas include housing, health programs such as Medicare and Medicaid, and mental health and chemical dependency services. Family violence is another area where federal, state, and local policies can promote or detract from the safety of family members. Family violence policies include domestic violence as well as child abuse and neglect. The final policy area identified by DiNitto and Gustavsson is family planning and reproductive rights, where debate occurs routinely at all levels of government. Decisions at any of these levels can determine whether family members have the right to decide if and when they want to be parents. Because of the immense importance of these policies, it is crucial that social workers not sit on the sidelines but rather become advocates for programs and policies that strengthen and support families.

A critical area for the future of family practice and other mental health treatment modalities is the issue of managed care. Governmental and professional policies notwithstanding, information shared with the practitioner can end up in the wrong hands. As Nichols and Schwartz (2001) observe, "It's no longer unusual for employers to learn about an employee's psychological treatment, and it isn't rare for such information to have a prejudicial impact on the employee's standing" (p. 9). In addition, practitioners find it increasingly frustrating to deal with bureaucratic levels that seemed focused on discouraging people from getting help. Often, the decisions of the social worker are second-guessed by individuals without any mental health training whatsoever.

Bagarozzi (1995) has listed some of the other problems associated with managed mental health care. These include the refusal of many such organizations to cover some types of mental health issues such as marital or family problems, parent–child difficulties, and bereavement. Other health care companies do not cover marital therapy because they do not view it as a legitimate service. The health care companies charge the client's employer sufficient amounts to recover their costs of maintaining a staff responsible for declining coverage to employees covered by the company's health care plan. Money that could be used to provide needed services to employees is spent on bureaucracy.

A reaction to such micromanaging of practice has been lawsuits by practitioner organizations hoping to leave more of the decision making about clients' care with the practitioner. Parity laws that require health insurers to provide the same level of coverage for mental health problems as for physical are often ineffective because of loopholes in the legislation. Another reaction is the attempt by some practitioners to try to get around the bureaucratic limitations by reinterpreting client problems and/or treatment being provided. This is a risky enterprise and it can lead to charges of criminal fraud. What is needed for the future health of family practice is for social workers and other family practitioners to become politically active around issues that threaten their ability to help families. If mental health services are not covered, or are covered only to a limited degree, the consequences are dire for both families and practitioners. Sitting on the sidelines and hoping a benevolent system will operate in the best interests of clients is a critical and potentially devastating mistake.

References

Achenbach, T. M. (1991). *Manual for the Child Behavior Checklist/4-18 and 1991 Profile*. Burlington, VT: University of Vermont Department of Psychiatry.

Ackerman, N.W. (1966). *Treating the troubled family.* New York: Basic Books.

Administration on Children, Youth and Families, Foster Care Maintenance Payments, Adoption Assistance, and Children and Family Services. 45 CFR 1355.34, Title 45, Public Welfare. Office of Human Development Services, Department of Health and Human Services, Subchapter G, PART 1355, General 1355.34 Criteria for determining substantial conformity. 2421 words, Code of Federal Regulations.

Adoption Assistance and Child Welfare Act of 1980, Pub. L. No. 96-272, 96 Stat. 500 (1980).

Adoption and Safe Families Act of 1997, Pub. L. No. 105-89, 111 Stat. 2215 (1997).

Adoption and Safe Families Act of 1997, 42 U.S.C. _ 620 (2003).

Adoption and Safe Families Act of 1997, 42 USCS. _ 670 (2003).

Aldous, J., & Dumon, W. (1990). Family policy in the 1980s: Controversy and consensus. *Journal of Marriage and the Family, 52,* 1136–51.

Alfano, B., Evans, C., Huang, W., & Williams, D. (1990). *Empowerment-based practice in family preservation service: The "gumbo blend."* Unpublished master's thesis, Southern University, New Orleans, LA.

Allen, M., & Burrell, N. (1996). Comparing the impact of homosexual and heterosexual parents on children: Meta-analysis of existing research. *Journal of Homosexuality, 32,* 19–35.

Almeida, R., Woods, R., & Messineo, T. (1998). Contextualizing child development theory: Race, gender, class and culture. *Cultural Diversity and Mental Health.*

Altstein, H., & McRoy, R. (2000). *Does family preservation serve a child's best interests?* Washington, DC: Georgetown University Press.

American Public Welfare Association. (1990). *The National Commission on Child Welfare and Family Preservation: Factbook on public child welfare services and staff.* Washington, DC: American Public Welfare Association.

Anderson, C. M., Reiss, D., & Hogarty, B. (1986). *Schizophrenia and the family: A practitioner's guide to psychoeducation and management.* New York: Guilford Press.

Anderson, E. (2001). Getting to the first rung of the ladder. *Joint Center for Poverty Research Newsletter, 5*(6). University of Chicago.

Angela R. v. Clinton, No. LRC-91-415. (E.D. Ark. July 8, 1991).

Annie E. Casey Foundation. (2003a). Exploring the role of the faith community in family strengthening. *Casey Connects, Winter/Spring,* p. 1, 6.

Annie E. Casey Foundation. (2003b). *Kids Count 2003 Data book online.* Baltimore, MD: Author.

Anthony, E. J. (1987). Children at risk for psychosis growing up successfully. In E. J. Anthony & B. J. Cohler (Eds.), *The invulnerable child.* New York: Guilford.

Aponte, H., & VanDeusen, J. (1981). Structural family therapy. In A. Gurman, & D. Kniskern (Eds.), *Handbook of family therapy* (pp. 310–360). New York: Brunner/Mazel.

Armour, M. A. (1995). Family life cycle stages: A context for individual life stages. *Journal of Family Social Work, 1*(2), 27–42.

Atwood, J. D. (Ed.). (1992). *Family therapy.* Chicago: Nelson-Hall.

Bachelor, A. (1995). Clients' perception of the therapeutic alliance: A qualitative analysis. *Journal of Counseling Psychology, 42*(3), 323–337.

Bagarozzi, D. A. (1995). Evaluation, accountability and clinical expertise in managed mental health care: Basic considerations for the practice of family social work. *Journal of Family Social Work, 1*(2), 101–116.

Bailey, J., Bobrow, D., Wolfe, M., & Mikach, S. (1995). Sexual orientation of the adult sons of gay fathers. *Developmental Psychology, 31,* 124–139.

Baker, D. R. (June 26, 2000.) The new federal regulations on ASFA. *ABA Child Law Practice.* Retrieved October 16, 2004, from http://www.abanet.org/child/rclji/fedregsumm.pdf

Bandura, A. (1977). *Social learning theory.* Englewood Cliffs, NJ: Prentice-Hall.

Banks, J. A., & McGee-Banks, C. A. (1997). *Multicultural education: Issues and perspectives.* Needham Heights, MA: Allyn & Bacon.

Bargh, J., & Chartrand, T. (1999). The unbearable automaticity of being. *The American Psychologist, 54*(7), 462–479.

Barker, R. L. (1999). *The social work dictionary* (4th ed.). Washington, DC: NASW Press.

Barnum, B. D., Snyder, C. R., Rapoff, M. A., Mani, M. M., & Thompson, R. (1998). Hope and social support in the psychological adjustment of children who have survived burn injuries and matched controls. *Children's Health Care, 27,* 15–30.

Barret, B., & Logan, C. (2002). *Counseling gay men and lesbians.* Pacific Grove, CA: Brooks/Cole.

Barth, R. P., & Berry, M. (1994). Implications of research on the welfare of children under permanency planning. In R. P. Barth, J. D. Berrick, & N. Gilbert (Eds.). *Child welfare research review (Vol. 1, pp. 323–368).* New York: Columbia University Press.

Bartlett, M. (1993). *Married Widows: Wives of men in long-term care.* New York: Garland.

Barusch, A. S. (2002). *Foundations of social policy.* Belmont, CA: Wadsworth Publishing.

Bavolek, S. J. (1984). *Handbook for the Adult-Adolescent Parenting Inventory.* Eau Claire, WI: Family Development Associates.

Beach, S. (2003). Affective disorders. *Journal of Marital and Family Therapy, 29*(2), 247–261.

Beaver, M. L. (1990). The older person in the black family. In S. M. Logan, E. M. Freeman, & R. G. McRoy (Eds.), *Social work practice with black families.* White Plains, NY: Longman.

Beck, A. (1976). *Cognitive therapy and the emotional disorders.* Connecticut: International University Press.

Becvar, D. S., & Becvar, R. J. (2003). *Family therapy* (5th ed.). Boston: Allyn & Bacon.

Bednar, S. G. (2001). Reuniting families and breaking the cycle: A research note. *Marriage and Family Review. 33*(4): 107–112.

Behr, H. (1996). Multiple family group therapy: A group-analytic perspective. *Group Analysis, 29*(1), 9–22.

Bellah, R. N., Madsen, R., Sullivan, W. M., Swindler, A., & Tipton, S. M. (1985). *Habits of the heart: Individualism and commitment in American Life.* New York: Harper and Row.

Ben-Ari, A. (1995). The discovery that an offspring is gay: Parents', gay men's, and lesbians' perspectives. *Journal of Homosexuality, 30,* 89–112.

Benningfield, M. F. (1998). Addressing spiritual/religious issues in therapy: Potential problems and complications. *Journal of Family Social Work, 2*(4), 25–42.

Berg, I. K. (1994). *Family-based services.* New York: Norton.

Berg-Cross, L. (1988). *Basic concepts in family therapy.* New York: Haworth.

Berger, R. M. (1990). Men together, Understanding the gay couple. *Journal of Homosexuality, 19*(3), 31–49.

Bern-Klug, M., Gessert, C., & Forbes, S. (2001). The need to revise assumptions about the end of life: Implications for social work practice. *Health & Social Work, 26*(1).

Berrick, J. D., Barth, R. P., & Needell, B. (1994). A comparison of kinship foster homes and foster family homes: Implications for kinship foster care as family preservation. *Children and Youth Services Review, 16,* 33–63.

Bill Summary and Status for the 99th Congress H.R. 2020.

Blacker, L. (1999). The launching phase of the life cycle. In B. Carter & M. McGoldrick (Eds.), *The expanded family life cycle* (3rd ed., pp. 287–306). Boston: Allyn & Bacon.

Blair, J. (2003, May). It takes two. *Teacher Magazine, 14,* 7, 11.

Bloom, M., Fischer, J., & Orme, J. G. (1995). *Evaluating practice: Guidelines for the accountable professional* (2nd ed.). Needham, MA: Allyn & Bacon.

Blumstein, W. J., & Schwartz, P. (1983). *American couples.* New York: Morrow.

Blythe, B., & Jayaratne, S. (2002). *Michigan families first effectiveness study.* Retrieved October 16, 2004, from http://www.michigan.gov/fia/0,1607,7-124-5458_7695_8366-21887—,00.html

Bogard, M., (1990). Women treating men. *The Family Therapist Networker, 14*(3), 54–58.

Bolman, L. G., & Deal, T. E. (1997). *Reframing organizations.* San Francisco: Jossey-Bass.

Borden, W. (2002). Object relations psychology and psychosocial intervention. In A. R. Roberts & G. J. Greene (Eds.), *Social workers' desk reference* (pp. 153–157). New York: Oxford University Press.

Borduin, C. M., Heiblum, N., Jones, M. R., & Grabe, S. A. (2000). Community-based treatments of serious antisocial behavior in adolescents. In W. E. Martin Jr. & J. L. Swartz-Kulstad, (Eds.), *Person-environment psychology and mental health: Assessment and intervention* (pp. 113–141). Hillsdale, NJ: N. J. Lawrence Erlbaum Associates.

Boughner, S. R., Hayes, S. F., Bubenzer, D. L., & West, J. D. (1994). Use of standardized assessment instruments by marital and family therapists: A survey. *Journal of Marital and Family Therapy, 20,* 69–75.

Bowlby, J. (1980). *Attachment and loss, vol. 3-loss.* New York: Basic Books.

Boxer, A. M., Cook, J. A., & Herdt, G. (1991). Double jeopardy: Identify transitions and parent–child relations among gay and lesbian youth. In K. Pillemer & K. McCartney (Eds.), *Parent-child relations throughout life* (pp. 59–92). Hillsdale, NJ: Lawrence Erlbaum.

Branch, J. O. (1996). Effects of a multiple family group intervention with caregiving families of Alzheimer's disease patients. *Dissertation Abstracts International: Section B: The Sciences and Engineering, 56*(11-B), 6381.

Brennan, J. W. (1995). A short-term psychoeducational multiple-family group for bipolar patients and their families. *Social Work, 40,* 737–743.

Briar-Lawson, K., & Wiesen, M. (2001). What hurts and what helps: Listening to families to build 21st century child welfare reforms. In A. L. Sallee, H. A. Lawson, & K. Briar-Lawson (Eds.), *Innovative practices with vulnerable children and families* (pp. 229–244). Dubuque, IA: Eddie Bowers.

Bridgers, B., Brown, P. M., Breger, J., & Roark, H. A. (1997). Cross-cultural considerations in family preservation practice. *Journal of Family Social Work, 2*(2), 141–158.

Brieland, D., Costin, L. B., & Atherton, C. R. (1980). *Contemporary social work*. New York: McGraw-Hill.

Briere, J. (1996). A self-trauma model for treating adult survivors of severe child abuse. In J. Briere & L. Berliner, (Eds.), *The APSAC handbook on child maltreatment* (pp. 140–157). Thousand Oaks, CA: Sage.

Brock, G. W., & Barnard, C. P. (1999). *Procedures in marriage and family therapy* (3rd ed.). Boston: Allyn & Bacon.

Bronfenbrenner, U. (1979). *The ecology of human development: Experiments by nature and design*. Cambridge, MA: Harvard University Press.

Brown, G. W., Birley, J. L. T., & Wing, J. K. (1972). The influence of family life on the course of schizophrenic disorders: A replication. *British Journal of Psychology, 121*, 241–258.

Brown, J. H., & Brown, C. S. (2002). *Marital therapy.* Pacific Grove, CA: Brooks/Cole.

Brown, J. H., & Christensen, D. N. (1999). *Family therapy* (2nd ed.). Pacific Grove, CA: Brooks/Cole.

Brown, J. H., Eichenberger, S. A., Portes, S. A., & Christensen, D. N. (1991). Family functioning factors associated with the adjustment level of children of divorce. *Journal of Divorce and Remarriage, 17*, 81–95.

Brown, L. S. (1995). Therapy with same-sex couples. In M. S. Jacobson & A. S. Gurman, (Eds.), *Clinical handbook of couple therapy* (pp. 274–291). New York: Guilford.

Brown, R. A., & Hill, B. A. (1996). Opportunities for change: Exploring an alternative to residential treatment. *Child Welfare, 75*(1), 35–57.

Brown, R. I., Bayer, M. B., & Brown, P. M. (1992). *Empowerment and developmental handicaps: Choices and quality of life*. London: Captus University Publications.

Brucker-Gordon, F., Gangi, B. K., & Wellman, G. (1988). *Making therapy work*. New York: Harper and Row.

Bryant, A. S., & Demian. (1994). Relationship characteristics of American gay and lesbian couples: Findings from a national survey. *Journal of Gay and Lesbian Services, 1*(2), 101–117.

Bryson, K., & Casper, L. M. (1998). *Household and family characteristics: March 1997.* Washington, DC: U. S. Department of Commerce.

Bumpass, L. L. (1984). Children and marital disruption: A replication and update. *Demography, 21*, 71–82.

Bureau of Census. (1993). *We the . . . first Americans.* Washington, DC: U.S. Government Printing Office.

Burns, B. J., Schoenwald, S. K., Burchard, J. D., Faw, L., & Santos, A. B. (2000). Comprehensive community-based interventions for youth with severe emotional disorders: Multisystemic therapy and the wraparound process. *Journal of Child and Family Studies 9*(3), 283–314.

Buscaglia, L. (1983). *The disabled and their parents: A counseling challenge.* Thorofare, NJ: Slack.

Cain, J. D. (2003, March). Balancing act. *Essence, 33*(11), 192–194.

Campbell, J. A. (1988). Client acceptance of single-system evaluation procedures. *Social Work Research and Abstracts, 24*, 21–22.

Canda, E. R., & Furman, L. D. (1999). *Spiritual diversity in social work practice.* New York: Free Press.

Carroll, J. S., & Doherty, W. J. (2003). Evaluating the effectiveness of premarital prevention programs: A meta-analytic review of outcome research. *Family Relations, 52*(2), 105–118.

Carter, B., & McGoldrick, M., (1980). *The family life cycle: A framework for family therapy* (1st ed). New York: Gardner.

Carter, B., & McGoldrick, M. (1999). Coaching at various stages of the life cycle. In B. Carter & M. McGoldrick (Eds.), *The expanded family life cycle* (3rd ed.)(pp. 436–454). Boston: Allyn & Bacon.

Cervantes, R. C., Padilla, A. M., & Salgado de Snyder, N. (1991). Hispanic Stress Inventory: A culturally relevant approach to psychosocial assessment. *Psychological Assessment: A Journal of Consulting and Clinical Psychology, 3,* 438–447.

Charles, C. (1986). Mental health services for Haitians. In H. P. Lefley & P. B. Pedersen (Eds.), *Cross-cultural training for mental health professionals* (pp. 183–198). Springfield, IL: Charles C. Thomas.

Chasin, R., Roth, S., & Bograd, M.(1989). Action methods in systemic therapy: Dramatizing ideal futures and reformed pasts with couples. *Family Process, 28*(2), 121–136.

Chenven, M., & Brady, B. (2003). Collaboration across disciplines and among agencies within systems of care. In A. J. Pumariega & N. C. Winters (Eds), *The handbook of child and adolescent systems of care: The new community psychiatry* (pp. 66–81). San Francisco: Jossey-Bass.

Cherlin, A., Furstenberg, F. F., Chase-Lansdale, P. O., Kiernan, K. E., Robins, P. K., Morrison, D. R., et al. (1991). Longitudinal studies of effects of divorce in children in Great Britain and the United States. *Science, 252,* 1386–1389.

Cherlin, A. J. (1992). *Marriage, divorce, remarriage* (Rev. ed.). Cambridge, MA: Harvard University Press.

Cherlin, A. J., Chase-Lansdale, P. L., & McRae, C. (1998). Effects of parental divorce on mental health throughout the lifecourse. *American Sociological Review, 63,* 239–249.

Cheung, K. M., Leung, P., & Alpert, S. (1997). A model for family preservation case assessment. *Family Preservation Journal, 2*(2), 1–20.

Child Welfare League of America. (1995a). *Issues in lesbian and gay adoption.* Washington, DC: Author.

Child Welfare League of America. (1995b, November 15). *Foster family shortage.* Retrieved October 5, 1995, from http://www.handsnet.org//handsnet/handsnet2/Articles/art.816464005.html

Children's Defense Fund. (2003, May 26). *Home page.* Retrieved October 16, 2004, from http://www.childrensdefense.org/

Chipungu, S., Everett, J., Verduik, M., & Jones, J. (1998). *Children placed in foster care with relatives: A multi-state study* (Final Report, Executive Summary). Washington, DC: U. S. Department of Health and Human Services, Administration for Children and Families.

Chiriboga, D. A. (1982). Adaptation to marital separation in later and earlier life. *Journal of Gerontology, 37*(1), 109–114.

Choi, G. (1997). Acculturative stress, social support, and depression in Korean American families. *Journal of Family Social Work, 2*(1), 81–97.

Christian, S. (1999, March). 1998 State legislative response to the adoption of the adoption and safe families act. *State Legislative Report, 24*(5).

Christian-Michaels, S. (1995). Psychiatric emergencies and family preservation: Partnerships in an array of community-based services. In L. Combrinck-Graham (Ed.), *Children in families at risk: Maintaining the connections* (pp. 56–79). New York: Guilford.

Cissna, K. N., Cox, D. E., & Bocher, A. P. (1994). The dialectic of marital and parental relationships within the stepfamily. In G. Handel & G. C. Whitchurch. *The psychosocial interior of the family* (4th ed.)(p. 255–279). New York: Aldine de Gruyter.

Cituk, A., Graves, L., & Thompson Prout, H. (1999). Other approaches, techniques, and special situations. In H. Thompson Prout & D. Brown (Eds.), *Counseling and psychotherapy with children and adolescents.* New York: Wiley & Sons, Inc.

Clark, H. B., Lee, B., Prange, M. E., & McDonald, B. A. (1996). Children lost within the foster care system: Can wraparound service strategies improve placement outcomes? *Journal of Child and Family Studies, 5*(1), 39–54.

Clark, H. B., Prange, M. E., Lee, B., Stewart, E. S., McDonald, B. A., & Boyd, L. A. (1998). An individualized wraparound process for children in foster care with emotional/behavioral disturbances: Follow-up findings and implications from a controlled study. In M. H. Epstein & K. Kutash (Eds.), *Outcomes for children and youth with emotional and behavioral disorders and their families: Programs and evaluation best practices* (pp. 686–707). Austin, TX: PRO-ED.

Coates, J. F. (1999). What's ahead for families: Five major forces of change. In K. R. Gilbert (Ed.), *Annual editions: Marriage and family 99/00* (pp. 210–215). Guilford, CT: Dushkin/McGraw-Hill.

Cole, B., & Duva, J. (1990). *Family preservation: An orientation for administrators and practitioners*. Washington, DC: Child Welfare League of America.

Collins, D., Jordan, C., & Coleman, H. (1999). *An introduction to family social work*. Itasca, IL: Peacock.

Committee for Economic Development (CED), Research and Policy Committee. (2000). *Welfare reform and beyond: Making work, work*. Committee for Economic Development.

Congressional Record. (1997). *Adoption Promotion Act*. 143 Cong Rec S 12198.

Conrad, C. (1995, October). Is your employer family friendly? *Black Enterprise, 26*(3), 27–31.

Constantino, G., Malgady, R. G., & Rogler, L. H. (1992). *TEMAS: Tell me a story*. Los Angeles: Western Psychological Services.

Cook-Morales, V. J. (2002). The home–school–agency triangle. In D. T. Marsh & M. A. Fristad (Eds.), *Handbook of serious emotional disturbance in children and adolescents*. (pp. 392–411). New York: John Wiley & Sons.

Coontz, S. (2000). Historical perspectives on family diversity. In D. H. Demo, K. R. Allen, & M. A. Fine (Eds.), *Handbook of family diversity* (pp. 15–31). New York: Oxford University Press.

Corcoran, J. (2002). Using standardized tests and instruments in family assessment. In A. R. Roberts & G. J. Greene (Eds.), *Social workers' desk reference*. New York: Oxford.

Corcoran, K., & Vandiver, V. (1996). *Maneuvering the maze of managed care*. New York: Free Press.

Corcoran, M., Duncan, G. J., Gurin, G., & Gurin P. (1985). Myth and reality: The causes and persistence of poverty. *Journal of Policy Analysis and Management, 4*(4), 516–536.

Corey, M. S., & Corey, G. (2002). *Groups: Process and practice*. Pacific Grove, CA: Brooks/Cole.

Cowger, C. (1997). Assessing client strengths: Assessment for client empowerment. In D. Saleebey (Ed.), *The strengths perspective in social work practice* (pp. 59–73). New York: Longman.

Csokasy, J. (1998). An effectiveness study of wraparound care. *Dissertation Abstracts International: Section B: The Sciences and Engineering, 58*(8-B), 4441.

Cuellar, I., Arnold, B., & Maldonado, R. (1995). Acculturation Rating Scale for Mexican Americans-II: A revision of the original ARSMA scale. *Hispanic Journal of Behavioral Sciences, 17*(3), 275–304.

Dain, N. (1980). *Clifford W. Beers: Advocate for the insane*. Pittsburgh: University of Pittsburgh Press.

David C. v. Leavitt, No. 93-C-206W (D.Ut. February 25, 1993).

Davis, A. (1973). *American heroine: The life and legend of Jane Addams*. New York: Oxford University Press.

De Jong, P., & Berg, I. K. (2002). *Interviewing for solutions* (2nd ed.). Pacific Grove, CA: Brooks/Cole.

Dell, P. F. (1989). Violence and the systemic view. *Family Process, 28*, 1–14.

Diller, J. V. (1999). *Cultural diversity*. Belmont, CA: Wadsworth.

DiNitto, D. M., & Gustavsson, N. S. (1999). The interface between family practice and family policy. In C. Franklin & C. Jordan (Eds.). *Family practice* (pp. 341–393). Pacific Grove, CA: Brooks/Cole.

Dollinger, S. A. (1998). The multisystemic treatment of an adolescent suicide attempter: A case study. *Dissertation Abstracts International, 58*(10-B), 5641.

Downs, S. W., Costin, L. B., & McFadden, E. J. (1996). *Child welfare and family services: Policies and practice.* White Plains, NY: Longman.

Dryfoos, J. G. (1998). *Full-service schools : A revolution in health and social services for children, youth, and families.* New York: Jossey-Bass.

Dubowitz, H., Feigelman, S., Harrington, D., Starr Jr., R., Zuravin, S., & Sawyer, R. (1994). Children in kinship care: How do they fare? *Children and Youth Services Review, 16,* 85–106.

Dubowitz, H., Feigelman, S., & Zuravin, S. (1993). A profile of kinship care. *Child Welfare*, 72, 153–169.

Dudley, J. R., & Stone, G. (2001). *Fathering at risk.* New York: Springer.

Duerr-Berrick, J., & Barth, R. P. (1994). Research on kinship foster care: What do we know? Where do we go from here? *Children and Youth Services Review, 16,* 1–5.

Duerr-Berrick, J., Barth, R. P., & Needell, B. (1994). A comparison of kinship foster homes and foster family homes: Implications for kinship foster care as family preservation. *Children and Youth Services Review, 16,* 33–63.

Duhl, F., Kantor, D., & Duhl, B. (1973). Learning, space, and action in family therapy: A primer of sculpture. In D.A. Block (Ed.), *Techniques of family psychotherapy: A primer* (pp. 167–183). New York: Grune & Stratton.

DuongTran, Q., Lee, S., & Khoi, S. (1996). Ethnic and gender differences in parental expectations and life stress. *Child and Adolescent Social Work Journal 13*(6), 515–26.

Dyck, D. G., Hendryx, M. S., Short, R. A., Voss, W. D., & McFarlane, W. R. (2002). Service use among patients with schizophrenia in psychoeducational multiple-family group treatment. *Psychiatric Services, 53*(6), 749–754.

Dyck, D. G., Short, R. A., Hendryx, M. S., Norell, D., Myers, M., Patterson, T., et al. (2000). Management of negative symptoms among patients with schizophrenia attending multiple-family groups. *Psychiatric Services, 51*(4), 513–519.

Eber, L, & Nelson, C. M. (1997). School-based wraparound planning: Integrating services for students with emotional and behavioral needs. *American Journal of Orthopsychiatry, 67*(3), 385–395.

Eber, L., Osuch, R., & Redditt, C. A. (1996). School-based applications of the wraparound process: Early results on service provision and student outcomes. *Journal of Child and Family Studies, 5*(1), 83–99.

Eber, L, Sugai, G., Smith, C. R., & Scott, T. M. (2002). Wraparound and positive behavioral interventions and supports in the schools. *Journal of Emotional and Behavioral Disorders, 10*(3), 171–180.

Edin, K., & Lein, L. (1997). *Making ends meet: How single mothers survive welfare and low-wage work.* New York: Russell Sage Foundation.

Egan, G. (1999). *The skilled helper* (4th ed.). Pacific Grove, CA: Brooks/Cole.

Ehrle, J., Green, R., & Clark, R. (2001). Children cared for by relatives: Who are they and how are they faring? Washington, DC: Urban Institute.

Ellis, A. (1977). The nature of disturbed marital interactions. In A. Ellis & R. Greiger (Eds.), *Handbook of rational-emotive therapy* (pp. 77–92). New York: Springer.

Ellison, J. (1984, June). The seven frames of mind. *Psychology Today,* 21–26.

Emery, R. E. (1988). *Marriage, divorce, and children's adjustment.* Newbary Park, CA: Sage.

Emery, R. E. (1994). *Renegotiating family relationships: Divorce, child custody, and mediation.* New York: Guilford.

Emery, R. E. (1998). *Marriage, divorce, and children's adjustment* (Rev. Ed.). Beverly Hills, CA: Sage.

Epstein, N., Baldwin, L., & Bishop, D. (1983). The McMaster Family Assessment Device. *Journal of Marital and Family Therapy, 9,* 171–180.

Epstein, N., Schlesinger, S. E., and Dryden, W. (Eds.). (1988). *Cognitive-behavior therapy with families.* New York: Brunner/Mazel.

Equal Employment Opportunity Commission (EEOC) and the U.S. Department of Justice. (1991). *Americans with Disabilities Act handbook.* Washington, DC: U.S. Government Printing Office.

Erikson, E. H. (1950). *Childhood and society* (2nd rev. ed., enlarged). New York: Norton.

Evenson, R. C., Binner, P. R., Cho, D. W., Schicht, W. W., & Topolski, J. M. (1998). An outcome study of Missouri's CSTAR alcohol and drug abuse programs. *Journal of Substance Abuse Treatment 15*(2), 143–150.

Ewalt, P. L., & Mokuau, N. (1996). Self-determination from a Pacific perspective. In P. L. Ewalt, E. M. Freeman, S. A. Kirk, & D. L. Poole (Eds.), *Multicultural issues in social work* (pp. 255–268). Washington, DC: NASW Press.

Faiver, C., Ingersoll, R. E., O'Brien, E., & McNally, C. (2001). *Explorations in counseling and spirituality.* Belmont, CA: Wadsworth.

Falloon, I. R. (1991). Behavioral family therapy. In A. S. Gurman & D. P. Kniskern (Eds.), *Handbook of family therapy, vol. 2* (pp. 65–95). Philadelphia: Brunner/Mazel.

Family Support America. (2002). *Home page.* Retrieved October 16, 2004, from http://www.familysupportamerica.org

Fennell, M. J., & Teasdale, J. D. (1987). Cognitive therapy for depression: Individual differences and the process of change. *Cognitive Therapy and Research, 11,* 253–271.

Ferreira, A. J. (1963). Rejection and expectancy of rejection in families. *Family Process, 2*(2), 235–244.

Fine, M. A., Demo, D. H., & Allen, K. R. (2000). Family diversity in the 21st century: Implications for research, theory, and practice. In D. H. Demo, K. R. Allen, & M. A. Fine (Eds.), *Handbook of family diversity* (pp. 440–448). New York: Oxford University Press.

Fischer, J., & Corcoran, K. (2000). *Measures for clinical practice: A sourcebook Volume I: Couples, families and children* (3rd ed.). New York: Free Press.

Fong, R. (1997). Child welfare practices with Chinese families: Assessment issues for immigrants from the People's Republic of China. In P. M. Brown & J. S. Shalett (Eds.), *Cross-cultural practice with couples and families* (pp. 33–47). Binghampton, NY: Haworth Press.

Fong, R., & Furuto, S. (Eds.) (2001). *Culturally competent practice.* Boston: Allyn & Bacon.

Fournier, R. R. (1997). *The role of spiritual well-being as a resource for coping with stress in bereavement among suicide survivors.* Boston: Boston College.

Frankl, B. R., & Piercy, F. P. (1990). The relationship among selected supervisor, therapist, and client behaviors. *Journal of Marital and Family Therapy, 16,* 407–421.

Franklin, C. & Jordan, C. (1999). *Family practice.* Pacific Grove, CA: Brooks/Cole.

Freeberg, A. L., & Stein, C. (1996). Felt obligation toward parents in Mexican-American and Anglo-American young adults. *Journal of Social and Personal Relationships, 13,* 457–471.

Freedman, J., & Combs, G. (1996). *Narrative therapy: The social construction of preferred realities.* New York: Norton.

Gallup, G. H., & Newport, F. (1990, June 4). Parenthood—A (nearly) universal desire. *San Francisco Chronicle, B-3, B-4.*

Garbarino, J. (1992). Children and families in the social environment (2nd ed.). New York: Aldine de Gruyter.

Gardner, H. (1983). *Frames of mind: The theory of multiple intelligences.* New York: Basic Books.

Garfield, R. (1982). Mourning and its resolution for spouses in marital separation. In J. C. Hansen & L. Messinger (Eds.). *Therapy with remarriage families* (pp. 1–16). Rockville, MD: Aspen Systems Corporation.

Garner, H. (1983). *Frames of mind: The theory of multiple intelligences.* Fontana Press.

Gehart, D. R., & Tuttle, A. R. (2003). *Theory-based treatment planning for marriage and family therapists.* Pacific Grove, CA: Brooks/Cole.

Geismar, L. L. & La Sorte, M. A. (1964). *Understanding the multi-problem family: A conceptual analysis and exploration in early identification.* New York: Association Press.

Generations United. (2003). *Fact sheet: Grandparents and other relatives raising children: Challenges of caring for the second family.* Washington, DC: Author.

Genovese, F. (1992). Family therapy and bereavement counseling. In J. Atwood (Ed.), *Family therapy* (pp. 298–320). Chicago: Nelson-Hall.

Germain, C. B. (1991). *Human behavior in the social environment.* New York: Columbia University Press.

Gilbert, N., & Terrell, P. (2002). *Dimensions of social welfare policy* (5th ed). Boston: Allyn & Bacon.

Gilbert, R., Christensen, A., & Margolin, G. (1984). Patterns of alliances in nondistressed and multiproblem families. *Family Process, 23,* 75–87.

Ginsburg, G. S., & Schlossberg, M. C. (2002). Family-based treatment of childhood anxiety disorders. *International Review of Psychiatry, 14,* 143–154.

Gladstone, J. W. (1995). The marital perceptions of elderly persons living or having a spouse living in a long-term care institution in Canada. *Gerontologist, 35*(1), 52–60.

Gleeson, J. (1995). Kinship care and public child welfare: Challenges and opportunities for social work education. *Journal of Social Work Education, 31*(2), 182–193.

Gleeson, J.P., & Craig, L. C. (1994). Kinship care in child welfare: An analysis of states' policies. *Children and Youth Services Review, 16*(1-2), 7–31.

Gleeson, J., Jackson, H. J., Stavely, H., & Burnett, P. (1999). Family intervention in early psychosis. In P. D. McGorry, & H. J. Jackson (Eds.), *The recognition and management of early psychosis: A preventive approach* (pp 376–406). New York: Cambridge University Press.

Goldenberg, H. & Goldenberg, I. (1999). Current issues and trends in family therapy. In D. M. Lawson & F. F. Prevatt (Eds.), *Casebook in family therapy* (pp. 327–328). Pacific Grove, CA: Brooks/Cole.

Goldenberg, H., & Goldenberg, I. (2002). *Counseling today's families* (4th ed.). Pacific Grove, CA: Brooks/Cole.

Goldenberg, I., & Goldenberg, H. (1991). *Family therapy.* Pacific Grove, CA: Brooks/Cole.

Goldman, D. (1997). *Emotional intelligence.* New York: Bantam.

Goldstein, M. J., Rodnick, E. H., Evan, J. R., May, P. R., & Steinberg, M. (1978). Drug and family therapy in the aftercare treatment of acute schizophrenia. *Archives of General Psychiatry. 35,* 1169–1177.

Gonzalez, S., Steinglass, P., & Reiss, D. (1989). Putting the illness in its place: Discussion groups for families with chronic medical illnesses. *Family Process, 28,* 69–87.

Goodman, C. C. (1992). Social support networks in late life divorce. *Family Perspective, 26*(1), 61–81.

Gordon, T. (1973). *Parent effectiveness training.* New York: Peter Wyden.

Gottman, J. (1994). *Why marriages succeed or fail.* New York: Simon & Schuster.

Gottman, J. (1999). *The marriage clinic: A scientifically-based marital therapy.* New York: Norton.

Gottman, J., Markman, H., & Notarius, C. (1977). The topography of marital conflict: A sequential analysis of verbal and nonverbal behavior. *Journal of Marriage and the Family, 39*(3), 461–477.

Green, J. (2003). *Family theory and therapy.* Pacific Grove, CA: Brooks/Cole.

Greenberg, M. (2001). From caseload reduction to poverty reduction. *Joint Center for Poverty Research Newsletter, 5*(6), University of Chicago.

Greene, B. (1994). African-American women. In L. Diaz & B. Greene (Eds), *Women of color: A portrait of heterogeneity* (pp. 10–29). New York: Guilford.

Greene, B. (2000). African American families. In K. R. Gilbert (Ed.), *Annual editions: marriage and family 99/00* (pp. 26–29). Guilford, CT: Dushkin/McGraw-Hill..

Greene, R. A., & Kropf, N. P. (1999). A family case management approach for level I needs. In A. C. Kilpatrick & T. P. Holland (Eds.), *Working with families* (2nd ed., pp. 82–99). Boston: Allyn & Bacon.

Grogan-Kaylor, A. (2000). Who goes into kinship care? The relationship of child and family characteristics to placement into kinship foster care. *Social Work Research, 24*(3), 132–141.

Grundle, T. J. (2002). Wraparound care. In D. T. Marsh & M. A. Fristad (Eds.), *Handbook of serious emotional disturbance in children and adolescents* (pp. 323–333). New York: John Wiley & Sons.

Gurman, A. S., & Knudson, R. M. (1978). Behavioral marriage therapy: A psychodynamic systems analysis and critique. *Family Process, 17,* 121–138.

Hale-Benson, J. E. (1986). *Black children: Their roots, culture and learning styles.* Baltimore: Johns Hopkins University Press.

Haley, J. (1976). *Problem-solving therapy.* San Francisco: Jossey-Bass.

Halley, A. A., Kopp, J., & Austin, M. J. (1998). *Delivering human services: A learning approach to practice* (4th ed.). New York: Longman.

Hammonds, K. H. (1997). Business gives caregivers a leg up. *Business Week, 3528,* 88–90.

Hanna, S. M., & Brown, J. H. (1999). *The practice of family therapy: Key elements across models* (2nd ed.). Belmont, CA: Wadsworth.

Hare-Mustin, R. (1978). The problem of gender in family theory. *Family Process, 26,* 15–28.

Harper-Dorton, K. V., & Herbert, M. (1999). *Working with children and their families.* Chicago: Lyceum.

Hartman, A. (1978). Diagrammatic assessment of family relationships. *Social Casework, 59,* 465–474.

Harvey, D. M., & Bray, J. H. (1991). Evaluation of an intergenerational theory of personal development: Family process determinants of psychological and health distress. *Journal of Family Psychology 4*(3), 298–325.

Hawkins, C. A., & Bland, T. (2002). Program evaluation of the CREST Project: Empirical support for kinship care as an effective approach to permanency planning. *Child Welfare, 31*(2), 271–292.

Hegar, R. L., & Scannapieco, M. (1998). *Kinship foster care: Practice, policy, research.* New York: Oxford University Press.

Hegar, R. L., & Scannapieco, M. (2000). Grandma's babies: The problem of welfare eligibility for children raised by relatives. *Journal of Sociology and Social Welfare, 37*(3), 153–171.

Hellenbrand, S. (1987). Termination in direct practice. In *Encyclopedia of social work* (18th ed., vol. 2, pp. 765–770). Silver Springs, MD: National Association of Social Workers.

Helton, L. R., & Jackson, M. (1997). *Social work practice with families.* Boston: Allyn & Bacon.

Hendricks, G., & Wills, R. (1975). *The centering book.* New Jersey: Prentice-Hall.

Heneghan, A. M., Horwitz, S. M., & Leventhal, J. M. (1996). Evaluating intensive family preservation services: A methodological review. *Pediatrics, 97*(4), 535–542.

Hepworth, D. H., Farley, O. W., & Griffiths, J. K. (1995). Clinical work with suicidal adolescents and their families. In F. Turner (Ed.), *Differential diagnosis and treatment in social work* (4th ed., pp. 684–695). New York: Free Press.

Hepworth, D. H., Rooney, R. H., & Larsen, J. A. (1997). *Direct social work practice.* Pacific Grove, CA: Brooks/Cole.

Herek, G. (1989). Hate crimes against lesbians and gay men. *American Psychologist, 44,* 948–955.

Herz, F. M., & Rosen, E. J. (1982). Jewish families. In M. McGoldrick, J. K. Pearce, & J. Giordano (Eds.), *Ethnicity and family therapy* (pp.364-392). New York: Guilford.

Hess, H., & Hess, P. (1994). Termination in context. In B. R. Compton & B. Galaway (Eds.), *Social work processes* (pp. 484–497). Pacific Grove, CA: Brooks/Cole.

Hetherington, E. M. (1989). Coping with family transitions: Winners, losers, and survivors. *Child Development, 60,* 1–14.

Hetherington, E. M., & Stanley-Hagan, M. (2000). Diversity among stepfamilies. In D. H. Demo, K. R. Allen, & M. A. Fine (Eds.), *Handbook of family diversity* (pp 173–196). New York: Oxford University Press.

Hitchcock, D. I. (1998). Asian crisis is cultural as well as economic. *Christian Science Monitor,* (4–9/98), 7.

Ho, M. K. (1987). *Family therapy with ethnic minorities.* Newbury Park, CA: Sage.

Hofferth, S. L. (1996). Child care in the United States today. *Financing Child Care, 6*(2), 41–61.

Holland, T. P., & Kilpatrick, A. C. (1999). An ecological systems–social constructionism approach to family practice. In A. C. Kilpatrick & T. P. Holland (Eds.), *Working with families* (2nd ed., pp. 16–36). Boston: Allyn & Bacon.

Hollander, D. (2002). Sexual risks are increased for women who were ever in foster or kinship care. *Perspectives on Sexual & Reproductive Health, 34*(1), 55.

Hooyman, N. R. (1994). Diversity and populations at risk: Women. In F. G. Reamer (Ed.), *The foundations of social work knowledge* (pp. 309–340). New York: Columbia University Press.

House Committee on Ways and Means. (1997, April 28). H. Rpt. 105-77 on H.R. 867, *Adoption Promotion Act.of 1997.* CIS NO: 97-H783-5.

Hoyert, D. L., Kochanek, K. D., & Murphy, S. (1999). *Deaths: Final data for 1997. National Vital Statistics Report, 47 (19).* Hyattsvill, MD: National Center for Health Statistics.

Hubble, M. A., Duncan, B. L., & Miller, S. D. (1999). *The heart and soul of change: What works in therapy.* Washington, DC: American Psychological Association.

Hudson, W. W. (1992). *The WALMYR Assessment Scales scoring manual.* Tempe, AZ: WALMYR Publishing.

Huffine, J. L. (2002). Family empowerment in an integrated system of care: The family mosaic project. *Dissertation Abstracts International: Section B, The Sciences and Engineering, 63*(5), 2652.

Ihinger-Tallman, M., & Pasley, K. (1987). *Remarriage and stepparenting: Current research and theory.* New York: Guilford.

Ilardi, S. S., & Craighead, W. E. (1994). The role of nonspecific factors in cognitive-behavior therapy for depression. *Clinical Psychology: Science and Practice, 1.* 138–156.

Imber-Black, E. (1999). The power of secrets. In K. R. Gilbert (Ed.), *Annual editions marriage and family 99/00* (pp. 216–219). Guilford, CT: Dushkin/McGraw Hill.

Imber-Black, E., & Roberts, J. (2000). Rituals for our times. In K. R. Gilbert (Ed.), *Annual editions marriage and family 00/01* (pp. 220–224). Guilford, CT: Dushkin/McGraw Hill.

Jacobson, N. S., & Addis, M. E. (1993). Research on couple therapy: What do we know? Where are we going? *Journal of Consulting and Clinical Psychology, 61*(1), 85–93.

Jansson, B. S. (2001). *The reluctant welfare state* (4th ed.). Pacific Grove, CA: Brooks/Cole.

Janzen, C., & Harris, O. (1997). *Family treatment in social work practice* (3rd ed.). Itasca, IL: F. E. Peacock.

Jay, K., & Young, A. (1979). *The gay report.* New York: Summit Books.

Jemerin, J. M., & Philips, I. (1988). Changes in inpatient child psychiatry: Consequences and recommendations. *Journal of the American Academy of Child and Adolescent Psychiatry, 27,* 397–403.

Jenny, C., Roesler, T., & Poyer, K. (1994). Are children at risk for sexual abuse by homosexuals? *Pediatrics, 94*(1), 41–44.

Johnson, B. B. (1981). The Indian Child Welfare act. *Child Welfare, 60*(7), 435–445.

Johnson, D. (1987). Professional–family collaboration. *New Directions for Mental Health Services, 34,* 73–79.

Johnson, L. (1998). *Social work practice: A generalist approach.* Boston: Allyn & Bacon.

Johnson, L. C., & Yanca, S. J. (2001). *Social work practice: A generalist approach* (7th ed.). Boston: Allyn & Bacon.

Johnson, R. A. (1992). *Owning your own shadow.* San Francisco: HarperCollins.

Jones, A. C. (2003). Restructuring the stepfamily: Old myths, new stories. *Social Work, 48*(2), 228–236.

Jones, J. M. (1991). Psychological models of race. In J. D. Goodchilds (Ed.), *Psychological perspectives on human diversity in America* (pp. 3–46). Washington, DC: American Psychological Association.

Jordan, C., & Franklin, C. (1995). *Clinical assessment for social work.* Chicago: Lyceum.

Jordan, C., & Franklin, C. (1999). *Clinical assessment for social work.* Chicago: Lyceum.

Jordan, J. (1984). Empathy and self boundaries. *Stone Center Works in Progress, 16,* 1–14.

Kadushin, A. (1990). *The social work interview.* New York: Columbia University Press.

Kamradt, B., & Meyers, M. J. (1999). Curbing violence in juvenile offenders with serious emotional and mental health needs: The effective utilization of wraparound approaches in an American urban setting. *International Journal of Adolescent Medicine and Health, 11*(3–4), 381–399.

Kanfer, F. H. & Schefft, B. K. (1988). *Guiding therapeutic change.* Champaign, IL: Research Press.

Kaplan, L. W. (1984). *The multi-problem family phenomenon: An interactional perspective.* A PhD dissertation submitted to the graduate school of the University of Massachusetts.

Karger, H. J., & Stoesz, D. (2002). *American social welfare policy. A pluralist approach.* Boston, MA: Allyn & Bacon.

Kelly, P. (2002). Narrative therapy. In A. R. Roberts & J. R. Greene (Eds.), *Social worker's desk reference* (pp. 121–124). Oxford, England: Oxford Press.

Kilpatrick, A. C., & Holland, T. P. (1999). *Working with families* (2nd ed.). Boston: Allyn & Bacon.

Kinney, J., Haapala, D., & Booth, C. (1991). *Keeping families together.* Hawthorne, NY: Aldine de Gruyter.

Kirk, R. S. (2002). *A critique of the evaluation of family preservation and reunification programs: Interim report.* Retrieved October 15, 2004, from http://www.nfpn.org/resources/articles/critique.html

Kirst-Ashman, K. K., & Hull Jr., G. H. (2002). *Understanding generalist practice.* Pacific Grove, CA: Brooks/Cole.

Knox, S., Hess, S. A., Petersen, D. A., & Hill, C. E. (1997). A qualitative analysis of client perceptions of the effects of helpful therapist self-disclosure in long-term therapy. *Journal of Counseling Psychology, 44*(3), 274–283.

Kruk, E. (1994). The disengaged noncustodial father: Implications for social work practice with the divorced family. *Social Work, 39*(1), 15–25.

Kurdek, L. A. (1995). Lesbian and gay close relationships. In A. R. D'Augelli & C. J. Patterson (Eds.), *Lesbian and gay identities over a lifespan: Psychological perspectives on personal, relational, and community processes* (pp. 243–261). New York: Oxford University Press.

Laird, J. (1994). Lesbian families: A cultural perspective. In M. P. Mirkin (Ed.), *Women in context: Toward a feminist reconstruction of psychotherapy* (pp. 118–148). New York: Guilford Press.

Lambert, M. J., & Anderson, E. M. (1996). Assessment for the time-limited psychotherapies. *Annual Review of Psychiatry, 15,* 23–47.

Lavee, Y. (1997). The components of health marriages: Perceptions of Israeli social workers and their clients. In P. M. Brown & J. S. Shalett (Eds.), *Cross-cultural practice with couples and families* (pp. 1–14). Binghamton, NY: Haworth.

Laveman, L. (2000). The Harmonium Project: A macrosystemic approach to empowering adolescents. *Journal of Mental Health Counseling, 22*(1), 17–31.

LaVigna, G. W., Christian, L., Liberman, R. L., & Camacho, E. (2002). Rehab rounds: Training professionals in use of positive methods for community integration. *Psychiatric Services, 53*(1), 16–18.

Lawson, D. (1994). Identifying pretreatment change. *Journal of Counseling and Development,* 72. 244–248.

Leacock, E. (1971). *The culture of poverty: A critique.* New York: Simon & Schuster.

Lebow, J. L. (1995). Research assessing couple and family therapy. *Annual Review Psychology, 46,* 27–57.

Leighninger, L. (2000). *Creating a new profession: The beginnings of social work education in the United States.* Alexandria, VA: Council on Social Work Education.

LeVay, S., & Hamer, D. (1994). Evidence for a biological influence in male homosexuality. *Scientific American, 270,* 20–25.

LeVine, E. S., & Sallee, A. L. (1999). *Child welfare: Clinical theory and practice.* Dubuque, IA: Eddie Bowers.

Lewis, J. J. (2004). *Future quotes.* Retrieved October 18, 2004, from http://www.wisdomquotes.com/cat_future.html

Lewis, M., & Haviland, J. M. (Eds.) (1993). *Handbook of emotions.* New York: Guilford Press.

Lewis, R. E., Walton, E., & Fraser, M. W. (1995). Examining family reunification services: A process analysis of a successful experiment. *Research on Social Work Practice, 5*(3), 259–282.

Lewit, E. M., & Baker, L. S. (1996). Homeless families and children. *Financing Child Care, 6*(2), 146–158.

Lindsey, E. W. (1997). The process of restabilization for mother-headed homeless families: How social workers can help. *The Journal of Family Social Work, 2*(3), 49–72.

Littell, J. H., & Schuerman, J. R. (1995). *A synthesis of research on family preservation and family reunification programs.* Chicago: Westat, Bell Associates, and The Chapin Hall Center for Children at the University of Chicago.

Logan, S. M. L., Freeman, E. M., & McRoy, R. G. (1990). *Social work practice with black families.* White Plains, NY: Longman.

Long, J. K. (1996). Working with lesbians, gays, and bisexuals: Addressing heterosexism in supervision. *Family Process, 35,* 377–388.

Loyola University, New Orleans. (2002). *New Orleans Resolving Conflict Creatively Program.* Retrieved March 2002, from http://www.loyno.edu/twomey

Lynch, J. M. (2000). Considerations of family structure and gender composition: The lesbian and gay stepfamily. *Journal of Homosexuality, 40*(2), 81–95.

Mackelprang, R., & Salsgiver, R. (1999). *Disability.* Pacific Grove, CA: Brooks/Cole.

MacKenzie, P. & McLean, M. (1992). Altered roles: The meaning of placement for the spouse who remains in the community. *Journal of Gerontological Social Work, 19*(2), 107–120.

Magura, S., Silverman-Moses, B., & Jones, M. A. (1987). *Assessing risk and measuring change in families: The family risk scales.* Washington, DC: Child Welfare League of America.

Majors, R., & Mancini, J. (1992). *Cool pose: The dilemmas of black manhood in America.* New York: Lexington Books.

Maluccio, A. N., Ainsworth, F., & Thoburn, J. (2000). *Child welfare outcome research in the United States, the United Kingdom, and Australia.* Washington, DC: Child Welfare League of America.

Manalo, V., & Meezan, W. (2000). Toward building a typology for the evaluation of service in the family support programs. *Child Welfare, 79*(4), 405–430.

Marlow, L. (1992). The family therapist and divorce mediation. In J. D. Atwood (Ed.), *Family therapy.* Chicago: Nelson-Hall.

Martin, T., & Bumpass, L. L. (1989). Recent trends in marital disruption. *Demography, 26,* 37–51.

Marziali, E. (1995). Borderline personality disorder. In F. Turner (Ed.), *Differential diagnosis and treatment in social work* (pp. 329–347). New York: Free Press.

Mason, M. A., & Mauldon, J. (1996). The new stepfamily requires a new public policy. *Journal of Social Issues, 52,* 11–27.

Mather, J. H., & Lager, P. B. (2000). *Child welfare: A unifying model of practice.* Pacific Grove, CA: Brooks/Cole.

Mattison, A. M., & McWhirter, D. P. (1994). Serodiscordant male couples. *Journal of Gay and Lesbian Social Services, 1*(2), 83–99.

Mauldon, J., London, R. Fein, D., & Bliss, S. (2002, November). *What Do They Think? Welfare Recipients' Attitudes Toward Marriage and Childbearing.* A Research Brief from the Welfare Reform and Family Formation Project. Research Brief #2.

Maurrasse, D. J. (2001). *Beyond the campus: How colleges and universities form partnerships with their communities.* NewYork: Routledge.

McCarthy IV, R. (2001). Universities and community-based economic development. *Blueprint of Social Justice, LIV*(10).

McCubbin, H. I., Boss, P. G., Wilson, L. R., & Dahl, B. B. (1991). Family coping inventory. In H. I. McCubbin & A. I. Thompson (Eds.), *Family assessment inventories for research and practice* (pp. 266–271). Madison: University of Wisconsin Press.

McCubbin, M. A., McCubbin, H. I., & Thompson, A. I. (1991). Family hardiness index. In H. I. McCubbin & A. I. Thompson (Eds.), *Family assessment inventories for research and practice* (pp. 286–288). Madison: University of Wisconsin Press.

McDonnell, M. G., Short, R. A., Berry, C. M., & Dyck, D. G. (2003). Burden in schizophrenia caregivers: Impact of family psychoeducation and awareness of patient suicidality. *Family Process, 42*(1), 91–103.

McFarlane, W. R. (1991). Family psychoeducational treatment. In A. S. Gurman & D. P. Kniskern (Eds.), *Handbook of family therapy* (vol. 2, pp. 363–395). New York: Brunner-Mazel.

McFarlane, W. R. (1997). Family psychoeducation: Basic concepts and innovative applications. In S. W. Henggeler & A. B. Santos (Eds.), *Innovative approaches for difficult to treat populations* (pp. 211–238). Washington, DC: American Psychiatric Association.

McFarlane, W. R., Link, B., Dushay, R., Marchal, J., & Crilly, J. (1995). Psychoeducational multiple family groups: Four-year relapse outcome in schizophrenia. *Family Process, 34* 127–144.

McGee, M. P. (1997). Cultural values and domestic violence. *Journal of Family Social Work, 2*(2), 129–140.

McGoldrick, M., & Carter, B. (1999). Self in context. In B. Carter & M. McGoldrick (Eds.), *The expanded family life cycle* (3rd ed., pp. 27–46). Boston: Allyn & Bacon.

McGoldrick, M., & Walsh, F. (1999). Death and the family life cycle. In B. Carter & M. McGoldrick (Eds.), *The expanded family life cycle* (3rd ed., pp. 185–201). Boston: Allyn & Bacon.

McGowan, B. (1990). Family-based services and public policy. In J. Whittaker, J. Kinney, E. Tracy, & C. Booth (Eds.), In *Reaching high-risk families* (pp. 81–82). New York: Aldine de Gruyter.

McKay, M. M., Gonzales, J., Quintana, E., Kim, L., & Abdul-Adil, J. (1999). Multiple family groups: An alternative for reducing disruptive behavioral difficulties of urban children. *Research on Social Work Practice, 9*(5), 593–607.

McKay, M. M., Harrison, M. E., Gonzales, J., Kim, L., & Quintana, E. (2002). Multiple family groups for urban children with conduct difficulties and their families. *Psychiatric Services, 53*(11), 1467–1468.

McLanahan, S. S., & Garfinkle, I. (1989). Single mothers, the underclass and social policy. *Annals of the American Academy of Political and Social Science, 501*, 92–104.

Means-Christensen, A. J., Snyder, D. K., & Negy, C. (2003). Assessing nontraditional couples: Validity of the Marital Satisfaction Inventory—Revised with gay, lesbian, and cohabiting heterosexual couples. *Journal of Marital and Family Therapy, 29*(1), 69–83.

Melaville, A. (1998). *Learning together: The developing field of school–community initiatives.* University of Chicago: Charles Stewart Mott Foundation.

Miedzian, M. (1991). *Boys will be boys: Breaking the link between masculinity and violence.* New York: Doubleday.

Miller, S. D., Hubble, M. A., & Duncan, B. L. (1996). *Handbook of solution-focused brief therapy.* San Francisco: Jossey-Bass.

Minuchin, S. (1974). *Families and family therapy.* Cambridge, MA: Harvard University Press.

Minuchin, S., & Nichols, M. (1993). *Family healing: Tales of hope and renewal from family therapy.* New York: Free Press.

Minuchin, S., Rosman, B., & Baker, L. (1978). *Psychosomatic families: Anorexia nervosa in context.* Cambridge, MA: Harvard University Press.

Moore, K. A., & Vandivere, S. (2000). Stressful family lives: Child and parent well being. *Assessing the New Federalism Project's National Survey of America's Families.* No. B-17, Policy Briefs. Washington, DC: Urban Institute.

Morgan, H., & Tucker, K. (1991). *Companies that care: The most family-friendly companies in America: What they offer and how they got that way..* New York: Simon and Schuster.

Morgan, K. S., & Nerison, R. M. (1993). Homosexuality and psychopolitics: An overview. *Psychotherapy, 30,* 133–140.

Morrison-Velasco, S. (2002). The role of empathy in the wraparound model. In P. R. Breggin & G. Breggin (Eds.), *Dimensions of empathic therapy* (pp. 79–88). New York: Springer.

Mrazek, P. J., & Haggerty, R. J. (Eds.). (1994). *Reducing risks for mental disorders.* Washington, DC: National Academy Press.

Mullen, A., Murray, L, & Happell, B. (2002). Multiple family group interventions in first episode psychosis: Enhancing knowledge and understanding. *International Journal of Mental Health Nursing, 11*(4), 225–232.

Multiethnic Placement Act of 1994. Public Law 103–382.

Murphy, B. C. (1989). Lesbian couples and their parents. *Journal of Counseling and Development, 68,* 46–51.

Murphy, B. C. (1994). Difference and diversity: Gay and lesbian couples. *Journal of Gay & Lesbian Social Services, 1*(2), 5–31.

Murray, C. (1984). *Losing ground: American social policy, 1950–1980.* New York: Basic Books.

Myaard, M. J., Crawford, C., Jackson, M., & Alessi, G. (2000). Applying behavior analysis within the wraparound process: A multiple baseline study. *Journal of Emotional and Behavioral Disorders, 8*(4), 216–229.

NASW. (1993). *Social work with older people: It could be for you.* Washington, DC: Author.

National Center for Health Statistics. (1996). *Vital statistics of the United States, 1992. Vol. 2,* part A. Hyattsville, MD: Author.

NCCPR. (2003). *Foster care vs. family preservation: The track record on safety.* Retrieved October 17, 2004, from http://www.nccpr.org/newissues/1.html

NCDSS. (2001). *IFPS FY 2000-2001 Annual Report.* Retrieved October 17, 2004, from http://www.dhhs.state.nc.us/dss/childrensservices/fampres/index.htm

Negroni-Rodriguez, L. K., & Morales, J. (2001). Individual and family assessment skills with Latino/Hispanic Americans. In R. Fong, & S. Furuto (Eds.), *Culturally competent practice* (pp. 132–146). Boston: Allyn & Bacon.

Newman, K. S. (1994). The downwardly mobile family. In G. Handel & G. C. Whitchurch (Eds.), *The psychosocial interior of the family* (4th ed., pp. 561–584). New York: Aldine de Gruyter.

Nichols, M. P. (1999). *Inside family therapy.* Boston: Allyn & Bacon.

Nichols, M. P., & Schwartz, R. C. (2001). *Family therapy* (5th ed.). Boston: Allyn & Bacon.

Obiakor, F. E., Utley, C. A., Smith, R., & Harrie-Obiakor, P. (2002, September). The comprehensive support model for culturally diverse exceptional learners: Intervention in an age of change. *Intervention in School and Clinic, 38*(1), 14–28.

O'Conner, A. (2001). *Poverty knowledge: Social science, social policy, and the poor in Twentieth-century U.S. history.* Princeton, NJ: Princeton University Press.

Odden, E. B. (1995). Making school-based management work. *Educational Leadership Journal of the Association of Supervision and Curriculum, 53*(5), 32–37.

Okun, B. R. (1992). *Effective helping: Interviewing and counseling techniques* (4th ed.). Pacific Grove, CA: Brooks/Cole.

Olson, D. H., Porter, J., & Ravee, Y. (1985). *FACES I.* St. Paul: Family Social Science, University of Minnesota.

O'Malley, K. D. (2003). Youth with comorbid disorders. In A. J. Pumariega & N. C. Winters (Eds.), *The handbook of child and adolescent systems of care: The new community psychiatry* (pp. 276–315). San Francisco: Jossey-Bass.

Omnibus Reconciliation Act of 1993. Public Law 103-55.

O'Neal, V. P., Brown, P. M., & Abadie, T. (1997). Treatment implications for interracial couples. In P. M. Brown & J. S. Shalett (Eds.), *Cross-cultural practice with couples and families* pp. 15–31). New York: Haworth.

Ooms, T. (2002). *Marriage and Government: Strange Bedfellows.* Policy Brief: Couples and Marriage Series. Center for Law and Social Policy. August 2002, Brief No. 1.

O'Shea, M. D., & Phelps, R. (1985). Multiple family therapy: Current status and critical appraisal. *Family Process, 24,* 555–582.

Ostroff, J., & Steinglass, P. (1996). Psychosocial adaptation following treatment: A family systems perspective on childhood cancer survivorship. In L. Baider & C. L. Cooper (Eds.), *Cancer and the family* (pp. 129–147). Oxford, England: John Wiley & Sons.

Pam, A. (1998). *Splitting up: Enmeshment and estrangement in the process of divorce.* New York: Guilford.

Paniagua, F. A. (1998). *Assessing and treating culturally diverse clients: A practical guide* (2nd ed.). Thousand Oaks, CA: Sage.

Parke, R. D., & Kellam, S. G. (1994). *Exploring family relationships with other social contexts.* Hillsdale, NJ: Lawrence Erlbaum Associates.

Parker, G., Tupling, H., & Brown, L. B. (1979). A parental bonding instrument. *British Journal of Medical Psychology, 52,* 1–10.

Parkes, C. M., &. Weiss, R. S. (1983). *Recovery from bereavement.* New York: Basic Books.

Pasamanick, B. (Ed.). (1959). *Epidemiology of mental disorders.* Washington, DC: The American Association for the Advancement of Science.

Patterson, C. J. (1992). Children of lesbian and gay parents. *Child Development, 63,* 1025–1042.

Patterson, C. J. (1994). Lesbian and gay couples considering parenthood: An agenda for research, service, and advocacy. *Journal of Gay and Lesbian Social Services 1*(2), 33–55.

Patterson, J., & Garwick, A. (1994). Levels of meaning in family stress theory. *Family Process, 33,* 287–304.

Paul, N. (1967). The use of empathy in the resolution of grief. *Perspectives in Biology and Medicine, 11,* 153–169.

Penn, P. (1998). Rape flashbacks: Constructing a new narrative. *Family Process, 37*(3), 299–310.

Peplau, L. A., Cochran, S., Rook, K., & Padesky, C. (1978). Loving women: Attachment and autonomy in lesbian relationships. *Journal of Social Issues, 34*(3), 7–27.

Peplau, L. A, Veniegas, R. C., & Campbell, S. M. (1996). Gay and lesbian relationships. In R. C. Savin-Williams & K. M. Cohen (Eds.), *The lives of lesbians, gays, and bisexuals: Children to adults* (pp. 250–273). Fort Worth, TX: Harcourt Brace.

Pierce, W. J., & Elisme, E. (1997). Understanding and working with Haitian immigrant families. *Journal of Family Social Work, 2*(1), 49–66.

Pillari, V. (2002). *Social work practice.* Boston: Allyn & Bacon.

Pine, B. A. (1986). Child welfare reform and the political process. *Social Service Review, 60*(3), 339–359.

Plomin, R., & Asbury, K. (2001). Nature and nurture in the family. *Marriage and Family Review, 33*(2–3), 273–281.

Popple, P. R., & Leighninger, L. (2002). *Social work, social welfare, and American society* (5th ed.). Boston: Allyn & Bacon.

Potocky-Tripodi, M. (2002). Effective practice with refugees and immigrants. In A. R. Roberts & G. J. Greene (Eds.), *Social workers' desk reference* (pp. 628–632). New York: Oxford.

Quinn, W. H., VanDyke, D. J., & Kurth, S. T. (2002). A brief multiple family group model for juvenile first offenders. In C. R. Figley (Ed.), *Brief treatments for the traumatized: A project of the Green Cross Foundation* (pp. 226–251). Westport, CT: Greenwood Press.

Rands, M. (1986). Changes in social networks following marital separation and divorce. In R. M. Milardo (Ed.), *Families and social networks* (pp. 127–146). Beverly Hills, CA: Sage.

Rank, M. (2000). Poverty and economic hardship in families. In D. H. Demo, K. R. Allen, & M. A. Fine (Eds.), *Handbook of family diversity* (pp. 293–315). New York: Oxford University Press.

Ray, J., Stromwell, L. K., Neumiller, S., & Roloff, M. (1998). A community response to tragedy: Individualized services for families. *Child and Adolescent Social Work Journal, 15*(1), 39–54.

Red Horse, J. (1997). Traditional American Indian family systems. *Families, Systems & Health, 15*(3), 243–250.

Reed-Ashcraft, K. B., Kirk, R. S., & Fraser, M. W. (2001, July). The reliability and validity of the North Carolina Family Assessment Scale. *Research on Social Work Practice, 11*(4), 503–520.

Richmond, M. (1917). *Social diagnosis.* New York: Russell Sage Foundation.

Robbins, S. P., Chatterjee, P., & Canda, E. R. (1998). *Contemporary human behavior theory.* Boston: Allyn & Bacon.

Robinson, B., Walters, L., & Skeen, P. (1989). Response of parents to learning that their child is homosexual and concern over AIDS: A national study. *Journal of Homosexuality 18,* 59–80.

Rogers, C. (1957). The necessary and sufficient conditions of therapeutic personality change. *Journal of Consulting Psychology, 22,* 95–103.

Roland, A., (1988). *In search of self in India and Japan: Toward a cross-cultural psychology.* Princeton, NJ: Princeton University Press.

Rolland, J. S. (1990). Anticipatory loss: A family systems developmental framework. *Family Process, 29,* 229–244.

Rooney, R. H. (1992). *Strategies for work with involuntary clients.* New York: Columbia University Press.

Rosman, E., McCarthy, J., & Woolverton, M. (2001). *Adults with Mental Health Needs and Children with Special Needs: Describing the Families.* Issue Brief #1. Georgetown University Child Development Center, Washington, D.C.

Ross, J. L. (1994). Challenging boundaries: An adolescent in a homosexual family. In G. Handel & G. C. Whitchurch (Eds.), *The psychosocial interior of the family* (4th ed., pp. 159–175). New York: Aldine de Gruyter.

Royse, D., & Thyer, B. A. (1996). *Program evaluation: An introduction* (2nd ed.). Chicago: Nelson-Hall.

Royse, D. (2004). *Research methods in social work*. Pacific Grove, CA: Brooks/Cole.

Rutter, V. (1999). Lessons from stepfamilies. In In K. R. Gilbert (Ed.), *Annual editions marriage and family 99/00* (pp. 176–181). Guilford, CT: Dushkin/McGraw Hill.

Saetersdal, B. (1997). Forbidden suffering: The Pollyanna syndrome of the disabled and their families. *Family Process 36,* 431–435.

Saks, J. C. (1999). Adolescents with physical disabilities and their families: The impact of a short-term multiple-family group. *Dissertation Abstracts International: Section B: The Sciences and Engineering, 60*(5-B), 2365.

Saleebey, D. (Ed.). (1997). *The strengths perspective in social work practice* (2nd ed.). White Plains, NY: Longman.

Salts, C. J. (1985). Divorce stage theory and therapy: Therapeutic implications through the divorcing process. In D. H. Sprenkle (Ed.), *Divorce therapy* (pp. 13–23). New York: Haworth.

Samantrai, K. (2004). *Culturally competent public child welfare.* Pacific Grove, CA: Brooks/Cole.

Satir, V. M. (1967). *Conjoint family therapy.* Palo Alto, CA: Science & Behavior Books.

Satir, V. M., Stachowiak, J., & Taschman, H. (1975). *Helping families to change.* New York: Jacob Aronson.

Savin-Williams, R. C. (1998). The disclosure to families of same-sex attractions by lesbian, gay, and bisexual youths. *Journal of Research in Adolescence, 8,* 49–68.

Savin-Williams, R. C., & Esterberg, K. G. (2000). Lesbian, gay and bisexual families. In D. H. Demo, K. R. Allen, & M. A. Fine (Eds.), *Handbook of family diversity* (pp. 197–215). New York: Oxford University Press.

School Mental Health Project/Center for Mental Health in Schools. (2003). Safe students/healthy schools: A collaborative process. *Addressing barriers to learning. 8*(2), 1–12.

Schor, E., & Gorski, P. (1995, May). The pediatrician's role in family support programs. *Pediatrics, 95*(5), 781–784.

Schuerman, J. R., Rzepnicki, T. L., & Littell, J. H. (1994). *Putting families first: An experiment in family preservation.* New York: Aldine de Gruyter.

Schwebel, A., & Fine, M. (1992). Cognitive-behavioral family therapy. *Journal of Family Psychotherapy, 3*(1) 73–91.

Sergiovanni, T. J. (1992). Why we should seek substitutes for leadership. *Educational Leadership Journal of the Association of Supervision and Curriculum. 50*(4), 63–69.

Seybold, E. D. (2002). Treatment of externalizing behavior disorders in a comprehensive, continuum of care program. *Dissertation Abstracts International: Section B, The Sciences and Engineering, 63*(4-B), 2074.

Shamai, M., & Sharlin, S. A. (1996). Who writes the 'therapeutic story' of families in extreme distress: Overcoming the coalition of despair. *Journal of Family Social Work,* 1(4), 65–82.

Sharlin, S. A., & Shamai, M. (1990). *Families in extreme distress (FED): Identification and intervention.* Haifa: The Center for the Research and Study of the Family, University of Haifa.

Sharlin, S. A., & Shamai, M. (2000). *Therapeutic intervention with poor, unorganized families.* New York: Haworth.

Shebib, B. (2003). *Choices: Counseling skills for social workers and other professionals.* Boston: Allyn & Bacon.

Sheridan, M. J. (2002). Spiritual and religious issues in practice. In A. R. Roberts & G. J. Greene (Eds.), *Social workers' desk reference.* New York: Oxford.

Shlonsky, A. R., & Berrick, J. D. (2001). Assessing and promoting quality in kin and nonkin foster care. *Social Service Review, 75*(1), 60–84.

Shulman, L. (1999). *The skill of helping individuals, families, groups, and communities* (4th ed.). Itasca, IL: Peacock.

Sidell, N. L. (2000). Factors that explain marital happiness when a spouse lives in a nursing home: Married but living apart. *Journal of Family Social Work, 4*(2), 3–20.

Simmons, H. C. (1998). Spirituality and community in the last stage of life. *Journal of Gerontological Social Work, 29*(2/3), 73–91.

Simons, R. L., Johnson, C., & Lorenz, F. O. (1996). Family structure differences in stress and behavioral predispositions. In R. Simons & Associates (Eds.), *Understanding differences between divorced and intact families: Stress, interaction, and child outcome* (pp. 45–63). Thousand Oaks, CA: Sage.

Skiba, R. J., & Nichols, S. D. (2000). What works in wraparound programming. In M. P. Kluger & G. Alexander (Eds.), *What works in child welfare* (pp. 23–29). Washington, DC: Child Welfare League of America.

Sloman, L., Springer, S., & Vachon, M. L. (1993). Disordered communication and grieving in deaf member families. *Family Process, 32,* 171–183.

Small Business Protection Act of 1996. Public Law 104-188.

Spalding, A. D., & Mertz, G. J. (1997). Spirituality and quality of life in Alcoholics Anonymous. *Alcoholism Treatment Quarterly, 15*(1), 1–14.

Spanier, G. B. (1999). *Dyadic adjustment scale manual.* Toronto, Ontario: Multi-Healthsystems.

Spark, G. M., & Brody, E. M. (1970). The aged are family members. *Family Process, 9,* 195–210.

Sprenkle, D., Blow, A., & Dickey, M. (1999). Common factors and other non-technique variables in marriage and family therapy. In M. A. Hubble, B. L. Duncan, & S. D. Miller (Eds.), *The heart and soul of change: What works in therapy* (pp. 3–24). New York: Guilford.

Stinnett, N., Sanders, G., & DeFrain, J. (1981). Strong families: A national study. In N. Stinnett, J. Defrain, K. King, P. Knaub, & G. Rowe (Eds.), *Building family strengths: Roots of well being*. Lincoln: University of Nebraska.

Stone, S., McKay, M. M., & Stoops, C. (1996). Evaluating multiple family groups to address the behavioral difficulties of urban children. *Small Group Research, 27,* 398–415.

Straus, M., Hamby, S., Boney-McCoy, S., & Sugarman, D. (1996). The revised conflict tactics scales (CTS2). *Journal of Family Issues, 17,* 283–316.

Straus, M. A., & Gelles, R. J. (1990). *Physical violence in American families: Risk factors and adaptations to violence in 8,145 families*. New Brunswick, NJ: Transaction.

Stuart, R. B., & Stuart, F. (1972). *Marital pre-counseling inventory.* Champaign, IL: Research Press.

Sundelin, J., & Hansson, K. (2000). Intensive family therapy: A way to change family functioning in multi-problem families. *Journal of Family Therapy, 21,* 419–432.

Taylor, M. J., Barusch, A., Vogel-Ferguson, M. B. (2002). *The dynamics of leaving welfare: A study of ong-term welfare recipients in Utah*. College of Social Work-Social Research Institute, University of Utah.

Teresa, Mother. (1997). *No greater love*. Novato, CA: New World Library.

Teyber, E. (1997). *Interpersonal process in psychotherapy* (3rd. ed.). Pacific Grove, CA: Brooks/Cole.

Thayne, T. R. (1997). Opening space for client's religious and spiritual values in therapy: A social constructionist perspective. *Journal of Family Social Work,* 2(4), 13–23.

Thibault, J., & Kelley, H. (1959). *The social psychology of groups*. New York: Wiley.

Thomlison, B. (2002). *Family assessment handbook*. Pacific Grove, Ca: Brooks/Cole.

Thomson, B. (2000). The healing power of intimacy. In K. R. Gilbert (Ed.), *Annual editions marriage and family 99/00* (pp. 95–99). Guilford, CT: Dushkin/McGraw Hill.

Thorngren, J. M., & Kleist, D. M. (2002). Multiple family group therapy: A postmodern/interpersonal approach. *The Family Journal, 10* (2), 167–176.

Title IV-E Foster Care Eligibility Reviews and Child and Family Services State Plan Reviews, Part IV 63 FR 50058, Proposed Rules, Department of Health and Human Services (HHS) Office of Human Development Services Administration for Children and Families Administration on Children, Youth and Families (ACYF), 45 CFR Parts 1355 and 1356, RIN 0970-AA97, Friday, September 18, 1998, ACTION: Notice of proposed rulemaking., FEDERAL REGISTER Vol. 63, No. 181.

Title IV-E Foster Care Eligibility Reviews and Child and Family Services State Plan Reviews, Part II 65 FR 4020, Rules and Regulations, Department of Health and Human Services (HHS) Office of Human Development Services Administration for Children and Families Administration on Children, Youth and Families (ACYF), 45 CFR Parts 1355, 1356 and 1357, RIN 0970-AA97, Tuesday, January 25, 2000, ACTION: Final Rule., FEDERAL REGISTER Vol. 65, No. 16.

Toseland, R. & Rivas, R. (1998). *An introduction to group work practice* (3rd ed.). Boston: Allyn & Bacon.

Tracy, E. M., & Whittaker, J. K. (1990). The Social network map: Assessing social support in clinical practice. *Families in Society,* 463, 466.

Trattner, W. I. (1984). *From poor law to welfare state*. New York: Free Press.

Treadway, D. (1989). *Before it's too late: Working with substance abuse in the family.* New York: Norton.

Tripodi, T. (1994). *A primer on single-subject design for clinical social workers*. Washington, DC: NASW Press.

Truax, C. G., & Carkhuff, R. E. (1967). *Toward effective counseling and psychotherapy.* Chicago: Aldine.

Tzeng, J. M., & Mare, R. D. (1995). Labor market and socioeconomic effects on marital stability. *Social Science Research, 24,* 329–351.

Umbarger, C. (1983). *Structural family therapy.* New York: Grune & Stratton.

Umberson, D. (1992). Relationships between adult children and their parents: Psychological consequences for both generations. *Journal of Marriage and the Family, 54,* 664–685.

Umberson, D. (1996). Demographic position and stressful midlife events: Effects on the quality of parent–child relationships. In C. D. Ryff & M. M. Seltzer (Eds.), *The parental experience in midlife* (pp. 493–532). Chicago: University of Chicago Press.

United States Department of Commerce. (1996). *How we're changing.* Washington, DC: Author.

United States Department of Health and Human Services. (1997, November 19). *Public Law 105-89 (H.R. 867).* Retrieved April 9, 2003, from http://www.hhs.gov/

United States Department of Health and Human Services, Administration on Children, Youth, and Families. (2001). *Child maltreatment 2001.* Washington, DC: U.S. Government Printing Office.

United States Department of Health and Human Services. (2004). *The 2001 HHS poverty guidelines.* Retrieved October 17, 2004, from http://aspe.hhs.gov/poverty/01poverty.htm

United States Department of Housing and Urban Development. (2002). *Lasting engagement: Building and sustaining a commitment to community outreach, development and collaboration* (Vol. 1). Washington, DC: Author.

United States General Accounting Office (USGAO). (1997, February). *Child welfare: States' progress in implementing family preservation and support services* (GAO/HEHS-97-34). Washington, DC: Author.

United States General Accounting Office. (2002, December) *Welfare reform: Former recipients with impairments less likely to be employed and more likely to receive federal supports.* Washington, DC: Author.

U.S. Census Bureau. (2000). America's families and living arrangements. *Current Population Reports.* Washington, DC: Author.

U.S. Census Bureau. (2001). *Current population reports.* Washington, DC: Author.

U.S. Department of Health and Human Services. (1994). *Promoting safe and stable families.* Washington, DC: Author.

U.S. Department of Health and Human Services. (2000). Final rule implementing child welfare laws aims to improve outcomes for children and families. Washington, DC: Author.

U.S. House of Representatives Committee on Ways and Means. (1998). *Background material and data on programs within the jurisdiction of the Committee on Ways and Means: The 1998 Green Book.* Washington, D.C.: U.S. Government Printing Office.

Valentine, D. R. (1996). Effect of family education and family therapy on spouses of alcoholics' coping behavior and perceptions of family environment. *Dissertation Abstracts International: Section B: The Sciences and Engineering, 56*(9-B), 5188.

Van Den Bergh, N., & Cooper, L. B. (Eds.). (1986). *Feminist visions for social work.* Silver Springs, MD: National Association of Social Workers Press.

Van Hook, M., Hugen, B., & Aguilar, M. (2001). *Spirituality within religious traditions in social work practice.* Pacific Grove, CA: Brooks/Cole.

Van Wormer, K., Wells, J., & Boes, M. (2000). *Social work with lesbians, gays, and bisexuals: A strengths perspective.* Boston: Allyn & Bacon.

Videon, T. (2002). The effects of parent–adolescent relationships and parental separation on adolescent well-being. *Journal of Marriage & Family, 64*(2), 489–504.

Visher, E. B., & Visher, J. S. (1982). Stepfamilies in the 1980s. In J. C. Hansen & L. Messinger (Eds.), *Therapy with remarriage families* (pp. 105–119). Rockville, MD: Aspen Systems Corporation.

Visher, E. B., & Visher, J. S. (1988). Treating families with problems associated with remarriage and step relationships. In C. S. Chilman, E. W. Nunnally, & F. M. Cox (Eds.), *Variant family forms* (pp. 222–244). Newbury Park, CA: Sage.

Vosler, N. R. (1996). *New approaches to family practice.* Thousand Oaks, CA: Sage.

Wallerstein, J. S. (1983). Children of divorce: Stress and developmental tasks. In N. Garmezy & M. Rutter (Eds.), *Stress, coping and development in children* (pp. 265–302). New York: McGraw-Hill.

Wallerstein, J. S. (1986). Women after divorce: Preliminary report from a ten-year follow-up. *American Journal of Orthopsychiatry, 56*(11), 65–77).

Wallerstein, J. S. (1989). *Second chances: Men, women and children a decade after divorce.* New York: Ticknor & Fields.

Wallerstein, J. S., & Johnston, J. R. (1990). Children of divorce: Recent findings regarding long-term effects and recent studies of joint and sole custody. *Pediatric Review, 11,* 197–204.

Walsh, F. (1999). Families in later life. In B. Carter & M. McGoldrick (Eds.), *The expanded family life cycle* (3rd ed., pp. 307–326). Boston: Allyn & Bacon.

Walton, E., & Denby, R. W. (1997). Targeting families to receive intensive family preservation services: Assessing the use of imminent risk of placement as a service criterion. *Family Preservation Journal, 2*(2), 53–70.

Ward, K. M., & Bosek, R. L. (2002). Behavioral risk management: Supporting individuals with developmental disabilities who exhibit inappropriate sexual behaviors. *Research and Practice for Persons with Severe Disabilities, 27*(1), 27–42.

Weaver, N. N., & White, B. J. (1997). The Native American family circle: Roots of resiliency. *Journal of Family Social Work, 2*(1), 67–79.

Weinberg, M. S., Williams, C. J., & Pryor, D. W. (1994). *Dual attraction.* New York: Oxford University Press.

Weiss, R. L., & Perry, B. A. (1979). *Assessment and treatment of marital dysfunction.* Eugene, OR: Marital Studies Program.

Weiss, R. S. (1994). A different kind of parenting. In G. Handel & G. C. Whitchurch (Eds.), *The psychosocial interior of the family* (4th ed., pp. 609–639): New York: Aldine de Gruyter.

Wenger, C. B., Elbaz, S., Stewart, C., Bravender, H., Griffin, L., & Keith, E. (2001). University community outreach for developing information skills on the south side of Chicago. *Illinois Libraries, 83*(3), 15–36.

Werner, E. E. (1993). Risk resilience, and recovery: Perspectives from the Kauai Longitudinal Study. *Development and Psychopathology 5,* 503–515.

Werner, E. E. (1999). Resilience in development. In K. R. Gilbert (Ed.), *Annual editions marriage and family 99/00* (pp. 142–145). Guilford, CT: Dushkin/McGraw Hill.

Westat. (2002). *Evaluation of family preservation and reunification programs: Final report.* Retrieved from http://aspe.hhs.gov/hsp/evalfampres94/final/

Whitaker, C. (1977). Process techniques of family therapy. *Interaction, 1.* 4–19.

Whitaker, C. (1982). The ongoing training of the psychotherapist. In J.R. Neill & D. P. Kniskern (Eds.), *From psyche to system: The evolving therapy of Carl Whitaker* (pp. 121–138). New York: Guilford Press.

Whitaker, C., & Keith, D. (1981). Symbolic-experiential family therapy. In A. Gurman & D. Kniskern (Eds.), *Handbook of family therapy.* Brunner/Mazel, New York.

Whitam, F., Diamond, M., & Martin, J. (1993). Homosexual orientation in twins: A report on 61 pairs and three triplet sets. *Archives of Sexual Behavior, 22*(3), 151–170.

Wilcoxon, A. (1991). Grandparents and grandchildren: An often-neglected relationship between significant others. In J. Veevers (Ed.), *Continuity and change in marriage and the family* (pp. 342–345). Toronto: Holt, Rinehart & Winston of Canada.

Wilk, R. J. (1986). The Haitian refugee: Concerns for health care providers. *Social Work in Health Care, 11*(2), 61–74.

Williams, J. M. (1998). Clearing up the confusion on hiring the disabled. *Nation's Business, 86*(12), 55–59.

Williams, L. F. (1990). Working with the black poor: Implications for effective theoretical and practice approaches. In S. M. L. Logan, E. M. Freeman, & R. G. McRoy (Eds.). *Social work practice with black families* (pp. 169–192). New York: Longman.

Witkin, S. L., (1989). Towards a scientific social work. *Journal of Social Service Research, 12*(3/4), 83–98.

Woellert, L. (2001, May 14). The shape of school reform. *Business Week, 3732*(84), 20, 1C.

Wolin, S. J., & Wolin, S. (1993). *The resilient self: How survivors of troubled families overcome adversity.* New York: Villard.

Worden, M. (1994). *Family therapy basics.* Pacific Grove, CA: Brooks/Cole.

Worden, M. (1999). *Family therapy basics.* Pacific Grove, CA: Brooks/Cole.

Worden, M. (2003). *Family therapy basics.* Pacific Grove, CA: Brooks/Cole.

Yegidis, B. L., Weinbach, R. W., & Morrison-Rodriguez, B. (1999). *Research methods for social workers.* Boston: Allyn & Bacon.

Zill, N., & Schoenborn, C. (1991). Developmental, learning, and emotional problems: Health of our nation's children, United States, 1988. (*Advance data from vital and health statistics* No. 190). Monograph. Hyattsville, MD: National Center for Health Statistics.

Zlotnik, J. L. (1995). Families in the 1990s—The changing picture of who we are. In W. J. O'Neill Jr. (Ed.), *Family: The first imperative* (pp. 333–344). Cleveland, OH: William J. and Dorothy K. O'Neill Foundation.

Zucal, B. (1992). Gender issues in couple therapy. In J. D. Atwood (Ed.), *Family therapy* (pp. 59–69). Chicago: Nelson-Hall.

Zuravin, S. J., Benedict, M., & Somerfield, M. (1997). Child maltreatment in family foster care: Foster home correlates. In R. P. Barth, J. D. Berrick, & N. Gilbert, (Eds.), *Child welfare research review* (vol. 2, pp. 189–200). New York: Columbia University Press.

Name Index

Subject Index

TO THE OWNER OF THIS BOOK:

I hope that you have found *Understanding Generalist Practice with Families* useful. So that this book can be improved in a future edition, would you take the time to complete this sheet and return it? Thank you.

School and address: ______________________________

____

Department: ______________________________

Instructor's name: ______________________________

1. What I like most about this book is: ______________________________

____

____

2. What I like least about this book is: ______________________________

____

____

3. My general reaction to this book is: ______________________________

____

____

4. The name of the course in which I used this book is: ______________________________

____

5. Were all of the chapters of the book assigned for you to read? ______________

   If not, which ones weren't? ______________________________

6. In the space below, or on a separate sheet of paper, please write specific suggestions for improving this book and anything else you'd care to share about your experience in using this book.

____

____

TAPE HERE.
DO NOT STAPLE.

TAPE HERE.
DO NOT STAPLE.

FOLD HERE

NO POSTAGE
NECESSARY
IF MAILED
IN THE
UNITED STATES

BUSINESS REPLY MAIL

FIRST-CLASS MAIL PERMIT NO. 102 MONTEREY CA

POSTAGE WILL BE PAID BY ADDRESSEE

Attn: *Lisa Gebo, Executive Editor*

BrooksCole/Thomson Learning
60 Garden Ct Ste 205
Monterey CA 93940-9967

FOLD HERE

OPTIONAL:

Your name:______________________________________ Date: ______

May we quote you, either in promotion for *Understanding Generalist Practice with Families*, or in future publishing ventures?

Yes: _______________ No: _________

Sincerely yours,

Grafton H. Hull, Jr. and *Jannah Mather*